ZAGATSURVEY®

2002 America's Top Restaurants

As a valued Chase Banking cardholder, we are delighted to present you with this 2002 Top Restaurants Zagat Guide. This 2002 Edition of the Zagat Survey® is your compact-yet-comprehensive guide to America's Top Restaurants – perfect for evenings with friends, vacation or a night on the town. It is our special gift to you.

This guide is just one of the benefits of using your Chase Banking Card. Remember to use your card for all of your purchases instead of cash and checks, and you'll enjoy the convenience, flexibility and security that it provides. Your Chase Banking Card lets you:

- Make purchases wherever MasterCard® is accepted.
- Choose to sign, swipe and go or enter your PIN.
- Enjoy the benefits of a credit card without finance charges or bills to pay.
- Feel secure in the knowledge that you have $0 liability* for purchases made by unauthorized individuals.

* If (1) your account is in good standing; (2) you have no more than two incidents of unauthorized use involving your account in the last 12 months; and (3) you used reasonable care in safeguarding your Card.

CHASE

THE RIGHT RELATIONSHIP IS EVERYTHING.®

ZAGATSURVEY®

2002

AMERICA'S TOP RESTAURANTS

Editors: Sinting Lai and Troy Segal

Published and distributed by
ZAGAT SURVEY, LLC
4 Columbus Circle
New York, New York 10019
Tel: 212 977 6000
E-mail: americastop@zagat.com
Web site: www.zagat.com

Acknowledgments

Our special thanks to the thousands of surveyors who have shared their views with us and made this nationwide *Survey* possible. We would also like to thank our editors and coordinators in each city: Angela Allen, Michele Axley, Karen Berk, Olga Boikess, Margaret Luellen Briggs, Kristine Britton, Mark Brown, Nikki Buchanan, Teresa Byrne-Dodge, Lauren Chapin, Suzi Forbes Chase, Jane Cisneros, Andrea Clurfeld, Chris Cook, Pat Denechaud, Victoria Elliott, Jeanette Foster, Connie Frost, Norma Gottlieb, Lisa Gray, Meesha Halm, Pam Harbaugh, Carolyn Heller, the late Suzanne Hough, Judy Houston, Philip Innes, Max Jacobson, Marty Katz, Michael Klein, Kathryn Kurtz, Gretchen Kurz, Ruth Lando, Sharon Litwin, John McDermott, Carolyn McGuire, Lori Midson, Colleen Moore, Maryanne Muller, David Nelson, Kristine Nickel, Sharon Niederman, Cynthia Nims, Jan Norris, Mary Orlin, Jennifer Pavlasek, Ann Lemons Pollack, Joe Pollack, Virgina Rainey, Susan Safronoff, Barbara Schmiett, Maura Sell, Merrill Shindler, Shelley Skiles Sawyer, Victoria Spencer, Mary Stagaman, Muriel Stevens, Bill St. John, Steve Stover, Deirdre Sykes Shapiro, Steve Stover, Jill Van Cleave, Phil Vettel, Carla Waldemar, Cheryl Walsh, Julie Wilson, Kay Winzenried and Nancy Zimmerman.

This guide would not have been possible without the hard work of our staff, especially: Betsy Andrews, Catherine Bigwood, Deirdre Bourdet, Phil Cardone, Reni Chin, Larry Cohn, Erica Curtis, Carol Diuguid, Jessica Fields, Jeff Freier, Curt Gathje, Randi Gollin, Jessica Gonzalez, Diane Karlin, Natalie Lebert, Mike Liao, Dave Makulec, Donna Marino, Lorraine Mead, Laura Mitchell, Andrew O'Neill, Rob Poole, Brooke Rein, Benjamin Schmerler, Robert Seixas, Daniel Simmons, Yoji Yamaguchi and Sharon Yates.

Very special thanks to Anne Cole and Michelle Gallagher, whose conscientious labor were invaluable in the preparation of this book.

Contents

What's New

As we go to press, the U.S. lies gripped in the aftermath of the terrorist attacks on New York City and Washington, DC. Under the circumstances, it may seem frivolous to discuss such things as dining trends and the most popular eateries – especially the special-occasion restaurants highlighted in this *Survey*. But to eat is to live; celebrating good food, preferably in good company, can be the most life-affirming of experiences. One could argue that it's even a patriotic duty to dine out. Not only does it raise individual spirits, it supports an industry that has suffered deeply from the recent tragedies. And most of all, it proves the resilience of America's way of life.

Food Without Frontiers: Once, fine dining in the U.S. meant French cuisine. Certainly, that perennial is still riding high – among the 41 regions included in this *Survey*, 39 percent of the restaurants rated No.1 for Food offer cooking *à la française*. But, increasingly, diners are embracing flavors from all over the world, and while that's nothing new for a coastal cosmopolis, dishes once considered 'foreign' now find favor in the meat-and-potatoes heartland as well. St. Louis surveyors, for example, rate Indian, Mexican and Vietnamese restaurants among their city's top choices, while Caribbean, Eurasian and Pan-Asian establishments are featured in the Columbus, OH section for the first time.

Rise of the Regional: Still, for many diners, there's no place like home – cooking, that is. From elk (a Rocky Mountain specialty) to Cajun crawfish étouffée, humble examples of regional cooking are now proudly served in professional kitchens. To wit: Nearly one-third of the restaurants in Seattle reviewed in this year's *Survey* focus on Northwest dishes, compared with only 10 percent in our first *America's Tops* a decade ago.

Best Brand Names: Not that there isn't common ground in our national tastes. Americans love steak – especially Ruth's Chris Steakhouse, which ranks high in 12 regions. We also enjoy putting on the Ritz: This hotel chain's French dining rooms dazzle with Top Food experiences in Atlanta, Chicago, San Francisco and Tampa. Entreprenurial chefs franchising their restaurants seems to be a winning formula: Nobu's Japanese-Peruvian menu wows them both east and west of the Rockies; Roy's Hawaiian fusion fare garners applause from the Atlantic (Palm Beach) to the Pacific (San Diego).

Adventuresome Appetites: Asian delicacies, French classics, indigenous delights – America's dining options have never been more eclectic, and our palates remain eager to experiment. It is this diversity that keeps our country strong. Not to mention well-fed.

New York, NY
November 5, 2001

Nina and Tim Zagat

About This Survey

Here are the results of our *2002 Zagat Survey of America's Top Restaurants*, covering some 1,222 restaurants in 41 U.S. regions. This book represents a compilation of the best restaurants selected by tens of thousands of *Survey* participants. For each area, we have included a list of the top restaurants (based on the results of our most recent *Surveys* in that area) as well as a list of "Additional Noteworthy Places" chosen by our local editors.

By regularly surveying large numbers of avid local restaurant-goers about their collective dining experiences, we hope to have achieved a uniquely current and reliable guide. In producing the reviews contained in this guide, our editors have done their best to accurately synopsize our surveyors' opinions, with their exact comments shown in quotation marks.

Because this guide is based on the ratings and reviews of our surveyors, we must first thank them. This guide is really theirs. Of course, we are also grateful to our local editors, who are usually professional food writers in their home cities. It was they who helped us choose the restaurants to be surveyed and edited the *Survey* results.

To help guide our readers to America's top restaurants, we have prepared two separate lists. See Top Food Rankings by Area (page 7) and Most Popular Places by Area (page 10). To assist readers in finding the cuisine they want in any region, without wasting time, we have also provided handy indexes.

To join any of our upcoming *Surveys,* you can request a ballot by e-mailing customerservice@zagat.com or using the pull-out card that's in this book. Each participant will receive a free copy of the resulting guide when it is published.

Your comments, suggestions and even criticisms of this *Survey* are also solicited. There is always room for improvement with your help. You can contact us at americastop@zagat.com or by mail at Zagat Survey, 4 Columbus Circle, New York, NY 10019. We look forward to hearing from you.

New York, NY
November 5, 2001

Nina and Tim Zagat

Key to Ratings/Symbols

Name, Address & Phone Number

Zagat Ratings

Hours & Credit Cards

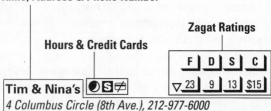

F	D	S	C
▽ 23	9	13	$15

Tim & Nina's ◗ 🅂 ⊄

4 Columbus Circle (8th Ave.), 212-977-6000

◪ Open 24/7, this "literal dive" is located in the IND station under Columbus Circle; as NY's first subway "soul pizza" stand, it offers "suckulent" slices with toppings of BBQ sauce, pork or fried chicken to harried strap-hangers "for little dough"; but for the "cost of your MetroCard" and the "need to shout your order" when the A train comes in, this would be "some trip."

Review, with surveyors' comments in quotes

Before each review a symbol indicates whether responses were uniform ■ or mixed ◪.

Hours: ◗ serves after 11 PM
🅂 open on Sunday

Credit Cards: ⊄ no credit cards accepted

Ratings: Food, Decor and Service are rated on a scale of **0** to **30**. The Cost (C) column reflects our surveyors' estimate of the price of dinner including one drink and tip.

F	Food	D	Decor	S	Service	C	Cost
23		9		13		$15	

0–9	poor to fair	**20–25**	very good to excellent
10–15	fair to good	**26–30**	extraordinary to perfection
16–19	good to very good	▽	low response/less reliable

A place listed without ratings is either an important **newcomer** or a popular **write-in**. For such places, the estimated cost is indicated by the following symbols.

I	$15 and below	**E**	$31 to $50
M	$16 to $30	**VE**	$51 or more

Top Food Rankings by Area

Atlanta
- **28** Bacchanalia
  Ritz-Carlton Buck. Din. Rm.
- **27** Soto
  Brasserie Le Coze
  Seeger's

Atlantic City
- **27** Le Palais
- **26** Medici
  White House
- **25** Chef Vola's
  Savaradio

Baltimore/Annapolis
- **28** Lewnes'
  Prime Rib
  Hampton's
- **27** Antrim 1844
  Inn at Perry Cabin

Boston
- **28** L'Espalier
  Aujourd'hui
  Caffe Bella
- **27** Hamersley's Bistro
  Olives

Chicago
- **28** Carlos'
  Ritz-Carlton Din. Rm.
  TRU
  Ambria
- **27** Seasons

Cincinnati
- **28** Maisonette
- **27** Palace
- **26** Dewey's Pizza
- **25** Daveed's at 934
  Precinct

Cleveland
- **28** Johnny's Bar
- **27** Baricelli Inn
  Phnom Penh
  Giovanni's Ristorante
- **26** Oz Bar & Bistro

Columbus, OH
- **28** Handke's Cuisine
- **27** Refectory
  L'Antibes
  Rigsby's
- **26** Yard Club at O'Toole's

Connecticut
- **28** Jean-Louis
  Thomas Henkelmann
- **27** Da Pietro's
  Ondine
  Restaurant du Village

Dallas
- **28** French Room
  Riviera
- **27** Mansion on Turtle Creek
  Cafe Pacific
  Bob's Steak & Chop

Denver/Mountain Resorts
- **28** Keystone Ranch
  Highlands Garden Cafe
  Mizuna
  Grouse Mountain Grill
  Tante Louise

Detroit
- **28** Lark
  Emily's
- **27** Zingerman's
- **26** Tribute
  Common Grill

Fort Lauderdale
- **27** Darrel & Oliver's Cafe Maxx
  Mark's Las Olas
  Casa D'Angelo
  Cafe Martorano
- **26** Cafe Seville

Fort Worth
- **28** Saint-Emilion
- **27** Del Frisco's
  La Piazza
- **26** Cacharel
  Randall's Cafe

Honolulu
- **27** Alan Wong's
- **26** La Mer
  Roy's
  Hoku's
  Ruth's Chris

Houston
- **28** Mark's
  La Réserve
- **27** Ruth's Chris
- **26** Cafe Annie
  Rotisserie/Beef & Bird

Kansas City

26 Stroud's
  American Restaurant
  Plaza III
25 Starker's Reserve
  Stolen Grill

Las Vegas

28 Renoir
  Aqua
27 Picasso
  Andre's
  Le Cirque

Long Island

28 Mill River Inn
27 Mirabelle
  Kotobuki
  Mirepoix
  Peter Luger

Los Angeles

28 Matsuhisa
  Sushi Nozawa
27 Chinois on Main
  Belvedere, The
  Water Grill

Miami

27 Chef Allen's
  Romeo's Cafe
  Palm
  Norman's
26 Osteria del Teatro

Minneapolis/St. Paul

27 Goodfellow's
  La Belle Vie
26 Bayport Cookery
  D'Amico Cucina
  Lucia's

New Jersey

28 Ryland Inn
  Daniel's on Broadway
27 Cafe Panache
  Sagami
  Saddle River Inn

New Orleans

27 Bayona
  Brigtsen's
  Gabrielle
  Grill Room
  Artesia

New York City

28 Daniel
  Chanterelle
  Le Bernardin
  Nobu
  Jean Georges

Orange County, CA

28 Pavilion
  Pinot Provence
  Napa Rose
27 Ritz
  Aubergine

Orlando

29 La Coquina
  Louis' Downtown
28 Victoria & Albert's
  Le Coq au Vin
  Del Frisco's

Palm Beach

29 Chez Jean-Pierre
27 Cafe L'Europe
  La Vieille Maison
  New York Prime
  Four Seasons

Philadelphia

29 Le Bec-Fin
  Fountain
28 Le Bar Lyonnais
27 Swann Lounge
  Susanna Foo

Phoenix/Scottsdale

28 Mary Elaine's
27 Marquesa
  Vincent Guerithault
26 T. Cook's
  RoxSand

Portland, OR

28 Genoa
  Paley's Place
  Tina's
27 Joel Palmer House
  Cafe des Amis

Salt Lake City/Mtn. Resorts

27 Seafood Buffet
  Fresco Italian Cafe
  Metropolitan
  Mariposa
  Tree Room

San Diego
27 Sushi Ota
El Bizcocho
WineSellar & Brasserie
Pamplemousse Grille
26 George's at the Cove

San Francisco Bay Area
29 French Laundry
28 Gary Danko
Ritz-Carlton Din. Rm.
Le Papillon
Chez Panisse

Santa Fe
27 Old House
Geronimo
26 Santacafe
Cafe Pasqual's
25 Ristra

Seattle
29 Rover's
28 Herbfarm
27 Salumi
Georgian Room
Mistral

So. New York State
29 Xaviar's at Piermont
Xaviar's at Garrison
28 Freelance Café
La Panetière
27 Escoffier

St. Louis
26 Sidney Street Cafe
Trattoria Marcella
25 Crossing
Tony's
Zinnia

Tampa Bay/Sarasota
29 Ritz-Carlton Din. Rm.
28 Caffe Paradiso
Lafite at the Registry
Blue Heron
27 Peter's La Cuisine

Tucson
28 Ventana Room
27 Dish
Janos
25 Cafe Poca Cosa
Le Rendez-Vous

Washington, DC
29 Inn at Little Washington
28 Makoto
27 Kinkead's
Citronelle
Gerard's Place

Most Popular by Area

Atlanta
1. Bacchanalia
2. Brasserie Le Coze
3. Bone's
4. Canoe
5. Seeger's

Atlantic City
1. Ram's Head Inn
2. Le Palais
3. White House
4. Renault Winery
5. Capriccio

Baltimore/Annapolis
1. Prime Rib
2. Tio Pepe
3. Charleston
4. Linwood's
5. Ruth's Chris

Boston
1. Aujourd'hui
2. Blue Ginger
3. Olives
4. Hamersley's Bistro
5. L'Espalier

Chicago
1. Charlie Trotter's
2. Ambria
3. TRU
4. Everest
5. mk

Cincinnati
1. Maisonette
2. Precinct
3. Montgomery Inn
4. Sturkey's
5. Palomino Euro Bistro

Cleveland
1. Sans Souci
2. Lola
3. Johnny's Bar
4. Blue Pointe Grill
5. Baricelli Inn

Columbus, OH
1. Refectory
2. Rigsby's
3. Columbus Fish Market
4. Lindey's
5. Handke's Cuisine

Connecticut
1. Jean-Louis
2. Mayflower Inn
3. Thomas Henkelmann
4. Rebeccas
5. Baang Café & Bar

Dallas
1. Mansion on Turtle Creek
2. Cafe Pacific
3. French Room
4. Riviera
5. Abacus

Denver/Mountain Resorts
1. Papillon Café
2. Highlands Garden Cafe
3. Barolo Grill
4. Strings
5. Briarwood Inn

Detroit
1. Lark
2. Tribute
3. Whitney
4. Capital Grille
5. Zingerman's

Fort Lauderdale
1. Ruth's Chris
2. Mark's Las Olas
3. Darrel & Oliver's Cafe Maxx
4. Charley's Crab
5. Outback Steakhouse

Fort Worth
1. Bistro Louise
2. Del Frisco's
3. Saint-Emilion
4. La Piazza
5. Angeluna

Honolulu
1. Alan Wong's
2. Hoku's
3. Roy's
4. 3660 on the Rise
5. Indigo

Houston
1. Cafe Annie
2. Brennan's
3. Mark's
4. Anthony's
5. Rotisserie/Beef & Bird

Kansas City
1. Fiorella's Jack Stack
2. Stroud's
3. Lidia's
4. Plaza III
5. McCormick & Schmick's

Las Vegas
1. Picasso
2. Rosemary's
3. Andre's
4. Palm
5. Steak House

Long Island
1. Peter Luger
2. Mill River Inn
3. Mirabelle
4. Panama Hatties
5. Bryant & Cooper

Los Angeles
1. Café Bizou
2. Spago
3. Campanile
4. Bel-Air Hotel
5. Patina

Miami
1. Joe's Stone Crab
2. Norman's
3. Cheesecake Factory
4. Pacific Time
5. Chef Allen's

Minneapolis/St. Paul
1. Oceanaire
2. Kincaid's
3. Goodfellow's
4. D'Amico Cucina
5. Lucia's

New Jersey
1. Ryland Inn
2. Scalini Fedeli
3. Saddle River Inn
4. Manor
5. Highlawn Pavilion

New Orleans
1. Commander's Palace
2. Galatoire's
3. Bayona
4. Brigtsen's
5. Grill Room

New York City
1. Union Square Cafe
2. Gramercy Tavern
3. Daniel
4. Gotham Bar & Grill
5. Peter Luger

Orange County, CA
1. Cheesecake Factory
2. Ruth's Chris
3. California Pizza Kitchen
4. Il Fornaio
5. El Cholo

Orlando
1. California Grill
2. Outback
3. Le Coq au Vin
4. Del Frisco's
5. Ruth's Chris

Palm Beach
1. Cafe L'Europe
2. Chez Jean-Pierre Bistro
3. Cheesecake Factory
4. La Vieille Maison
5. Cafe Chardonnay

Philadelphia
1. Le Bec-Fin
2. Fountain
3. Buddakan
4. Brasserie Perrier
5. Susanna Foo

Phoenix/Scottsdale
1. Lon's at the Hermosa
2. RoxSand
3. T. Cook's
4. Vincent Guerithault
5. Ruth's Chris

Portland, OR
1. Genoa
2. Wildwood
3. Higgins
4. Paley's Place
5. Castagna

Salt Lake City/Mtn. Resorts
1. New Yorker Club
2. Fresco Italian Cafe
3. Metropolitan
4. Tuscany
5. Log Haven

San Diego
1. George's at the Cove
2. Laurel
3. Pamplemousse Grille
4. Mille Fleurs
5. Tapenade

San Francisco Bay Area
1. Boulevard
2. Gary Danko
3. French Laundry
4. Jardinière
5. Aqua

Santa Fe
1. Geronimo
2. Santacafe
3. Cafe Pasqual's
4. Coyote Cafe
5. Old House

Seattle
1. Wild Ginger
2. Dahlia Lounge
3. Rover's
4. Metropolitan Grill
5. Canlis

So. New York State
1. La Panetière
2. Crabtree's Kittle House
3. Xaviar's at Piermont
4. La Crémaillère
5. American Bistro, An

St. Louis
1. Trattoria Marcella
2. Sidney Street Cafe
3. Harvest
4. Tony's
5. Bar Italia Ristorante

Tampa Bay/Sarasota
1. Michael's on East
2. Ophelia's
3. Bern's Steak House
4. Beach Bistro
5. Café L'Europe

Tucson
1. Ventana Room
2. Janos
3. Cafe Poca Cosa
4. Anthony's/Catalinas
5. Café Terra Cotta

Washington, DC
1. Kinkead's
2. L'Auberge Chez François
3. Inn at Little Washington
4. Galileo/Il Laboratorio
5. D.C. Coast

Restaurant Directory

Atlanta

TOP 20 FOOD RANKING

Restaurant	Cuisine Type
28 Bacchanalia	New American
Ritz-Carlton Buck. Din. Rm.	Classic French
27 Soto	Japanese
Brasserie Le Coze	New French/Seafood
Seeger's	Continental
Chops/Lobster Bar	Steakhouse/Seafood
Pano's & Paul's	Continental
La Grotta	N&S Italian
26 Sushi Huku	Japanese
Bone's	Steakhouse
Nikolai's Roof	Classic French/Russian
Park 75	New American
Ritz-Carlton Buck. Café	Continental/Provençal
Sia's	Asian/Southwestern
Tamarind	Thai
25 Hashiguchi	Japanese
Nava	Southwestern
dick & harry's	New American
Food Studio	New American
Floataway Cafe	French Bistro/N&S Italian

ADDITIONAL NOTEWORTHY PLACES

Abruzzi	N&S Italian
Aria	New American/Southern
Atlanta Fish Market	Seafood
Babette's Cafe	Continental/International
BluePointe	New American
Buckhead Diner	New American
Canoe	New American
Eno	Mediterranean
Haru Ichiban	Japanese
Harvest	American
Kamogawa	Japanese
Morton's of Chicago	Steakhouse
Mumbo Jumbo	New American
103 West	New French/Continental
Oscar's	New American
Prime	Steakhouse/Seafood
Sotto Sotto	N&S Italian
Tierra	Latin American/Fusion
Van Gogh's	New American
Watershed	New American

Abruzzi
24 | 19 | 24 | $44

Peachtree Battle Shopping Ctr., 2355 Peachtree Rd. NE (Peachtree Battle Ave.), 404-261-8186

■ "Buckhead matrons" at lunch and a "who's who" of "regulars" at dinner patronize this "upscale" Italian for "excellent" fare and "gracious" service by a "professional staff" and "delightful" owner in a "warm", "clubby" setting.

Aria
– | – | – | M

490 E. Paces Ferry Rd. (Maple Dr.), 404-233-7673

This jewel box of a space in Buckhead may have finally found its groove with this stylish spot that smartly sports tiered leather walls and metal drapery; diners can tell that Gerry Klaskala is in the kitchen after just one taste of his succulent slow-roasted offerings from the New American menu with a Southern twist.

Atlanta Fish Market [S]
23 | 20 | 20 | $32

265 Pharr Rd. (bet. Peachtree St. & Piedmont Rd.), 404-262-3165

■ Packed to the gills, this "first-class" Buckhead seafood palace is so "busy" that some worry "it'll single-handedly deplete the ocean"; the "impressive case" displays "many choices" of the "freshest" fish, each "always cooked just right", leading finatics to aver "if I were a fish, I'd want to be prepared here."

Babette's Cafe [S]
24 | 20 | 22 | $28

573 N. Highland Ave. (Freedom Pkwy.), 404-523-9121

■ "Charming all around", this Poncey-Highlands Continental-International bistro offers a "unique menu" of "fabulous", "classy European comfort food" served by a "knowledgeable" staff in a renovated house with a "romantic" ambiance; scores of devotees promise it's "worth the trip" to "delight" in this "wonderful" "gem", especially since it now takes reservations.

Bacchanalia
28 | 24 | 26 | $59

1198 Howell Mill Rd. (14th St.), 404-365-0410

■ Ranked once again as Atlanta's Most Popular restaurant, this "heavenly" New American that's "in a class by itself" is "where Bacchus himself would eat"; also rated No. 1 for Food, it combines an "incredible" menu and an "extraordinary wine list" with cutting-edge warehouse-chic decor and "seamless" service to create the "best magic in town"; N.B. they're now open for lunch.

BluePointe [S]
– | – | – | E

3455 Peachtree Rd. (Lenox Rd.), 404-237-9070

Blue bloods, businessmen and Buckhead Life Group boosters eager for a bite of this white-hot scene stream into a soaring space appointed with sensuous curves and flattering lighting; it's an eye-catching backdrop for chef Ian Winslade's New American dishes tweaked with Asian accents, so if you can put up with the crush, this big-city spot may be worth the wait.

Bone's [S]
26 | 22 | 25 | $47

3130 Piedmont Rd. (Peachtree Rd.), 404-237-2663

■ "When money and cholesterol are no object", "old Atlanta" heads to this "essential Buckhead power center" for "huge portions" of some of the "best steaks anywhere"; expect "lavish service", as well as a "he-man" atmosphere and lots of "cigar smoke"; though a few quibble that it's "too clubby", "regulars" are more than happy to keep up this "favorite" "tradition."

Brasserie Le Coze 27 | 24 | 24 | $38

Lenox Sq., 3393 Peachtree Rd. (Lenox Rd.), 404-266-1440

■ "You could be in Paris" at this "sophisticated" New French bistro in Buckhead, where the seasonal menu is "exceptional"; as it's run by the owners of NYC's top-rated Le Bernardin, it's no surprise that the seafood here is "perfect"; along with "stunning" decor and "professional" service, it adds up to a "memorable" experience that'll make diners "forget they're at Lenox Square."

Buckhead Diner ◐ [S] 23 | 22 | 21 | $29

3073 Piedmont Rd. NE (Pharr Rd.), 404-262-3336

◪ Whether you're there to "see and be seen" or to impress "your out-of-town guests", this "upscale" Buckhead New American diner has long been a "favorite" thanks to its "creative" dishes, "glitzy atmosphere" and "marvelous service", though critics carp about the "no-reservations" policy and accuse it of "living on its past reputation"; N.B. recent updates to the menu and dining room may enhance the above food and decor scores.

Canoe [S] 24 | 26 | 22 | $38

Vinings on the River, 4199 Paces Ferry Rd. (I-75), 770-432-2663

◪ Romantics love to stroll in the garden at this "bucolic" "delight" "on the banks of the Chattahoochee" in Vinings, which showcases ironwork that's as "beautiful" as its "gorgeous landscaping"; factor in "outstanding", "innovative" New American dishes and "excellent" service, and the result is an "impressive" "class act"; critics, however, detect "way too much attitude" and warn that it can be "incredibly noisy."

Chops/Lobster Bar [S] 27 | 25 | 25 | $47

Buckhead Plaza, 70 W. Paces Ferry Rd. (Peachtree Rd.), 404-262-2675

■ Upstairs at this Buckhead standout is a "hearty men's-club steakhouse" that delivers "great" beef and an "excellent wine list" to a "power" business crowd; downstairs at the "glitzy" Lobster Bar, an arched white-tile ceiling makes for "romantic grotto" dining over sublime seafood; a few spoilers sniff about "snooty" service, but for most it's all a "real treat."

dick & harry's 25 | 20 | 22 | $36

Holcomb Woods Village, 1570 Holcomb Bridge Rd. (½ mi. east of GA 400), Roswell, 770-641-8757

■ Anticipate a "great culinary adventure" at the Marmulstein brothers' "refreshing" New American "destination", which is "worth a trip" to Roswell for their "trendsetting menu" that ensures "incredible" "flavor combinations" (the "seafood is a must"); the "upscale, modern interior" complements the chef's "innovative presentations", and though it can get "noisy", it's still a "delight."

Eno [S] – | – | – | E

800 Peachtree St. (5th St.), 404-685-3191

In an up-and-coming area of Midtown that's on the verge of trendy, accomplished chef Jamie Adams turns out zesty Mediterranean fare – from bar nibbles to appetizers to entrees – that's perfectly backed up by the well-stocked wine cellar (100 or so choices by the taste or the glass); it's a prime pick for a romantic dinner or pre-theater meal.

Floataway Cafe 25 | 21 | 21 | $37

1123 Zonolite Rd. (at int. of Briarcliff & Johnson Rds.), 404-892-1414

◪ Bacchanalia's "funky little sister", this "edgy" yet "sophisticated" French-Italian bistro set in a "converted warehouse" near Emory sports polished metals and airy cloud paintings; the less enchanted "don't like" the "cold" surroundings or the "servers with way too much attitude", but just about everyone appreciates the "amazing" cooking that relies on "fresh" ingredients; be warned, though, of the decibel level ("how does great food make so much noise?").

Food Studio [S] 25 | 26 | 23 | $38

King Plow Art Ctr., 887 W. Marietta St. (bet. Ashby St. & Howell Mill Rd.), 404-815-6677

■ "Feast your eyes and your mouth" at this "stunning" New American located in a turn-of-the-century West Midtown loft that was once a farm equipment factory; old brick walls and flickering candlelight create a "hyper-romantic" mood in which to sample the "inventive", "awesome" menu of chef Christopher Brandt, complemented by a wine list that's "nothing short of perfect"; add on "attentive" service, and the result is a dining experience that's "fabulous all the way."

Haru Ichiban [S] – | – | – | M

36-46 Satellite Blvd. (Pleasant Hill Rd.), Duluth, 770-622-4060

While its setting may be a typical suburban mall space, this tastefully appointed Japanese neophyte in Duluth is anything but ordinary when it comes to its glorious array of authentic sushi and traditional seasonal cooking; owner Yukio Watanabe is delighting expats from the homeland, as well as local foodies, who are willing to make the drive here from all over Atlanta.

Harvest [S] 24 | 22 | 22 | $30

853 N. Highland Ave. (St. Charles Ave.), 404-876-8244

■ Delighted diners shovel heaps of praise on this "romantic" Va-Highlands American "gem" quartered in a "cozy" old house "enhanced" by "great" Arts and Crafts details and six working fireplaces; admirers savor "generous portions" of "imaginative", "exceptional" dishes crafted with "loving attention to detail", and since the service is "friendly" to boot, this "true joy" "has all the bases covered"; P.S. don't miss the "scrumptious" Sunday brunch.

Hashiguchi 25 | 18 | 20 | $24

The Terrace, 3000 Windy Hill Rd. (Powers Ferry Rd.), Marietta, 770-955-2337

Hashiguchi Jr.

3400 Wood Dale Dr. (Peachtree St.), 404-841-9229

■ Boosters bow in honor of this "family-style" Japanese duo in Marietta and Buckhead that showcases "first-rate sushi and sashimi" (one of the "best deals we've found") and "pleasing" cooked dishes in a "simple" (or "bland"?) setting; factor in a "nice" staff that's "not pretentious" and it's easy to see why it's an "authentic" "favorite" for many "regulars."

Kamogawa 24 | 23 | 20 | $36

Grand Hyatt Atlanta, 3300 Peachtree Rd. NE (Piedmont Rd.), 404-841-0314

■ "Wonderful" Japanese food, including some of the "best sushi in the Southeast", is the hallmark of this South Buckhead "classic"; it's "pricey", but the "fresh" fish proffered by a "great" staff in refined surroundings is "perfect, just perfect."

La Grotta 27 | 22 | 26 | $44

2637 Peachtree Rd. (bet. Lindbergh Dr. & W. Wesley Rd.), 404-231-1368

Crowne Plaza Ravinia Hotel, 4355 Ashford Dunwoody Rd. (Hammond Dr.), 770-395-9925

■ Once again ranked the top Italian in Atlanta, this "lovely" pair promises "one of the finest dining experiences anywhere", since it "maintains its standards year after year"; while the Buckhead flagship is most "romantic", the Dunwoody offshoot is "delightful" too, and both showcase "incredible" "classic" dishes that "just get better with time", complemented by a "superb" staff that's "professional all the way"; the impeccable reputation of this Atlanta "mainstay" is clearly "well deserved."

Morton's of Chicago [S] 24 | 21 | 22 | $45

3379 Peachtree Rd. (Lenox Rd.), 404-816-6535

303 Peachtree Center Ave. (Baker St.), 404-577-4366

◪ "You expect the best and you get it" at the Downtown and Buckhead outposts of these "upper-class" steakhouses, "the best of the chains by far" according to partisans, where "outsized portions" of "great meat" are the norm; loyal locals who prefer other "high-priced" beef barns insist that it's "overrated" and "brutally overpriced", but if you "go on someone else's ticket", it's definitely easy to "enjoy."

Mumbo Jumbo [S] 22 | 24 | 19 | $35

89 Park Pl. NE (Auburn Ave.), 404-523-0330

◪ "Splashy" decor sets the stage at this "hip", "high-energy" New American with a "great bar" and "superb" cooking from chef Shaun Doty, whose presentations "deserve photographing" (the dishes "taste as good as [they] look"); dissenters, however, find it "uneven", and even fans who dub it the "best Downtown" mumble that it needs to "lose the attitude."

Nava [S] 25 | 27 | 23 | $37

Buckhead Plaza, 3060 Peachtree Rd. NW (W. Paces Ferry Rd.), 404-240-1984

■ "This sexy Southwestern success" story is "still inventive and fun" thanks to "great" chef Kevin Rathbun's "spicy", "imaginative" creations; "fine service" and a "gorgeous" room only add to the "wonderful experience", and though a few grumble that it's just "another overrated Buckhead spot", the overwhelming majority likes being "in the hands of someone who knows what he's doing": "there's not an 'ok' thing on the menu – it's all superb."

Nikolai's Roof [S] 26 | 26 | 26 | $64

Atlanta Hilton, 255 Courtland St., 30th fl. (bet. Baker & Harris Sts.), 404-221-6362

◪ It's "hard to top the view" from this rooftop French with a decidedly Russian flair at Downtown's Atlanta Hilton, where "tourists", "expense-account crowds" and celebrants enjoy one of the "best dining experiences" in the city, from the "excellent" old-world service to the iced vodkas, silver domes and "great food", including classics such as piroshkis, borscht and caviar (but of course!); though many moan it's "horribly overpriced", it's "a treat" and "you have to go at least once."

103 West
24 | 23 | 25 | $49

103 W. Paces Ferry Rd. (Peachtree St.), 404-233-5993

☑ Renowned for its "romantic" "Victorian" setting appointed with "rococo furnishings", this "old-world charmer" is where Buckhead celebrates "special occasions"; the New French–Continental fare is "superb" (especially the "exceptional" fried lobster tail) and "beautifully served", but detractors find this place at once a "bit too formal" and "gaudy"; still, loyalists laud the "lavish" experience.

Oscar's
– | – | – | M

3725 Main St. (bet. Harvard & Princeton Aves.), College Park, 404-766-9688

In the heart of College Park, owner Oscar Morales has converted a turn-of-the-century building into this casual, cosmopolitan New American eatery where chef Todd Immel's (ex Mumbo Jumbo) stellar cooking has created a buzz among diners from far and wide (including lots of airport employees); a 1917 Coca-Cola sign and candy-striped light fixtures highlight the decor.

Pano's & Paul's
27 | 22 | 25 | $50

W. Paces Ferry Shopping Ctr., 1232 W. Paces Ferry Rd. (Northside Pkwy.), 404-261-3662

■ "Excellent for two decades", this "elegant" Buckhead "patriarch endures" thanks to "exquisite", "classic" Continental fare (don't miss its "famous fried lobster tail") that's proffered by a "friendly and efficient" staff; better "take $$$", but for a "romantic" "special-occasion" "treat", this "exceptional" "experience" is hard to beat.

Park 75 S
26 | 26 | 25 | $50

Four Seasons Atlanta, 75 14th St. (Peachtree St.), 404-253-3840

■ A "favorite" of gourmands, this New American showplace at the Four Seasons Atlanta in Midtown is among the "most exciting" in town; credit the "smoking menu" (the "delightfully innovative" dim sum–style Sunday brunch is a must), service that's just about "perfect" and a "great" setting appointed with palm trees, beautiful fabrics and oil paintings; N.B. the recent departure of chef Brooke Vosika may outdate the above food score.

Prime S
24 | 22 | 21 | $38

Lenox Sq., 3393 Peachtree Rd. (Lenox Rd.), 404-812-0555

■ "Can you believe this place is in a mall?" marvel boosters of this Lenox Square "hot spot" that offers "something for everyone" in a "beautiful" room that melds manly clubhouse with a light-filled Asian feel; an eager clientele gathers for "prime" cuts of meat and some of the "best fish you'll ever eat in a steakhouse", so though it may be "too noisy" and "overpriced" to some, most just sigh "sublime!"

Ritz-Carlton Buckhead Café S
26 | 26 | 26 | $39

Ritz-Carlton Buckhead, 3434 Peachtree Rd. NE (Lenox Rd.), 404-237-2700

■ "When you want to act grown-up", go straight to this "beautiful", "first-class" Continental-Provençal cafe at the Ritz-Carlton hotel in Buckhead, where "great food, service and dancing" are the norm and where they "set the standard for Sunday brunch"; despite quibbles that it's "a bit stuffy", the majority maintains it's a veritable "model to emulate."

Ritz-Carlton Buckhead Dining Room

F	D	S	C
28	27	27	$64

Ritz-Carlton Buckhead, 3434 Peachtree Rd. NE (Lenox Rd.), 404-237-2700

■ Tops for hotel dining in Atlanta, this "superlative" main room of the Ritz-Carlton Buckhead thrills with "exquisite" Classic French dishes sparked by Japanese accents; furthermore, an "attentive" staff makes patrons "feel like royalty", leaving them convinced that even "heaven can't get much better" than this "memorable" "experience"; N.B. the recent departure of chef Joël Antunes, along with an interior redo, may outdate the above food and decor scores; stay tuned.

Seeger's

F	D	S	C
27	26	26	$77

111 W. Paces Ferry Rd. (E. Andrews Dr.), 404-846-9779

◪ "What fine dining is all about, from top to bottom", cheer fans of this "world-class" restaurant in Buckhead set in a "sophisticated" space that makes an ideal backdrop for the modern Continental creations of "Atlanta's resident culinary genius", Guenter Seeger; some may gripe about "minute servings for a king's ransom" and "snobby service to boot", but connoisseurs, made to "feel like royalty", laud this "incomparable" "dining-as-theater" experience as "fabulous in every respect."

Sia's

F	D	S	C
26	24	25	$41

The Shoppes of St. Ives, 10305 Medlock Bridge Rd. (Wilson Dr.), Duluth, 770-497-9727

■ "Finally, a classy place outside the perimeter" of the city, this "suburban star" in Duluth is the "beautiful" brainchild of Sia Moshk (ex general manager of 103 West); in a "modern" cobalt-and-tangerine-colored room with warm cherrywood walls, chef Scott Serpas' "superb" Asian-Southwestern creations are brought to table by an "attentive" staff; keep an eye on this "outstanding" gem.

Soto ◐

F	D	S	C
27	14	15	$34

Kroger Shopping Ctr., 3330 Piedmont Rd. (Peachtree Rd.), 404-233-2005

■ This "modest" winner in Buckhead is renowned for preparing some of the "best sushi on the East Coast", crafted by one of the "most skilled and inventive chefs in the city"; the interior may be "unappealing" and you might want to "bring a book" (the "service is sooo slow" and "inattentive"), but the "exquisite" Japanese fare – when it arrives – compensates for all.

Sotto Sotto

F	D	S	C
23	19	18	$33

313 N. Highland Ave. (Elizabeth St.), 404-523-6678

◪ While this "trendy" Inman Park spot may be "harder to find than a native Atlantan", adventurers are "rewarded" with "authentic", zesty Italian food; frustrated fans gripe that "too much popularity can be a bad thing" (read: "long waits" and a "frenzied" pace), but more patient patrons urge "just go."

Sushi Huku [S]

F	D	S	C
26	19	23	$32

Powers Ferry Village, 6300 Powers Ferry Rd. (Northside Dr.), 770-956-9559

■ "Feel like you've traveled to Japan" after dining at this Northside establishment that showcases not only some of "the best sushi in Atlanta" – "fresh and well prepared" – but also "authentic" cooked dishes, including "excellent tempura"; most of the customers are Japanese, but the "friendly" staff makes everyone feel welcome.

Tamarind [S] 26 | 21 | 22 | $26

80 14th St. NW (bet. Spring & Williams Sts.), 404-873-4888

■ "Clearly the leader" in "gourmet" Thai, this Midtown treasure attracts a following that likes to "relax" in its "beautiful", "peaceful" room while nibbling on "unusual", "flavorful" and "well-presented" fare; a "family-run" establishment, it also earns nods for "courteous service" – small wonder it's at the "top of the heap."

Tierra [S] 23 | 19 | 20 | $28

1425-B Piedmont Ave. (Westminster Dr.), 404-874-5951

■ "Terrific Latin American fusion at the edge of Piedmont Park" is creating a stir among aficionados of this "interesting concept" from chef-owners Ticha and Dan Krinsky, who employ "fresh, unique ingredients" to interpret the "flavors of the Americas"; the "charming" interior and "nice patio" provide pleasant backdrops for the "great" food and "reasonably priced wines" – all reasons fans fear that "crowds will overwhelm" this "tiny", "bright" gem.

Van Gogh's [S] 24 | 23 | 22 | $34

70 W. Crossville Rd. (Crabapple Rd.), Roswell, 770-993-1156

■ "Gogh, gogh, gogh!" urge boosters of this New American "gourmet delight" as they paint a glowing picture of its "creative" menu, "charming" atmosphere and "wonderful service"; ever a "trendsetter", it remains one of the "best in Roswell" and well "worth the drive."

Watershed 23 | 20 | 19 | $22

406 W. Ponce de Leon Ave. (Commerce Dr.), Decatur, 404-378-4900

■ "How creative can you get?" marvel adventurous admirers of this "fabulous" New American set in a "cool" renovated garage in Decatur; let the "knowledgeable" staff advise on chef Scott Peacock's "unique" menu of "divine" dishes, which are paired with a "top-notch wine selection"; though a few nitpick that it's a bit "expensive for what you get", most savor this "breath of fresh air."

Atlantic City

TOP 10 FOOD RANKING

	Restaurant	Cuisine Type
27	Le Palais	New French
26	Medici	Southern Italian
	White House	Sandwich Shop
25	Chef Vola's	N&S Italian
	Savaradio	Eclectic
	Ram's Head Inn	American
	Tre Figlio	N&S Italian
	Capriccio	N&S Italian
24	Brighton	Steakhouse
	Renault Winery	American

F	D	S	C

Brighton Steak House **S**

24	23	24	$47

Sands Casino Hotel, Indiana Ave. (Brighton Park), 609-441-4300
■ "Stop gambling losses" with a time-out at this Sands steakhouse where the beef is "wonderful", the service is "top-notch" and the "live piano music" sweetly embellishes the "elegant atmosphere"; high rollers, however, warn if you can't "get comped", better bring a "hefty wallet."

Capriccio **S**

25	25	24	$48

Resorts, 1133 Boardwalk (North Carolina Ave.), 609-340-6789
■ "Eat like royalty" (especially at a table "overlooking the ocean") at this "top-scale" Italian ristorante at the Resorts casino and hotel, where the "luscious dining" "never fails to deliver" and service is "classy" and "polite"; of course, the food tastes even better if you're using a "twofer" coupon.

Chef Vola's **S**⇗

25	12	22	$39

111 S. Albion Pl. (Pacific Ave.), 609-345-2022
■ It helps to "know someone" at this Italian BYO, since it's so tough to snag a reservation, but if you're lucky enough to get inside this "happening basement", you'll be rewarded with "superb", "can't-be-beat" cooking, service so "personal" that "they make you feel like family" and a "noisy", convivial scene; N.B. cash only.

Le Palais **S**

27	28	27	$51

Resorts, 1133 Boardwalk (North Carolina Ave.), 609-340-6400
■ "Get lucky at the tables and pick up the check" at this "posh", "first-class" New French bastion at the Resorts casino and hotel, where "fabulous, synchronized" service complements the kitchen's "elegant" fare (rated No. 1 for Food in Atlantic City) and ultra-"romantic" setting; it's clearly a "place to celebrate something special"; P.S. open only at limited times, so call ahead.

Medici   26 | 26 | 25 | $48

Sands Casino Hotel, Indiana Ave. (Brighton Park), 609-441-4200

■ "If you're in Atlantic City with an expense account", consider this Southern Italian at the Sands that boasts a "creative bread basket" and enough "excellent" options for admirers to regard it as one of the "best restaurants in South Jersey"; the "romantic" environs and "excellent service" earn high marks too.

Ram's Head Inn **S**   25 | 27 | 25 | $47

9 W. White Horse Pike (bet. Garden State Pkwy S. & Rte. 30), Absecon, 609-652-1700

■ "Escape from Atlantic City schlock" at this "finely decorated" American country inn in Absecon that's "one of the few class acts in South Jersey", which may explain why it was voted the Most Popular restaurant in this resort town; you can "relax knowing the food and service will be superb", so "if you can afford only one expensive meal a year, this is the place to go."

Renault Winery **S**   24 | 25 | 23 | $40

72 N. Bremen Ave. (Moss Mill Rd.), Egg Harbor, 609-965-2111

■ An "enchanting atmosphere inside and out" awaits at this "romantic" American set in an Egg Harbor winery and offering "great multi-course meals"; it's a "fun out-of-the-way place for a special date", with decor so wonderful it elevates the entire experience "up a notch."

Savaradio **S**⊉   25 | 17 | 20 | $34

5223 Ventnor Ave. (Little Rock Ave.), Ventnor, 609-823-2110

■ This "different and delicious" Ventnor Eclectic BYO comes courtesy of talented chef-owner Lisa Savage, whose "delightful presentations" taste "even better" than they look; it's a "terrific, trendy spot" and "worth the 15-minute drive" from Atlantic City, even though the constant crowds virtually guarantee that you'll "brush elbows with your fellow eaters."

Tre Figlio **S**   25 | 21 | 23 | $39

500 W. White Horse Pike (Mannheim Ave.), Egg Harbor, 609-965-3303

■ Admirers say it's "always a pleasure" to dine at this Egg Harbor Italian since the "attentive" staff is most "accommodating"; in addition, the "authentic" fare (especially the "super veal chop" and lobster ravioli) pairs nicely with the noteworthy wine list at this "hidden winner" that's a "must when in the Atlantic City area."

White House **S**⊉   26 | 12 | 18 | $13

2301 Arctic Ave. (Mississippi Ave.), 609-345-1564

■ "Hoagies from heaven" make this sandwich shop a "culinary icon" in Atlantic City, so despite the name, it earns bipartisan plaudits; "check out all the pictures of famous people who've stopped here", then get in line for "hall-of-fame" grinders that "can be an addiction" because they're so damn "sub-lime."

Baltimore/Annapolis

TOP 10 FOOD RANKING

Restaurant	Cuisine Type
28 Lewnes'/A*	Steakhouse
Prime Rib	Steakhouse/Seafood
Hampton's	New American
27 Antrim 1844	New American
Inn at Perry Cabin/A	Continental
Charleston	New American/Southern
Rudys' 2900	Continental/New American
26 Linwood's	New American
208 Talbot/A	New American
Boccaccio	Northern Italian

ADDITIONAL NOTEWORTHY PLACES

Black Olive	Greek/Seafood
Helmand	Afghan
Kelly's	American
Milton Inn	American/Continental
Petit Louis	French Bistro
Pierpont	Chesapeake/Seafood
Polo Grill	American/Continental
Ruth's Chris	Steakhouse
Samos	Greek/American
Tio Pepe	Spanish/Continental

F	D	S	C

Antrim 1844 Country Inn 🄢   27 | 28 | 27 | $55

30 Trevanion Rd. (Rte. 140), Taneytown, 410-756-6812

■ "Perfect in every way" rhapsodize visitors to this pre–Civil War mansion near Gettysburg that's graced with "magnificent" gardens; inside, the "opulent" dining room filled with "many roaring fires and 19th-century period pieces" sets the mood for "superb" prix fixe New American meals; no wonder couples find it ideal for the seduction, the engagement and the wedding itself.

Black Olive 🄢   25 | 18 | 21 | $41

814 S. Bond St. (bet. Lancaster & Thames Sts.), Baltimore, 410-276-7141

☑ "*The* place to go for fresh fish" is this "sophisticated" Fells Point Greek taverna where a "charming" family gives a "pick-your-own" "tour" of the exotic seafood (including "fish we've never heard of!") displayed in the open kitchen that is then cooked simply and paired with fine wines; despite the "exceptional" quality, some quip it's "cheaper to cruise Greece" than pay premium prices for what they see as "plain" fare served in a "casual" setting (now expanded to next door).

---

* A=Annapolis/Eastern Shore

Boccaccio [S] 26 | 24 | 24 | $44

925 Eastern Ave. (bet. Exeter & High Sts.), Baltimore, 410-234-1322

■ "It's hard to be the best", especially if you're Baltimore's top Italian ristorante, but this "*primo*" Little Italy "power" place has proven yet again that it "can't be beat" by continuing to showcase "first-class" cooking "impeccably served" in an "elegant" setting; if they actually started "honoring reservation times", they might win even greater accolades.

Charleston 27 | 26 | 26 | $47

1000 Lancaster St. (bet. Central & Exeter Sts.), Baltimore, 410-332-7373

■ "Baltimore's answer to NYC and San Francisco" (and that's not just local pride talking) is this "fabulous" Inner Harbor East New American "gem" owned by chef Cindy Wolf and her husband, Tony Foreman; her "innovative" Southern-accented fare is "queen", while his "monumental wine cellar" and expertise is "king"; add on "handsome" surroundings and "pampering" service proffered by an intelligent staff and the result is a dining experience that "wows" just about everyone; it's "worth" the "splurge."

Hampton's [S] 28 | 29 | 27 | $58

Harbor Court Hotel, 550 Light St. (bet. Conway & Lee Sts.), Baltimore, 410-347-9744

■ "Never less than excellent", Baltimore's "best" hotel dining establishment impresses with "world-class" service, a "gorgeous" room and "beautiful harbor views" that complement the "top-notch" seasonal New American fare; one of Charm City's foremost sites for "special occasions", it's "almost perfect."

Helmand [S] 26 | 21 | 23 | $23

806 N. Charles St. (Madison St.), Baltimore, 410-752-0311

■ Combine a "wonderful" adventure for "bored taste buds", an intriguing ambiance, "helpful staff" and "reasonable prices" and you'll usually wind up with a "full house", like at this popular Mount Vernon Afghan; it "wins over" most anyone who wants to break timid friends into "exotic" dining, "delight" a date or dig into the "best rack of lamb."

Inn at Perry Cabin [S] 27 | 29 | 26 | $60

308 Watkins Ln. (Talbot St.), St. Michaels, 410-745-2200

■ This luxurious Eastern Shore retreat is "an elegant experience from start to finish"; everyone's treated like a "celebrity", and a meal in its modern Continental restaurant is "one that you won't forget"; though a few quibble about "pretentious" pampering, most just wish they lived "closer" so they could "visit more often", especially for the "wonderful" formal tea served on the patio, which boasts a spectacular view of the water.

Kelly's ◐[S] ▽ 19 | 10 | 16 | $18

2108 Eastern Ave. (bet. Chester & Duncan Sts.), Baltimore, 410-327-2312

■ Kelly and Mary Sheridan's "great" "watering hole" in Southeast Baltimore is a classic "neighborhood bar"; folks flock here for the "best [steamed] crabs and camaraderie in town", other "home-cooked" American eats, "cheap" tabs and loud "fun", especially once the karaoke starts.

Lewnes' Steakhouse S
28 23 26 $45

401 Fourth St. (Severn Ave.), Annapolis, 410-263-1617
■ Proving beyond any doubt that diners still love "prime steaks" and "great wines", this "locally owned" "gentlemen's club" in Eastport is ranked No. 1 for Food in the *Baltimore/Annapolis Survey*; well-hooved carnivores gather here for hefty portions of "really outstanding beef", accompanied by traditional sides; yes it's "pricey", but it's well "worth it", as it's "excellent on all fronts."

Linwood's S
26 26 25 $43

McDonough Crossroads, 25 Crossroads Dr. (McDonough & Reisterstown Rds.), Owings Mills, 410-356-3030
■ Linwood Dame "gets it all right" at his "prestigious" Owings Mills New American, which features a "creative" menu, an "accommodating" staff and a "clubby, cozy" setting that works equally well for casual bar dining or "special occasions" when elegant "ambiance and service count"; though it's too "pricey" and "stuffy" to some, the "worldly" set lauds it as a "class act" with "city sophistication."

Milton Inn S
25 27 24 $48

14833 York Rd. (3 mi. north of Shawan Rd.), Sparks, 410-771-4366
■ "Class and character" plus "excellent" American fare with Continental touches proffered in an 18th-century "*Masterpiece Theatre*" manor setting sum up this "special-occasion" mecca in North Baltimore County; though it's "expensive", few places anywhere can match its "romantic" ambiance, and most laud the owners for striving to continually "improve" its "quality"; P.S. the prix fixe Sunday–Friday makes it possible to dine here without taking out a "bank loan."

Petit Louis S
– – – E

4800 Roland Ave. (Upland Ave.), Baltimore, 410-366-9393
A sophisticated uptown crowd fills Charleston's boisterous young offshoot, set in the restored former Morgan-Millard in Roland Park, for hearty Parisian bistro fare, matched by Tony Foreman's wine picks and delivered by suave servers; it's settling down to a smooth (but energetic) stride and worth keeping an eye on.

Pierpoint S
24 16 20 $37

1822 Aliceanna St. (bet. Ann & Wolfe Sts.), Baltimore, 410-675-2080
■ "Fells Point at its best" rave fans of chef-owner Nancy Longo's "hip, sophisticated" "small bistro with big seafood" flavor; expect "innovative", reinterpreted Maryland classics like smoked crab cakes and a "relaxing atmosphere", though some critics object to the "close" seating.

Polo Grill S
26 25 24 $47

Doubletree Inn at the Colonnade, 4 W. University Pkwy. (bet. Canterbury Rd. & N. Charles St.), Baltimore, 410-235-8200
■ "Baltimore's 'who's who'" and "new money" congregate at this "handsome" "public club" near Roland Park "to be seen", as well as to enjoy the "wonderful" American-Continental cooking ("great fried lobster tail") prepared by chef Michael Rork (ex Hampton's) and served by a "veteran" staff; some note the "serious $$$" and "noise", but most chorus "if someone else is buying, I'm there!"

Prime Rib ●☐☐   28 | 26 | 27 | $51

Horizon House, 1101 N. Calvert St. (Chase St.), Baltimore, 410-539-1804

■ Voted the Most Popular restaurant in the *Baltimore/Annapolis Survey* (and ranked No. 2 among steakhouses), this Downtown retro supper club with a "swank", big-city feel proves that dressing up for a great evening of martinis, fine wines and red meat has enduring appeal; while it sets "the standard" for beef and seafood (the crab dishes are as notable as the signature prime rib), its "superior" service and "'50s-era" "glamour" make any occasion a truly "special" experience.

Rudys' 2900 ☐   27 | 22 | 25 | $42

2900 Baltimore Blvd. (Rte. 91), Baltimore, 410-833-5777

■ "Way, way out" in Finksburg, this Continental-American has cultivated a discriminating coterie that's willing to make the trip to partake of the "consistently" excellent performance of the "Rudy and Rudi twosome" (chef/co-owner Rudy Speckamp cooks up "inspired" "gourmet and regional favorites" that please both "steak-and-potato guys" and lovers of haute cuisine, while co-owner Rudi Paul provides "great personal attention"); though it has a "nice country ambiance", it could possibly use a third Rudy to do some "redecorating."

Ruth's Chris Steak House ☐   25 | 23 | 23 | $47

1777 Reisterstown Rd. (Hooks Ln.), Pikesville, 410-837-0033
600 Water St. (bet. Gay St. & Market Pl.), Baltimore, 410-783-0033
301 Severn Ave. (3rd St.), Annapolis, 410-990-0033

■ No "need to ask where's the beef?" at this "clubby", Big Easy–style steakhouse chain – it's drenched in butter and sizzling on your plate, hauled out by "courteous" servers; while these "top-drawer" "guy" havens are beacons for travelers elsewhere, they rank below Prime Rib in this region's power stakes.

Samos ⊅   25 | 9 | 19 | $15

600 S. Oldham St. (Fleet St.), Baltimore, 410-675-5292

■ Embraced as Baltimore's top Hellenic treasure, this corner rowhouse in Greektown delivers an "enormous variety" of tasty, "authentic" dishes (some American eats too) at prices that make it "value-driven eating"; owner Nick Georgales and his "friendly" crew gained "some breathing room" with an expansion next door (not yet reflected in the above decor score).

Tio Pepe ☐   25 | 22 | 23 | $42

10 E. Franklin St. (bet. Charles & St. Paul Sts.), Baltimore, 410-539-4675

☑ Perennially popular, this Downtown Spanish-Continental with an "underground mystique" (it's housed in a "noisy cellar") is a "happy-occasion" fiesta for many aficionados, who "go back" (and back) for "excellent" paella, suckling pig and other "decadent" dishes; lots of complaints, however, surface about the "ridiculous" "wait, even with a reservation", as well as the feeling that "rudeness rules" if you're not a regular.

208 Talbot ☐   26 | 23 | 24 | $45

208 N. Talbot St. (bet. Dodson Ave. & North St.), St. Michaels, 410-745-3838

■ Join the Shore's "upper crust" at this "romantic" New American "hideaway" in St. Michaels, where the "beautiful presentations" of "innovative" dishes amount to "art on your plate"; "extremely well-run", it's definitely a "worthy" "destination" in this charming town.

Boston

TOP 20 FOOD RANKING

Restaurant	Cuisine Type
28 L'Espalier	New French
Aujourd'hui	New American
Caffe Bella	Mediterranean
27 Hamersley's Bistro	French Bistro/New American
Olives	Mediterranean
Il Capriccio	Northern Italian
Prezza	N&S Italian
Saporito's	Northern Italian
26 Icarus	New American
Yanks	American/Californian
Julien	New French
Rialto	Mediterranean
Blue Ginger	Asian/Eclectic
La Campania	N&S Italian
Bistro 5	Northern Italian
Morton's of Chicago	Steakhouse
Radius	New French
No. 9 Park	New American
Mistral	Classic/New French
Lumière	New French

ADDITIONAL NOTEWORTHY PLACES

Ambrosia on Huntington	New French/Asian
Biba	New American
Blue Room	Eclectic
Bonfire	International/Steakhouse
Centro	N&S Italian
Clio	New French
East Coast Grill & Raw Bar	Barbecue/Seafood
Evoo	Eclectic
Federalist	New French
Ginza	Japanese
Grill 23 & Bar	American/Steakhouse
Harvest	American
Maison Robert	Classic French
Mantra	Classic French/Indian
Oleana	Med./Middle Eastern
Perdix	New American
Pigalle	Classic French
Rowes Wharf	New England
Salamander	Asian/Eclectic
Salts	New American/E. European

Ambrosia on Huntington [S] 24 | 24 | 23 | $50

116 Huntington Ave. (bet. Exeter & W. Newton Sts.), 617-247-2400

◪ Savor the "food of the gods" at this "hip" Back Bay "scene", which tantalizes curious palates with "inventive" New French–Asian "fusion" "combinations that push the envelope" ("like having a party in your mouth"); not only is the "dramatic" setting "drop-dead" "gorgeous" but the service is "silky smooth", the "people-watching is a treat" and "great noshing" is available "at the bar"; cynics, however, are turned off by the "pretentious" staff and warn that the prices at least are "certainly Olympian."

Aujourd'hui [S] 28 | 28 | 28 | $64

Four Seasons Hotel, 200 Boylston St. (bet. Arlington & S. Charles Sts.), 617-351-2071

■ "Simply glorious", this "total treat for the body and heart" at the Four Seasons was not only voted the Most Popular restaurant in Boston but it was also rated tops for service; "when you have the urge to splurge", this "formal" room will "make any celebration spectacular" ("ask for a window table" overlooking the Public Garden); "such care, such flair" is clearly evident in the "exquisite" French-influenced New American dishes executed by chef Edward Gannon and brought to table by an "impeccable" staff, so though it's "pricey", this is the "pinnacle" of fine dining.

Biba [S] 24 | 24 | 22 | $51

272 Boylston St. (bet. Arlington & S. Charles Sts.), 617-426-7878

◪ Admirers "moan with delight" at the "quirky", "intriguing flavors" produced by this "avant-garde" New American kitchen where chefs Lydia Shire and Susan Regis – the "grandes dames" of the local dining scene – execute "impressive", "one-of-a-kind" Eclectic creations; even if the "complex combinations" are "occasionally preposterous", it's always "an adventure for the taste buds" and well enhanced by the "dramatic" room with a "front-row view" of the Public Garden.

Bistro 5 26 | 17 | 23 | $31

5 Playstead Rd. (High St.), West Medford, 781-395-7464

■ "An amazing restaurant in West Medford, of all places" gush boosters of chef-owner Vittorio Ettore's Tuscan-style "charmer" where his "gourmet" Northern Italian cooking "excites the palate" with "creative food pairings" and "big tastes"; though a "VW may have more room" than this "tiny storefront", satisfied surveyors say it's "worth the squish", while the BYO policy (it helps keep prices quite "reasonable") makes it even more of "a great find."

Blue Ginger 26 | 23 | 23 | $43

583 Washington St. (Rte. 16), Wellesley, 781-283-5790

◪ "Rising above the fusion fray", chef-owner Ming Tsai "sets the standard for East-meets-West cuisine" with a "transcendent" menu that "more than lives up to" "the buzz"; no wonder it's immensely "challenging to get a reservation" – "even diners from Boston do the reverse commute" to this "sleek" suburban "phenomenon" where it's so perpetually packed "wall-to-wall" that you may "have to beg to be waited on"; though skeptics insist that "in LA, it'd be no big deal", plenty of groupies only hope that "the Ming dynasty continues to reign in Wellesley."

Blue Room [S] 25 | 21 | 22 | $36

1 Kendall Sq. (bet. Broadway & Portland St.), Cambridge, 617-494-9034

■ "Definitely a favorite", this "casually chic" Kendall Square "winner" is "full of energy", a "just right" showcase for chef Steve Johnson's "adventurous" Eclectic menu; whether you settle in for the "awesome" Sunday brunch, "make a meal" of the "fabulous appetizers" or tuck into a "grillfest like no other", you'll be treated to "divine" Asian-influenced dishes that yield "an intriguing mix of flavors"; "considering the high level" of quality and the "well-informed" service, it adds up to "an exceptional value."

Bonfire ◐[S] – | – | – | E

Park Plaza Hotel, 64 Arlington St. (St. James St.), 617-426-2000

Scheduled to open shortly after we go to press, this latest venture by chef-owner Todd English, quartered in the Park Plaza Hotel, is a Latin-themed homage to beef, showcasing an International menu inspired by all the cattle-ranging regions around the world – from Argentine strip loin to Seoul-style short ribs to New York steak; not only will diners be able to see their meats being grilled on long swords that ring a vertical fire in the open kitchen but there's also a taqueria that'll offer light bites.

Caffe Bella 28 | 19 | 23 | $36

19 Warren St. (bet. Main St. & Rte. 139), Randolph, 781-961-7729

■ "What an amazing find!" fawn followers of this "exceptional" "suburban" "surprise" "hidden" "in a dingy little strip mall"; "once inside, you'll forget that you're in Randolph" because you've found the "best spot between Boston and the Cape"; Patrick Barnes, "a master of the culinary world", has designed a Mediterranean menu "so enticing that it's hard to choose", but "everything is of the freshest quality", and it's all served by a "knowledgeable" staff.

Centro [S] 24 | 19 | 20 | $33

720 Mass Ave. (bet. Inman & Prospect Sts.), Cambridge, 617-868-2405

■ Admirers of this "cramped" yet "swank" newcomer in Central Square "hate to get the word out" about its "creative" Italian bistro cooking that's "so understated but so good" (the "memorable" menu was designed by "can't-be-topped" Rene Michelena, who has passed the toque to Brian Maxwell); because of the "no-reservations" policy (except for parties of six or more), prepare to cool your heels in the adjacent bar.

Clio [S] 25 | 26 | 24 | $58

Eliot Suite Hotel, 370A Commonwealth Ave. (Mass Ave.), 617-536-7200

◪ Among "the most creative chefs in Boston", Ken Oringer "rules", conjuring up a "handsome", "high-style" Back Bay showplace for his "artfully prepared" New French dishes that "challenge the palate" and make any meal a "sublime" "special occasion"; backed by "terrific" service, it's an "extraordinary" "NYC-style experience", even though you should prepare for "micro portions at macro prices"; still, devotees are always "ready to spend the bucks" to join in this "phenomenal" "orgy of dining bliss."

East Coast Grill & Raw Bar [S]
25 | 18 | 20 | $32

1271 Cambridge St. (Prospect St.), Cambridge, 617-491-6568

■ "No wimps allowed" warn those addicted to the "dazzling, bold flavors" produced by owner Chris Schlesinger's crew at this "jumping" Inman Square joint that's always "packed to the gills" (insiders advise "ask for the lava lounge", as it's a notch less "cacophonous" and you can "sit next to a volcano" – "beat that for kitsch"); not only does the kitchen prepare "sophisticated BBQ" that's the "best spicy food in town" but it's also renowned for "fantastically fresh seafood" dishes; "a favorite year after year", "this grill still thrills."

Evoo
24 | 21 | 22 | $38

118 Beacon St. (Washington St.), Somerville, 617-661-3866

■ Each "delicious", "luscious" taste savored at this "intimate" Eclectic bistro in Somerville "reveals chef Peter McCarthy's imagination"; contributing to the "exciting" experience are "understated" surroundings with an "urban edge" and a staff that exemplifies a "passion for food and service", so "though the name's a bit much" (it stands for 'extra virgin olive oil'), "every neighborhood should be so lucky" as to have such "a gifted chef."

Federalist ◐ [S]
24 | 25 | 23 | $62

XV Beacon Hotel, 15 Beacon St. (Bowdoin St.), 617-670-2515

◪ "Worth the splurge", a meal at this "opulent" Beacon Hill paean to power "isn't just dinner, it's an event"; from the "spectacular" decor to the "polished", "officious" service, each "extravagant" detail makes you "feel special"; equally "a beautiful treat" is the "exquisite" New French menu, matched with one of the "most extensive wine lists in Boston"; though "you may need to take out a mortgage", this is a "truly swanky" "place to impress those snobby out-of-town guests"; N.B. the post-*Survey* departure of chef Eric Brennan may outdate the above food score.

Ginza [S]
25 | 17 | 19 | $29

16 Hudson St. (bet. Beach & Kneeland Sts.), 617-338-2261 ◐
1002 Beacon St. (St. Mary's St.), Brookline, 617-566-9688

■ Afishionados insist that it'd be "a sin to order anything but the unparalleled sushi" at this "traditional" Japanese duo in Chinatown and Brookline, renowned for "expertly preparing" raw fish that's "absolutely the best" in Boston – so "ultra-fresh" that "you can taste the sea"; though "getting a table is like a cattle call", the Hudson Street flagship is a "late-night" "lifesaver."

Grill 23 & Bar [S]
26 | 24 | 24 | $50

161 Berkeley St. (Stuart St.), 617-542-2255

■ Just about "Boston's best" chophouse, this "boisterous" "Back Bay power scene" not only delights old-school carnivores with the "most tender steaks in town" but chef Jay Murray has made some "exciting" "updates" to the traditional American menu with "superb" results (particularly the "exquisite" seafood); the "knowledgeable, courteous" staff and "stellar sommelier" "treat you like a king" amid "elegant" appointments that lend the room "a gentlemen's club feel", making it a "great place to bring clients", while the upstairs bar "is a welcome addition" "for the boys and their cigars."

Hamersley's Bistro S
27　24　25　$53

553 Tremont St. (Clarendon St.), 617-423-2700

■ "Transcendent" French–New American "bistro cooking by someone who gets it" distinguishes this "class-act" "splurge" in the South End, where chef/co-owner Gordon Hamersley "reigns supreme" with "perfectly prepared", "soul-warming" signatures including his "melt-in-your-mouth" roasted chicken; an "eclectic wine list" complements the "unfussy" yet "imaginative" cooking, while a "professional" staff works a room marked by "elegant simplicity"; "a favorite since it opened in the '80s", it's "still among the very best" in all of Boston.

Harvest S
25　22　23　$43

44 Brattle St. (Church St.), Cambridge, 617-868-2255

☑ "Aging well, like its own exceptional wines", this Harvard Square "institution" "has regained its former splendor", showcasing a "first-class" menu of "updated" American cooking in a "clubby setting" graced with an "understated elegance" (think "all beiges" and dark woods); "managers who know how to run the show" oversee an "efficient" staff, so even if a minority laments "it used to be unique and now it's just another expensive restaurant", most declare "it keeps getting better and better."

Icarus S
26　25　25　$49

3 Appleton St. (bet. Arlington & Berkeley Sts.), 617-426-1790

■ "Wow!" exclaim elated epicures about this "well-appointed" South End luminary where the "modern renditions of classic cuisine" soar like its winged namesake; "Chris Douglass is a star chef without attitude", and his "artful" New American "creations" are "served with finesse" in a "serene", "rich-looking room" that resembles a "grand supper club"; though you may need to cash in "your 401(k) to pay" the bill, this is one of "the finest restaurants in Boston" in which "to celebrate a special evening."

Il Capriccio
27　22　25　$46

888 Main St. (Prospect St.), Waltham, 781-894-2234

■ "Worth the trip" to Waltham, this "refined" Northern Italian is "excellent by any standard, not just for the suburbs"; there may well be "too many praises to sing" here, but we'll try: chef/co-owner Richard Barron's "superlative" specialties are a "dreamy" "culinary treat", beautifully complemented by a "wonderful wine selection" (the list must've been "compiled by a fanatic") and delivered by a "knowledgeable" staff that adds a "personal" touch; this is a "place you want to return to" time and again – "how could you not love it?"

Julien
26　27　26　$58

Le Meridien Hotel, 250 Franklin St. (bet. Oliver & Pearl Sts.), 617-451-1900

■ Bringing "a touch of France to the Financial District", this "opulent" "star" in Le Meridien Hotel is a "classy" "place for a celebration" or "romantic" dinner served by an "outstanding but not overbearing" staff in a "formal", "dramatic space"; chef Dominique Rizzo's "imaginative" New French menu brims with "sumptuous" selections, so despite the "astronomical prices", this is a truly "memorable" experience – "what more could one wish?"

La Campania 26 | 23 | 23 | $42

504 Main St. (bet. Cross & Heard Sts.), Waltham, 781-894-4280

■ Evocative of a "rustic cafe" "in Tuscany", this "Waltham jewel" is "a special treat", tantalizing with Italian food so "mouthwatering" you "could lick the plate"; an "amiable" staff "treats you as a beloved guest" in a teeny room with "charming country-kitchen decor", which helps explain why despite "Downtown prices", it's always "hard to get in"; fans have just one question: "is there a way to make it bigger?"

L'Espalier 28 | 28 | 28 | $71

30 Gloucester St. (bet. Commonwealth Ave. & Newbury St.), 617-262-3023

■ "Absolute bliss" rhapsodize euphoric devotees of this "exquisite" Back Bay "stunner", a "lavish treat" "for any special occasion"; "extraordinary" chef Frank McClelland executes "inventive", "seriously" "gourmet" New French dishes (rated No. 1 for Food in Boston) that are "elegant in every way" and turned out in a "romantic", "luxurious" townhouse setting that's equally "divine"; consider too the "unsurpassed" "personal attention" from the "unbelievable" staff and you'll concur that it justly "deserves all its acclaim."

Lumière [S] 26 | 22 | 24 | $48

1293 Washington St. (bet. Waltham & Wilkes Sts.), West Newton, 617-244-9199

■ Arguably Newton's "best gastronomic contribution since the Fig Newton", this "sophisticated" "star" is a "suburban restaurant with city flavors"; chef-owner Michael Leviton's "exciting", "exceptional" New French dishes are served by an "impeccable" staff in "intimate" surroundings with an ambiance of "easy elegance"; it's "a delectable experience in every way" – you just "have to plan weeks in advance", since it may be "harder to get into than Harvard."

Maison Robert 24 | 24 | 24 | $48

Old City Hall, 45 School St. (bet. Beacon & Tremont Sts.), 617-227-3370

◩ "One of the first really gourmet restaurants" in the city, this "bastion of old Boston" remains an enduring "favorite that never disappoints"; "elegant and sophisticated", "with all the finishing touches" – from the "superior" Classic French cuisine to the "grand" setting to the "thoughtful" service – it's "impressive" for a "special occasion"; trendoids may find it "conservative", but the chocolate soufflé surely "makes up for any sins."

Mantra ◐ – | – | – | VE

52 Temple Pl. (bet. Tremont & Washington Sts.), 617-542-8111

Boasting a hookah den with fruit-scented tobaccos and comfy red couches, this chichi Downtown newcomer is already topping the local hip meter; the elegant quarters retain all the marble and granite trappings of the bank that used to occupy this space, while the polished service recalls the days of the raj; it's a smart backdrop for chef Thomas John's Classic French–Indian menu, which proves that this eclectic fusion really can work.

Mistral S   26 25 24 $54

223 Columbus Ave. (bet. Berkeley & Clarendon Sts.), 617-867-9300

☑ "Trendy to the last detail", this "glamorous" "hot spot" situated where the Back Bay meets the South End lures hipsters who swoon over chef Jamie Mammano's Provençal-inspired dishes that are "guaranteed fab"; "lots of pretty people" "in little black dresses" gather not only for the "memorable" fare but also for the "sexy", "très chic" "see-and-be-seen" "scene", made even more "seductive" by the "elegantly" "cosmopolitan" setting; "if you can get over the hype", consider it for a "decadent celebration" – just don't forget to "bring your attitude."

Morton's of Chicago S   26 20 23 $50

1 Exeter Plaza (bet. Boylston & Exeter Sts.), 617-266-5858

☑ "A real steak in all its Midwestern glory", combined with an "opulent power-dining" setting with a "manly" atmosphere, makes this "clubby" Chicago import in the Back Bay a "big hit with the business crowd"; though a minority grumbles that this "stodgy" "high-priced chain" "can't hold a charcoal" to the top homegrown temples of meat in town, contented carnivores can't wait to tuck into "huge portions" of the "best-quality cow" and scoff "love it or leave it, baby."

No. 9 Park   26 23 24 $54

9 Park St. (bet. Beacon & Tremont Sts.), 617-742-9991

☑ "Viva Barbara Lynch" cheer followers of the chef-owner whose "skill and imagination are evident in every dish" prepared at her "memorable" boîte in the shadow of the State House; the "low-key elegance" of the "swanky" yet "simple" interior "allows you to focus" on her "creative" New American "culinary masterpieces" inspired by France and Italy; if some wish they'd "lighten up", finding it "too precious and pricey", most just get turned on by this "orgasm for the taste buds."

Oleana S   26 23 22 $39

134 Hampshire St. (bet. Columbia & Prospect Sts.), Cambridge, 617-661-0505

■ At this "promising newcomer", "a hip place to be" near Inman Square, "the excitement is palpable"; credit Ana Sortun, who "was born to cook" and who brings her considerable Mediterranean expertise to this "darling" room, executing "intriguing" dishes enlivened by "surprising", "exotic" Middle Eastern flavors; whether indoors or out on the lovely patio, you'll be well taken care of by an "unpretentious, welcoming" staff.

Olives   27 22 23 $48

10 City Sq. (bet. Main & Park Sts.), Charlestown, 617-242-1999

☑ "Please let this be where I eat my last meal on earth" pray fanatical worshipers of chef-owner Todd English's Mediterranean flagship in Charlestown, where his "big, bold, in-your-face" dishes are based upon "creative" – even "crazy" – "concoctions" that make the "taste buds dance"; sure, it's "too frantic" and some are put off by the staff's "attitude", while the "no-reservations" policy (for parties smaller than six) "makes it a real hassle", but still, this "extravaganza dazzles" and "deserves every accolade."

Perdix [S] – | – | – | E

597 Centre St. (bet. Pond & Spencer Sts.), Jamaica Plain, 617-524-5995

"Food is the star" at this "wonderful" new bistro, a "tiny treasure" in Jamaica Plain that's easily "a cut above other local eateries"; chef-owner Tim Partridge's (ex the East Coast Grill) "first-rate" New American cooking is full of "bold flavors", delivered to a handful of tables less than a stone's throw from the "open kitchen" (clearly, there's "no pretense" here); "intimate" and "welcoming", it brings "a touch of friendly elegance" to town.

Pigalle [S] 25 | 23 | 23 | $50

75 Charles St. S. (bet. Stuart St. & Warrenton Pl.), 617-423-4944

■ "Bravo" for this "brilliant newcomer" in the Theater District, the "most exciting French restaurant to open in Boston" in quite some time; chef-owner Marc Orfaly's classic dishes are "elegant and flavorful" and served in a "dark", "intimate" setting that seems to "suggest illicit activity"; not only is it "*très romantique* and *très cher*" but the servers are "knowledgeable" and "everything they do has a personal touch"; P.S. "make reservations for after 8 PM", when the "curtain crowd departs."

Prezza 27 | 24 | 25 | $46

24 Fleet St. (Hanover St.), 617-227-1577

■ Opened not too long ago, this "polished North End newcomer" is already the "best" Northern-Southern Italian restaurant in Boston; credit chef-owner Anthony Caturano's "unique", "modern" interpretations (don't pass up the "awe-inspiring desserts", "artistic masterpieces" all), "fabulously presented" and matched with an "outstanding wine list"; kudos too to the "friendly" staff that works the "sophisticated", "inviting" room and "can't do enough to please"; this "winner" is for keeps.

Radius 26 | 25 | 25 | $57

8 High St. (bet. Federal & Summer Sts.), 617-426-1234

■ "Eating in Boston is glamorous again" thanks to this "sleek", "chic" Financial District destination that's "among the best in the city"; chef Michael Schlow's "intriguing", "meticulously prepared" New French dishes are "more like an artistic experience" than a mere meal, delivered by a "polished" staff whose "professionalism" and "attention to detail are evident everywhere"; thus, despite "minimalist" decor that some find rather "stark", the "beautiful people" and "power brokers" "spend here till it hurts."

Rialto [S] 26 | 25 | 24 | $53

Charles Hotel, 1 Bennett St. (Harvard Sq.), Cambridge, 617-661-5050

■ "Harvard Square's ritziest restaurant", this cherished "favorite for grand occasions" remains at "the top level" of Boston dining rooms; chef "Jody Adams is a goddess", crafting "exceptional" Mediterranean fare that's "always gratifying" and "sophisticated", "delivered with joie de vivre" by an "impeccable" staff in a "sumptuous", "modern" setting that's "a shrine to understated good taste"; the consensus: "love it."

Rowes Wharf [S] 24 | 27 | 24 | $52

Boston Harbor Hotel, 70 Rowes Wharf (Atlantic Ave.), 617-439-3995

■ Boasting "unbeatable harbor views", an "elegant" room and "formal" service that proffers the "royal treatment", this "must do" at the Boston Harbor Hotel is a "relaxing place to be pampered"; it's a tough job to compete with such a "gorgeous" setting, but chef Daniel Bruce's daily changing menu of "classy", "rich", contemporary New England dishes shows "respect for simplicity and quality" and features lots of "local ingredients", particularly seafood; all in all, "superbly done" and "worth every $100 bill."

Salamander [S] 23 | 24 | 23 | $51

Trinity Pl., 1 Huntington Ave. (Dartmouth St.), 617-451-2150

◪ Now settled into "swanky new digs" in Copley Square, Stan Frankenthaler's wildly "inventive" contemporary Asian stunner has cemented his reputation as "one of Boston's more talented chefs"; "every dish" on his "eclectic" menu is a "medley" of "bold, assertive flavors", delivered in a "minimalist", "high-tech" room by a "crackerjack" staff; dismayed diners, however, say the "complex" creations "have too much going on", resulting in "weird" concoctions that are "shockingly expensive"; P.S. for a lighter bite, check out the "awesome satay bar."

Salts 26 | 21 | 25 | $45

798 Main St. (Windsor St.), Cambridge, 617-876-8444

■ At this "engaging" New American bistro in Cambridge, Steve Rosen's "unique" menu seeks inspiration from the East, though in this case it's Eastern Europe and the results are "inspired" – dishes that are "restrained yet flavorful and offered in interesting combinations without any excess distractions"; despite the "understated elegance" of the petite room, diners may feel a little "jammed in", but the chef and his wife are a "charming couple who make this spot shine" and "they aim to please", making it "a real find for a romantic evening."

Saporito's [S] 27 | 18 | 24 | $40

11 Rockland Circle (George Washington Blvd.), Hull, 781-925-3023

■ If your "passion for Italian cuisine knows no obstacles", it's "worth the awful trip" to this "homey" "South Shore treasure" where the "entire menu" of "innovative" dishes is "skillfully prepared and presented"; "don't let the exterior put you off" (it's set in "an old beach house") because the "expert" kitchen inside is "a secret to be shared only with your best friends"; "even if it's way out in Hull", it's "one of the best in Boston."

Yanks [S] 26 | 23 | 23 | $49

717 Hale St./Rte. 127 (2nd Ave.), Beverly Farms, 978-232-9898

■ "Finally, refined food here on Cape Ann" swoon the cognoscenti about this "top-notch North Shore destination" distinguished by a "NYC sophistication"; "though the name suggests a staid Brahmin dining room serving pot roast and cod cakes", the "superior" menu – classical American updated with a "Californian influence" – and "bright, contemporary" decor couldn't feel more "upscale" and "urban"; backed by "exemplary" service, it "rivals some of Boston's best" and is "well worth the drive" to Beverly Farms.

Chicago

Restaurant	Cuisine Type
28 Carlos'	New French
Ritz-Carlton Din. Rm.	New French
TRU	New French
Ambria	New French
27 Seasons	New American
Everest	New French
Le Titi de Paris	Classic French
Trio	New French
Charlie Trotter's	New American
Tallgrass	New French
Topolobampo	Mexican
Les Nomades	Classic French
26 Arun's	Thai
302 West	New American
Spiaggia	N&S Italian
Courtright's	New American
mk	New American
Gabriel's	New French/N&S Italian
Frontera Grill	Mexican
Las Bellas Artes	Mexican

ADDITIONAL NOTEWORTHY PLACES

Atlantique	Seafood
Aubriot	New French
Avenues	New French/Med.
Blackbird	New American
Chilpancingo	Mexican
Crofton on Wells	American
D & J Bistro	French Bistro
Gibsons	Steakhouse
Harvest on Huron	New American
Joe's Seafood	Seafood/Steakhouse
Le Français	Classic French
Mirai Sushi	Japanese
MOD.	New American
Naha	New American
NOMI	Classic French/Asian
one sixtyblue	New American
Pasteur	Vietnamese
Spring	New American/Asian
Twelve 12	New American
Zealous	New American

Ambria 28 | 26 | 27 | $68

Belden-Stratford Hotel, 2300 N. Lincoln Park W. (Belden Ave.), 773-472-5959

■ "As always", this Lincoln Park New French is a "romantic" "oasis of luxury" where chef Anselmo Ruiz's "superb" execution is matched with "impeccable" service in an art nouveau setting that manages to be "dignified" and "elegant" without "pretense"; in sum, it's "a heavenly dining experience."

Arun's [S] 26 | 23 | 25 | VE

4156 N. Kedzie Ave. (bet. Belle Plaine & Berteau Aves.), 773-539-1909

◪ "Master chef" Arun Sampanthavivat is an "artist" whose "exquisite" presentations of "unique", "top-notch" Siamese fare entice the faithful to this "out-of-the-way" North Side "class act"; ordering is easy because a "breathtaking" $75 tasting menu is the only option, and if some are "alienated" by the "excessive" cost, admireres are convinced that there's "no better Thai" anywhere.

Atlantique [S] 24 | 19 | 23 | $40

5101 N. Clark St. (bet. Carmen & Foster Aves.), 773-275-9191

■ Chef-owner Jack Jones launches "another winner" at this Andersonville seafood house where "the freshest fish" makes for a "mouthwatering" meal served by a "welcoming" staff; marine mavens deem it "excellent", and high ratings buoy their claims.

Aubriot [S] 22 | 19 | 22 | $50

1962 N. Halsted St. (Armitage Ave.), 773-281-4211

◪ There's "no scene" at this Lincoln Park "gastronomic gem", just an "inventive" New French menu courtesy of "rising star" Eric Aubriot; his "fabulous" food is served "without attitude", though a few complain of "high prices" for "tiny portions"; N.B. dinner only.

Avenues [S] – | – | – | E

Peninsula Chicago, 108 E. Superior St. (bet. Michigan Ave. & Rush St.), 312-573-6754

The main dining room of the new Peninsula Chicago hotel, just off the Mag Mile, specializes in New French–Mediterranean seafood dishes (dubbed 'cuisine de mer' by consulting chef Yves Mattagne) served in deluxe surroundings that include an exhibition kitchen and a 400-bottle wine display – not to mention 5th-floor views of the cityscape.

Blackbird 24 | 19 | 21 | $47

619 W. Randolph St. (bet. Desplaines & Jefferson Sts.), 312-715-0708

◪ Contrasting "minimalist decor" with "maximal flavor", this "chic" West Loop New American with a French accent "would be at home in TriBeCa or South Beach"; "beautiful people" flock in to peck at "stellar" dishes served in "stark" surroundings, though phobes pass on the "pretentious" scene and seating that's "too close for comfort."

Carlos' [S] 28 | 25 | 27 | $69

429 Temple Ave. (east of Waukegan Ave.), Highland Park, 847-432-0770

■ Rated No. 1 for Food in the *Chicago Survey*, this "North Shore dining temple" boasts "the ultimate hosts" in Carlos and Debbie Nieto and "outstanding" New French food and "professional" service; the cognoscenti agree that the "exquisite presentations" and "intimate setting" add up to a "truly magnificent dining" experience that's "worth every penny."

Charlie Trotter's 27 | 26 | 27 | VE

816 W. Armitage Ave. (Halsted St.), 773-248-6228

■ Once again voted the Most Popular restaurant in Chicago, this "world-class" Lincoln Park New American offers "exquisite" tasting menus (priced from $100 to $115) that exhibit the "limitless creativity" and "magnificent" flavor palette of chef-owner Charlie T.; detractors may decry it as "pricey" and "pretentious", but the consensus is that "on a scale of 1 to 10, this is a 20."

Chilpancingo [S] – | – | – | M

358 W. Ontario St. (Orleans St.), 312-266-9525

Named after the state capital of Guerrero on Mexico's Pacific coast, this upscale River North newcomer courtesy of chef-owner Genoroso 'Geno' Bahena is an elegant venue for his adventurous, regional south-of-the-border cooking, which reinterprets the classics based on his unique combinations of ingredients, as exemplified by his nuanced moles and array of *tacos al carbon.*

Courtright's [S] 26 | 26 | 25 | $45

8989 Archer Ave. (Willow Springs Rd.), Willow Springs, 708-839-8000

■ A "surprise in the Southwest Suburbs", this "exquisite" New American is proof that "brains and taste" can flourish even in the outskirts; the "truly gourmet" fare (particularly an "excellent *dégustation*" menu), backed by an "exceptional" wine list, is as captivating as the "elegant" room, which offers a "photo-op" view of a garden and "forest preserve."

Crofton on Wells 24 | 20 | 21 | $46

535 N. Wells St. (bet. Grand Ave. & Ohio St.), 312-755-1790

■ Chef-owner Suzy Crofton's "brilliance shines through" at this "outstanding" River North American; her "innovative menu" of "consistently high-quality" seasonal dishes served in a stylish, "intimate" setting makes it a "winner", though hedgers hint "lighten up on the attitude."

D & J Bistro [S] 25 | 21 | 23 | $35

First Bank Plaza, 466 S. Rand Rd. (Rte. 22), Lake Zurich, 847-438-8001

■ This "fetching" French bistro is a "hard-to-find" "treasure" in a Far Northwest strip mall that's built its reputation with a "terrific", "innovative menu" and "charming" service; the three-course, $26 prix fixe deal is nominated by many as the "best value in the metro area" – devotees only "wish it were in the city."

Everest 27 | 27 | 27 | $76

1 Financial Pl., 440 S. La Salle St., (Congress Pkwy.), 312-663-8920

■ The "dining is as spectacular as the view" at this 40th-floor New French in the Loop, where chef Jean Joho's "ethereal and beautiful" creations (backed by a "marvelous wine selection") set a culinary "standard"; with its "breathtaking" setting and "flawless" service, it's an acknowledged "pinnacle of haute cuisine."

Frontera Grill 26 | 22 | 22 | $33

445 N. Clark St. (bet. Hubbard & Illinois Sts.), 312-661-1434

■ "Rick Bayless is a master" according to admirers who cheer "olé" over his "amazing" River North Mexican grill, "a feast for the eyes and mouth" that ranks among the "best in the USA"; it's a "perennial favorite" for "unbeatable", "zesty" food matched with "margaritas from heaven", and though there's "always a wait", it "sure beats Taco Bell!"

Gabriel's   26 | 23 | 25 | $53
310 Green Bay Rd. (Highwood Ave.), Highwood, 847-433-0031
■ In the eyes of jealous urbanites, Gabriel Viti's namesake is "too good for the suburbs", though North Shore natives are tickled to call this "elegantly understated" "French-Italian crossover" their own; "spectacular" food and "meticulous" service make it a special-"occasion place" where patrons pay "out-of-sight prices" to "feel like a million bucks."

Gibsons Steakhouse ●S   25 | 20 | 22 | $47
1028 N. Rush St. (Bellevue Pl.), 312-266-8999
Doubletree Hotel, 5464 N. River Rd. (bet. Balmoral & Bryn Mawr Aves.), Rosemont, 847-928-9900
■ As a "hometown favorite", this pair of Gold Coast steakhouses gives the "beautiful people" a chance to "see and be seen" while indulging in "fabulous", "Flintstone-size" "hunks of meat" turned out by a highly "professional" staff; though it can be "bedlam", the "best steaks" are "worth the chaos"; N.B. the Rosemont offshoot is new and unrated.

Harvest on Huron   23 | 22 | 20 | $41
217 W. Huron St. (bet. Franklin & Wells Sts.), 312-587-9600
■ Expect "Chicago swagger" at this "chichi" River North New American where chef Allen Sternweiler concocts "exciting and different" dishes that are "creatively presented" and "delicious"; the "beautiful people" and "classy" room catch the eye, though it reaps complaints of "too much noise."

Joe's Seafood, Prime Steak &   – | – | – | E
Stone Crab S
60 E. Grand Ave. (Rush St.), 312-379-5637
There's more than just stone crab available at this River North spin-off of the original Joe's Stone Crab in Miami Beach, hence the mouthful of a name; though the costly crustaceans are the clear specialty, the steaks and other seafood options are good enough to keep customers lining up (reservations are tough to come by) early to snag a coveted table at one of restaurateur Rich Melman's latest ventures.

Las Bellas Artes S   26 | 22 | 23 | $36
112 W. Park Ave. (York St.), Elmhurst, 630-530-7725
◪ A "tiny gem worthy of major attention", this "unique and fabulous" West Suburban Mexican features "fantastic" "gourmet" cooking from chef-owner Gloria Duarte (including a *muy popular* Sunday brunch); the antique-filled room sets the scene for "subdued" dining backed by "attentive" service.

Le Français   – | – | – | VE
269 S. Milwaukee Ave. (bet. Dundee & Hintz Rds.), Wheeling, 847-541-7470
Legendary chef-owner Jean Banchet has retired – for good, this time – and sold his perennially top-rated Classic French gem in Wheeling to Phil Mott and chef Don Yamauchi (ex Carlos'); while the front-room staff remains virtually intact, Yamauchi has introduced contemporary flourishes to the menu like hot foie gras with dried cherries, toasted peanuts and mint.

Les Nomades
27 | 24 | 26 | $69

222 E. Ontario St. (bet. Franklin & Wells Sts.), 312-649-9010

■ Having relinquished control of Le Français, Roland and Mary Beth Liccioni's principal business is now this "elegant" Classic French in Streeterville that boasts "flawless haute cuisine", "exemplary" service and a "subtle" "Parisian ambiance"; it's a jacket-required "bastion of civility", and if some find it "a tad snooty", habitués appreciate it as "a refined dining experience."

Le Titi De Paris
27 | 25 | 26 | $58

1015 W. Dundee Rd. (Kennicott Ave.), Arlington Heights, 847-506-0222

■ "Toques off" to owner Pierre Pollin and chef Michael Maddox for presenting some of the "best-value haute French in Chicagoland" at this "charmer" in the Northwest, where the food is "masterful" and the wine selection is "outstanding"; that this "jewel" can thrive in its "dull suburban setting" is proof that a prime "location isn't always imperative."

Mirai Sushi S
▽ 26 | 22 | 22 | $35

2020 W. Division St. (Damen Ave.), 773-862-8500

■ "A worthy competitor to the established sushi" emporiums, this West Side Japanese has trendsetters labeling it *the* place for "delish" raw fish, including several "unusual" varieties, all "fresh" and "beautifully presented"; there's also a lounge upstairs that "caters to the 'in' crowd."

mk S
26 | 25 | 24 | $52

868 N. Franklin St. (bet. Chicago Ave. & Oak St.), 312-482-9179

■ Michael Kornick's "creative and cultured" Near North New American is "memorable" as a "hip place" that "doesn't take itself too seriously"; the "superb" dishes, spun with New French and Italian accents, perfectly complement the "sleek", "chichi" setting and "trendy", black-clad clientele; P.S. "there's nothing better than dessert" here, so "save room."

MoD. S
– | – | – | E

1520 N. Damen Ave. (North Ave.), 773-252-1500

Wicker Park's trendy set congregates at this New American over upscale, Alice Waters–inspired cooking courtesy of chef Kelly Courtney; the space-age setting features perforated wall dividers, futuristic furnishings and a riot of color, while those trapped in the present are grateful for free parking in the adjacent lot.

Naha
– | – | – | E

500 N. Clark St. (Illinois St.), 312-321-6242

Set in a minimalist, light-filled space in River North, this tastefully upscale New American showcases the assertive cooking of chef Carrie Nahabedian, whose impressive seasonal repertoire exhibits strong Mediterranean and Californian influences; P.S. ask for a window to take in the city skyline.

NoMI S
– | – | – | VE

Park Hyatt Chicago, 800 N. Michigan Ave. (Chicago Ave.), 312-335-1234

As the showpiece of the Park Hyatt Chicago on the Mag Mile, this luxe French-Asian pulls out all the stops with a Tony Chi–designed dining room, polished-steel open kitchen, stunning views, a 3,000-bottle wine cellar and picture-perfect dishes from Sandro Gamba.

one sixtyblue
24 | 25 | 22 | $53

160 N. Loomis St. (Randolph St.), 312-850-0303
■ Bringing together a "most beautiful" Adam Tihany–designed room and "brilliant cooking", this West Loop New American achieves "a perfect blend" of food and mood; it offers "stylish" "dining at the highest level" and yet "another reason to love Michael" (silent partner Michael Jordan, that is); N.B. the food score does not reflect the departure of Patrick Robertson and the arrival of chef Martial Noguier.

Pasteur S
23 | 22 | 19 | $31

5525 N. Broadway (Bryn Mawr Ave.), 773-878-1061
■ Quite a few admirers call this "beautiful and romantic" "gem" in Edgewater "the best Vietnamese in the area", citing "delicious" food delivered by a "pleasant" staff; the "pretty room" features wicker chairs and slow-spinning ceiling fans ("just like Saigon, right?"), but some warn that the "intimate" space gets "very noisy."

Ritz-Carlton Dining Room S
28 | 27 | 28 | $66

Ritz-Carlton Hotel, 160 E. Pearson St. (Michigan Ave.), 312-573-5223
■ Chicago's premier showcase for hotel dining continues to "impress in every way": chef Sarah Stegner's "stellar" New French menu "never ceases to amaze", the "opulent" environment is an "experience in luxe" and the service is simply "superb"; here's a chance to feel "pampered" over an "outstanding" dinner.

Seasons S
27 | 27 | 27 | $61

Four Seasons Hotel, 120 E. Delaware Pl., 7th fl. (bet. Michigan Ave. & Rush St.), 312-649-2349
■ "Want to impress?" – then visit this "gracious" Four Seasons New American with French and Asian accents, "a delight for all the senses"; chef Mark Baker's "superb" dishes are "so delicious you'll lick the plate clean", and they're served in a "magnificent room" by an "exceptional" staff; not only is it an "elaborate" "tribute to Chicagoland dining" but the Sunday brunch is just "out of this world."

Spiaggia S
26 | 27 | 25 | $60

1 Magnificent Mile Bldg., 980 N. Michigan Ave., 2nd fl. (Oak St.), 312-280-2750
■ With the departure of chef Paul Bartolotta, it's up to successor Tony Mantuano to maintain this "elegant" Gold Coast Italian's "superb" standards in the kitchen; the "superior" staff is still in place, along with the "breathtaking" decor and a view that "alone makes it outstanding" – just bring "lots of lire"; N.B. the chef change is not reflected in the above food score.

Spring S
– | – | – | E

2039 W. North Ave. (Milwaukee Ave.), 773-395-7100
Ex Trio chef Shawn McClain has converted a vintage Bucktown bathhouse into this minimalist yet eye-catching New American, which specializes in Asian-influenced seafood dishes; the Far Eastern accents begin at the Zen garden off the entrance and continue through such menu items as lemongrass-coconut soup and a Chinese-style tea service, though a Western sensibility is evident behind the carefully chosen wine list and creative desserts; by all accounts, this Spring has certainly sprung.

Tallgrass [S] 27 | 24 | 26 | $62

1006 S. State St. (10th St.), Lockport, 815-838-5566

■ In the "exurban" locale of Lockport, this "charming" New French is an "intimate" Victorian showcase for chef Robert Burcenski's "innovative", "picture-perfect" culinary creations; his menu typically offers a choice of "excellent" three-, four- or five-course prix fixe extravaganzas that are "well worth the long ride" (and the "pricey" tab); N.B. jacket required.

302 West 26 | 24 | 25 | $47

302 W. State St. (3rd St.), Geneva, 630-232-9302

■ Situated in an "old bank building" in the Far Western suburbs, this low-lit, "high-class" destination is a very "romantic" "gem" where there's "always something great" on the "creative" seafood-leaning New American menu; "delicious desserts" and an all-American wine list that spotlights "small vineyards" further leave admirers feeling like a million.

Topolobampo 27 | 23 | 25 | $46

445 N. Clark St. (bet. Hubbard & Illinois Sts.), 312-661-1434

■ "Unique and outstanding" flavors make Rick Bayless' "gourmet" Mexican in River North the "best of the breed"; the "fancy" counterpart to Frontera Grill, it offers "haute cuisine versions" of regional dishes (including a $59 tasting menu that's "worth every penny") in a "high-class" room – just call it 'Tops' for short.

Trio [S] 27 | 25 | 27 | $70

Homestead Hotel, 1625 Hinman Ave. (Davis St.), Evanston, 847-733-8746

■ "Daring food combinations" offer devotees a taste of "gourmet heaven" at this "magnificent" New French on the North Shore; it's a "refined experience" where "cuisine as art" meets "superb" service in a "serene" setting; deep-pocketed regulars report that the "tasting menu is the way to go"; N.B. chef Grant Achatz has succeeded Shawn McClain, which may outdate the food score.

TRU 28 | 27 | 27 | $88

676 N. St. Clair St. (bet. Erie & Huron Sts.), 312-202-0001

■ Truly "lush and luscious", this "exciting" Streeterville star is "one of the best in town"; Rick Tramonto's and Gale Gand's New French cooking elevates "food to an art form" (their signature caviar staircase leads straight "to heaven"), and it's only enhanced by the "spectacular" decor and "excellent" service; even if it's a "wallet-breaker", believers observe "perfection" rarely comes cheap.

Twelve 12 – | – | – | E

1212 N. State Pkwy. (Division St.), 312-951-1212

What was briefly known as the State Room has undergone a quick transformation into this less-flamboyant Gold Coast New American helmed by chef David Shea, whose sophisticated dishes draw a dress-to-thrill crowd.

Zealous ▽ 23 | 20 | 21 | $52

419 W. Superior St. (Hudson Ave.), 312-475-9112

■ "Brilliant cooking without a safety net" is how supporters sum up the New American style of Charlie Trotter protégé Michael Taus, who's flying high at this River North sophisticate; thanks to a substantial "no-expense-spared" upgrade, the "dramatic" setting now nearly rivals the food that simply "rocks", even if a few are less than zealous about the "undersized portions."

Cincinnati

TOP 10 FOOD RANKING

	Restaurant	Cuisine Type
28	Maisonette	Classic French
27	Palace	New American
26	Dewey's Pizza	Pizza
25	Daveed's at 934	Eclectic
	Precinct	Steakhouse/Seafood
	Ambar India	Indian
	Phoenix	Continental/American
24	China Gourmet	Chinese
	Pacific Moon Cafe	Pan-Asian
	JUMP Café & Bar	New American

ADDITIONAL NOTEWORTHY PLACES

Aioli	French Bistro/N&S Italian
Beluga	Eurasian
Brown Dog Cafe	New American
Chez Alphonse	Classic French
Jeff Ruby's	Steakhouse
Montgomery Inn	Barbecue
Nicola's	N&S Italian
Palomino Euro Bistro	Mediterranean
Primavista	Northern Italian
Sturkey's	New American

	F	D	S	C
Aioli	23	17	16	$31

700 Elm St. (7th St.), 513-929-0525

■ Julie Francis, a chef-owner "destined for culinary greatness", presides at this "nice addition to the Downtown scene" that offers "tempting", "well-prepared" "imaginative presentations" of French-Italian fare; though some cite a need for "improved service", the "casual, comfortable" ambiance and a thoughtful list of *vins de pays* keep city-dwellers coming back for "affordable" meals that are "perfect before the opera or symphony."

	F	D	S	C
Ambar India [S]	25	9	16	$18

350 Ludlow Ave. (Clifton Ave.), 513-281-7000

■ "There's always a crowd" at this "bustling" "Clifton favorite" where the "scrumptious" fare (including "lots of wonderful vegetarian dishes" and "amazing naan") will "transport you right to India"; the "decor's nonexistent" and the "speedy service" can be "choppy", but if you want "great food and fair prices, this is the place to go."

Beluga ◐ 21 25 18 $39

3520 Edwards Rd. (Erie Ave.), 513-533-4444

■ "Contemporary with a minimalist mindset" sums up this "inviting, sleek" East Side bistro where a "helpful", "good-looking" staff ministers to the way-cool crowd with martinis and Eurasian fare that offers "a new twist on sushi"; if it's all a bit "pricey" – well, a "hip location" near tony Hyde Park doesn't come cheap.

Brown Dog Cafe 23 14 19 $35

Pfeiffer Commons, 5893 Pfeiffer Rd. (bet. I-71 & Kenwood Rd.), Blue Ash, 513-794-1610

■ "Who woulda thunk" you'd find a "really neat funky gourmet" New American with "artfully prepared" "inventive cuisine" in a plain-Jane strip mall in suburban Blue Ash; the "attentive" staff manages to create "a friendly atmosphere" in the "tastefully decorated" space hung with chef-owner Mary Swortwood's paintings; perhaps it's "a bit overpriced", but "as neighborhood restaurants go, this one's a keeper."

Chez Alphonse 22 20 23 $44

654 Highland Ave. (Grand Ave.), Ft. Thomas, KY, 859-442-5488

◪ "Out-of-the-way" Fort Thomas is the surprising setting for "an experience that comes as close to authentic French dining as you can find"; *amis* assert the expensive but "unforgettable" meals are served in a "formal" atmosphere enlivened with the "perfect personal touch" from owners Alphonse and Christine Kaelbel; *ennemis* insist it's "stuffy" and "not worth the drive", but even they may be won over by the low-cost bistro menu served weeknights.

China Gourmet 24 16 21 $32

3340 Erie Ave. (Marburg Ave.), 513-871-6612

■ Gourmets guarantee that the Moy family dynasty continues to operate "the best Chinese in Cincinnati", with a "refined and restrained menu" that "rises above" "other Asian establishments"; "charming service by a loyal staff" "makes you feel like an honored guest", even if the rooms replete with rosewood "could use some help"; regulars of this Hyde Park veteran know to "go with the waiter's recommendations", though they tend to be "quite pricey."

Daveed's at 934 [S] 25 21 19 $49

934 Hatch St. (Louden St.), 513-721-2665

◪ A "trendy but casual" ambiance permeates the "cozy" rooms in this renovated Mt. Adams townhouse (try snagging a banquette for "good people-watching"); a majority agrees that "Cincinnati's most creative chef", David Cook, satisfies "sophisticated palates" with his "daring", "exceptional" Eclectic cooking, but critics claim the "food isn't enough to overcome the belittling feeling", and "small portions at big prices" are a turnoff too.

Dewey's Pizza [S] 26 15 16 $16

Oakley Sq., 3014 Madison Rd. (Markbreit Ave.), 513-731-7755
Shops at Harper's Point, 11338 Montgomery Rd. (Kemper Rd.), Symmes, 513-247-9955

■ The "best pizza in town" can be found at this pair of "crowded" Oakley Square meccas where pie-heads purr over the "endless combinations" of "tasty and innovative" "gourmet" toppings, plus red sauce with a "nice little kick to it"; they also save room for the "fantastic" house salad and the "good wine-by-the-glass list."

Jeff Ruby's
23 | 26 | 24 | $54

700 Walnut St. (7th St.), 513-784-1200

■ Ok, so Jeff Ruby's Downtown steakhouse is somewhat "over the top" – how could it be otherwise when the "beautiful art deco decor" is so "flamboyant" and the "fantastic" dry-aged beef is displayed in a streetside meat locker?; what's more, the "portions are huge" (cut of choice: a 32-ounce bone-in rib-eye) and the wine list is 21 pages long; a handful gripe that it's "overpriced", but who can resist when the waiters make "you the star attraction?"

JUMP Café & Bar ◐
24 | 24 | 22 | $48

1203 Main St. (12th St.), 513-665-4677

■ "Jump to it" Over-the-Rhine locals say – this "hip spot" offers "terrific and imaginative" New American food accented with "nice little touches" like homemade bread with savory spreads; the "to-die-for decor" is part New York chic, part California casual, with "the best seats in the house" at the food bar "with a view of the kitchen" or at "the private table in the old elevator shaft"; it's "very pricey", but the main gripe is that the upstairs restaurant gets "overwhelmed" by the noise "from the bar below."

Maisonette
28 | 27 | 27 | $64

114 E. Sixth St. (bet. Main & Walnut Sts.), 513-721-2260

■ After 51 years, this French Downtowner remains the "traditional choice for wow occasions", as well as Cincinnati's Most Popular and No. 1 for Food; a "lighter, modern" approach to "the crème-de-la-crème" cuisine and a freshening of the "warm, elegant decor" (still full of "fine artwork and soothing lighting") only augment other strengths: the "unobtrusive" staff that puts you "totally at ease" and a tab that may be "the best fine-food bargain in the U.S."; P.S. the departure of "longtime chef Jean-Robert de Cavel" may outdate the food score.

Montgomery Inn ⬚
20 | 17 | 17 | $30

9440 Montgomery Rd. (Milford Rd.), Montgomery, 513-791-3482

Montgomery Inn at the Boathouse ⬚
925 Eastern Ave. (I-471), 513-721-7427

■ "Gazillions of customers" say "you just can't beat" these "blue-collar gourmet" shrines known for "massively meaty bones" and homemade Saratoga chips; while waits for a table "can be over two hours" (offering time to study the "sports memorabilia" at both the Montgomery and the Downtown riverfront-with-a-view locations) and service can be "rushed", tourists and locals agree this "Cincinnati tradition" is "mmm" good.

Nicola's
23 | 19 | 16 | $39

1420 Sycamore St. (Liberty St.), 513-721-6200

■ "Near the entertainment" district, this sophisticate serves up "very creative Italian" delicacies that are "worth the time" it takes to prepare them; owner Nicola Pietoso and his "informed and friendly" servers operate in a "lovely, airy room" in a historic building full of "eclectic touches" like old clockworks and local artwork; given the "wonderful food and ambiance", regulars can't figure out why it "doesn't get the crowds it deserves" (perhaps the edgy Over-the-Rhine "location keeps timid people away").

Pacific Moon Cafe S

24 | 14 | 19 | $25

Market Pl., 8300 Market Place Ln. (Montgomery Rd.), Montgomery, 513-891-0091

■ For those sick of the "same old, same old offerings", this popular Pan-Asian cafe in suburban Montgomery offers one of the "most diversified" and "creative" menus in town, including "outstanding dim sum on weekends" that many partisans feel is "the only one to try in the tri-state area"; sure, "it's a little expensive", but this is "where the Chinese community eats" – preferably on the "cozy little patio."

Palace S

27 | 27 | 26 | $52

Cincinnatian Hotel, 601 Vine St. (6th St.), 513-381-6006

■ "Luxurious" and "refined", this "perennial favorite" Downtown shatters any lingering stereotypes about hotel dining thanks to its "inventive and delicious" New American menu; its other "key elements" are more traditional: "serene" surroundings and "impeccable service" ("they go out of the way to make an evening special for you"); P.S. while the main room remains the place to go if you're "celebrating or trying to impress someone", the adjacent Cricket Lounge hits just the right note for a "reasonably priced" late-night bite.

Palomino Euro Bistro S

21 | 24 | 18 | $34

Fountain Pl., 505 Vine St. (5th St.), 513-381-1300

■ "Above-average creativity" on an "eclectic menu", a "vibrant and exciting" atmosphere and a "knowledgeable" staff may be why this Downtown Mediterranean decorated with vivid Northwestern art and blown glass "doesn't seem like a chain"; it's always crowded with "Cincinnati's elite" and conventioneers who clamor for the rotisserie-cooked meats and the "best mushroom soup ever" while they compete for the window tables that provide a "perfect perch" "to watch the happenings on the square."

Phoenix

25 | 27 | 24 | $39

812 Race St. (9th St.), 513-721-8901

■ "Elegant", "old-fashioned" surroundings with lovely Victorian appointments and a "gracious, club-like atmosphere" make this Downtown Continental-American a "good place to carry on a conversation" or to have a memorable "night out"; "exceptional pricing" (especially on the wine list), "beautifully served, rich" dishes and "hardly any turnover" among the experienced staff all ensure "you'll always feel special" here.

Precinct S

25 | 20 | 22 | $48

311 Delta Ave. (Columbia Pkwy.), 513-321-5454

■ While it's no crime to call this "remodeled 19th-century police station" a "temple to steak", the raw bar and other seafood options are "just as impressive", and whatever you order, you get "a lot for your money"; yes, the "seating is cramped" in the warren of candlelit, mirrored rooms, but after 20 years on the East Side, this "clubby" "favorite" is still the best place "for a power dinner" or "to see celebrities and sports stars."

Primavista [S] 23 | 24 | 22 | $42

Queen's Tower, 810 Matson Pl. (bet. 8th St. & Price Ave.), 513-251-6467

■ "The name says it all" – "the absolutely best view" of the Ohio River valley and Downtown Cincinnati can be seen from this Price Hillsider that draws an "older, local crowd" "with a few heirs thrown in for good measure"; though the decor suggests an English tavern, the "extensive", "delicious" menu (strong on veal) is strictly Northern Italian; while you may pay a little extra for that prima vista, the cognoscenti claim it's still an "excellent value."

Sturkey's [S] 23 | 16 | 20 | $36

400 Wyoming Ave. (bet. Grove & Oak Aves.), Wyoming, 513-821-9200

■ Historic Wyoming village is the "beautiful" locale for chef-owners Paul and Pamela Sturkey's "creative but not conceited" New American where there's "something for everyone on the menu, from burgers to gourmet entrees" to "desserts to die for"; though some see a need "to soften the noise level" and warm up the "cold, modern decor", faithful followers agree that "the taste of the food outweighs everything."

Cleveland

TOP 10 FOOD RANKING

	Restaurant	Cuisine Type
28	Johnny's Bar	Continental/N. Italian
27	Baricelli Inn	Continental
	Phnom Penh	Asian
	Giovanni's Ristorante	Northern Italian
26	Oz Bar & Bistro	Continental/Eclectic
	Lola	New American
	Sans Souci	Mediterranean
25	Johnny's Downtown	Continental/N. Italian
	Parker's	New French
	Mise	Eclectic/New American

ADDITIONAL NOTEWORTHY PLACES

Blue Pointe Grille	Seafood
Century	Seafood
Chez François	Classic French
Circo Zibibbo	N&S Italian
Johnny's Bistro	French Bistro
Moxie	New American
One Walnut	New American
Sergio's	South American
Viva Barcelona	Spanish
Weia Teia	Asian

	F	D	S	C
Baricelli Inn	27	24	24	$59

Baricelli Inn, 2203 Cornell Rd. (Murray Hill Rd.), 216-791-6500

■ "Atmosphere abounds" at owner Paul Minnillo's "elegant", "upscale" eatery housed in a "historic" brownstone mansion near "picturesque Little Italy"; the "flawlessly served" selections – "creative" contemporary Continental dishes and a "wonderful selection of cheeses" – are among the reasons devotees deem this a "favorite" "place for a celebration of any sort, including being able to afford to dine here"; P.S. "stay overnight for a truly wonderful experience" (it's also a "quaint" B&B).

	F	D	S	C
Blue Pointe Grill [S]	24	23	22	$43

700 W. Saint Clair Ave. (6th St.), 216-875-7827

■ Chef Jim Gillison scores points for the "finest fish in Cleveland" (including "grouper perched atop primo lobster mashed potatoes") at this "refurbished" landmark "in the heart of the Warehouse District", where thirtysomething-and-up professionals converge for a "terrific bar scene" amid the "nautical decor"; despite gripes at the "outrageous prices", most rate this "elegant establishment" a "favorite" when they "want to impress."

Century 🅂   24 | 25 | 22 | $47 |
Ritz-Carlton Hotel, 1515 W. Third St. (Huron Rd.), 216-623-1300
■ "Exactly what you would expect from a Ritz-Carlton" say surveyors of this Downtowner whose "elegant", "sleek decor" "with a train motif" is "carpeted and draped so well you can actually carry on a conversation"; the "seafood-oriented menu" is "creative", while the "comprehensive sushi bar" and "cool" martini bar offer speedier options; opinions diverge on the service ("suave" vs. "overbearing"), but all agree the "huge swirl of cotton candy that arrives with the check is a great touch."

Chez François 🅂   ▽ 28 | 26 | 26 | $68 |
555 Main St. (Liberty Ave.), Vermilion, 440-967-0630
■ Whether they arrive by land or by sea – the restaurant offers docking, along with a "terrific view", on the Vermilion River – fans find "creative food", "top-notch service" and an all-around "truly wonderful French dining experience" at this "out-of-the-way" Far West "treat"; while prices can hit the high-water mark (even "some of the wealthiest are complaining"), the "special wine-pairing dinners" constitute the "best gourmet dining buy in northern Ohio."

Circo Zibibbo 🅂   20 | 24 | 17 | $44 |
1300 W. Ninth St. (Saint Clair Ave.), 216-575-0699
☑ "A rainbow of colored glass hanging from the ceiling and undulating along the walls" draws "fun crowds" to this "can-you-say-trendy?" spot "at the base of the Warehouse District"; the "jumping bar" is "more enjoyable than the restaurant", because while the "contemporary" Italian menu features some "truly inspired cooking", it's "overpriced" and "takes a looong time to arrive at table"; "but people come for the scene, not the food."

Giovanni's Ristorante   27 | 24 | 27 | $60 |
25550 Chagrin Blvd. (Richmond Rd.), Beachwood, 216-831-8625
■ "An oasis of quiet (some would say stuffiness) attracts well-dressed diners" to this "longtime favorite" in ritzy Beachwood; though "the epitome of expensive", it offers the "crème de la crème" in Northern Italian cuisine, served by an "attentive staff"; even if they "tend to overdo", "you can't go wrong" here.

Johnny's Bar   28 | 19 | 25 | $52 |
3164 Fulton Rd. (Trent Ave.), 216-281-0055
■ "Reminiscent of the '40s", this West Side spot is the oldest of the three Johnny's establishments, and as with many a trilogy, "the first is always the best" assert *amici* who have voted its "gorilla-size portions" of "fantastic" Continental–Northern Italian food No. 1; though "dark" and a bit "cramped" with "the crowd of Cleveland notables coming in and out", it's "still charming"– thanks to "superb service" – and "worth every cent."

Johnny's Bistro   24 | 27 | 23 | $56 |
1400 W. Sixth St. (bet. Saint Clair & Superior Aves.), 216-774-0055
☑ Co-owner Paul Anthony's latest Johnny's venture, this "elegant" French beckons "special-occasion" diners to the Warehouse District; advocates adore the "authentic dishes" ("if you don't try the truffled mashed potatoes, you've committed a culinary sin"), "plush atmosphere" and "fabulous service"; but naysayers snap that "bistro food should not be this expensive or served in such a snooty environment."

Johnny's Downtown 🇸 25 23 22 $51
1406 W. Sixth St. (bet. Saint Clair & Superior Aves.), 216-623-0055
☑ When they need a "reliable spot for an important business dinner", the Downtown "suits" march to this "nice little brother" of Johnny's Bar, followed by a stream of "slicks and trendies" seeking a "swank" setting and a "mouthwatering" Continental–Northern Italian meal to match; the bottom line is "expensive", though most say it's "worth it for the occasional splurge."

Lola Bistro & Wine Bar 🌑🇸 26 21 23 $46
900 Literary Rd. (Professor Ave.), 216-771-5652
■ He's posed naked with a Vita-Mix, he appears on the Food Network show *The Melting Pot* and still chef-owner Michael Symon has time to keep Tremont diners "oohing and ahhing" with his "not-for- the-timid" American menu that "makes food you don't think you like taste good"; "success hasn't spoiled" this "cutting-edge place", but it has made "reservations extremely necessary", so "call ahead" and come "wearing black."

Mise 25 22 26 $37
10427 Clifton Blvd. (bet. 104th & 105th Sts.), 216-651-6473
■ Chef-owner "Jeff Uniatowski has done a phenomenal job" say fans of this unexpectedly hip spot spanning two West Side storefronts; on the ever-evolving Eclectic–New American menu, surveyors single out "imaginative" mainstays like coffee-crusted sea scallops and a "don't-miss" "coffee and doughnuts dessert", dished up by "extremely knowledgeable servers"; just be warned the "creative" mise-en-scène gets "noisy."

Moxie 🇸 25 19 21 $44
3355 Richmond Rd. (Chagrin Blvd.), Beachwood, 216-831-5599
■ A "well-dressed", "table-hopping crowd" crams into this "East Side trendy" suburbanite, fondly deemed a "deli on steroids" for its "consistently excellent" New American classics like long-bone rib steak and "out-of-this-world baked hot chocolate" dessert; while the waiters sometimes resemble "the Sprockets skit from *Saturday Night Live*" and the "cavernous" space gets "oppressively loud", for most this "fun place" has plenty of moxie.

One Walnut 22 21 21 $46
Ohio Savings Bldg., 1 Walnut Ave. (bet. 9th & 12th Sts.), 216-575-1111
☑ "Pricey and proud of it", this New American Downtown represents the "latest incarnation of chef-owner Marlin Kaplan"; while the faithful rave that the "creative but classically inspired dishes" and "glitzy Gotham styling" represent a "great comeback", the less-reverent roar it's "overrated" ("decor leaves much to be desired, and the same with service") – especially considering "not everyone is on an expense account."

Oz Bar & Bistro 26 18 24 $37
2391 W. 11th St. (Kenilworth Ave.), 216-861-3734
■ "Forget home – there's no place like Oz" rave reviewers about this newcomer whose "trendy" Continental-Eclectic "menu fits perfectly into the trendy Tremont dining scene"; chef-owner Donna Chriszt (aka "the Wizard") "prepares awesome food" – the presentation alone "is worth a picture" – and the staff "tries hard to please"; the only doubts are over the "stark decor": "plastic patio chairs inside are tacky, not edgy."

Parker's S   25 | 18 | 21 | $49
2801 Bridge Ave. (28th St.), 216-771-7130

☑ "Chef-owner Parker Bosley brings semi-formal haute cuisine" to Ohio City at this "quiet and refined" New French where his "exquisite use of local ingredients" results in "small portions but huge taste"; "for pure food, it's top-shelf", but while converts chant "fresh, fresh, fresh", critics counter "so, so, so boring", turned off by the "simple, not baroque" cooking and "no glitz" atmosphere.

Phnom Penh S⊅   27 | 4 | 12 | $18
13124 Lorain Ave. (131st St.), 216-251-0210

■ The "best cheap eats in town" (certainly not the "what-a-dump" decor) draw diners who "line up outside" this West Side Asian "hole-in-the-wall"; the "wonderfully spicy" "extensive menu" emphasizes Cambodia and Vietnam, but extends to "almost anything from the region", which means don't ask for "hot" unless "you can handle it"; P.S. "no liquor service, but customers are encouraged to BYO."

Sans Souci S   26 | 27 | 25 | $47
Cleveland Renaissance Hotel, 24 Public Sq. (bet. Superior Ave. & 3rd St.), 216-696-5600

■ "Quiet rooms, an ever-changing menu and relaxed service . . . what could be better?"; nothing, and that's why reviewers have once again voted this Renaissance Hotel spot "overlooking Public Square" the Most Popular in town; there's "elegant, enticing" decor (think fireplace and countryside murals) and "hands down Cleveland's best Mediterranean" cuisine; "oozing with charm", "this is the place for that special someone."

Sergio's in University Circle S   24 | 17 | 21 | $38
1903 Ford Dr. (Bellflower Rd.), 216-231-1234

■ Brazilian influences shake up a menu that "never lets you down" at this "fascinating and flavorful" South American, "one of the better choices" in the arty "University Circle area"; live Latin-inspired jazz "makes the experience festive all the time", but on concert nights the pre-symphony crowd takes over the already-"cramped quarters", so be sure to "book in advance" or else "wait for patio weather."

Viva Barcelona S   ▽ 23 | 20 | 26 | $30
24600 Detroit Rd. (bet Clague & Columbia Rds.), Westlake, 440-892-8700

■ "Fine Spanish dining comes to the West Shore Suburbs" crow converts to this neophyte, whose "incredible" food is paired with "excellent sangria"; "exceptional service" from "tuxedo-clad waiters" and a "perfect atmosphere" (the "right mix of soft lighting and music") are further reasons to dub "the experience a real treat."

Weia Teia S   23 | 17 | 17 | $25
Great Northern Mall, 140 Great Northern Mall (Brookpark Rd.), North Olmsted, 440-716-8381

■ "All mall restaurants should be this good" say fans surprised to find an "inventive", "artful" and "funky" "Asian-inspired" (with New French and Italian influences) eatery so close to a Gap; its South Suburbs locale makes it a hot spot for lunchtime shoppers and diners looking for "a fusion experience", though more than a few think the "inattentive" service could use work.

Columbus, OH

TOP 10 FOOD RANKING

Restaurant	Cuisine Type
28 Handke's Cuisine	Continental/International
27 Refectory	Classic/New French
L'Antibes	Classic French
Rigsby's	Provençal/N. Italian
26 Yard Club at O'Toole's	Irish/American
25 Lindey's	American
Restaurant Japan	Japanese
Cameron's	New American
Morton's of Chicago	Steakhouse
La Tavola	Northern Italian

ADDITIONAL NOTEWORTHY PLACES

Alana's Food & Wine	Eclectic
Braddock's Grandview	Low Country
Columbus Fish Market	Seafood
Mitchell's	Steakhouse
Out On Main	International
Shoku	Pan-Asian
Starliner Diner	Cuban/Mexican
SuLan Eurasian Bistro	Eurasian
Tapatio	Caribbean/Mexican
Trattoria Roma	Northern Italian

F	D	S	C

Alana's Food & Wine

24	13	21	$31

2333 N. High St. (bet. Oakland & Patterson Aves.), 614-294-6783
☑ "Funky and strange yet comfortable", Alana Shock's (the "queen of flavor") "different" kind of eatery north of Ohio State's campus attracts "adventurous" appetites with her "innovative" Eclectic cooking (the "always-changing menu" "does well by vegetarians" too) matched by an "extensive" wine list with truly "great prices"; though a few find her "well meaning but cranky", supporters relish her "personalized" concept as a "refreshing" "diversion" and appreciate her "real commitment to quality ingredients."

Braddock's Grandview

22	17	20	$32

1470 Grandview Ave. (Ida Ave.), 614-487-0077
☑ Michael Braddock's "magic with pork dishes" (don't say no to his "flavorful" hickory-smoked chops) and other "tasty", "imaginative" Low Country interpretations (like the "wonderful salmon purse") keep loyalists returning to this "unpretentious" Southern treat on the main drag of the hip (yes, really) suburb of Grandview; it definitely "fills a niche" in the local dining scene, even if detractors gripe "lots of hype but not enough follow-through."

Cameron's S　　25　19　22　$32
2185 W. Dublin-Granville Rd. (Linworth Rd.), Worthington,
614-885-3663
■ Columbus restaurateur Cameron Mitchell clearly "knows the
business" well, which explains why this "friendly neighborhood"
bistro in quaint Worthington, his first local venture, is "still going
strong"; while it may be "less flashy" than some of his later
restaurants, it remains an "all-time favorite" thanks to a New
American menu that's "consistently" "awesome" and includes
some "very unique items" and a "super" staff; granted, it can get
"crazy loud", but plenty of enthusiasts just "love" this place.

Columbus Fish Market S　　24　20　20　$31
40 Hutchinson Ave. (Rte. 270), 614-410-3474
1245 Olentangy River Rd. (bet. 3rd & 5th Aves.), 614-291-3474
☑ Schools of fin fanatics seek out this "hit" pair of seafood
houses (courtesy of Cameron Mitchell) with an "active, urbane"
atmosphere in North Columbus and in the Crosswoods area for
"excellent fish" ("flown in fresh daily" and prepared with a "lively
flair") that landlocked diners "can rely on"; the "unimpressed",
however, say "good but never spectacular, and way too noisy."

Handke's Cuisine　　28　25　24　$47
520 S. Front St. (bet. Beck & Blenkner Sts.), 614-621-2500
■ Certified Master Chef Hartmut Handke is the "genius" behind
this "charming" "special-occasion" destination in the Brewery
District, which has again been ranked No. 1 for Food in Columbus;
featuring "unique subterranean dining" in a restored 19th-century
rathskeller with vaulted ceilings, it provides a "superb" Continental-
International "feast for the eyes as well as the palate" (including
"incredible" buffalo tenderloin steak and crème brûlée "that might
be the best in the world"), along with "attentive" service; of course
it's "expensive", but this "class act" is "still the best in town."

L'Antibes　　27　22　24　$45
772 N. High St. (Warren St.), 614-291-1666
■ "Very small and intimate", this Short North "gem" is "a definite
asset" to Columbus because chef/co-owner Dale Gussett "knows
what we want in fine dining" – "phenomenal" Classic French
fare ("go for the veal sweetbreads", "the best in town") proffered
in an "elegant" environment with a "romantic" ambiance by a
"professional" staff that satisfies "your every whim"; "expect a
leisurely dinner" – there's "no rushing" here.

La Tavola　　25　10　19　$22
33 Beech Ridge Dr. (Powell Rd.), Powell, 614-848-4231
■ "From the outside, you'd never guess that this building is home
to the best Italian food in town (the inside isn't much to look at
either)", but this "family-run" trattoria in the Northwest delivers
"truly outstanding", "authentic" Northern Italian cooking that's the
real deal (plus, the menu offers "half-size" helpings for smaller
appetites, "a wonderful idea"), paired with a "great" all-Italian
wine list that's "priced around retail"; to boot, the atmosphere is
"laid-back" and the staff "super-friendly."

Lindey's [S] 25 | 24 | 22 | $37

169 E. Beck St. (Mohawk St.), 614-228-4343

◪ Even after two decades, "the beautiful people" still flock to this "lively" American bistro situated in a 19th-century building in German Village because it's a "long-standing favorite" "institution that doesn't fail"; a "great gathering place" with "lots of action" at the bars and "interesting people-watching", it features a "wonderful variety" of "can't-go-wrong" dishes (though "nothing will knock your socks off"), but dissenters find it "overhyped" and "pretty snotty."

Mitchell's Steakhouse [S] 24 | 26 | 22 | $45

45 N. Third St. (bet. Gay & Lynn Sts.), 614-621-2333

◪ "Movers and shakers" patronize this "classy" steakhouse set in a "wonderful old bank building" in the heart of Downtown; it's a prime power place to "take clients" thanks to its "beautiful", spacious surroundings, "clubby feel" and an "excellent" staff that "treats you right", not to mention "well-prepared" aged cuts like its signature Kansas City strip; critics, however, who think that namesake restaurant mogul Cameron Mitchell "may be spreading himself too thin" charge "overrated."

Morton's of Chicago [S] 25 | 20 | 21 | $50

2 Nationwide Plaza (High St.), 614-464-4442

◪ "More-than-generous portions" of "melt-in-your-mouth" aged porterhouses and "good" sides ("you could feed three kids with one potato") satisfy cadres of carnivores at this "traditional" Downtown chophouse; though fans praise the experience as "gluttony at its best", detractors shrug "more of the same" and surmise that this "expense-account" chain link is "not as big a standout as in other cities because there are plenty of good steakhouses" in Columbus.

Out On Main [S] 23 | 20 | 23 | $33

122 E. Main St. (bet. 3rd & 4th Sts.), 614-224-9510

■ "Fun, hip and gay", this "lighthearted" Downtown alternative is where the "'in' crowd goes out" "with a group" for a "unique" "good time"; amid an "incredible" (or "distracting"?) "collection of memorabilia", an "arty", "friendly" staff serves a "wide variety" of "inventive", "surprisingly excellent" International dishes (the signature Louisiana "crawfish cakes are delish"); "no matter your sexual orientation, everyone feels welcome" here.

Refectory 27 | 26 | 26 | $48

1092 Bethel Rd. (Kenny Rd.), 614-451-9774

■ "The ecclesiastical atmosphere matches the heavenly food" at this "sumptuous", "flawless" French "benchmark" housed in a restored Northwest church with an air of "quiet elegance"; given "superb" chef Richard Blondin's "masterful" execution of both the classics and modern interpretations, beautifully accompanied by an "award-winning wine list" and brought to table by an "exquisite" staff "that's never intrusive", is it any revelation that it was yet again voted the Most Popular restaurant in Columbus by faithful worshipers?; P.S. a "bargain" three-course prix fixe bistro menu is available in the lounge.

Restaurant Japan [S] 25 15 19 $25

1173 Old Henderson Rd. (Kenny Rd.), Upper Arlington, 614-451-5411

■ "One bite of the sublime spicy tuna roll will convince anyone that this is the best Japanese food in Columbus"; not only will the "expertly prepared, melt-in-your-mouth sushi make you an addict", but this "busy" Upper Arlington "real deal" also features "top-notch" cooked dishes including "heavenly tempura and perfect noodles"; granted, the digs are strictly "no-frills" and it's "a little too bright", but the "great value" keeps fans coming back.

Rigsby's Cuisine Volatile 27 23 23 $38

698 N. High St. (Lincoln St.), 614-461-7888

■ "A happy place to eat", this "modern", "stylish" Provençal–Northern Italian in the trendy Short North district offers "lots of lively kitchen action on view and fun things on the menu"; chef Christian Hatterman's "exciting" cooking yields "complex flavors" that are "sometimes unusual but always good", so though "it may be the place to be seen, unlike restaurants that focus on form over substance", this "adventure in food" "delivers consistently excellent" fare "artfully presented" in a "metropolitan" ambiance by a "superb" staff.

Shoku [S] 23 20 20 $32

1312 Grandview Ave. (3rd Ave.), 614-485-9490

■ "Good, if not great", sushi in "chic", "dramatic" environs beckon scenesters to this "pleasant" Grandview Pan-Asian "favorite" replete with a "spacious" patio that affords a prime "people-watching" view; though a few feel that the service can "vary", the majority recommends this "relaxing and enjoyable experience."

Starliner Diner [S] 24 13 18 $17

5240 Cemetery Rd. (east of Main St.), Hilliard, 614-529-1198

■ "Kitschy" "treasures" (think eccentric holiday ornaments, a collection of clocks from the '60s, etc.) earn this "down 'n' dirty" Hilliard diner acclaim as a "favorite funky place" to scarf down "huge portions" of "hearty", "out-of-this-world" Cuban-Mexican food, "wonderfully spiced" and "unusually good"; though there's often "a wait", when you "want to have some fun" and eat cheap ethnic, this "kooky" "oddball" satisfies.

SuLan Eurasian Bistro [S] 23 27 18 $35

2894 E. Main St. (east of Roosevelt Ave.), Bexley, 614-338-0788

■ "What a space" exclaim enthusiasts of this "trendy" "rising star" in affluent Bexley, which distinguishes itself with a "fabulous interior design" and "soothing" ambiance; it's a "really cool" backdrop in which to sample a "smashing variety" of "creative", "exotic" even, Eurasian dishes; "a great addition to the Columbus scene", this "wonderful experience" just "keeps getting better."

Tapatio [S] 22 18 17 $28

491 Park St. (Spruce St.), 614-221-1085

◪ Better "watch out for the peppers" at this "lively" Short North "favorite" because the kitchen "really knows how to spice things up" and offers "interesting choices" influenced by the cuisines of Mexico, the Caribbean and the Southwest and spun "with a twist"; though "disappointed" diners deem it "not as good as its reputation" and warn about "spotty" service, aficionados "enjoy this change" of pace.

Trattoria Roma
24 | 17 | 18 | $32

1447 Grandview Ave. (5th Ave.), 614-488-2104

■ Providing an "authentic Italian experience in Grandview", this "delightful" "treat" pleases with "inspired preparations" like "perfect al dente" "homemade pastas" with "incredible sauces" and "melt-in-your-mouth fish"; the "crowded" conditions and "noisy" room are "the only unfortunate distractions from the food", but at least "you can eat out front" on the sidewalk patio during nice weather.

Yard Club at O'Toole's S
26 | 22 | 21 | $26

4065 Main St. (Norwich St.), Hilliard, 614-771-1400

■ Thanks to "a chef who thinks", the "surprisingly innovative" Irish-American selections offered at this "fun" hang (set in an 1883 building registered with the National Historic Preservation Society) in old Hilliard are far "more gourmet" than the "pub grub you might expect from its name"; though the "service can be a little questionable at times", the "quality of the food" "makes up for it"; it's still an "underappreciated" "secret", which suits just fine the insiders who only "hope the word doesn't get out."

Connecticut

TOP 20 FOOD RANKING

Restaurant	Cuisine Type
28 Jean-Louis	New French
Thomas Henkelmann	Classic French
27 Da Pietro's	N. Italian/Classic French
Ondine	New French
Restaurant du Village	Classic French
Cavey's	N. Italian/New French
Max's Oyster Bar	Seafood
Frank Pepe Pizzeria	Pizza
Rebeccas	New American
La Colline Verte	New French
26 Métro Bis	New American
Bernard's Inn	Classic French
Valbella	Northern Italian
Jeffrey's	Continental/New American
Quattro's	N&S Italian
Sally's Apizza	Pizza
Meson Galicia	Spanish
Max Downtown	New American
Peppercorn's Grill	N&S Italian
Stonehenge	Continental

ADDITIONAL NOTEWORTHY PLACES

Ann Howard Apricots	New American/Continental
Baang Café & Bar	Californian/Asian
Cafe Routier	French Bistro
Carole Peck's	New American
Elms	American
Gennaro's	N&S Italian
Golden Lamb Buttery	American
Great Taste	Chinese
Max Amoré	Northern Italian
Mayflower Inn	American/Continental
Miramar	Mediterranean
Piccolo Arancio	N&S Italian
Restaurant Bricco	N. Italian/Med.
Roger Sherman Inn	Continental
Roomba	Nuevo Latino
Ruth's Chris	Steakhouse
Steve's Centerbrook	New American
Terra Mar Grille	New American
Union League Cafe	French Bistro
West Street Grill	New American

Ann Howard Apricots S   24 | 22 | 23 | $38
1593 Farmington Ave. (Rte. 4), Farmington, 860-673-5405
■ "You'll love it even if you hate apricots" (from those "on the walls to the chocolate-covered [ones] delivered at the end of the meal") assert advocates of this New American–Continental that some call "the definitive New England restaurant"; "enjoy drinks outside", then "ask for a table by the window" in the "romantic" dining room for a "grand view" of the Farmington River; some wallet-watchers prefer the "fun" pub purveying less expensive food than is found upstairs.

Baang Café & Bar S   24 | 21 | 19 | $41
1191 E. Putnam Ave. (I-95, exit 5), Greenwich, 203-637-2114
■ "Still hopping and happening" after seven years, this "Greenwich hot spot" is where "super-cool people" convene for "inventive", "expensive" Cal-Asian cooking (like firecracker shrimp rolls) in a "modern minimalist" space; there are "long waits", the tables are "too close together" and the "noise level is painful", but that's exactly why "folks who want NY attitude and aura" head here.

Bernard's Inn S   26 | 24 | 24 | $53
20 West Ln. (Rte. 33), Ridgefield, 203-438-8282
■ Loyalists laud this Ridgefield landmark now helmed by top toque team Bernard and Sarah Bouissou as "French elegance at its finest", offered in a "picture-perfect New England setting"; the cooking is so "heavenly", it "forces you to reset your standards" (especially notable is the "wonderful array of appetizers"), and it's all served by a "superb, professional" staff; clearly, there are "no weaknesses" here.

Cafe Routier S   25 | 18 | 22 | $35
1080 Boston Post Rd. (Oyster River Rd.), Old Saybrook, 860-388-6270
■ "An unlikely surprise in a modest" Old Saybrook location, this "intimate" Post Road French bistro delights devotees who dine at either "the beautiful copper [wine] bar" or the dining room on the "steak frites of my dreams" and other "incredibly consistent" dishes; with "good prices" and "great wine", regulars say "it's like coming home."

Carole Peck's Good News Cafe S   25 | 19 | 21 | $38
694 Main St. S./Rte. 6 (Rte. 64), Woodbury, 203-266-4663
■ The "food is very good news" at this Woodbury New American "gem" where "Connecticut's Alice Waters" has a "deft hand" with "fresh from the farm" ingredients, which results in "innovative but not coy" "takes on new and classic dishes"; a "gregarious crowd" finds it "well worth the drive" as well for the "professional service" and "chic", "casual setting"; P.S. "yes, that was Helen Hunt."

Cavey's   27 | 24 | 25 | $51
45 E. Center St. (Main St.), Manchester, 860-643-2751
■ "Black-tie service and blue-ribbon food in a blue-collar town" sums up the sentiment about this "close-to-perfect" "seasoned veteran" in Manchester that's a "delightful" Northern Italian upstairs and a "formal but not pretentious" New French downstairs; enhanced by "excellent wine selections" and "step-back-in-time decor", it's "great for special occasions."

Da Pietro's
| 27 | 20 | 25 | $54 |

36 Riverside Ave. (Boston Post Rd.), Westport, 203-454-1213

■ "Pietro's [Scotti] makes you feel like a guest in his house" pronounce those passionate about his Northern Italian–French in Westport, where the creative, "flawless" dishes are "worth a drive from anywhere in the tri-state area"; though "romantic", the "tiny" storefront is "uncomfortably cramped" for some.

Elms S
| 24 | 23 | 23 | $46 |

Elms Inn, 500 Main St./Rte. 35 (Gilbert St.), Ridgefield, 203-438-9206

■ Reviewers rave about "highly acclaimed" chef-owner Brendan Walsh and his "special-occasion" place in a landmark Ridgefield inn; it's "two restaurants in one", both serving "American food with a delicious twist", but the "beautiful" "dining room is formal", while the tavern with a "fireside setting" is" more affordable."

Frank Pepe Pizzeria S⊅
| 27 | 12 | 16 | $17 |

157 Wooster St. (bet. Brown & Olive Sts.), New Haven, 203-865-5762

■ Reviewers only wrangle about whether the white clam pie at New Haven's "king of pizza" is "the single best on earth", "in the galaxy", "from heaven" or "of all time"; the "wait is unbelievable" ("bring *War and Peace*"), and "service is brusque, but don't take it personally"; old hands advise calling for takeout – "if you can get someone to answer the phone."

Gennaro's Ristorante D'Amalfi
| 25 | 20 | 23 | $35 |

937 State St. (bet. Bishop & Humphrey Sts.), New Haven, 203-777-5490

■ "Home is where the heart is, and the owners are all heart" at this New Haven Italian rated "excellent" by regulars who return for "an abundance of good choices" that includes "always great veal", "good red sauce" and "great desserts."

Golden Lamb Buttery ⊅
| 25 | 27 | 25 | $54 |

499 Wolf Den Rd. (Bush Hill Rd.), Brooklyn, 860-774-4423

■ For over 40 years, husband-and-wife owners Bob and Jimmie Booth have overseen a "once-in-a-lifetime experience" that includes pre-dinner "horse-drawn sleigh rides in winter" and "fall hayrides" ("you can see dinner frolicking in the fields") on their 1,000-acre Brooklyn farm; the American menu features "superb food", especially in summer, when "fresh, fresh" vegetables turn up on the table; just one caveat: it's "country cooking at city prices."

Great Taste S
| 25 | 24 | 24 | $24 |

597 W. Main St. (Corbin Ave.), New Britain, 860-826-8988

■ Respondents rave about this "aptly named" New Britain Chinese, calling it an "ultra-reliable" "gem" ("try the Peking duck") and the "best use yet of an old IHOP"; the "owner's strong hand is evident in everything", and "service is splendid."

Jean-Louis
| 28 | 25 | 26 | $62 |

61 Lewis St. (bet. Greenwich Ave. & Mason St.), Greenwich, 203-622-8450

■ At the "La Grenouille of Greenwich" and the No. 1 rated restaurant for Food and Popularity in the *Connecticut Survey*, Jean-Louis Gerin, the "chef-owner, gets better every year", the New French food is "superb" and the "wine list would give any sommelier goose bumps"; the setting is "intimate" and "elegant" ("even the lighting is exquisite"), and service is "perfection"; it's "pricey", but "from the warm welcome to the chef waving goodbye at the door", "it doesn't get any better than this."

Jeffrey's
26 | 23 | 26 | $37

501 New Haven Ave. (Old Gate Ln.), Milford, 203-878-1910

■ "You'd never expect to find" "such incredible food" "in a little restaurant with an unassuming exterior on the side of a busy [Milford] road" say surveyors about this Continental–New American "class act" with "inspired", "fresh ideas"; "Jeffrey is a perfect host", and "friendly, professional service and soft piano music" "enhance" the experience.

La Colline Verte [S]
27 | 25 | 26 | $52

Greenfield Hill Shopping Ctr., 75 Hillside Rd. (Bronson Rd.), Fairfield, 203-256-9242

■ Critics chorus "kudos" to the owner of this "surprising-for-a-shopping-mall" New French where "fine cuisine, elegant decor and superlative service equal an Olympic Gold"; "though prices aren't cheap", the equivalent experience is "higher at other spots", plus it provides "some of the best people-watching in Fairfield County" – "we've seen both Newman and Redford here."

Max Amoré Ristorante [S]
25 | 22 | 22 | $31

Somerset Sq., 140 Glastonbury Blvd. (Main St.), Glastonbury, 860-659-2819

■ "Big fans of the Max chain" find this "trendy" Glastonbury Northern Italian that "feels like a California version of a Tuscan farmhouse" a "consistently great" "scene to be seen"; "your taste buds will do back flips" over "delicious food" ("pasta perfect") while you "shout over the din and stuff yourself."

Max Downtown [S]
26 | 24 | 24 | $43

City Pl., 185 Asylum St. (bet. Haynes & Trumbull Sts.), Hartford, 860-522-2530

■ "Don't save it for a special occasion" encourage admirers of Hartford's "power place", a Downtown New American that's "very NYC" and the "place to go" for "dinner with friends" or "the corporate bigwigs from out of town"; "steaks like buttah" and "other man-size meat dishes" share the table with the "best sea bass", while "the bar is fully stocked with both liquor and patrons"; if a minority is "Maxed out" over the prices, they're outvoted.

Max's Oyster Bar [S]
27 | 26 | 25 | $44

964 Farmington Ave. (S. Main St.), West Hartford, 860-236-6299

■ "Snazzy", cathedral-ceilinged "addition to the Max empire" that hit happening West Hartford and is making a huge splash with "excellent" chilled shellfish 'hi-rise' platters, the "best" baked swordfish and other superlative seafood; it's "noisy", "packed", "pricey" and very "hot."

Mayflower Inn [S]
26 | 28 | 27 | $57

118 Woodbury Rd./Rte. 47 (Rte. 109), Washington, 860-868-9466

■ If you're longing for "textbook country chic" with "pristine flower beds", "beautiful grounds" and an "elegant" "*Masterpiece Theatre*" interior presided over by an "impeccable" staff, then this Washington Continental-American is the place; the fare is always "excellent", but a meal is especially delightful on the terrace in summer, so it's not surprising that thoroughly enchanted correspondents conclude "I could live here."

Meson Galicia [S] 26 21 23 $44

10 Wall St. (bet. High & Knight Sts.), Norwalk, 203-866-8800

■ "*Numero uno*" for Spanish food in Connecticut, Norwalk's "classic Madrid" mainstay still "maintains its edge", serving "pricey but delicious tapas" ("great small doses for pregnancy cravings"), "outstanding paella" and "perfectly prepared squid"; a "solicitous" staff presides over "pleasant" country inn–like surroundings, so "it pleases every time."

Métro Bis 26 21 24 $41

Simsburytown Shops, 928 Hopmeadow St./Rte. 202 (Massaco St.), Simsbury, 860-651-1908

■ "Who would think a Simsbury strip-mall storefront could hide such great food and wine?" ask surveyors who were "tempted to lie" so this New American "gem wouldn't be discovered"; conscience must have prevailed, because they report that chef-owner Christopher Prosperi oversees a "consistently enticing, innovative menu" that just "keeps getting better."

Miramar [S] 26 26 24 $54

Inn at National Hall, 2 Boston Post Rd./Rte. 1 (Rte. 33), Westport, 203-222-2267

■ Todd English's "creative" Med menu melds "unusual flavors to create wonderful dishes that are exciting to eat" in a "festive" Westport setting presided over by an "attentive staff"; while some critics call it an "overrated, overpriced" "Manhattan-chic wanna-be", most maintain "it's expensive" but "exceptional" and "worth it" for a "special occasion" or "expense-account" evening.

Ondine [S] 27 26 26 $50

69 Pembroke Rd./Rte. 37 (Wheeler Dr.), Danbury, 203-746-4900

■ "Worth the drive" to its "out-of-the-way" Danbury setting, this Contemporary Gallic destination is situated in a "romantic old house" with "paradigmatic Country French" ambiance ("look no further for Provence"); moreover, the "first-class" prix fixe menu has "many choices" and the service is "professional"; P.S. save room for the "must-try molten-chocolate dessert."

Peppercorn's Grill 26 22 22 $40

357 Main St. (bet. Buckingham St. & Capital Ave.), Hartford, 860-547-1714

■ What voters vow is "Hartford's best non-traditional Italian" dishes up both "classic and trendy" meals made from "hard-to-find ingredients"; this "edgy, smart" "happening place" is considered "expensive but not overly" so by fans who rave that they "love everything about" the "absolutely fabulous experience."

Piccolo Arancio 25 20 23 $38

819 Farmington Ave./Rte. 4 (Rte. 10), Farmington, 860-674-1224

■ With Peppercorn's Grill as its papa, no wonder this "romantic", rustic Italian serves "sleepy Farmington" "consistently excellent" "food that's too good to drive by"; "every bite" of its "awesome pastas", "innovative pizzas" and "fabulous salads" is a "Tuscan-style" "delight" at this "cozy", "comfortable" culinary keeper that's "easy to visit often."

Quattro's S   26 | 18 | 21 | $35
*Strawberry Hill Plaza, 1300 Boston Post Rd. (Long Hill Rd.), Guilford,
203-453-6575*

■ An "amazing selection" of "delectable specials" plus a "terrific
wine list" has "junkies" of this "outstanding" Guilford Italian
"addiction" vouching for its "quite excellent reputation" as "*the*
restaurant on the shoreline", but be forewarned that the "delicious
creations" are served in a "tight and noisy" space.

Rebeccas S   27 | 21 | 22 | $55
265 Glenville Rd. (Riversville Rd.), Greenwich, 203-532-9270

☑ A "delicious" "NYC pulse beats" at this "sophisticated" New
American in Greenwich "with strong European influences"; it's "a
real showstopper on the rise", serving many surveyors' "absolute
favorite best food"; if one glance at "the parking lot full of Mercedes
and BMWs" "makes the prices more understandable", co-owner/
manager Rebecca Kirhoffer "makes you feel like a VIP even if
you pulled up in a Honda", though "snotty" servers and "austere
decor" might make some wish it were drive-thru.

Restaurant Bricco S   25 | 21 | 21 | $37
78 LaSalle Rd. (Farmington Ave.), West Hartford, 860-233-0220

■ Duplicitous diners "want to give a poor review to keep people
away" from this West Hartford Northern Italian–Med "hot spot",
but most surveyors can't help "fawning" over the "fabulous"
"world-class" "creations" from a "menu that changes frequently";
chef/co-owner Billy Grant has won fans galore amid the "social
climbers in attendance" at this "loud, hectic" "yuppie nirvana."

Restaurant du Village S   27 | 24 | 26 | $49
59 Main St. (Maple St.), Chester, 860-526-5301

■ It may be "the poor man's substitute for a trip to France", but
boosters of this "cozy, quaint" Country French in the "cute village"
of Chester are far from *les misérables*; "extraordinary" Alsatian
and Provençal provender accompanied by "fabulous bread" "will
knock your socks off", albeit in a "quiet and *tranquille*" way, at
this "small, calm" "special-occasion" "oasis" with "music and
candlelight" that's "true to its" Gallic "origins."

Roger Sherman Inn S   25 | 26 | 24 | $50
195 Oenoke Ridge/Rte. 124 (Holmewood Ln.), New Canaan, 203-966-4541

■ "Visiting is like being a guest in a private home" with a colonial
pedigree at this seventysomething New Canaan Continental in a
"clubby country inn"; it's an "elegant" "gem" with a patio and
"smoker's-heaven piano bar" that's "perfect", particularly at
"scrumptious" Sunday brunch or the "great-value prix fixe dinner",
though hipsters heckle it as "fuddy-duddy" and warn "wear your
plaid pants to fit in with" the "mainly blue-rinse crowd."

Roomba S   25 | 25 | 23 | $38
1044 Chapel St. (bet. College & High Sts.), New Haven, 203-562-7666

■ "The beat goes on" at this "hip and hot" New Haven Nuevo
Latino where a "waterfall" "cools" the "fun Cubano" decor; in
the "classy outdoor seating area" and "at the counter watching
the chefs", the "noisy, lively" "killer-drink" crowd cries "*me gusta
mucho*" about "quirky combinations of tastes" in a riot of "tutti-
frutti" colors that makes "plates look like a party."

Ruth's Chris Steakhouse 🅂   25 | 20 | 22 | $46
2513 Berlin Tpke./Rte. 515 (Kitts Ln.), Newington, 860-666-2202
■ "For 'meatatarians', a real feast" can be found at what the
Newington crew of carnivores calls the "best of the chain steak
places"; if flesh is your fancy, you "can't miss" the "tender" beef
"cooked in butter" accompanied by "side dishes big enough for
two"; however, the fact that there's "no atmosphere" could account
for wallet-conscious cries of "too expensive."

Sally's Apizza 🅂⊘   26 | 11 | 15 | $17
237 Wooster St. (Olive St.), New Haven, 203-624-5271
■ "A testament to New Haven pizza", the "delicious" brick-oven
offerings at this Wooster Street 64-year-old are "good enough to
make Hillary want to run for Senator from Connecticut" claim
"best-clam-pie"-shop partisans; if she did campaign, she could
pump hands in the "two- to three-hour" lines "where waiting is
part of the mystique."

Steve's Centerbrook Cafe 🅂   25 | 24 | 24 | $43
78 Main St./Rte. 154 (Rte. 80), Centerbrook, 860-767-1277
■ A "wonderful menu and wine list" enhanced by the "lovely,
intimate ambiance" of a "cozy old house" earn high marks for chef-
owner Steve Wilkinson's "elegant" New American in Centerbrook;
with its "attentive service", "fantastic food" and "reasonable
prices", it's become a "favorite" for many – "we bring friends."

Stonehenge 🅂   26 | 26 | 25 | $54
Stonehenge Inn, 35 Stonehenge Rd. (Rte. 7), Ridgefield, 203-438-6511
■ "Civilized" "classic that's still at the top" and a "real treat for
your entire being" is just a sampling of the superlatives surveyors
lavish on this "great old dame" graced with a "wonderful setting"
in Ridgefield and pretty "lake views" that enhance its "luxurious"
Continental menu and "lovely service"; a "special-occasion"
destination for "a romantic evening", it's even better if you "stay
over" at the inn and enjoy the "perfect brunch."

Terra Mar Grille 🅂   25 | 26 | 24 | $45
Saybrook Point Inn & Spa, 2 Bridge St. (Rte. 154), Old Saybrook, 860-388-1111
■ Admirers "sail up and enjoy welcoming service" at this "classy",
"romantic" waterside New American in the Saybrook Point Inn
with "fantastic views" of Long Island Sound and "high-quality,
well-executed" "gourmet" fare; with "great cocktails" at the bar
and a "very good" Sunday brunch, what's not to like?; "wonderful
everything" sums it up.

Thomas Henkelmann 🅂   28 | 28 | 27 | $64
*Homestead Inn, 420 Field Point Rd. (bet. Bush Ave. & Horseneck Ln.),
Greenwich, 203-869-7500*
■ This "truly elegant" French in Greenwich's Homestead Inn is
"*the* place for that special occasion"; a "temple of tradition" where
"the elite meet to eat", it garners "bravos!" for its "beautiful
surroundings", "gentlemanly waiters" and "unparalleled" food,
including "the best roast duck of all time"; so "hold on to your
hats and your wallets too – it's flawless, but perfection comes at
a high price."

Union League Cafe 25 | 25 | 24 | $41

1032 Chapel St. (bet. College & High Sts.), New Haven, 203-562-4299

■ Take "a step back in time to when food tasted as good as it looked" at this "oasis of elegance" and "consistently excellent", "authentic French bistro" that many call "the best New Haven has to offer"; both the "classy", "top-notch" service and the "beautiful" "surroundings make you feel like someone special", so even if it's "a little pricey", it's "absolutely worth it."

Valbella 26 | 23 | 25 | $53

1309 E. Putnam Ave./Rte. 1 (Sound Beach Ave.), Riverside, 203-637-1155

■ Fans find more than a "bit of Tuscany" in the "superb" cuisine at this "upscale" Riverside favorite; the "specials are so good" some "never use" the "excellent menu", but those who do find an "incredible breadth" of Northern Italian dishes complemented by an "awesome wine list" and "seamless service"; savvy surveyors suggest you savor your "memorable dinner" "downstairs" in the "intimate setting" of the "must-see wine cellar."

West Street Grill [S] 25 | 20 | 21 | $44

43 West St. (bet. Rtes. 118 & 202), Litchfield, 860-567-3885

■ "Spot movie stars, authors or just your friends" experiencing "first-class" "fine dining" at this "culinary mecca" on the green in the "Hallmark-card town" of Litchfield; loyalists "love the variety" of "delicious", "deftly prepared" dishes delivering "creative twists on" New American "standards", though many find the prices "a bit over the top" and suggest the sometimes "charming service" can suffer "if you're not part of the 'in' crowd."

Dallas

TOP 20 FOOD RANKING

Restaurant	Cuisine Type
28 French Room	New French/American
Riviera	Classic French/Med.
27 Mansion on Turtle Creek	Southwestern
Cafe Pacific	Seafood
Bob's Steak & Chop	Steakhouse
26 Hôtel St. Germain	New French/Continental
Pyramid Grill	New American
Nana Grill	New American
Green Room	New American
Pappas Bros.	Steakhouse
Del Frisco's	Steakhouse
Old Warsaw	Classic French/Continental
Star Canyon	Southwestern
Mi Piaci	Northern Italian
Abacus	New American
25 Modo Mio	Northern Italian
Tei Tei Robata Bar	Japanese
City Cafe	New American
Chamberlain's	Steakhouse
Capital Grille	Steakhouse

ADDITIONAL NOTEWORTHY PLACES

Al's Prime Steaks & Seafood	Steakhouse/Seafood
Arcodoro/Pomodoro	N&S Italian
Citizen	Pan-Asian
Ciudad	Mexican
Fogo de Chão	Brazilian
Grape	New American/Eclectic
Il Sole	Mediterranean
Jeroboam	French Bistro
Lawry's	Steakhouse
Lola	New American
Mercury	New American
Nick & Sam's	Steakhouse
Salve!	Northern Italian
Sea Grill	Seafood
Sevy's Grill	New American
Sonny Bryan's	Barbecue
Steel	Pan-Asian
Tramontana	New American
Voltaire	New French/New American
York St.	New American

Abacus 26 | 27 | 23 | $58

4511 McKinney Ave. (Knox St.), 214-559-3111

■ "If I could afford it, I'd eat here every night" gush acolytes of chef-owner Kent Rathbun's Uptown New American where "novel appetizers" like "delicious lobster shooters", dazzling tasting menus and an "interesting wine list" are complemented by a "visually stunning", geometrically themed interior with "lovely orchids" on every table; in short: a smart choice for a "special occasion."

Al's Prime Steaks & Seafood [S] 23 | 23 | 23 | $49

4217 Oak Lawn Ave. (Herschel Ave.), 214-219-2201

◪ "Personal attention" from "consummate host-owner" Al Biernat wins over many at this Oak Lawn surf 'n' turf house where patrons dress up and "ask for a booth" to best take in the boisterous, "see-and-be-seen" scene; "delicious salads" and "huge portions" of great beef go a long way as well, though a few tough-to-please types note that the service is "better when they know you."

Arcodoro/Pomodoro ◐ [S] 22 | – | 19 | $30

2708 Routh St. (McKinney Ave.), 214-871-1924

■ These two longtime Uptown Italian favorites have joined forces and moved a few blocks east to a new space that's been renovated to resemble an Italian villa; they now share a kitchen and the same Sardinian menu, with the exception of the popular wood-oven pizzas, which are served only in Arcodoro, the more casual bar-and-cafe area.

Bob's Steak & Chop House 27 | 22 | 25 | $47

4300 Lemmon Ave. (Wycliff Ave.), 214-528-9446

■ "As close as you can get to a private club without paying dues" is how close-knit regulars describe this "dark" Lemmon Avenue steakhouse, which serves "the best prime beef in Dallas", as well as critically acclaimed lamb chops and enormous glazed carrots that are "out of this world"; N.B. while sensitive types may object to walking through the cigar smoke–filled bar, the dining rooms are well-ventilated.

Cafe Pacific 27 | 25 | 26 | $42

Highland Park Village, 24 Highland Park Village (Mockingbird Ln. & Preston Rd.), 214-526-1170

■ "Blue bloods and high-maintenance women" agree that this Highland Park seafood "institution" is "always at the top of its game" thanks to marvelous "maitre d' and local legend" Jean-Pierre Albertinetti, a "professional staff with personality and polish", an old-world setting that feels "like a private club", an "impressive wine list" and "the freshest fish in landlocked Dallas" (don't miss the "heavenly sole").

Capital Grille [S] 25 | 26 | 25 | $46

Crescent Shops & Galleries, 500 Crescent Ct. (bet. Cedar Springs Rd. & McKinney Ave.), 214-303-0500

■ "You know the drill" at this "quiet" Uptown outpost of a steakhouse chain: expect the "best liver and onions" (just ask Neiman's Stanley Marcus), "great" cuts of beef like aged prime sirloin, a comprehensive wine list, an unobtrusive and "well-taught" staff and "classy", "clubby" quarters appointed with animal heads, comfortable booths and a piano lounge; in sum, it's a true masculine "power trip" and a slice of "high-roller heaven."

Chamberlain's S
25 | 22 | 23 | $46

5330 Belt Line Rd. (east of N. Dallas Tollway), Addison, 972-934-2467

■ "Always a class act", "charming" chef-owner Richard Chamberlain's smartly located Addison steakhouse wins over patrons with a "killer corn side dish", some of the "best crab cakes" around and superior cuts of beef; a "warm", "professional" staff, mahogany paneling and original lithographs from the '20s further explain why this is "where all the big-name people eat" (including Chuck Norris and Hulk Hogan), as well as tourists.

Citizen S
24 | 25 | 21 | $39

Two Turtle Creek, 3858 Oak Lawn Ave. (bet. Blackburn & Irving Sts.), 214-522-7253

■ "Chic and delicious" declare denizens of this "loud" Oak Lawn Pan-Asian that's a darling of the "go-to-be-seen" crowd thanks to a "dramatic", "contemporary" interior that gives off an "LA look and feel"; every bit as stylish as the decor is the "inventive" cooking influenced by every corner of Asia and "presented with flair."

City Cafe S
25 | 20 | 23 | $33

5757 W. Lovers Ln. (N. Dallas Tollway), 214-351-2233

■ "Consistently one of the finest in the city", this Lovers Lane New American offers the "comfortable" "feel of a neighborhood" eatery but with "first-class food and service"; its menu of "uniquely prepared" and "creatively presented" dishes "changes often enough to pique your curiosity", while the crowning touch is an "exquisite" wine list that oenophiles rank among "the best" in town.

Ciudad S
21 | 22 | 21 | $30

1 Turtle Creek, 3888 Oak Lawn Ave. (bet. Blackburn & Irving Sts.), 214-219-3141

■ "Wow" – it's "almost ahead of its time" marvel admirers of the both "creative and authentic" Mexican dishes at this "upscale", "trendy" Oak Lawn addition, which features flavors from the Yucatán and Mexico City (try the red mole–braised veal short ribs); it also cultivates friends with "warm" service and a "fun" atmosphere, though it's often "very loud" "unless you sit outside" on the "great patio."

Del Frisco's Double Eagle Steak House
26 | 24 | 24 | $53

5251 Spring Valley Rd. (N. Dallas Pkwy.), 972-490-9000

▣ Some of "the best steaks in the West" come off the grill at this "prime" North Dallas chophouse that's simply "tops", from its "perfectly cooked" beef and 850-bottle wine list to its clubby, high-"energy" environs and "superior" service; there's a price for being this "near to heaven", however: hefty tabs make it "strictly for the expense-account crowd", and its popularity means there's often a "long wait for a table", even "with a reservation."

Fogo de Chão S
25 | 21 | 24 | $41

4300 Belt Line Rd. (Midway Rd.), Addison, 972-503-7300

■ "Nirvana for carnivores", this Addison Brazilian churrascaria presents "food with a show", as "fantastic" gaucho-clad waiters serve unlimited quantities of "excellent" skewered meats and poultry until you flip your coaster from green to red and beg them to stop; an "outstanding" salad bar only adds to the "gluttony", so "skip breakfast and lunch" before Chao-ing down here.

French Room   28 | 29 | 28 | $69

Hotel Adolphus, 1321 Commerce St. (Akard St.), 214-742-8200

■ Elected No. 1 for Food in Dallas, this Downtown New French–American "throwback to more elegant times" is "magnificently" appointed with a cherub-painted ceiling, soft candlelight and beautiful flowers; factor in "impeccable" service from a staff that makes you "feel like a king or queen" and "fabulous", exquisitely plated dishes and you have the city's "perfect" spot for "special-occasion dining"; N.B. gourmet diners on a budget should consider the prix fixe menus.

Grape S   25 | 20 | 22 | $30

2808 Greenville Ave. (Vickery Blvd.), 214-828-1981

■ Going on 30 years old, this "romantic" New American–Eclectic bistro on Greenville has been "a perennial winner" from day one thanks to a renowned mushroom soup (the "best I ever ate"), an award-winning wine list and "attentive" service; close tables, however, mean "unavoidable eavesdropping", which is just fine if you have a dull "first-date dinner" companion.

Green Room S   26 | 19 | 23 | $40

2715 Elm St. (Crowdus St.), 214-748-7666

■ Put away those jackets and ties because this "noisy" Deep Ellum New American is a "brash", "refreshingly casual" spot where twentysomethings lap up chef Marc Cassel's "magnificent", "innovative" dishes, revel in a "delightfully funky" atmosphere and bond with the appropriately "trendy" staff; P.S. to best take advantage of this "bohemian" experience, consider the "superb" 'Feed Me, Wine Me' menu offered at "cherry-picking prices."

Hôtel St. Germain   26 | 28 | 26 | VE

2516 Maple Ave. (bet. Cedar Springs Rd. & McKinney Ave.), 214-871-2516

■ "Escape from reality" to this "quaintly European" Uptown New French–Continental whose mutely lit, widely spaced tables are staffed by attentive white-gloved waiters; "the ultimate place for an intimate celebration", it exclusively offers a multicourse tasting menu ("a bargain at $85"), so à la carte cats should consider rendezvousing at the Champagne Bar, which serves an array of appetizers and desserts.

Il Sole S   23 | 23 | 21 | $38

Travis Walk, 4514 Travis St. (Armstrong Ave.), 214-559-3888

■ This "romantic" Mediterranean in Knox/Henderson features a second-story patio perfect for people-watching and a subdued, soothing atmosphere; it draws a "classy, not flashy" group of regulars who love the award-winning wine list (especially the smart offerings "by the glass or even half-glass") and the menu filled with "delicious" options like "to-die-for" calamari and a perfect maple crème brûlée.

Jeroboam S   – | – | – | E

Kirby Bldg., 1501 Main St. (Akard St.), 214-748-7226

Already hailed as a Downtown destination, this sleek brasserie (the sibling of the Green Room) uncorks casual French fare, including such favorites as pâté, cassoulet and selections from the cheese cart; regulars also know that the curried cauliflower soup is the way to start a meal.

Lawry's the Prime Rib Ⓢ ___25_ _23_ _24_ _$38_
14655 Dallas Pkwy. (bet. Belt Line & Spring Valley Rds.),
972-503-6688
■ "The definitive prime rib" carved tableside, "great creamed spinach" and a famous 'spinning bowl salad' are the highlights of this upscale North Dallas chain link; granted, trendy types might think the decor "could use updating" and find the staff uniforms "hokey", but it's still an enduring "favorite for celebrations" and an "excellent lunch value."

Lola ___–_ _–_ _–_ _E_
2917 Fairmont St. (Cedar Springs Rd.), 214-855-0700
This Uptown New American serves innovative prix fixe meals in two, three or four courses by a suave staff in a house-turned-restaurant setting with a romantic atmosphere; N.B. owner Van Roberts has assembled an award-winning collection of wines, which he's eager to discuss with oenophiles and novices alike.

Mansion on Turtle Creek Ⓢ ___27_ _28_ _27_ _$64_
2821 Turtle Creek Blvd. (Gillespie Ave.), 214-559-2100
■ Once again voted the Most Popular restaurant in Dallas and the "gold standard" in its category, this Downtown Southwestern features acclaimed chef Dean Fearing's "consistently innovative" combinations, which may leave you "speechless"; moreover, the "outstanding" staff provides a "never-ending flow of attention" and the "beautiful rooms" convey an "exclusive feel" that's "like dining in someone's house"; in sum, a "first-class night out", even if the "amazing wine list" is "overpriced."

Mercury Ⓢ ___25_ _22_ _22_ _$42_
11909 Preston Rd. (Forest Ln.), 972-960-7774
6121 W. Park Blvd. (Dallas Pkwy.), Plano, 469-366-0107
■ For "fine food in an improbable strip-mall location", head to this North Dallas New American where "innovative" dishes "dazzle the senses" and a "trendy" clientele looks glamorous in the understated, modern setting; the only quibble: it's "one of the loudest restaurants" around; N.B. an offshoot just opened in Plano.

Mi Piaci Ristorante Ⓢ ___26_ _24_ _23_ _$38_
14854 Montfort Rd. (Belt Line Rd.), Addison, 972-934-8424
■ "Luscious ingredients, creative combinations and lovely presentations" add up to "absolutely spectacular" dining at this "upscale" Addison Northern Italian known for its "marvelous risotto" and osso buco; its "sophisticated", "sleek" and "open" room "overlooking the water" (a man-made duck pond) and "exemplary" service also win kudos; P.S. a small dining room in the wine cellar can be rented out for private parties.

Modo Mio Cucina Rustica Italiana ___25_ _21_ _22_ _$35_
Frankford Crossing, 18352 Dallas Pkwy. (Frankford Rd.), 972-671-6636
■ Rino Brigliadori (chef-owner) and his son, Rino Jr. (manager), "make a welcoming team" at this "great neighborhood" Northern Italian trattoria in North Dallas, where the "fantastic", "authentic" dishes (including sea bass that's the "best ever") are always served "with a smile"; given this "warm an atmosphere", no one minds much if it can get a bit "crowded" and "noisy."

Nana Grill S   26 27 25 $54
Wyndham Anatole Hotel, 2201 N. Stemmons Frwy. (Market Center Blvd.), 214-761-7470

■ "What a view" exclaim enthusiasts admiring the vista from this Downtown New American favorite; its "luxurious room" is "where you go to impress someone", and the "excellent food and service" complement the "wonderful atmosphere" (enhanced by live jazz Wednesday–Saturday); fans also recommend it for the "best brunch in Texas", a buffet replete with "buckets of champagne"; N.B. it's undergoing renovations but plans to reopen shortly after we go to press.

Nick & Sam's S   24 24 23 $50
3008 Maple Ave. (Oak Lawn Ave.), 214-871-7444

☑ This "see-and-be-seen" Uptown steakhouse attracts followers with amenities such as a rolling caviar cart, a grand piano in the open kitchen and "smart, sophisticated decor"; beef takes center stage, of course, but the lamb and fish dishes are also "excellent"; detractors, however, caution that it's "incredibly loud" and "priced for a roaring economy."

Old Warsaw S   26 24 23 $56
2610 Maple Ave. (McKinney Ave.), 214-528-0032

☑ An "elegant and romantic hideaway", this Uptown French-Continental has been exuding "old-world charm" for more than 50 years and not long ago received a much-needed remodeling (don't miss the shark tank); the "superb" food (including "the best chocolate soufflé ever made") is formally served, but wallet-watchers warn "take your heaviest credit card."

Pappas Bros. Steakhouse   26 25 24 $47
10477 Lombardy Ln. (I-35 & Northwest Hwy.), 214-366-2000

■ "Outstanding every time" declare devotees of this Northwest Dallas jewel in the crown of the Pappas family restaurant empire, which is "Texas to the core" and features "Lone Star State–size drinks, big steaks and great Southwestern decor"; a "huge wine selection" ("from $25 to $70,000") and practically "flawless service" add to its reputation – just get "someone else to pay."

Pyramid Grill S   26 26 24 $54
(fka Pyramid Room)
Fairmont Hotel, 1717 N. Akard St. (Ross Ave.), 214-720-5249

■ Formerly called the Pyramid Room, this elegant Uptown New American is still "one of our favorite" places "to celebrate an anniversary or promotion" thanks to well-spaced tables, "terrific" courtly service, "excellent" grilled fare and many swell touches from its previous incarnation, such as sorbets presented in lighted ice sculptures.

Riviera   28 25 26 $60
7709 Inwood Rd. (Lovers Ln.), 214-351-0094

■ Chef Michael Marshall (ex Hôtel St. Germain) is now behind the stove at this "cosmopolitan" North Dallas French-Mediterranean stalwart, which is where celebration-minded diners go "when they want to be pampered" by a "graceful, welcoming" European-style staff serving "superb" fare (notably "to-die-for Dover sole" and rack of lamb); decor that's "like walking into a room in Provence" merely adds to its "fancy-shmancy" allure.

Salve! S   24 | 24 | 22 | $48
2120 McKinney Ave. (Pearl St.), 214-220-0070
■ "Dallas' most sophisticated restaurant", this "exceptional" Uptown Italian from Mi Piaci duo Phil and Janet Cobb features a "sleek", angular setting, a truly "outstanding", "diverse menu of upscale" Tuscan food and an impressive all-Italian wine list.

Sea Grill S   – | – | – | M
17617 Dallas Pkwy. (Trinity Mills Rd.), 972-733-4904
Fully settled into its North Dallas digs, this casual seafood house relocated from Plano now offers a broader range in triple the space; chef Andy Tun continues to perform his piscine magic with a Pan-Asian flair, executing a variety of simple fish dishes that can be ordered grilled, blackened, broiled, sautéed or steamed, all priced moderately; the only major complaint: it's very loud.

Sevy's Grill S   23 | 22 | 22 | $33
8201 Preston Rd. (Sherry Ln.), 214-265-7389
■ "All the essential elements" of a successful restaurant can be found at this Park Cities New American "favorite", which features a mission-style interior, a martini bar that's "quite the gathering place", two hands-on, entertaining owners and "impressive" food (especially "if you like roasted or wood-fired anything").

Sonny Bryan's Smokehouse   21 | 12 | 15 | $13
2202 Inwood Rd. (Harry Hines Blvd.), 214-357-7120 S
Macy's at Galleria Mall, 13375 Noel Rd. (bet. LBJ Frwy. & N. Dallas Tollway), 972-851-5131 S
Frankford Crossing, 4701 Frankford Rd. (bet. Dallas Pkwy. & Pear Ridge Rd.), 972-447-0102 S
302 N. Market St. (Pacific Ave.), 214-744-1610 S
Republic Towers, 325 N. St. Paul St. (bet. Bryan St. & Pacific Ave.), 214-979-0102
5519 W. Lovers Ln. (Inwood Rd.), 214-351-2024 S
■ The "funky, original" Inwood locale "will always be the best" branch of this famous BBQ chain, which has long been revered for its "enormous onion rings" and "tender", hickory-smoked brisket, pulled pork and ribs.

Star Canyon S   26 | 26 | 24 | $48
Centrum Bldg., 3102 Oak Lawn Ave. (Cedar Springs Rd.), 214-520-7827
■ Superstar kitchen wizard Stephan Pyles has moved on, but "executive chef Matthew Dunn [keeps things] humming" at this Oak Lawn destination that "sets an example for great Southwestern food", ranging from "innovative" dishes like "fantastic *cuitlacoche* enchiladas" to classics like the "awesome bone-in rib-eye"; reviewers also rave about the "Texas-perfect decor, right down to the ceiling tiles branded with town names."

Steel   – | – | – | E
Centrum Bldg., 3102 Oak Lawn Ave. (Cedar Springs Rd.), 214-219-9908
Cloaked in metal, stone and cherrywood, this smart Pan-Asian addition to Oak Lawn presents an ambitious and interesting menu inspired by China, Japan, Korea and Southeast Asia and turned out with a bold flair; quickly emerging as a notable gathering place, it's become quite the hot table thanks to its assortment of lacquered bento boxes and steaming clay pots, while its hyperactive sushi and sake bars pull in the urban-chic demographic.

Tei Tei Robata Bar [S] 25 | 23 | 23 | $42

2906 N. Henderson Ave. (Willis Ave.), 214-828-2400

■ "Hip patrons and trendy decor" are just the appetizers at this "pricey" Knox/Henderson Japanese where a "world-class chef" prepares "fresh sushi and sashimi"; a "tremendous array" of *robata* (grilled) dishes also explains why some addicts will "travel 150 miles" to satisfy their yen here.

Tramontana 25 | 18 | 22 | $36

Preston Ctr., 8220B Westchester Dr. (Lemmon Ave.), 214-368-4188

■ "A tiny, romantic hideaway", this North Dallas New American bistro gets tons of accolades for its "superior", "inventive" cooking tweaked with French and Italian accents; surveyors add that "super-nice" chef-owner James Neel is a "treasure" whose skills are "moving this storefront to the forefront."

Voltaire 25 | 27 | 23 | $62

5150 Keller Springs Rd. (N. Dallas Tollway), 972-239-8988

◪ "Wow" swoon aesthetes over this "gorgeous" French–New American in North Dallas, where trendsetters go to ogle "fabulous" Dale Chihuly glass sculptures, as well as the "beautiful" patrons; while some diners delight in the "excellent", "creative" fare and "fantastic", "extensive" wine list, others find it "pretentious" and ask "what's the fuss?"

York St. 25 | 20 | 24 | $47

6047 Lewis St. (Skillman St.), 214-826-0968

■ Admirers say that "every intimate restaurant should aspire" to be this "enchanting" New American "tucked inside an old house" in East Dallas; amid an unhurried pace, a "superb" staff provides angelic attention while delivering a "slice of culinary heaven" from new chef-owner Sharon Hage's "interesting", market-fresh menu.

Denver Area & Mountain Resorts

TOP 20 FOOD RANKING

Restaurant	Cuisine Type
28 Keystone Ranch	Rocky Mountain
Highlands Garden Cafe	New American
Mizuna	New American
Grouse Mountain Grill	Rocky Mountain
Tante Louise	Classic French
27 Del Frisco's	Steakhouse
Micole	New American
Papillon Café	New French
Alpenglow Stube	Rocky Mountain
Charles Court	Continental/New American
Palace Arms	Continental/New American
Cafe Brazil	South American
Piñons	Rocky Mountain
Sweet Basil	New American
Wildflower	New American
Full Moon Grill	Northern Italian
Flagstaff House	Continental
Penrose Room	Continental/New French
Renaissance	Med./New American
Left Bank	Classic French

ADDITIONAL NOTEWORTHY PLACES

Bang!	American
Barolo Grill	Northern Italian
Beano's Cabin	New American
Briarwood Inn	Continental/American
Conundrum	New American
Domo	Japanese
Fourth Story	New American
Hilltop Café	New American
India's	Indian
John's	Eclectic
Kevin Taylor	New American
La Petite Maison	New American
Mel's	Med./New American
Potager	New American
Q's	New American
Splendido	New American
Strings	New American
Sushi Den	Japanese
240 Union	New American/Seafood
Vesta Dipping Grill	New American

Alpenglow Stube [S]
27 | 28 | 26 | $63

Keystone Resort, 154 Soda Ridge Rd. (top of North Peak Mtn.), Keystone, 970-496-4386

■ A blizzard of praise surrounds this high-end Rocky Mountain "fine dining experience", the nation's highest restaurant at 11,444 feet, set on North Peak Mountain in the Keystone Resort; take the "romantic gondola" to the top where you're "greeted with warm, fuzzy slippers" and "the best setting in the state" – it's a "cool adventure" that almost feels "fairy tale-ish"; the "fabulous old-world service" also makes it "an incredible place to break for lunch during your ski day"; N.B. open for dinner only Thursday–Sunday during the summer.

Bang!
26 | 18 | 20 | $19

3472 W. 32nd Ave. (bet. Julian St. & Lowell Blvd.), 303-455-1117

■ "Explosive, down-home" traditional American fare lures locals to this "funky", "laid-back" "gem" in North Denver; surveyors squeeze inside the "crowded" digs for "creative combinations" of "soul-soothing" "comfort" food that "highlights seasonal ingredients" (go ahead, "try the ever-popular meat loaf"), all served in an "upbeat, colorful and kooky" atmosphere; a few are "disappointed that prices have risen" after a recent move to some "little bigger and little nicer quarters" down the street, but you still get lots of "bang for the buck."

Barolo Grill
25 | 25 | 24 | $39

3030 E. Sixth Ave. (bet. Milwaukee & St. Paul Sts.), 303-393-1040

■ This "warm, inviting" East Denver "place to be" dishes out "the most authentic ambiance" and Northern Italian cuisine "in the Rockies"; "it's in a class by itself" thanks to the "fabulous food" and a "wine list that will knock your socks off" with plenty of offerings from the Barolo region; while most applaud the "intelligent", "knowledgeable" and, above all, vintage-"savvy" servers, a few miffed reviewers say they're "heavy-handed" and "snobbish" and should "get over themselves."

Beano's Cabin [S]
24 | 28 | 24 | $62

Beaver Creek Resort, 1 Beaver Creek Pl. (Avon Rd.), Avon, 970-949-9090

■ "The trip up Vail mountain is worth the price of the meal" say fans of this "enchanting" Beaver Creek New American set in an "intimate, woodsy", "gorgeous log cabin"; "the resident porcupine welcomes" trekkers to this "ultimate romantic dinner date" (yes, it's "an adventure"), accessible by a "wonderful sleigh ride" in winter, horse in summer, and anchored by an "elaborate and creative" fixed-price menu and extensive global wine list.

Briarwood Inn [S]
25 | 27 | 26 | $41

1630 Eighth St. (bet. Hwy. 58 & US 6), Golden, 303-279-3121

■ The "food is phenomenal" at this "exquisite", "expensive and worth it" Golden Continental-American, "the classic place to go to celebrate a special occasion" or "save for guests you wish to impress"; the "delicious" fare comes in "huge portions" and is served in "old-fashioned", "homelike surroundings" that make you feel "like you're having dinner with your aged, widowed aunt."

Cafe Brazil ∅
27 18 23 $28

3611 Navajo St. (W. 36th Ave.), 303-480-1877

■ It's "back to Rio" for revelers of this affordable, "hard to find, hard to forget" North Denver South American, an "out-of-the-ordinary" "way funky" locale featuring "fantastic", "flavorful" ethnic fare brimming with a "riot of flavors"; insiders suggest you "reserve two weeks in advance" to sit in what some call a "cute little quaint place" (not unlike "someone's kitchen"), but a few consider it a "spartan", "claustrophobic", "tiny shoebox."

Charles Court S
27 28 28 $51

Broadmoor Hotel, 1 Lake Ave. (Mesa Ave.), Colorado Springs, 719-634-7711

■ Visitors to Springs' venerable Broadmoor resort deem this get-out-the-wallet Continental-New American "a must" for "classic", "exceptional" "fine dining" that includes an "excellent wine selection" plus "professional" but "relaxed" service that offers "all the right pampering"; admirers adore the "small cozy" room but say the "lakeside patio is great" as well, making this "wonderful special occasion" destination "worth the drive from Denver"; N.B. jackets suggested.

Conundrum S
26 25 24 $54

325 E. Main St. (bet. Mill & Monarch Sts.), Aspen, 970-925-9969

■ It's no brain-teaser – followers fawn over this Aspen heavy-hitter because the "excellent" "New American cuisine is prepared by a talented crew" and served in a "chic", "hip", "high-energy" setting that "evokes autumn colors" with some of the "best people-watching around"; "the dessert and coffee are as fantastic as the entrees", plus there's a "great wine list" – all delivered by a "professional, hospitable" staff.

Del Frisco's
Double Eagle Steak House
27 25 26 $50

Denver Tech Ctr., 8100 E. Orchard Rd. (I-25), Greenwood Village, 303-796-0100

☑ "As good as it gets" bellow "beef eaters" over this Greenwood Village franchise where "manly", "football-size steaks" that "melt in your mouth" are carried out by "top-shelf" servers; it's a "local favorite with sports figures" and "expense-account types" who also gather in the "dimly lit cigar bar"; detractors declare it's "for people with more money than sense" – "no one can eat that much" – adding "you're paying to see the glitterati."

Domo
24 27 20 $26

1365 Osage St. (Colfax Ave.), 303-595-3666

■ "You'd have to go" to the Far East "to get more authentic" food claim admirers who head to this almost-"sushi-free zone" near Downtown for "Japanese country cooking" that's "indescribably delicious"; the "homestyle" dishes are a "refreshing change", "different than any other restaurant" and served in a "magical" "place that just oozes atmosphere", with the "most beautiful and unique decor", "peaceful gardens" and "fascinating museum" right on the grounds; a few diners, however, are less than "enchanted" by the "always slow service" and a "no-reservations policy that's a drag."

Flagstaff House [S] 27 | 28 | 27 | $50

1138 Flagstaff Rd. (on Flagstaff Mtn.), Boulder, 303-442-4640

◪ "The ultimate expensive-but-worth-it special occasion place to go" fawn fans of this Continental stalwart, Boulder's mountainside "treat", set in what was once a cabin, offering "breathtaking views" of the city below and surrounding wildlife; surveyors say the "imaginative" "intricately prepared" fare, boasting Asian touches, is "world-class" and suggest you "ask for a tour of the wine cellar", home to 20,000 bottles.

Fourth Story [S] 24 | 25 | 23 | $32

Tattered Cover Bookstore, 2955 E. First Ave. (Milwaukee St.), 303-322-1824

■ "Curl up in a booth" with a "literary classic", dine on New American eats "among the stacks" or "smooch between the books" at this "handsome" "local treasure" "perched atop" – and accessorized by – the famed Tattered Cover Bookstore, a "popular gathering place" in Cherry Creek; the "delicious" weekend brunch, "interesting seasonal menus" and "decadent desserts" are a "joy to the palate" and the "top wine bar" offers "flights of fancy wines", all delivered by a "meticulous" staff; P.S. it's also the spot to tune in to "Denver's best jazz."

Full Moon Grill [S] 27 | 21 | 24 | $33

Village Shopping Ctr., 2525 Arapahoe Ave. (bet. Folsom & 28th Sts.), Boulder, 303-938-8800

■ It's *amore* all around for adoring admirers smitten by this "usually packed" moderately priced Boulder Northern Italian, a "terrific discovery" "tucked in a strip mall"; lovers laud the "interesting variations" of "inventive", "consistently" "delicious" fare", including "great specials", as well as the "friendly, accommodating" servers; while followers find the "pleasant" "unassuming" quarters "intimate", a handful consider it "crowded with too many tables."

Grouse Mountain Grill [S] 28 | 26 | 26 | $54

Beaver Creek Resort, 141 Scott Hill Rd. (Village Rd.), Avon, 970-949-0600

■ There's little to grouse about at this "superior" Beaver Creek Resort spot where "flawless food" from a Rocky Mountain menu, including "excellent meat" entrees and "great side dishes", is served in "hearty", "huge portions", bolstered by a "great wine list"; an "absolutely perfect" staff that's at "the top of its game", as well as "beautiful outdoor dining" and "stunning views" of the Valley, only adds to the luster of this "gem."

Highlands Garden Cafe 28 | 27 | 26 | $37

3927 W. 32nd Ave. (bet. Osceola & Perry Sts.), 303-458-5920

■ Gastronomes go gaga for this "garden of eating", a North Denver New American "beauty" where the "amazing" flowers are matched by the "inventive cuisine" and "impeccable service"; it's "stellar in all respects" and the two "quaint", "cute as a button" "old houses" provide a "lovely refuge" any season, while patio dining by the greenery is a definite "summer must"; in a word, "perfect"; N.B. as we go to press, the restaurant is scheduled to become mostly a special-event venue, though it will be open to the public on a limited basis; call for details.

Hilltop Café   26 ┃ 22 ┃ 24 ┃ $30 ┃
1518 Washington Ave. (16th St.), Golden, 303-279-8151
■ It's a "great addition to the suburbs" say locals who head west to this "quaint", "attractive" "Golden nugget" for "expertly crafted New American" fare with "innovative" Asian touches served in a "charming" "Victorian-era residence"; it's a "delicious fine dining" experience "with no pretensions" say admirers who adore the "artistic" and "fabulous presentations" of "exciting new combos", all brought to the table by "impeccable" servers who provide "incredible customer attention."

India's 🄂   26 ┃ 20 ┃ 19 ┃ $25 ┃
Tamarac Sq., 3333 S. Tamarac Dr. (Hampden Ave.), 303-755-4284
■ "Still the standard for Indian food in Denver" chant devotees of this Southeast Denver mecca who pay homage to the "consistently delicious" and "most authentic" fare that's "worlds above and beyond" the competition; while most say the service is "very friendly" and appreciate the "warm decor", a few sniff that the staff is "apathetic" and the setting is no Taj Mahal – "the look is tired" and the "strip-mall location is a turnoff."

John's   26 ┃ 23 ┃ 25 ┃ $39 ┃
2328 Pearl St. (bet. 23rd & 24th Sts.), Boulder, 303-444-5232
■ "Intimate dining at its finest" say surveyors who offer universal praise for this "unrivaled" Eclectic Boulder "treasure" where "personal care is taken with each" and every "creative" dish; the adventure unfolds in a "cozy", "cute" and "romantic" "lovely old house" that makes you feel like you're "dining at a friend's" place, with "great service" to boot; for some, though, "it's a little too homey" – "good, but not truly exceptional", plus "the portions are small for a lot of moola."

Kevin Taylor   26 ┃ 26 ┃ 24 ┃ $53 ┃
Hotel Teatro, 1106 14th St. (Arapahoe St.), 303-820-2600
■ "Paris, New York, San Francisco and London dining come to Denver" rave fans of this "*très* $$$" Downtown New American, a "grown-up's restaurant" set in the "gorgeous" art deco Hotel Teatro; chef-owner Kevin Taylor's "sublime" fare is a "superb" counterpoint to the "awesome wine list", so "go for an expense-account dinner" and "impress" clients and friends with this "over-the-top" experience, though some caution about "uptight", "snobby" waiters.

Keystone Ranch 🄂   28 ┃ 28 ┃ 28 ┃ $61 ┃
Keystone Resort, 154 Soda Ridge Rd. (top of North Peak Mtn.), Keystone, 970-496-4386
■ "The elk melts" in your mouth "like butter" say worshipers who make the pilgrimage for seasonal Rocky Mountain fare to this "grand" 1930s Keystone ranch homestead, rated No. 1 for Food in this state's *Survey*; the "extraordinary" "exotic dishes", wild game and "delectable desserts" are served in a "quiet and relaxed atmosphere", complemented by a "superb" "rustic mountain setting"; it's an "expensive treat", however, so "take a big sack of money."

La Petite Maison — 26 | 23 | 25 | $37

1015 W. Colorado Ave. (bet. 10th & 11th Sts.), Colorado Springs, 719-632-4887

■ "Keep on keeping on" cheer fans who deem this "consistently wonderful" Colorado Springs New American veteran with a "Classic French influence" their "all-time favorite"; "it's outstanding in every respect", with "excellent", "innovative" fare served by a staff that's "never stuffy" in a "quiet and relaxed" Victorian cottage (circa 1894), appointed with two "small dining rooms that make it very intimate."

Left Bank [S]⊭ — 27 | 24 | 24 | $49

Sitzmark Lodge, 183 Gore Creek Dr. (Bridge St.), Vail, 970-476-3696

■ Vail's "top authentic" and "very traditional", "quiet and elegant French" standby "has become the standard by which to evaluate" all others gush Gallic-philes who consider it a "great" respite from the area's "nouveau places"; the "classic" expensive fare, such as rack of lamb and soufflés, is "delicious", and "beautiful" to look at too; while some say "it's truly the best in service", a few snipers say it's "snooty", like "Paris with an attitude"; "bring cash" because "they still don't take credit cards – maybe next century."

Mel's Bar & Grill [S] — 25 | 22 | 23 | $34

235 Fillmore St. (bet. 2nd & 3rd Aves.), 303-333-3979

◪ An "easygoing" but "upscale" atmosphere marks this "steady" Med–New American "standby" in Cherry Creek, where "creative dishes" (including "mussels to die for"), served by a "very friendly staff" that "has excellent knowledge" of "the great wine list", may be eclipsed by "better-than-Broadway" people-watching at the bar (though a few whine that "over-the-hill" "regulars seem to get all the attention"); it's a "winner" weigh in worshipers, who concur "live jazz makes the experience."

Micole — 27 | 24 | 25 | $48

1469 Pearl St. (W. Colfax Ave.), 303-744-1940

■ It's "heaven for the hedonist" trumpet fans who deem this "sophisticated prix fixe" Washington Park New American the "best new restaurant in Denver"; the chef's "risks pay off", with the "most inventive", "deliriously wonderful" "terrific gourmet choices" and "plate presentations like miniature Renoirs" toted to the tables by an "attentive", "knowledgeable staff"; the "magnetic ambiance" and "comfy chairs" help make this "one of the most appealing dining rooms in town."

Mizuna — 28 | 23 | 27 | $41

225 E. Seventh Ave. (bet. Grant & Sherman Sts.), 303-832-4778

■ Chef Frank Bonnano has a "ton of talent" declare devotees dazzled by this moderately expensive Capitol Hill New American, a "gustatory bonanza" considered one of the "finest new restaurants in town"; "mom didn't make macaroni and cheese (with lobster) like this" crow connoisseurs who concur that the "menu is clever" and the "beautiful" "food is fabulous" – a study in "culinary artistry", with "elegant service" to boot; a handful gripe that "cozy" quarters make for "cramped dining."

Palace Arms S
27 | 28 | 27 | $50

Brown Palace Hotel, 321 17th St. (bet. Broadway & Tremont Pl.), 303-297-3111

■ If you want "hoity-toity", this "regal" Continental–New American, a Downtown "Denver landmark" set in the 109-year-old Brown Palace Hotel (frequented by President and Mrs. Eisenhower) delivers with "classic cuisine" ("like you died and went to heaven") and "exquisite" service; "it's the epitome of old-world dining elegance, complemented by daring nouveau regional fare", a selection of 1,500 wines and "oh, those macaroons!"; while most adore the "one-of-a-kind French Empire decor" (some antiques date back to Napoleon's era), some sniff that it's "stuffy."

Papillon Café S
27 | 24 | 24 | $41

250 Josephine St. (bet. 2nd & 3rd Aves.), 303-333-7166

■ "Great French fare with an Asian twist" served in a "chic setting" draws an "upscale crowd" with "varied palates" to this Cherry Creek "dining adventure", the Most Popular restaurant in the Colorado *Survey*; the "impressive presentation of well-designed food", including "unbelievable lobster ravioli", "creative fish dishes" and "great desserts", is enhanced by the "incredibly deep and broad wine list at fair prices"; while most rave about the "attentive but not interruptive" service and "stimulating" atmosphere, naysayers find the staff "arrogant" and advise "get earplugs" because the room becomes "rather noisy."

Penrose Room S
27 | 28 | 28 | $50

Broadmoor Hotel, 1 Lake Ave. (Lake Circle), Colorado Springs, 719-634-7711

■ "Elegance, ambiance and excess" characterize this Continental–New French "resort tradition", a "romantic", "perfect for special occasions" spot with "breathtaking views" of Colorado Springs and Cheyenne Mountain; the "spectacular", "imaginative cuisine", "featuring some dishes prepared tableside", rises to the "high Broadmoor Hotel standards", and so does the "outstanding service"; there's also live dinner music, including a pianist and "great jazz for dancing", every night except Sunday.

Piñons S
27 | 25 | 26 | $56

105 S. Mill St. (Main St.), Aspen, 970-920-2021

■ Perhaps "Aspen's best" encore enthusiasts who adore the "great" Rocky Mountain cuisine at this "always reliable" spot that's "dressed up" to the nines in "cowboy chic" style ("the most elegant of Western settings"); the "food is terrific", with simply "marvelous" elk and "incredibly delicious lobster strudel" set off by an "excellent wine list" and "service with a smile"; "go there for special nights."

Potager
24 | 21 | 22 | $33

1109 Ogden St. (bet. 11th & 12th Aves.), 303-832-5788

■ "Pound for pound" it's one of "the best restaurants in Denver" state loyalists about this Capitol Hill New American "neighborhood hangout" and its "monthly menu based on the availability of seasonal ingredients"; it's "simple, yet stellar" with "healthy preparations" of "fresh, adventurous" fare and an "excellent wine list", plus the "patrons are as attractive as the food"; it's a "cool scene", augmented by "beautiful garden seating", but grumblers grouse about the "no-reservations policy" and "tightly crammed tables": "you come and leave with two, but you eat with six."

Q's S
26   24   24 $38

Boulderado Hotel, 2115 13th St. (Spruce St.), Boulder,
303-442-4880

■ Reviewers recommend this "way good" Boulder New American for its "sublime" selection of "dynamic, modern" food served by a "very well-trained staff" in an "elegant dining room"; epicureans enthuse the "emu is incredible" and the tasting menu is an "indulgent splurge", while grazers find "an appetizer or two, a dessert, plus wine equals heaven!"; a recent move makes for "a true class act in an even classier location" – the antique-filled "historic Boulderado Hotel."

Renaissance S
27   25   26 $63

304 E. Hopkins Ave. (bet. Mill & Monarch Sts.), Aspen,
970-925-2402

■ Instead of making it a "once-in-a-lifetime dinner" patrons of this "pricey" Med–New American in Aspen say go often to sample the "daring" seasonal dishes that are "always pushing the envelope"; it's "outstanding on all fronts", including a "tasting menu that's A-plus" and a wine list that features 450 selections; the "sumptuous, romantic decor" in the main dining room is offset by the newly remodeled private dining room upstairs.

Splendido S
26   26   25 $59

The Chateau at Beaver Creek Resort, 17 Chateau Ln. (Scott Hill Rd.), Avon,
970-845-8808

■ Raves abound for this "stunningly superlative" New American at the Chateau in Beaver Creek and its "warmly romantic" setting and "impeccably professional", "intelligent and informed staff"; it's among the "best dining and wining experiences in Colorado" – there's "such attention to detail" that it's "even better than its glowing reviews"; yes, it's "very expensive", in fact, "the locals call it Spendido – and spend you will."

Strings S
26   24   24 $36

1700 Humboldt St. (17th Ave.), 303-831-7310

■ "It's impossible to have a less than perfect meal" at this "groovy" Uptown destination, rave reviewers who rally for the combination of New American with Mediterranean and Californian influences served in "chic surroundings"; the "modern, fresh" and "fabulous food presentations" are "hard to beat", and it's an especially "premium experience" if "you want to see the beautiful people"; while it's "dependable when entertaining or doing business", a few squawk it's "too yuppie."

Sushi Den S
27   23   20 $33

1487 S. Pearl St. (Florida Ave.), 303-777-0827

■ If you're lucky enough to snag "a table as a walk-in, buy a lottery ticket later" advise fans of this "jam-packed", "always noisy", "no reservations" Japanese near Washington Park, where the "ecstasy" of the "awesome sushi and sashimi" more than makes up for the "frustration of waiting"; the combo of "see and be seen" "crowds of people with cell phones", "remarkably fresh fish" and "scrumptious" "dishes for all palates" means "you'll enter with a frown but leave with a smile."

Sweet Basil S
27 | 24 | 24 | $43

193 E. Gore Creek Dr. (Bridge St.), Vail, 970-476-0125

■ "No wonder reservations are hard to come by" say regulars who cherish this New American Vail Village "mountain favorite" "supernova" for its "brilliant food", "kick-ass wine list", "relaxed atmosphere" and "wonderful" "view of Gore Creek"; "it's the quintessence of interesting, fabulous dining" thanks to "unique, creative dishes" with a smidge of an "Asian influence" served by a "smiling, terrific staff" that's "attentive to every detail"; even after 20-plus years, it's still a "chichi scene."

Tante Louise
28 | 27 | 27 | $45

4900 E. Colfax Ave. (Eudora St.), 303-355-4488

■ A French "treasure with history, style and sensational cuisine", this East Denver "gem" is set in a "perfectly intimate", "romantic" "comfortable country"-style inn that's "simultaneously quaint and fabulous, high-class and warm"; the "delectable", "impeccably prepared" "classic" Gallic fare, served by a "civilized", "friendly and unpretentious" staff, makes for a "memorable experience"; while a few gripers grumble that "the old lady has lost a step", supporters counter "it's our favorite."

240 Union S
26 | 22 | 24 | $34

240 Union Blvd. (bet. Alameda Pkwy. & 6th Ave. Frwy.), Lakewood, 303-989-3562

■ One of the "best bets in West Denver" chorus customers who congregate at this Lakewood spot for "refreshingly delightful" New American and seafood fare delivered by "pleasant" servers in a "comfortable on the eye" setting graced with "zippy decor"; it's that "rare combo: a fun place with good food" – perhaps "the best fish in town" – so no wonder it's a solid "business dining" destination and "wonderful for a high-end lunch"; everyone also agrees that "the noise is horrendous" – "if it was any louder you'd need earplugs."

Vesta Dipping Grill S
25 | 25 | 22 | $32

1822 Blake St. (bet. 18th & 19th Sts.), 303-296-1970

■ "Whether you're on a date or looking to find one", head to this "sexy, sexy, sexy" New American "LoDo tastefest", a "hip", "stylishly funky outpost" with a "really enjoyable bar" packed with "young, trendy, pretty people"; the "international flavors" of "mix-and-match entrees and sauces", "phenomenal grilled meats", "excellent soundtrack" and "helpful servers" conspire to make this a "unique, divine" "dining experience", even if the "dipping theme seems gimmicky" to some.

Wildflower S
27 | 27 | 25 | $49

The Lodge at Vail, 174 E. Gore Creek Dr. (base of Vail Mtn.), Vail, 970-476-5011

■ "Like a precious perennial", this "stunning" New American set in The Lodge at Vail is a "blue-ribbon experience" with "superb", "sophisticated" fare (including "the absolute most sybaritic brunch ever), "a "delightful atmosphere" and "impeccable service"; worshipers are also wowed by the "wonderful room", while in the summertime the "terrific" lunches served on the patio near the "beautiful flower" garden are a "special treat."

TOP 10 FOOD RANKING

Restaurant	Cuisine Type
28 Lark	New French
Emily's	Med./New French
27 Zingerman's	Deli
26 Tribute	New French/Asian
Common Grill	Eclectic
25 Il Posto Ristorante	N&S Italian
Mon Jin Lau	Pan-Asian
Cafe Bon Homme	New French
24 Daniel's on Liberty	New American
Capital Grille	Steakhouse

ADDITIONAL NOTEWORTHY PLACES

Annam	Vietnamese
Café Cortina	N&S Italian
Earle	Classic French/N&S Italian
Five Lakes Grill	New American
Golden Mushroom	Continental
Morels	American
Opus One	New American
Ritz-Carlton Grill	American/Continental
Steve's Backroom	Middle Eastern
Whitney	New American

F	D	S	C

Annam

▽ | 26 | 20 | 23 | $23 |

22053 Michigan Ave. (bet. Mason & Monroe Sts.), Dearborn, 313-565-8744

■ "The first place we take out-of-town guests" is this still-being-discovered Dearborn Vietnamese with a big-city, small-restaurant feel "reminiscent of a cramped auberge in Paris" (French-speaking owner Phuong Nguyen hails from Europe); in a "serene" room appointed with beautiful table settings and simple floral displays, a polished staff turns out "absolutely wonderful", "elegant" fare, resulting in a "sensational" meal, notwithstanding the "tiny" quarters ("it's worth the squeeze").

Cafe Bon Homme

| 25 | 21 | 23 | $47 |

844 Penniman Ave. (bet. Harvey & Main Sts.), Plymouth, 734-453-6260

■ Marked by lots of "European touches and flavors", this "quaint" "little" "jewel" in "small town" Plymouth is a "classy" yet "relaxing" nook in which to "enjoy" "original", "outstanding" New French fare served by a "courteous" staff; "warm, intimate and romantic", it's "a great place for a casually formal rendezvous" and "a guaranteed good meal."

Café Cortina | 23 | 21 | 20 | $45

30715 W. 10 Mile Rd. (Orchard Lake Rd.), Farmington Hills, 248-474-3033

■ Ask for a "table near the fireplace" in the winter and a seat near the garden (once an apple orchard and now the site where the restaurant "grows its own vegetables" and herbs) in summer to best savor the dining experience at this "upscale" Italian in suburban Farmington Hills, long cherished for its "wonderful" menu of "cooked-just-right" pastas and "rich" entrees; combined with "tasteful" decor, "terrific" service and "owners who make patrons feel very welcome", it adds up to "a real treat."

Capital Grille [S] | 24 | 23 | 23 | $54

Somerset Collection, 2800 W. Big Beaver Rd. (bet. Coolidge & Crooks Rds.), Troy, 248-649-5300

◪ "The ultimate businessman's expense-account restaurant", this "masculine" steakhouse with a "private club" feel pulls in movers and shakers as well as the "ladies who lunch" to Troy's tony Somerset Collection mall with its "tried-and-true" menu of dry-aged prime cuts, served in an "inviting", "swanky" setting by a staff that's "attentive without being obvious"; what's more, the bar is a "happening spot" for the "single senior" crowd, so though it's a chain, it's a "perennial favorite" because it's a "capital idea."

Common Grill [S] | 26 | 19 | 23 | $32

112 N. Main St. (bet. Middle & South Sts.), Chelsea, 734-475-0470

■ Occupying a pair of 1800s brick storefronts in the charming village of Chelsea, this "casual-chic" Eclectic grill shines with a "gourmet" menu of "scrumptious seafood" that's "always well-prepared"; chef-owner Craig Common's "distinctly uncommon" dishes ("inventive though not so far out that the flavors don't mix") are "impressively presented" in a "lovely", "boisterous" room by "friendly" folks; for such "excellent food without the attitude", admirers insist it's well "worth the scenic drive", but "plan on a wait at this popular" "getaway."

Daniel's on Liberty | 24 | 23 | 23 | $40

(fka Moveable Feast)

326 W. Liberty St. (2nd St.), Ann Arbor, 734-663-3278

■ Set in an "old Victorian house" in Ann Arbor, this New American "treat" is still an "outstanding place to entertain" or "celebrate a special day" because new owners Daniel and Carol Huntsbarger "carry on the tradition of excellence"; the fare is "always fabulous" and "lovingly prepared" and "sometimes surprisingly cross-cultural", served by a "personable", "knowledgeable" staff in a series of "cozy, intimate" rooms (read: "tiny, so be prepared to like the couple sitting next to you") with "understated" decor.

Earle [S] | 23 | 20 | 21 | $41

121 W. Washington St. (Ashley St.), Ann Arbor, 734-994-0211

■ A "true gem amid the collegiate chaos of Ann Arbor", this beloved "tradition" (a classic that never seems stale) "warmly" appointed with exposed brick and dim lighting has long been acclaimed for its live jazz, but its menu hits the right notes too (fans vote it "the winner of the best-food-in-a-dark-basement category"); inspired by the provinces of France and Italy, the kitchen's country cooking is so "fabulous" that "it's all I could do not to lick my plate", and it's accompanied by a "grand" 1,400-bottle wine list.

Emily's　　　　28 | 23 | 26 | $56
505 N. Center St. (8 Mile Rd.), Northville, 248-349-0505

■ Anticipate "a brilliant experience" in dining at this "cozy" "oasis" quartered in an old house in "the little hamlet of Northville", where chef-owner Rick Halberg's "imaginative" French-accented Med menu promises to "make a foodie's heart sing" (don't miss the "best duck in Detroit", glazed with balsamic vinegar and paired with sweet potato–vanilla bean puree); not only is "everything prepared to order" and served by a staff that "takes care of you as if you were a guest in their home", but the "monthly wine dinners are not to be missed."

Five Lakes Grill　　　　24 | 17 | 20 | $41
424 N. Main St. (Commerce St.), Milford, 248-684-7455

■ "Bustling with friendly, noisy people who don't feel at all intimidated by the greatness" of "hardworking" chef-owner Brian Polcyn's New American cooking, this "storefront" "treasure" is "worth the drive" to the "picturesque" village of Milford way north of Detroit; the "fantastic" menu changes seasonally, but it always offers "interesting choices from the traditional to the nouveau", all based on "local" ingredients and prepared with "a lot of flair"; "tell all your friends about this must" "destination."

Golden Mushroom　　　　23 | 18 | 21 | $55
18100 W. 10 Mile Rd. (Southfield Rd.), Southfield, 248-559-4230

◪ Specializing in mushrooms, natch, and wild game ("love the pheasant"), this "perennial" Continental "favorite" in Southfield maintains a loyal following that relies on it as "a sure thing for a special occasion", praising its "classic old-school" menu and "quiet", "upscale" ambiance; "disappointed" dissenters, however, who lament that it's slipped "down a notch from its starry past" sigh this "old dame has lost her luster."

Il Posto Ristorante　　　　25 | 23 | 25 | $57
29110 Franklin Rd. (Northwestern Hwy.), Southfield, 248-827-8070

◪ "Reminiscent of Italy without any Americanization", this "beautiful" "special-occasion" destination in Southfield boasts the "best" Italian food in the Detroit area, pleasing with a "marvelous" "gourmet" menu presented by "charming" waiters imported from the motherland (let them "steer you in the right direction" when ordering), who provide European-style kitchen-to-cart-to-table service; its "magnificent" appointments "set the mood for a romantic meal", though keep in mind that this is "definitely an expense-account type of place."

Lark　　　　28 | 28 | 28 | $85
6430 Farmington Rd. (north of Maple Rd.), West Bloomfield, 248-661-4466

■ Voted both No. 1 for Food and the Most Popular restaurant in Detroit, this "memorable" country inn in West Bloomfield is "absolutely the best in the metro" region thanks to proprietors Jim and Mary Lark, who "do everything to make your visit a special occasion"; equal raves go to chef Marcus Haight's "seductive", "exquisite" New French fare (don't miss his "bountiful appetizer cart", "superb" rack of lamb Genghis Khan or Austrian soufflé) and the "impeccable" tuxedoed staff; though some detect a "pompous" air, devotees insist this is "a must."

Mon Jin Lau ◐ [S] 25 | 16 | 19 | $32

1515 E. Maple Rd. (Stephenson Hwy.), Troy, 248-689-2332

■ Daringly "imaginative", this "lively" "Nouvelle" Asian fusion "surprise" in Troy is "a big step up from your typical everyday Chinese"; chef-owner Marshal Chin's "unique approach" allows curious "taste buds to experiment" with "haute" dishes that are "always changing but always really delicious"; backed by an "unexpectedly good", eclectic wine list, a staff that's "usually right on" and "fine value for the quality", it's constantly "packed" with adventurous types who gather to "meet, greet" and eat.

Morels 22 | 22 | 21 | $43

Bingham Office Park, 30100 Telegraph Rd. (bet. 12 &13 Mile Rds.), Bingham Farms, 248-642-1094

◪ "A mushroom-lover's paradise", this "pretty" American bistro "built around an atrium" garden in a Bingham Farms office complex is a "dependable" bet for "a guaranteed good meal"; the menu offers "lots of nice choices" that "emphasize Michigan specialties" (order anything with the namesake morels in it) and it's enhanced by an "excellent wine list"; "you won't find any eyebrow-raising exotic items" emerging from the kitchen, but the service is "pleasant", if somewhat "spotty", resulting in an "enjoyable" experience for most.

Opus One 23 | 22 | 23 | $61

565 E. Larned St. (Beaubien St.), 313-961-7766

◪ "Downtown politicos" and "business leaders" "meet frequently" at this "elegant" New American power-lunch haunt where the "high-caliber" fare, "fine" weekly changing wine list, "classy" surroundings and "unobtrusive" service help to "close the deal"; in the evening, it's a "great place to have dinner before the theater, as they offer package deals and a shuttle service", as well as live piano music, so even if doubters are "not sure what the appeal is here", fans appreciate it as "a dress-up-and-enjoy kind of place."

Ritz-Carlton Grill [S] 23 | 26 | 26 | $56

Ritz-Carlton Hotel, Fairlane Plaza, 300 Town Center Dr. (Hubbard Dr.), Dearborn, 313-441-2100

◪ "Living up to the Ritz's high level of quality and service", this "sedate" American-Continental grill in Dearborn pays "attention to every detail", proffering an "excellent, classic" menu in "luxurious" environs appointed with mahogany and warmed by a fireplace; the service is "impeccable", if "stiff", but the unimpressed say that though there's "nothing to really complain about, there's no special reason to go either."

Steve's Backroom 23 | 11 | 18 | $21

19872 Kelly Rd. (bet. 7 & 8 Mile Rds.), Harper Woods, 313-527-7240

■ "Hidden" away in the back of an ethnic market in Harper Woods, this "small" Middle Eastern "storefront" beckons with "absolutely first-rate" "treats" that attract even the tony crowd from the affluent suburbs across town; despite its humble digs ("the decor could use an upgrade") and "no ambiance", it's a real "find" for "fresh", "flavorful" cooking at "bargain" prices, and "on your way out the front door you can buy some of the great foods you sampled."

Tribute | 26 | 26 | 25 | $78

31425 W. 12 Mile Rd. (Orchard Lake Rd.), Farmington Hills, 248-848-9393

■ "A strong contender for the best in Michigan", this "grand" Farmington Hills "award winner" promises "a dining experience to remember", boasting "outstanding" Franco-Asian "fusion" cuisine courtesy of Takashi Yagihashi that's a sheer "tribute to food" ("go for the chef's table in the kitchen for a really big show"); with "unsurpassed presentations", his "artistically prepared" "creations" are turned out in "stunning" surroundings by a "thoughtful and attentive" staff overseen by Mickey Bakst, "the best maitre d' in town"; "for a wow dinner, this is the place."

Whitney [S] | 22 | 28 | 23 | $58

4421 Woodward Ave. (bet. Mack & Warren Aves.), 313-832-5700

◪ "Could any decor be better" than that of this "breathtakingly lovely" "step back in time" housed in a "restored" Victorian mansion? – not in Detroit attest admirers of this "special-occasion" Downtown "landmark" that ensures "truly elegant dining"; "in the main, it deserves its reputation as one of the fine restaurants in the area", though the New American menu and the service clearly "don't do justice" to the "enchanting" setting; still, it's "well worth a visit to take a look around and retire upstairs for dessert, coffee or after-dinner drinks."

Zingerman's [S] | 27 | 14 | 19 | $16

422 Detroit St. (Kingsley St.), Ann Arbor, 734-663-3354

■ "Always a madhouse, always a treat" sums up "positively the greatest deli in the Midwest", located in a brick storefront a few blocks off the University of Michigan's Ann Arbor campus; it's "a must" for an "outstanding selection" ("if you can't find it here, it doesn't exist") of "world-class breads, pastrami" and other goodies, making it "a very special place for food lovers"; this is "a classic that does it right and doesn't mess with success", thankfully; the only caveat: "beware of the long lines."

Fort Lauderdale

TOP 10 FOOD RANKING

	Restaurant	Cuisine Type
27	Darrel & Oliver's Cafe Maxx	New American
	Mark's Las Olas	New American
	Casa D'Angelo	N&S Italian
	Cafe Martorano	N&S Italian
26	Cafe Seville	Spanish
	Eduardo de San Angel	Mexican
	By Word of Mouth	New American
	Hobo's Fish Joint	Seafood
	Canyon	Southwestern
	Silver Pond	Chinese

ADDITIONAL NOTEWORTHY PLACES

Armadillo Cafe	Southwestern
Baraka	Kosher
Black Orchid Cafe	Continental
Cafe Vico	Northern Italian
Charley's Crab	Seafood
La Ferme	Classic/New French
Outback	Steakhouse
Primavera	Northern Italian
Ruth's Chris	Steakhouse
Sunfish Grill	Seafood

	F	D	S	C
Armadillo Cafe [S]	26	19	23	$42

3400 S. University Dr. (Frontage Rd.), Davie, 954-791-5104
■ For a "fun adventure" "involving all the taste buds", "go with a group of foodies" to this "radical Southwestern" freshly relocated to "larger quarters" on South University Drive; the Davie den delivers a "wide variety" of "always interesting", "delicious" dishes "cooked and served with pride", from "outstanding fish" to "awesome chocolate fritters"; the new space has a private dining room as well as a separate bar where, at press time, there are plans to open for lunch.

Baraka [S]	–	–	–	E

3025 N. Ocean Blvd. (E. Oakland Park Blvd.), 954-567-2525
This new upscale kosher restaurant in northeast Fort Lauderdale isn't well-known by surveyors yet, but it should soon garner a loyal following for signature sea bass and other "truly gourmet" dishes; take advantage of prix fixe specials while dining on the patio in good weather, but don't try to eat here on Friday evening when it's closed for Shabbat, and leave the jacket at home since this one's casual.

Black Orchid Cafe S   25 | 23 | 23 | $47
2985 N. Ocean Blvd. (south of E. Oakland Park Blvd.), 954-561-9398
☑ Surveying safari hunters with "tastes that lean toward venison, ostrich and other game come home" to this Continental cafe in Central Broward where the menu blooms with "wonderful" "exotica"; the beach location, "candles and jazz guitar set the right mood" for "romantic" dining, though critics with contemporary tastes say "outdated" cuisine and decor make a meal at this "overpriced" place feel like "a time warp back to 1978."

By Word of Mouth   26 | 16 | 24 | $39
3200 NE 12th Ave. (E. Oakland Park Blvd.), 954-564-3663
■ Word of mouth has it that this "tiny" "culinary hot spot" in Northeast Lauderdale offers one of "the most unique dining experiences ever"; there's "no menu" – they just "bring you to the showcase to let you see what they have for the day" – and though the New American "innovations" are "delicious", possibly "the best part" of the meal is when the "attentive servers" "entertain you by describing each dish."

Cafe Martorano   27 | 17 | 21 | $53
3343 E. Oakland Park Blvd. (N. Ocean Blvd.), 954-561-2554
■ "*Sopranos*-cool before *The Sopranos* was cool", this cafe "is where Sinatra and Pacino would eat" if they craved "awesome and abundant" "South Philly Italian" while in Fort Lauderdale; there are "no menus", so when you finally land a table, "just ask what" "food genius Steve Martorano" "is cooking today", and stick around for "late night, when the disco ball comes down and the music starts pumping" – "ba-da-bing!"

Cafe Seville   26 | 20 | 24 | $33
2768 E. Oakland Park Blvd. (Bayview Dr.), 954-565-1148
■ "Ask for extra bread to devour every drop" of *las comidas* at this "festive" Spanish "favorite" in Fort Lauderdale; the "friendly owner" "isn't shy about telling you what to eat", such as the signature paella or "some of the best fish specials in town"; he's such a "fantastic host" that even "kids" have "fun" here, though only adults have the pleasure of sipping on the house's "hit sangria."

Cafe Vico S   25 | 19 | 25 | $35
1125 N. Federal Hwy. (north of Sunrise Blvd.), 954-565-9681
■ "When you enter, you are immediately greeted" by the "gracious" owner and "made to feel like family" at this "intimate", "outstanding neighborhood Northern Italian" in central Fort Lauderdale; regulars rave about "some of the best ravioli" and "real-treat" specials around, though they "almost hate to say how good" this "reasonably priced", "enjoyable experience" is, since they "still want to get in."

Canyon S   26 | 22 | 23 | $39
1818 E. Sunrise Blvd. (N. Federal Hwy.), 954-765-1950
■ "Oooh!" – the happy-hour posse just "loves those prickly pear margaritas", but the "Southwestern charms" of this "funky" Fort Lauderdale "treasure" extend to its "inventive" meals as well; though the "bar noise" in the "crowded" yet "cozy" eatery can be "a bit loud", "unusual dishes packed with character and spice" speak boldly enough to keep your palate's attention.

Casa D'Angelo S
27 | 22 | 25 | $44

*Sunrise Sqare Plaza, 1201 N. Federal Hwy. (bet. E. Sunrise Blvd. &
NE 13th Ave.), 954-564-1234*

■ "Wonderful" chef-owner Angelo Elia uses "first-class
ingredients" for "truly fine quality" at this Fort Lauderdale casa
of "killer Italian"; the whole family pitches in at the "casual-dressy"
"favorite": Denise, "who greets you, is so nice she makes everyone
feel" "like an old friend", and in season, "mama comes from
Italy" to cook her "melt-away delicious" fusilli — though regulars
visit any time of year because "it always feels good to be here."

Charley's Crab S
21 | 21 | 21 | $38

3000 NE 32nd Ave. (E. Oakland Park Blvd.), 954-561-4800

Pal's Charley's Crab S

*Cove Shopping Ctr., 1755 SE Third Ct. (bet. Hillsboro Blvd. & S. Federal Hwy.),
Deerfield Beach, 954-427-4000*

◪ Charley's chums choose these "old, classic" seafood houses
along the Intercoastal "again and again for the view and the
vittles"; "grandparents" bring the kids for "family comfort" and a
"good early-bird value", while "out-of-towners" tout the "excellent
Sunday brunch"; picky patrons pout, however, that since owner
Chuck Muer was lost at sea in 1993, these crab "traps" have been
"fading into touristy blandness."

Darrel & Oliver's Cafe Maxx S
27 | 22 | 26 | $52

*2601 E. Atlantic Blvd. (east of N. Federal Hwy.), Pompano Beach,
954-782-0606*

■ Eighteen years marks one lengthy "orgasmic experience" for the
clientele of this "California-style, open-kitchen" New American
that was voted No. 1 for Food in the *Fort Lauderdale Survey*; if the
"ordinary decor" and "strip-mall" setting fail to romance design
divas, time and again Pompano Beach foodies "come back to see
what's new" on the "daily changing menu" of "delectable dishes."

Eduardo de San Angel
26 | 23 | 24 | $46

*2822 E. Commercial Blvd. (bet. Bayview Dr. & 28th Ave.),
954-772-4731*

■ "It's so nice to not have to scream over music" when you want
to discuss how "marvelous every dish is" at this "quiet" "nouveau
Mexican" in Fort Lauderdale; "forget your preconceived notions",
settle into a "postage stamp–size table" and savor the kitchen's
"masterful" "fusion of all things from Baja to the Yucatan" at
this beer-and-wine-only "shining" "gem" amid the dross of the
"Taco Bell world."

Hobo's Fish Joint S
26 | 18 | 22 | $40

*10317 Royal Palm Blvd. (Coral Springs Dr.), Coral Springs,
954-346-5484*

■ "One thing about Florida" lecture locals "is that a strip-mall
location means nothing as far as quality"; case in point: this
"creative" Coral Springs finster that drops its line "where you
least expect it" to reel in "serious fish eaters" for a "wide variety"
of "fresh" ocean treats served in a choice of "interesting ways";
hook a hungry friend and "tramp over" to "share their seafood
sampler" with "homemade ketchup and tartar sauce."

La Ferme S   25 | 21 | 23 | $41

1601 E. Sunrise Blvd. (16th Ave.), 954-764-0987

■ The "very, very friendly" Marie-Paule Terrier is "still the loveliest hostess" in Broward according to locals, and her husband, chef Henri, turns out "unbeatable", "sophisticated French" fare at this "favorite" East Sunrise bistro; the "warm, delightful" place is decked out in "old-style" reds and boasts a private dining room in an adjacent historic house.

Mark's Las Olas S   27 | 24 | 24 | $52

1032 E. Las Olas Blvd. (bet. 10th & 11th Sts.), 954-463-1000

■ Fort Lauderdale's "people-watching headquarters" is this "trendy" downtown New American where "chef Mark Militello's flair" for "fab" fare finds fans among the "hip and happening"; if so many "moguls on phones" makes the atmosphere too "New York" and the "noise quotient a bit high" for your tastes, "head for one of the booths in back" to enjoy signature crab-crusted grouper and other "delicious" "culinary treats" in relative peace.

Outback Steakhouse S   19 | 16 | 18 | $25

6201 N. Federal Hwy. (bet. E. Cypress Creek Rd. & E. McNab Rd.), 954-771-4390
1801 SE 10th Ave. (17th St. Causeway), 954-523-5600
650 Riverside Dr. (W. Atlantic Blvd.), Coral Springs, 954-345-5965
7841 Pines Blvd. (N. University Dr.), Pembroke Pines, 954-981-5300
1823 Pine Island Rd. (Sunrise Blvd.), Plantation, 954-370-9956

◪ "Crikey!" cry reviewers, "are onions supposed to bloom?" – who knows, but who cares when they taste so "great, mate" at this "solid-value", "family-oriented chain" chophouse that pals opine "will stun you with mouthwatering delights" from Down Under; a "party atmosphere" means they're "always packed", but critical carnivores wonder why anyone would be "prepared to wait" at the "glorified Denny's" for "slabs o' meat" they say "belong in a shoe factory."

Primavera S   26 | 22 | 22 | $45

Primavera Plaza, 830 E. Oakland Park Blvd. (west of N. Dixie Hwy.), 954-564-6363

◪ Skip the local "rip-offs" and "step into a whole other scene past the portals" of this "small and warm" Northern Italian "favorite" in Oakland Park where "nearly perfect, artfully crafted" pasta, seafood and seasonal game are complemented by an extensive wine list; the room is "elegant and romantic", but a "stuffy" staff that "fawns over regulars" and is "cold" to "newcomers" is only appealing "when you miss New York snobbery."

Ruth's Chris Steakhouse S   25 | 23 | 24 | $49

2525 N. Federal Hwy. (bet. Oakland Park & Sunrise Blvds.), 954-565-2338

■ "Sizzle, sizzle!" – "despite being a chain", this "solid" Lauderdale "steak joint" "has the right formula" to please "good old-fashioned meat lovers"; "huge portions" of "the best trimmings around" like "great creamed spinach" and "thin, crispy onions" can be had here, but "nothing can match the arrival" of "delicious", "buttery" beef in a "nice atmosphere" "without the men's club decor"; though "big taste" comes at a "big price", loyalists insist that "Ruth's superior selections" are worth it.

Silver Pond ⬤⧉S 26 | 12 | 17 | $25

4285 N. State Rd. 7 (south of Commercial Blvd.), Lauderdale Lakes,
954-486-8885

■ "New Yorkers have no need to go back home" – for "the best
Chinese for the price this side of Manhattan's Chinatown", they
can dive into this "authentic" spot in Lauderdale Lakes; "even if
English is a challenge", the "informed, friendly staff" helps to select
"incredible Hong Kong–style" dishes in a "modest" joint where the
best way to stomach the "awful decor" is to "not look around."

Sunfish Grill 25 | 18 | 23 | $44

2771 E. Atlantic Blvd. (Intracoastal Waterway), Pompano Beach,
954-788-2434

■ "One nibble and you're hooked" as surely as the "fabulous"
"local fish" at this "little jewel tucked away near the Intracoastal";
chef-owner Tony Sindaco's "lovingly prepared seafood" and
"outrageous desserts" are "world-class" at this "charming and
colorful" Pompano Beacher; diners would even dare to "show up
in the middle of a hurricane" to be "blown away from start to finish"
by "the outstanding" meals.

Fort Worth

TOP 10 FOOD RANKING

Restaurant	Cuisine Type
28 Saint-Emilion	Classic French
27 Del Frisco's	Steakhouse
La Piazza	N&S Italian
26 Cacharel	Classic French
Randall's Cafe	Eclectic
25 Bistro Louise	Mediterranean
Kincaid's	Burgers
Railhead Smokehouse	Barbecue
23 Angelo's Barbecue	Barbecue
Angeluna	Eclectic/International

ADDITIONAL NOTEWORTHY PLACES

Café Ashton	New American
Café on the Green	New American
Classic Cafe	New American
Cool River Cafe	Southwestern
Escargot	Classic French
Grape Escape	Eclectic
Lonesome Dove	Western
Pegasus	International/Med.
Rough Creek Lodge	New American
Ruffino's	N&S Italian

F	D	S	C

Angelo's Barbecue ⌀

23	14	17	$14

2533 White Settlement Rd. (University Dr.), 817-332-0357

■ "A tattered stuffed bear still greets you at the door" of this "no-frills", mesquite smoke–filled Northwest BBQ "institution", famous for serving the "coldest beers in town" and "great chopped beef" and brisket to "lots of guys wearing cowboy hats"; P.S. "get plenty of napkins."

Angeluna S

23	23	21	$35

215 E. Fourth St. (bet. Calhoun & Commerce Sts.), 817-334-0080

☑ "Convenient" before or after an event at Bass Performance Hall, this "cutting-edge" entry showcases a global menu of "artistically presented fusion dishes" ("Texas meets Asia and the angels sing") amid "cool" decor highlighted by a skylike ceiling covered with eclectic images (from Marilyn Monroe to Mr. Potato Head); still, spoilers shout that it's "so noisy I wanted to cry."

Bistro Louise
25 24 23 $37

Stonegate Commons, 2900 S. Hulen St. (Oak Park Ln.), 817-922-9244

■ Sharing the No. 1 spot for Popularity in Fort Worth, chef Louise Lamensdorf's Mediterranean bistro is praised by admirers as one of the "best in the Metroplex" given its "wonderful brunch", a menu that "challenges the local steak mentality" and a "newly improved wine list"; the "casually elegant", Provençal-themed setting attracts a lot of well-heeled locals to the Southwest side, so don't be surprised if "you always see someone you know."

Cacharel
26 25 25 $44

Brookhollow Tower Two, 2221 E. Lamar Blvd. (bet. Ballpark Way & Hwy. 360), Arlington, 817-640-9981

■ An Arlington office tower surrounded by amusement parks and fast-food chains is the unusual location for this high-achieving Classic French grande dame, which offers pampered patrons an "intimate, posh" dining room with an illuminated skyline view, plus a choice between a three-course prix fixe menu and à la carte selections; either way, the "great soufflés" should be a de rigueur sweet finale.

Café Ashton 🅂
– – – E

Ashton Hotel, 610 Main St. (6th St.), 817-332-0100

While this New American bistro is set in a prestigious Downtown landmark building, now home to the luxurious new Ashton boutique hotel, all historical overtones end at the glass front doors; inside is a streamlined space appointed with creamy yellow walls, bright-blue opera chairs and modern artwork, making for a sleek backdrop for chef Diarmuid Murphy's cooking, which mixes hints of his Irish roots with tropical nuances; the piano bar is just a bonus.

Café on the Green 🅂
▽ 24 23 21 $47

Four Seasons Resort & Club, 4150 N. MacArthur Blvd. (Northgate Dr.), Irving, 972-717-2420

■ "Better than any of the private country clubs" reflects surveyors' regard for this Las Colinas venue whose New American offerings range from spa selections and à la carte options to a sumptuous buffet and "absolutely divine brunch", all of which can be enjoyed in a sunny, window-filled room.

Classic Cafe
▽ 25 18 22 $39

504 N. Oak St. (Denton St.), Roanoke, 817-430-8185
621 E. Southlake Blvd. (Byron Nelson Pkwy.), Southlake, 817-410-9001

■ While contrasting greatly in size – the candlelit, intimate Roanoke original seats about 90, the modern Southlake outlet 300 – both turn out "salmon at its best" and other "exceptional" New American dishes; hands-on service and "friendly" managers who "always remember returning guests" further explain their popularity.

Cool River Cafe ◑🅂
21 23 19 $33

1045 Hidden Ridge Rd. (MacArthur Blvd.), Irving, 972-871-8881

■ This Rocky Mountain–themed lodge set amid the Los Colinas/Valley Ranch sprawl is a convivial gathering spot for dot-com survivors, corporate climbers and "beautiful women" who make the "bar scene"; since it's fully stocked with large-screen TVs, billiard tables and a cigar/cognac lounge, the Southwestern food may not be the focus, but it scores well, especially the rib-eye, which alone is "worth the trip."

Del Frisco's
Double Eagle Steak House   27 | 26 | 26 | $57
812 Main St. (8th St.), 817-877-3999
■ Tied for No. 1 in Popularity in the *Fort Worth Survey*, this
Downtown steakhouse chain link wows surveyors with "the
clubbiest environs", "wonderful sides", some of "the best red meat
you'll ever eat", a showstopping wine list and "impeccable"
service; so don your sports jacket and cowboy boots, double-
check that "expense-account" limit and prepare for an "elegant
power dinner"; N.B. reservations are essential on weekends.

Escargot S   ▽ 26 | 24 | 23 | $37
Chitcosky's Shopping Ctr., 3427 W. Seventh St. (Montgomery St.),
817-336-3090
■ Frédéric Angevin's "wonderful new" Cultural District French
entry is quickly becoming a "favorite" thanks to his "outstanding"
food; decorated in an "elegant", understated style, the narrow
slice of a dining room is tended to by wife Michele; yes, "prices
are high" and it can get "crowded", but that's to be expected for
such a classy operation.

Grape Escape Wine Bar S   20 | 22 | 21 | $26
500 Commerce St. (4th St.), 817-336-9463
◪ Small plates of Eclectic nibbles are creatively teamed with
flights of global wines at this compact Downtown tasting bar that
makes for a "nice place to converse" after a concert at nearby
Bass Performance Hall; while sour grapes whine "overpriced"
with "not much food" to choose from, most say "we need more
places like this."

Kincaid's Hamburgers ⊭   25 | 14 | 17 | $10
4901 Camp Bowie Blvd. (Eldridge St.), 817-732-2881
■ "Excellent", "lean, juicy burgers" "dripping with mustard" and
delivered in white paper sacks generate long lines at this peerless
patty joint on the West Side, which draws patrons from as far as
"140 miles away"; "while it's not much for decor" (just picnic tables
and stand-up counters), the staff's "old-fashioned friendliness"
more than compensates.

La Piazza S   27 | 26 | 24 | $49
University Park Village, 1600 S. University Dr. (I-30), 817-334-0000
◪ Though clearly "the best Italian in Fort Worth", this "expensive",
"dressy" University Park Village destination is not without some
controversy: while a "who's who" of regulars are welcomed as
warmly as arriving relatives and whisked to prime tables to enjoy
"a fabulous meal" based on the "freshest ingredients" (try the
veal tenders with porcini mushrooms), a minority of frustrated
outsiders chafes over the owner's playing favorites.

Lonesome Dove Western Bistro ▽ 23 | 18 | 20 | $33
2406 N. Main St. (24th St.), 817-740-8810
■ Chef Tim Love has set up his camp stove in the Stockyards with
this "good new addition" featuring polished Western ranch-style
vittles turned out in a small, saloon-like room with plank doors,
burlap draperies and a quintessential Western sunset painting;
granted, fine linens, pewter platters and stemware are not typical
chuck wagon accessories, nor is the grilled quail quesadilla or BBQ
duck spring rolls, but culinary cowboys will easily adapt.

Pegasus
▽ | 24 | 25 | 22 | $35 |

2443 Forest Park Blvd. (Park Hill Dr.), 817-922-0808

■ This elegant newcomer to Forest Park "shows promise out of the gate", what with its "cool", minimalist decor and an "interesting" Mediterranean-influenced global menu; first-time visitors should consider ordering some meze and entrees like the sumac-crusted filet mignon, Persian-spiced osso buco or duck with a fruit mole.

Railhead Smokehouse
| 25 | 18 | 19 | $13 |

2900 Montgomery St. (I-30), 817-738-9808
5220 Hwy. 121 S. (Hall Johnson Rd.), Colleyville, 817-571-2525

■ Hot as the coals that smoke their meat is the "best BBQ" rivalry between this twosome and Angelo's; loyalists insist Railhead's ribs are "the final word" on the subject but add that "the brisket is out of this world" too (especially with "a tall schooner of Shiner Bock"); moreover, while the tables and patio perpetually overflow with patrons, the "cafeteria-style lines move quickly" and the "fun" atmosphere (T-shirts for sale read: 'Life Is Too Short To Live in Dallas') keeps the mood light.

Randall's Cafe
| 26 | 24 | 23 | $35 |

907 Houston St. (bet. 8th & 9th Sts.), 817-336-2253

■ This exposed-brick, white-tablecloth Eclectic cafe "tucked away on the nontouristy side of Downtown" features a daily changing menu of impressive preparations as well as a romantic "Paris meets New Orleans meets San Francisco meets Greenwich Village" setting; N.B. don't forget to end your meal with a creamy wedge of its famous cheesecake.

Rough Creek Lodge S
▽ | 29 | 29 | 29 | $54 |

County Rd. 2013 (US 67 S., 9 mi. south of Glen Rose), Glen Rose, 254-918-2550

■ Anticipate an "incredible experience" out on the "wide open prairie" at this haute hunting resort set in the shadow of Chalk Mountain; once seated in the elegant Western-accented room, saddled between a soaring, three-story limestone fireplace and a bustling open kitchen, you'll wax poetic over chef Gerard Thompson's intelligently stylish New American menu; P.S. "stay overnight" to avoid the long drive back.

Ruffino's Ristorante Italiano
▽ | 24 | 21 | 23 | $32 |

2455 Forest Park Blvd. (Park Hill Dr.), 817-923-0522

■ Brothers Franco and Bobby Albanese express their love of wine and "great food" ("never a dull meal" here) at this Forest Park cucina with golden-washed walls, starched linens and a piano player who hits all the classy, "romantic" notes; traditional favorites include grandma's lasagna and tiramisu.

Saint-Emilion
| 28 | 25 | 26 | $47 |

3617 W. Seventh St. (Montgomery Rd.), 817-737-2781

■ Voted No. 1 for Food in Fort Worth and embraced as "a French oasis in a steak-and-BBQ desert", owner Bernard Tronche's "romantic" bit of France set in a brick cottage near the Arts District showcases "first-rate", classically prepared dishes based on "quality" ingredients, as well as a top-notch wine list that favors its namesake region; while the menu advises diners to pace themselves for a leisurely meal, let the staff know that you're on an American schedule if you want them to speed it up.

Honolulu

TOP 10 FOOD RANKING

	Restaurant	Cuisine Type
27	Alan Wong's	Hawaiian Regional
26	La Mer	Classic French
	Roy's	Hawaiian/Fusion
	Hoku's	International
	Ruth's Chris	Steakhouse
25	Yohei Sushi	Japanese
	Orchids	International/Seafood
	Kyo-Ya	Japanese
	3660 on the Rise	Pacific Rim
	Hy's Steak House	Steakhouse

ADDITIONAL NOTEWORTHY PLACES

Bali-By-The-Sea	Eurasian
Chef Mavro's	New French/Hawaiian Reg.
Golden Dragon	Chinese
Indigo	Eurasian
OnJin's Cafe	Asian/French Bistro
Padovani's	Classic French/Med.
Palomino Euro Bistro	American/Med.
Pineapple Room	Hawaiian Regional
Prince Court	American/Japanese
Sansei	Hawaiian/Japanese

F | D | S | C

Alan Wong's [S] 27 | 20 | 25 | $48

McCully Ct., 1857 S. King St. (bet. Hauoli & Pumehana Sts.), 808-949-2526

■ Voted Honolulu's Most Popular restaurant as well as No. 1 for Food, this Hawaiian Regional standout boasts the "most creative chef" on the islands, Alan Wong, who is simply "da man" when it comes to "innovative" cooking; despite a "crowded", "uninspired" room, his "exceptionally exceptional" (albeit "pricey") fusion cuisine and "imaginative presentations" make this an "event" for locals and a "must-go for out-of-towners."

Bali-By-The-Sea 23 | 25 | 24 | $47

Hilton Hawaiian Village, 2005 Kalia Rd. (Ala Moana Blvd.), 808-941-2254

■ One of the islands' top "impress-your-date" restaurants, this "elegant yet comfortable" room set in a "romantic" Waikiki Beach locale specializes in "excellent" Eurasian cuisine with a Hawaiian accent courtesy of chef Jean-Luc Voegele; despite a few doubters ("a lot of hype"), most agree that the "super wine list and steward", "classy decor" and "great service" add up to an experience that's among "the best for special occasions."

Chef Mavro's §　　　　23 | 23 | 24 | $62
1969 S. King St. (McCully St.), 808-944-4714
☑ "Serious food for serious diners" is prepared by chef George Mavrothalassitis (ex La Mer) at this "superior" McCully New French–Hawaiian Regional where the "fabulous food-and-wine pairings" draw huzzahs; sure, it's "expensive with a capital E" and hearty eaters groan that the servings are "microscopic", but to its many fans, this "must-try" spot is simply "ahead of its time."

Golden Dragon §　　　　24 | 23 | 22 | $35
Hilton Hawaiian Village, 2005 Kalia Rd. (Ala Moana Blvd.), 808-946-5336
■ If you're seeking Oahu's "consummate" Chinese restaurant, look no further than this "superb" spot where "exquisite" dishes like "to-die-for" lobster curry are brought to table in a "beautiful" setting within a prestigious Waikiki hotel; it's "expensive", but for "truly gourmet" cooking, this "class act" is worth it.

Hoku's §　　　　26 | 26 | 25 | $48
Kahala Mandarin Oriental Hotel, 5000 Kahala Ave., 808-739-8779
■ The name means 'star' in Hawaiian, and surveyors say this "classy" International set in a top-drawer hotel is celestial in every way; "breathtaking views", "delicate, nonrushed" service and "amazing" food courtesy of Wayne Hirabayashi come together for a "first-class" "fine dining" experience; the only quibbles: "costly" tabs and "a little too much noise."

Hy's Steak House §　　　　25 | 23 | 23 | $42
Waikiki Park Heights Hotel, 2440 Kuhio Ave. (Uluniu Ave.), 808-922-5555
☑ "Top-of-the-line", this dinner-only homage to meat in Waikiki is done up like an "old boys' club", with "dark woods and a fireplace" that complement its "great steaks and chops"; though prices are on the "expensive" side, fans consider it "a solid value."

Indigo　　　　23 | 22 | 21 | $30
1121 Nuuanu Ave. (Hotel St.), 808-521-2900
■ "Always an adventure", this Eurasian "culinary treasure" in Chinatown offers a "unique" mix of "interesting" dishes – from potstickers to pizza – in a "Polynesian" setting complete with an "enchanting garden patio"; though many describe the food as "shockingly good", a vocal minority derides its "small portions/high cost" formula.

Kyo-Ya §　　　　25 | 25 | 23 | $38
2057 Kalakaua Ave., 808-947-3911
■ For an "excellent visual" experience, visit this "consummate" Japanese with "great decor" and "superb, beautifully served" fare; it's "pricey", but for "authentic" dining that's among the "classiest on Waikiki", admirers suggest you "splurge on a leisurely lunch."

La Mer §　　　　26 | 27 | 26 | $63
Halekulani Hotel, 2199 Kalia Rd. (Lewers St.), 808-923-2311
■ "Tops in all categories", this "legendary" Classic French is the "crème de la crème" of Waikiki, boasting a "fabulous" menu from chef Yves Garnier, "outstanding" service and a "*très* elegant" setting in the Halekulani resort; "bring lots of money", however – it just might be "the most expensive restaurant" around – and don't forget to "wear a sport coat" or long-sleeved dress shirt, required for entry.

OnJin's Cafe　　　　　　– | – | – | M

401 Kamakee St. (Kapiolani Blvd.), 808-589-1666
At this creative, upscale cafe near Ala Moana, look for filling,
satisfying Asian plate lunches by day and straightforward French
bistro-style preparations at night.

Orchids S　　　　　25 | 27 | 24 | $43

Halekulani Hotel, 2199 Kalia Rd. (Lewers St.), 808-923-2311
■ Located in a "beautiful", "romantic" Waikiki oceanfront hotel,
this International seafood house is an "oasis" where "five-star"
dishes are served by an "impeccable" staff; whether you opt for
a "delightful" lunch, "lovely" sunset dinner or "superior" Sunday
brunch, this exercise in "classic hedonism" is a "wonderful
splurge"; N.B. check out the seafood appetizer bar.

Padovani's Restaurant & Wine　　25 | 24 | 23 | $55
Bar S

*Doubletree Alana Hotel, 1956 Ala Moana Blvd. (Kalakaua Ave.),
808-946-3456*
☑ "First-class" chef Philippe Padovani (ex La Mer) has created
this "bright star" in Waikiki, a wine bar offering 35 vintages by
the glass and a "superb" Classic French–Med bistro menu with a
Hawaiian Regional influence; "impressive" decor (though there's
"no view") adds to the "quality" experience, thus most say the
"expensive" tabs are "worth every penny"; N.B. a mandatory
tipping policy has been scratched.

Palomino Euro Bistro S　　22 | 25 | 21 | $30

Harbor Sq., 66 Queen St. (bet. Bethel & Nimitz Sts.), 808-528-2400
■ "Stunning" decor and a "happening", "lively" atmosphere draw
"scenesters" to this "trendy" Downtown American-Mediterranean
where the "creative" cooking comes at "reasonable" prices; the
only drawback at this "oh-so-cosmopolitan" spot seems to be
the service, which some surveyors say "depends on who you are
or appear to be."

Pineapple Room S　　　　– | – | – | E

*Liberty House, Ala Moana Shopping Ctr., 1450 Ala Moana Blvd.
(Atkinson Dr.), 808-945-8881*
The remarkable Hawaiian Regional cooking of chef Alan Wong
can be sampled at breakfast, lunch or dinner at this airy, tropical
room complete with an exhibition kitchen on the third floor of a
department store at the Ala Moana Shopping Center; nothing here
is traditional, from the braised roast duck to the lobster pizza.

Prince Court S　　　　23 | 22 | 22 | $36

*Hawaii Prince Hotel Waikiki, 100 Holomoana St. (Ala Moana Blvd.),
808-944-4494*
■ This traditional American-Japanese palace overlooking the
Ala Wai Yacht Harbor remains a "favorite" for special occasions
and "expense-account" meals, even after the departure a couple
of years ago of popular chef Gary Strehl; credit its "impressive"
buffets and a "delicious", extensive Sunday brunch for making
this a "great dining experience."

Roy's S   26 | 20 | 23 | $42

6600 Kalanianaole Hwy. (Keahole St.), 808-396-7697

■ The "original" Hawaii Kai site of the global Hawaiian fusion chain founded by award-winning chef-owner Roy Yamaguchi is "still the best" thanks to always "innovative" cooking from the "wonderful" open kitchen, a "friendly" staff and the "best" sunset views around; the "packed-in tables" and "intolerable noise level" in the main dining room, however, make eating in the lounge an option to consider, short of bringing "earplugs."

Ruth's Chris Steak House S   26 | 20 | 23 | $42

Restaurant Row, 500 Ala Moana Blvd. (bet. Punchbowl & South Sts.), 808-599-3860

■ Carnivores crow that "you'll leave happy and full" after dining at this "high-energy" Restaurant Row chain chop shop where the "à la carte everything" menu includes "oh-so-tender" steaks that are excellent "100 percent of the time"; a "great wine list" ("three different Turley's – rare for Hawaii") rounds out this impressive, if "pricey", experience.

Sansei Seafood Restaurant & Sushi Bar S   – | – | – | E

Restaurant Row, 500 Ala Moana Blvd. (bet. Pohukaina & South Sts.), 808-536-6286

Foodies rejoice in the arrival of this cavernous crowd-pleaser on Restaurant Row, where creative chef D.K. Kodama offers a choice of three menus featuring Hawaiian classics (like ahi with shrimp cake), Japanese sushi (both traditional and innovative) and daily specials (such as *opakapaka* with *furikake* and curry vinaigrette); if you're interested, there's laser karaoke after 10 PM.

3660 on the Rise S   25 | 20 | 22 | $39

3660 Waialae Ave. (Wilhelmina Rise), 808-737-1177

■ "Nouvelle Pacific Rim cuisine at its best" wins raves for this "cutting-edge" Kaimuki entry led by "innovative", "outstanding" chef Russell Siu; after a redo, there are now more tables and "a more relaxing", "personable" ambiance, leading partisans to predict that this "consistent" "favorite" could "reach the top."

Yohei Sushi   25 | 16 | 19 | $31

Kokea Business Complex, 1111 Dillingham Blvd. (Kokea St.), 808-841-3773

◪ Despite an "out-of-the-way" location on the edge of Kalihi, reservations are strongly recommended for this "always crowded" Japanese seafood house with "one of the best sushi bars in town"; signature dishes include the bento box at lunch and tempura and broiled salmon at dinner.

Houston

Aldo's Dining con Amore 25 | 19 | 21 | $63

219 Westheimer Rd. (bet. Brazos & Taft Sts.), 713-523-2536

■ When you're "in the mood" for a truly "opulent experience", it's hard to beat this "intimate" Montrose Northern Italian where "the word 'no' does not exist" for chef-owner Aldo El-Sharif, who "caters to your every culinary whim" while his "attentive" staff will even "put the doggy bag in your car"; "be sure to ask the price" of the "exotic dishes" (like "kangaroo, zebra, lion") on his "spoken menu", however, lest your "jaw hit the floor" when the bill arrives.

Américas 24 | 26 | 21 | $35

The Pavilion, 1800 Post Oak Blvd. (bet. San Felipe St. & Westheimer Rd.), 713-961-1492

■ The "fantasy world" decor of this multi-level Latin American near the Galleria is so "amazing" it threatens to "overwhelm" chef Michael Cordúa's "innovative", "magically" presented and "drop-dead delicious" cooking; similarly diverting are the "beautiful patrons" who fill this "trendy" spot "to the brim", especially during the "fabulous tapas happy hours" in the "funky bar"; the only quibble: it gets "way too loud."

Amerigo's Grille [S] 25 | 22 | 24 | $34

Grogan's Park, 25250 Grogan's Park Dr. (Sawdust Rd.), The Woodlands, 281-362-0808

■ Those looking for a "reason to trek out to The Woodlands" should consider this "top-notch" Northern Italian, "one of the only" places in the area that's "quiet" (i.e. "few children" around) and offers "lots of elegance for the money"; best of all is its "fantastic" menu, which makes it "wonderful for special occasions"; P.S. check out the second-floor piano lounge.

Anthony's 26 | 24 | 24 | $46

Highland Village, 4007 Westheimer Rd. (Drexel Dr.), 713-961-0552

■ A "dream dinner" is an "experience worth the price" at this "elegant" Highland Village "classic", which Zagateurs count as one of the "top choices" in town for Continental-American "business power lunches", "special occasions" or prime "yuppie-watching" (it attracts a "hip, well-heeled crowd"); nearly as impressive as the "excellent" menu are the "beautiful bar and sunken dining room", though the "smooth" service strikes some as "snobbish."

Aries – | – | – | E

4315 Montrose Blvd. (Richmond Ave.), 713-526-4404

From the ashes of 43 Brasserie, Scott Tycer and his wife Annika (both born under the sign of Aries) have raised up this elegant New American in heartwarming homage to fresh Texas ingredients; the California-oriented wine list sports eye-opening picks, while exotic coffees and teas provide an ideal finale.

benjy's IN THE VILLAGE [S] 24 | 20 | 21 | $28

Rice Village, 2424 Dunstan St. (Kelvin Dr.), 713-522-7602

■ "Skinny people dressed in black" adore the "state-of the-art" decor and "trendy" atmosphere at this "popular" Rice Village New American whose "inventive" Asian-influenced dishes are only slightly upstaged by the stylish staff (the "waiters are even prettier than the food"); it's "crowded" and "noisy", but that's to be expected for an "LA-in-Houston" experience.

Brennan's Houston [S] | 26 | 27 | 26 | $44

3300 Smith St. (Stuart St.), 713-522-9711

■ About "as close to perfection as you can get", this Downtown cousin of New Orleans' Commander's Palace puts a Texas twist on Louisiana cuisine with Carl Walker's "over-the-top fabulous" Southwestern-Creole creations; ideal for "special occasions" and "wowing out-of-towners", this stalwart exemplifies "Southern charm" and "tradition" with its "sophisticated yet friendly" service, "wonderful atmosphere" and a "peaceful courtyard."

Cafe Annie | 26 | 26 | 25 | $53

1728 Post Oak Blvd. (San Felipe St.), 713-840-1111

◪ "Still elegant and chic" – and still the Most Popular restaurant in Houston – Robert Del Grande's "richly designed" ("who does those flower arrangements?") Tanglewood Southwestern sets "the standard that others must meet" thanks to chef Ben Berryhill's "fantastic", "avant-garde" creations presented like "works of art", an "ooh-la-la wine list" and "impeccable" service; given such a "world-class" experience, the "elite" crowd that flocks here doesn't seem to mind much if the tabs get "expensive."

Café Descours | 25 | 16 | 18 | $20

1330 Wirt Rd. (Westview Dr.), 713-681-8894

Pâtisserie Descours

1330 Wirt Rd. (Westview Dr.), 713-681-8894

■ "Desserts that'll make you change your lunch plans", as well as "fabulous breads and sandwiches", are the specialty of this "delightful" Spring Branch patisserie and next-door cafe (open evenings only), which for dinner serves "delicious" bistro favorites; despite its humble digs, it's a welcome source of "affordable fine French" fare and "a nice addition to the scene."

Cafe Red Onion | 25 | 15 | 18 | $18

3910 Kirby Dr. (Southwest Frwy./Hwy. 59 S.), 713-807-1122
12041 Northwest Frwy./Hwy. 290 (43rd St.), 713-957-0957

■ This "inspired" Latin American entry's "upscale", spacious Kirby offshoot may look completely different from the Highway 290 "hole-in-the-wall" original ("buy some tablecloths already!"), but both offer the same, "knock-your-socks-off" fusion cooking.

Capital Grille [S] | 25 | 25 | 24 | $48

5365 Westheimer Rd. (Yorktown St.), 713-623-4600

■ "Catering to power brokers", this "dark", "clubby" Galleria steakhouse with an "old-boy lawyer style" is a "No. 1 place to impress" clients with its "first-class" dry-aged beef, a winning wine list ("heavy and complete") and "stellar" service; it should be no surprise that the "prices match" the "premium" "quality" of the chops; P.S. there's also a "see-and-be-seen" scene at the "bar packed with singles" of the 40-plus persuasion.

Chez Nous | 26 | 22 | 25 | $48

217 S. Ave. G (Staitti St.), Humble, 281-446-6717

■ For that "special occasion", "when French classics are what you want", take the "drive from Houston" to this "beautiful" venue in Humble whose "unusual home" is a "converted church" – a fitting locale for its divine rack of lamb and "foie gras that's a life-altering experience"; for this "absolute treasure", "urban dwellers" are quite "willing to venture" far into "suburbia."

Churrascos 25 | 21 | 22 | $31

Shepherd Sq., 2055 Westheimer Rd. (S. Shepherd Dr.), 713-527-8300
9705 Westheimer Rd. (Gessner Rd.), 713-952-1988
1320 W. Bay Area Blvd. (bet. Baybrook Mall & Gulf Frwy./I-45 S.), Friendswood, 281-461-4100

◪ Carnivores reach "meat-eaters' paradise" at this South American steakhouse trio that always satisfies "cravings" for its namesake *churrasco* – "melt-in-your-mouth tender" beef anointed with "garlicky" *chimichurri* sauce – as well as "bring-more-please" plantain chips and "can't-be-beat" *tres leches* cake; surveyors deem it a "winner", despite some gripes that it's too "crowded."

Daily Review Cafe [S] 23 | 16 | 19 | $24

3412 W. Lamar St. (Dunlavy St.), 713-520-9217

■ "Filling a niche" in Montrose, this "sophisticated, metropolitan" cafe "hidden" down a side street is a "neighborhood hit" thanks to its "creative without being wacky" New American menu (top pick? – "what else but the chicken pot pie", though it's nothing like mom used to make), "happy atmosphere" and garden patio.

Da Marco 24 | 20 | 21 | $36

1520 Westheimer Rd. (bet. Mandell St. & Montrose Blvd.), 713-807-8857

■ Chef-owner Marco Wiles "is a genius" rave fans of this Montrose Italian "winner" where his "dazzlingly good" – make that "stellar" – cooking is fashioned from a palette of "authentic" Tuscan flavors; most everyone approves of the "class-act" staff that "aims to please", but the eye-popping golden-orange setting draws varying responses: admirers call it "cute" and "charming", while skeptics demand "explain the paint job."

Damian's Cucina Italiana 26 | 23 | 24 | $38

3011 Smith St. (Rosalie St.), 713-522-0439

■ "Dark and full of business suits", this Downtown "paragon" of "old-world elegance" and "sophisticated" Tuscan interpretations encourages loyalists to "linger" and "enjoy every minute" of the "expensive", "take-your-time dining" experience; the downside of such "pleasant" loitering: customers on the clock report that "the office wasn't happy" about the "three-hour lunch."

Goode Co. Barbeque [S] 24 | 17 | 17 | $14

8911 Katy Frwy./I-10 W. (Campbell Rd.), 713-464-1901
5109 Kirby Dr. (bet. Bissonnet St. & Westpark Dr.), 713-522-2530

■ Despite "lots of competition", owner Jim Goode's "not-to-be-missed" "cafeteria-style" smokehouse duo slow-cooks "the best BBQ in Houston", maybe even "in Texas"; what wins hearts here are the "incredible brisket sandwiches", "stellar turkey" and "coup de grâce" pecan pie, not to mention a "fabulous" staff.

Goode Co. Seafood [S] 23 | 18 | 20 | $21

2621 Westpark Dr. (Kirby Dr.), 713-523-7154
10211 Katy Frwy./I-10 W. (Gessner Dr.), 713-464-7933

■ "Thick and zesty" gumbo is what insiders seek "when it's cold" outside at this "bustling" pair of seafood diners (the "funky" railroad-car "classic" on Kirby and a newer, "more upscale" offshoot out on I-10); fin fans wonder could "there be anything better" than its "terrific" fried and oven-roasted oysters, mesquite-grilled fish or "extra-fantastic" seviche presented in a sundae glass?

Irma's 22 17 21 $16
22 N. Chenevert St. (Ruiz St.), 713-222-0767

◪ "Don't tell anyone else how good the food is here" plead amigos of this "funky" Warehouse District Tex-Mex where "sweet" Irma Galvan's lemonade quenches the thirst of the customers in her always "crowded" dining room; it's "perfect for a pre-game dinner", never mind if the "irritating" spoken menu of roughly "three dishes, no changes" prompts a few grumbles about "enchilada Nazis."

Khyber North Indian Grill [S] 22 17 19 $20
2510 Richmond Ave. (Kirby Dr.), 713-942-9424

■ Owner Mickey Kapoor "makes serious Indian food fun" at this River Oaks cafe where customers cheer the selection of spicy "grilled meats" and the "minimal use of oil" ("finally, healthy food with taste!"), as well as the "great prices" and "really nice" staff; while "the excellent lunch buffet is worth every penny", insiders prefer to ask for the "chef's assortment platter", which may be the "best item not on the menu."

La Griglia [S] 24 23 22 $32
River Oaks Ctr., 2002 W. Gray St. (McDuffie St.), 713-526-4700

■ When the "River Oaks crowd wants to be casual", it often heads to this Northern Italian prizewinner" courtesy of Tony Vallone, where the "funky interior" houses a "great kitchen", a staff that operates with "tag-team precision" and "the highest density of young, beautiful people" in town; no surprise that some down-to-earth types find it just "too noisy", too "snobby" and "too 'in.'"

La Mora Cucina Toscana 25 23 23 $32
912 Lovett Blvd. (Montrose Blvd.), 713-522-7412

■ "That's *amore*" sigh surveyors smitten with this "top-notch" Northern Italian "gem" that's "as romantic as it gets" thanks to its "serene", "lovely setting" in a "well-hidden" Montrose "villa"; chef-owner Lynette Mandola's "exquisite" Tuscan fare (such as "light and airy gnocchi" and the "best" *ribollita*) sets hearts aflutter, while the "charming" staff treats diners "like valued friends", all of which "makes the uncomfortable chairs worth sitting on."

La Réserve 28 27 26 $53
Omni Hotel, 4 Riverway (Woodway Dr.), 713-871-8177

■ "Serious" from its "quiet", "elegant ambiance" to chef Mercer Mohr's "outstanding", meticulously rendered Classic French menu, this "beautiful" Galleria hotel dining room "can't be beat" as a "place to dress up and have a special night out"; it boasts a "fabulous seasonal menu" backed by a "well-selected" list of wines and "professional" service, but better "bring your platinum" card; P.S. it features one of the "best Christmas buffets in town."

Mark's American Cuisine [S] 28 25 25 $43
1658 Westheimer Rd. (bet. Dunlavy & Ralph Sts.), 713-523-3800

■ "Feast at the altar of haute cuisine" at this "simply superlative" New American "cathedral of innovation" (voted No. 1 for Food in Houston) in Montrose, where acolytes report a near-"religious experience" thanks to "genius" chef-owner Mark Cox's "inspired" creations that find a fittingly "celestial" backdrop in this "chic" converted "brick church"; the only hint of impiety regards the "claustrophobically" "close quarters", though a recent renovation may be the answer to surveyors' prayers.

Morton's of Chicago [S]

25 | 23 | 24 | $48

Centre at Post Oak, 5000 Westheimer Rd. (Post Oak Blvd.), 713-629-1946

■ The "dark" lighting and "masculine atmosphere" at this Galleria link of the upscale chophouse chain (perhaps "the best thing Chicago ever exported") provide a "clubby" environment for its "fabulously presented", "superb steaks"; for many admirers, it adds up to the carnivorous "meal of the year" and the "No. 1 place" to visit when you "want to impress", but for the minority of the clientele not on "expense accounts", the "pretentious" experience may feel "overdone."

Mosquito Cafe [S]

25 | 20 | 21 | $18

628 14th St. (Church St.), Galveston, 409-763-1010

■ It's "worth seeking" this "out-of-the-way" "jewel" of an Eclectic cafe housed in a "hip, cute" renovated building in Galveston's historic district; on an island fusty with fried fish, its "inventive", "healthy food prepared with inspiration" is a "pleasant" "breath of fresh air" "for vegetarians" and carnivores alike.

Ouisie's Table

23 | 22 | 20 | $30

3939 San Felipe St. (bet. Drexel Dr. & Willowick Rd.), 713-528-2264

◪ There's "always something great on the chalkboard" at "nice lady" Elouise Cooper Jones' "welcoming" and "hip" Southern-Eclectic, which River Oaks denizens find "a pleasant lunch spot", as well as a "first-class" choice for "delicious" dinner dishes that spin "fresh takes on old favorites" (like shrimp-and-cheese grits and fried oysters); keep in mind, though, that the experience may "cost more than you'd expect."

Pappas Bros. Steakhouse

26 | 24 | 24 | $49

5839 Westheimer Rd. (Bering Dr.), 713-780-7352

■ Yes, "there are a lot of steakhouses in Houston", but this "handsome" Pappas family contender near the Galleria is "among the best"; "oil tycoons" appreciate the "impeccable service", "excellent wine list", "wonderful sides" and, of course, the "select" beef (though the place's cigar-friendliness prompts some to label it "more humidor than restaurant"); "just make sure someone else picks up the tab", because it can be "insanely expensive."

Rainbow Lodge [S]

23 | 27 | 21 | $40

1 Birdsall St. (Memorial Dr.), 713-861-8666

■ Enraptured visitors to this charmer beside Buffalo Bayou "can't say enough good things" about its "beautiful setting", a "country hunting lodge" filled with antiques, where diners "watch for peacocks" and wildlife while roaming a menu of "excellent game" and Gulf Coast seafood dishes; it's quite a "wonderful choice for romantic" meals (never mind if there are a few "too many prom dresses" within its "pretty" rooms).

Riviera Grill

26 | 17 | 23 | $37

Radisson Suites, 10655 Katy Frwy./I-10 W. (Sam Houston Pkwy.), 713-974-4445

■ "Master chef" John Sheely does such an "outstanding" job "with everything" on his "varied" New American–French menu that Westside locals swear "you wouldn't be able to get a table" if his eatery were located in a, ahem, "better facility"; housed in the Radisson Suites, it's "not much to look at, but what food!" (don't miss his signature pepper-crusted sea bass with tomato ragout), so get in on this "unpretentious", "wonderful surprise."

Rotisserie for Beef & Bird | 26 | 23 | 25 | $43

2200 Wilcrest Dr. (Westheimer Rd.), 713-977-9524

■ In this mad, mad world it's hard to find a restaurant that's been "very, very good" for a couple dozen years, but this "superb" Far West traditional American still garners raves from diners who indulge their "more exotic moods" with its "excellent wild game dishes" and "inspired wine list"; an "elegant dining atmosphere" rounds out the "delightful" experience at this "classic."

Ruggles Grill [S] | 25 | 18 | 17 | $33

903 Westheimer Rd. (Montrose Blvd.), 713-524-3839

■ At Bruce and Susan Molzan's Montrose mothership, "enormous helpings" of "adventurous" Southwestern–New American fare eventually land on your table after "always-long waits", "even with reservations"; for such an "awesome" meal, masochistic mavens are willing to "suffer" "claustrophobic" seating and "legendarily" "snobby" service, but not without griping that this is "not a tightly run ship."

Ruggles Grille 5115 | 25 | 25 | 21 | $36

Saks Fifth Avenue, The Galleria, 5115 Westheimer Rd. (bet. Post Oak Blvd. & Sage Rd.), 713-963-8067

■ Take a Galleria breather to "sink into a posh chair and dig into the richest desserts you've ever tasted", preceded by "creative" New American–French dishes served in "huge portions" at this "swanky sanctuary" tucked inside Saks; it's "a special place to dine within a special place to shop" say bag-laden buyers who bless this "oasis of peace" for service that's "much better than at the original."

Ruth's Chris Steak House [S] | 27 | 22 | 24 | $45

6213 Richmond Ave. (bet. Fountain View Dr. & Hillcroft Ave.), 713-789-2333
14135 Southwest Frwy./Hwy. 59 S. (bet. Dairy Ashford Rd. & Williams Trace Blvd.), Sugar Land, 281-491-9300

■ Houston's chophouse of choice, this "excellent" chain is simply "the best you're ever going to have" swear carnivores partial to these franchises west of the Galleria and in Sugar Land; "always perfect" and "sizzling" and accompanied by "fabulous" sides ("their asparagus – yum!"), the prime steaks are served in an "elegant" setting, offering a "quality" way to blow your oil millions.

Saba Blue Water Cafe | – | – | – | M

416 Main St. (bet. Prairie & Preston Sts.), 713-228-7222

A jaw-dropping beauty of an aquarium with a beachy backdrop mural of cavorting nudes dominates this techno-sleek Downtown diner, complementing the menu of sexy salads and entrees inspired by islands spanning the seas from Asia to the Caribbean.

Scott's Cellar | 24 | 25 | 24 | $50

(fka Scott Chen's)

6540 San Felipe Dr. (Voss Rd.), 713-785-8889

■ Supplicants "save up" for the "radical", "adventurous" Asian-Continental menu and a "wine list from the gods" at this chef-owned Memorial "fusion heaven"; the five-course "White Glove" tasting menu bestows "an evening's entertainment for the senses", stoking quiet foodie fervor amid the "beautiful" dining rooms and a "lounge with a fireplace"; bear in mind that the tabs "can really get expensive", but worshipers whisper it's "worth it" – "at any price."

Tony Mandola's Gulf Coast Kitchen [S]

23 | 18 | 21 | $27

River Oaks Ctr., 1962 W. Gray St. (McDuffie St.), 713-528-3474

■ Its West Gray locale is "perfect for a long lunch away from Downtown offices" say suits who "drop in" "at least once a week" at this "friendly, happy" Cajun-Italian "seafood heaven" and fight the "temptation to fill up on" the "outstanding appetizers" so that they'll have room for the "great variety" of "fresh" fish; with "excellent waiters" and "always-on-time reservations", no wonder its a "neighborhood favorite."

Tony Ruppe's

26 | 22 | 22 | $40

3939 Montrose Blvd. (bet. Richmond Ave. & W. Alabama St.), 713-852-0852

■ What style mavens label "'Montrose's fanciest restaurant' lives up to its reputation" for "fabulously crafted", "exquisitely good" New American cuisine "that's down-home but with class" enough to "hold its own in Manhattan"; "even the burgers are gourmet" thanks to the "hard work" and "passion" of "wonderful host" chef Tony Ruppe, who personally "checks on the progress and needs" of "relaxed" patrons in the dining room's minimalist "multi-story atrium."

Tony's [S]

26 | 25 | 26 | $60

1801 Post Oak Blvd. (San Felipe St.), 713-622-6778

■ "If God makes a reservation in Houston, it should be" at this Galleria Continental gush groupies of this "star of the Tony Vallone empire"; *the* place to "view Houston's society set in action", "Big T's" "continues to do a top-notch job" delivering "dreamy" dishes to the "diner who has everything", as well as to those who simply aspire to "feel like a baron or baroness" luxuriating in a "sexy" environment "where any request is greeted warmly."

Zula [S]

– | – | – | E

705 Main St. (Capitol St.), 713-227-7052

Thanks to the concerted efforts of owners Dave Edwards and Steve Fronterhouse and showy chef Lance Fegen, this flashy, multi-million-dollar, split-level Downtown haunt is absolutely fabulous, right down to its glossy black doggy boxes; spit-and-polish professionals flock for glam dinners of foie gras and lobster, while the budget-minded congregate at lunch.

TOP 10 FOOD RANKING

Restaurant	Cuisine Type
26 Stroud's	American
American Restaurant	New American
Plaza III	Steakhouse
25 Starker's Reserve	New American
Stolen Grill	New American
Metropolis	New American
Ruth's Chris	Steakhouse
Cafe Allegro	New American
Café Sebastienne	New American
Tatsu's	Classic French

ADDITIONAL NOTEWORTHY PLACES

Bristol Bar & Grill	Seafood
D'Bronx	Pizza/Sandwich Shop
Fiorella's Jack Stack	Barbecue
Garozzo's	N&S Italian
Grand St. Cafe	Eclectic
Grille on Broadway	New American
Le Fou Frog	French Bistro
Lidia's	Northern Italian
McCormick & Schmick's	Seafood
zin	New American

F	D	S	C

American Restaurant — 26 | 25 | 26 | $52

Crown Ctr., 200 E. 25th St. (Grand Ave.), 816-426-1133

■ As "romantic" as "a big Valentine", this "stunning" Downtown "icon" is the "perfect place if you're in the mood to be pampered"; "a favorite spot for a special occasion", it promises "a meal made in heaven" – a "fabulous", daily changing New American menu courtesy of new chef Celina Tio, paired with an "exquisite wine list" and proffered by an "impeccable" staff ("you won't get better service" in this town) in a "gorgeous room" with a "beautiful view" of the skyline.

Bristol Bar & Grill Ⓢ — 24 | 22 | 22 | $34

5400 W. 119th St. (Nall Ave.), Leawood, KS, 913-663-5777

■ "Fresh-from-the-oven" sugary biscuits that are "alone worth the trip", fish so pristine it "almost jumps off the plate" and a "glutton's delight" Sunday brunch draw discerning diners to Leawood to this "suburban reincarnation of a classic Plaza restaurant"; "one of the busiest places in town", it's well-manned by "enthusiastic" servers, but note that the room can get quite "noisy" because "a lot's going on."

Cafe Allegro
25 | 19 | 24 | $47

1815 W. 39th St. (bet. Bell St. & State Line Rd.), 816-561-3663

◪ "The long-standing grande dame of 39th Street's restaurant row has kept foodies' attention year after year" with "splendid" New American dishes "carefully prepared and appealingly presented" (don't miss the "decadent" signature 'hot and gooey chocolate soufflé'); while most concur that the fare "can stand toe-to-toe with any big-city fine-dining establishment", "disappointed" dissenters feel it's "overrated" and "way expensive for what you get" and reserve special barbs for the service that "borders on rude and abrasive."

Café Sebastienne [S]
25 | 24 | 21 | $31

Kemper Museum of Contemporary Art, 4420 Warwick Blvd. (45th St.), 816-561-7740

■ Chef Jennifer Maloney's "quirky and delicious" New American cooking, distinguished by "intriguing combinations of flavor", "takes full advantage of what's fresh and seasonal"; as befits its setting in the Plaza's Kemper Museum, the cafe is adorned with a monumental series of oil paintings by Frederick James Brown ("free art with every meal"), which results in a "unique refuge from the ordinary"; just one "regret": dinner is served only on Fridays and Saturdays, but the "menu changes weekly" and it makes for a "great end to a day of viewing beautiful works."

D'Bronx
24 | 12 | 15 | $11

3904 Bell St. (39th St.), 816-531-0550
Crown Ctr., 2450 Grand Ave. (25th St.), 816-842-2211 [S]

■ For "D'best" pizzas and deli sandwiches (notably a "Reuben to die for") "in town, period", head straight to one of these two "quintessential", "very busy" Italian joints ("run by a family loaded with personality") Downtown and in Midtown to "take a break from the diet your cardiologist prescribed"; since you're already not counting calories, top off the meal with a slice of the "amazing" sour cream apple pie; any wonder that you'll always find a "good cross section of Kansas City" "hanging" here?

Fiorella's Jack Stack [S]
24 | 21 | 20 | $20

13441 Holmes Rd. (135th St.), 816-942-9141
101 W. 22nd St. (Wyandotte St.), 816-472-7427
9520 Metcalf Ave. (95th St.), Overland Park, KS, 913-385-7427

■ "Don't wear your best shirt" if you're visiting this "killer" BBQ chainlet, voted the Most Popular restaurant in Kansas City, because the "amazing" vittles are finger-lickingly messy (especially the crown prime short ribs) and they're teamed with "out-of-this-world sides" (including "baked beans good enough to commit crimes for"); one caveat: no reservations accepted.

Garozzo's
22 | 15 | 19 | $24

526 Harrison St. (Missouri Ave.), 816-221-2455
12801 E. Hwy. 40 (Norfleet Rd.), Independence, 816-737-2400 [S]
1514 NE Rice Rd. (Hwy. 291), Lee's Summit, 816-554-2800 [S]
9950 College Blvd. (Mastin St.), Overland Park, KS, 913-491-8300 [S]

◪ "Frank Sinatra is always playing" in the background and the "garlic just won't stop" at this "big, hearty, old-style" Italian institution; it's "very noisy", "always busy" and the portions are so "large" they can "scare you", but you "won't find chicken *spiedini* as good anywhere else", nor servers as "entertaining."

Grand St. Cafe S   23 | 22 | 23 | $31 |
4740 Grand St. (47th St.), 816-561-8000

■ At this Plaza "jewel", the "wonderful variety" of "unique", "trend-conscious" Eclectic dishes "reflects the region's resources and tastes", making it "a good spot to take out-of-towners for a taste of Kansas City" ("you must try the huge pork chop" and "decadent phyllo brownie dessert"); combined with pleasant patio dining, "affable" service and live jazz, it adds up to "a relaxing and enjoyable place" that's "well above average across the board"; P.S. check out the "wonderful Sunday brunch."

Grille on Broadway   25 | 15 | 21 | $32 |
3605 Broadway (Valentine Rd.), 816-531-0700

■ "Tucked away in Midtown", this "cozy" "sleeper" is "one of the best spots for a romantic little getaway"; the New American menu emphasizes "excellent, creative seafood" dishes prepared "with flair" (while the "Chilean sea bass is always a winner" and the "crab cakes alone are worth the trip", "don't overlook the fish specials") and the "personable service reminds one of the days when unobtrusive friendliness was an art", but the quarters are "miniscule", so "claustrophobes" better "get used to very little elbow room."

Le Fou Frog S   24 | 15 | 20 | $40 |
400 E. Fifth St. (Oak St.), 816-474-6060

■ Don't be deterred by the "deceptively bland exterior" of this "cheeky" French bistro in the River Market area because the kitchen shows "a lot of dedication to food" and the "marvelous" cooking is well enhanced by a "smart wine list", which explains why "everyone from twentysomething hipsters to big-shot lawyers and judges eat here with gusto"; follow the lead of the "completely smitten" and just "relax and enjoy the hustle and bustle" of this "cozy, splendid little place" while "friendly, prompt" servers tend to your needs.

Lidia's S   22 | 27 | 21 | $32 |
101 W. 22nd St. (Baltimore Ave.), 816-221-3722

◪ Boasting a "drop-dead gorgeous" interior designed by David Rockwell, this "lively" Northern Italian set in an "old train depot" just north of Union Station is the co-creation of Lidia Bastianich; exuding "a sense of excitement and anticipation", it features "generously portioned" dishes at relatively "wallet-pleasing" prices, notably a daily changing "pasta sampler" for $12, along with a wine list where every bottle costs only $18; detractors, however, find it "disappointingly mediocre" and lament "if only the food could be stepped up a few notches to match the atmosphere."

McCormick & Schmick's S   24 | 25 | 22 | $36 |
448 W. 47th St. (Pennsylvania Ave.), 816-531-6800

■ "For landlocked Midwesterners", this "upscale" seafood house is "the answer", thrilling fin fanatics with a "selection bar none" of "fish so fresh it may still be jumping on your plate" and an "impressive" oyster bar that "must be a wonderful dream"; perhaps even more "fabulous" is the "extraordinary" interior appointed with a "majestic stained-glass dome", mahogany woodwork and brass fixtures, and the "picturesque" deck "overlooking the Plaza"; even those who are "totally against chains have to admit that this one does a great job."

Metropolis American Grill | 25 | 20 | 23 | $36

303 Westport Rd. (Central St.), 816-753-1550

■ A "popular outpost for the well-heeled set", this "tiny gem" in Westport attracts adventurous appetites with "inventive" New American dishes accented with "lots of ethnic influences" (think "phenomenal" tandoori sea bass and "memorable" wild mushroom strudel) and "uniquely presented"; while "this is definitely not Midwestern fare" (neither, perhaps, is the "super-cool" decor), this "indescribably good favorite is always a treat", and though the quarters are "small and tight", the "nicest" owners somehow "make the space sparkle."

Plaza III The Steakhouse | 26 | 23 | 24 | $42

Country Club Plaza, 4749 Pennsylvania Ave. (Ward Pkwy.), 816-753-0000

■ Though "the world may change", thankfully this Plaza palace of beef "stays the same" say longtime loyalists; "red meat rules here, so just leave the guilt at home" and fork into the "best steak in Kansas City", so "perfectly cooked" and "deliciously tender" that "cows should line up for the chance to be served"; rounding out the picture is an award-winning wine list, "throwback" "classic" setting and "knowledgeable", "polite" staff.

Ruth's Chris Steak House [S] | 25 | 21 | 22 | $46

700 W. 47th St. (Jefferson St.), 816-531-4800

◪ If you like your beef "sizzling, juicy" and "soaked in butter", amble over to this Plaza franchise, which has earned begrudging respect from many locals ("a chain steakhouse in Kansas City? – horrors!") and is "doing very well in a city that knows its meat"; "for the price, you may be able to buy your own cow", so "save this place for the expense account", though hometown supporters who are adamant that you "can find better chops" in this town conclude "an admirable effort, but not quite the prime cut of other mainstays."

Starker's Reserve | 25 | 23 | 24 | $43

Country Club Plaza, 201 W. 47th St. (Wyandotte St.), 816-753-3565

■ Overlooking Country Club Plaza, this "charming hideaway" appointed with country French decor is "renowned" for its "mind-boggling wine list", which beautifully accompanies a "quietly superb", regularly changing New American menu (the signature herb-roasted rack of lamb is "not to be missed") presented by a "classy" staff that "attends to every human need without hovering"; while a few find it all "a bit staid", admirers cherish it as a "special-occasion" "gem" that always promises a "magical evening."

Stolen Grill | 25 | 18 | 23 | $40

904 Westport Rd. (Southwest Trafficway), 816-960-1450

■ "Located just off the beaten path" in Westport, this "innovative and warmhearted" New American bistro is a "great discovery" say followers of "talented chef" Tim Doolittle, who executes a "limited" but "ever changing" menu of "flavorful dishes" that are "artfully presented"; it's set in an "intimate", "lovely" storefront with "exposed brick walls that give it a casual, big-city feel", and even if it could stand "a bigger room or fewer tables", the enchanted "can't recommend it highly enough."

Stroud's 🆂   26 13 20 $19

1015 E. 85th Ave. (Troost Ave.), 816-333-2132
5410 NE Oak Ridge Rd. (bet. I-35 & Vivion Rd.), 816-454-9600

■ "Forget your diet, forget your arteries" – "if it's pan-fried chicken
you want, this is the place" exclaim enthusiasts of this "campy"
pair of traditional American roadhouses on the South Side and
Northland, whose "down-home" cooking is so "mouthwatering"
(don't pass up the "absolutely sinful cinnamon rolls" either) that it
was voted No. 1 for Food in Kansas City; sure, "there's always a
line out the door", but "just bring a lawn chair, a novel and some
snacks to tide you over" – it's definitely "worth the wait."

Tatsu's   25 19 22 $36

4603 W. 90th St. (Roe Ave.), Prairie Village, KS, 913-383-9801

☑ "Consistently exquisite year after year after year", this "haute"
French grande dame in "out-of-the-way" Prairie Village appeals to
an "older crowd" with its "conservative" (or "overly traditional"?),
"rich" "classics" napped with "delectable sauces"; though it's a
"solid performer", detractors lament that it's "rarely exciting or
memorable" and suggest the "clichéd" "menu could use some
new life" (bigger portions too).

zin   24 23 22 $43

1900 Main St. (19th St.), 816-527-0120

☑ "For a meat 'n' potatoes town", this "happy, hopping" New
American addition to Downtown's Crossroads art district is "doing
very well" thanks to a "clever", "constantly changing" menu that's
always "a fresh surprise", teamed with a "brainy wine list" (natch,
as it's named after the diminutive term for Zinfandel) and turned
out in "swankily" "minimalist" environs; though dissenters find it
"a bit contrived" and warn about "small" portions ("plan to leave
hungry"), "nothing else in Kansas City feels as urban" as this
"one-of-a-kind" "up-and-comer."

Las Vegas

TOP 20 FOOD RANKING

Restaurant	Cuisine Type
28 Renoir	New French
Aqua	Seafood
27 Picasso	New French
Andre's	Classic French
Le Cirque	Classic French
Nobu	Japanese/Peruvian
Prime	Steakhouse
Morton's of Chicago	Steakhouse
26 Rosemary's	New American
Delmonico	Steakhouse
Steak House	Steakhouse
Mayflower Cuisinier	Chinese
Trumpets	New American
Michael's	American/Seafood
Wild Sage Cafe	New American
Palm	Seafood/Steakhouse
25 Emeril's New Orleans	Cajun-Creole/Seafood
Commander's Palace	Cajun/Creole
Hugo's Cellar	Continental/Steakhouse
Charlie Palmer	Steakhouse

ADDITIONAL NOTEWORTHY PLACES

Aureole	New American
Border Grill	Mexican
Cili	Pan-Asian/American
Eiffel Tower	Classic French
8-0-8	Pacific Rim/Fusion
Mon Ami Gabi	French Bistro
Napa	Californian/Classic French
NOBHILL	American
Osterio del Circo	Northern Italian
Piero's	Northern Italian
Piero Selvaggio Valentino	Northern Italian
Postrio	New American
Ruth's Chris	Steakhouse
Samba	Brazilian/Steakhouse
Spago	Californian/New American
Spiedini	N&S Italian
St. James at the London Club	International
Terrazza	Northern Italian
Top of the World	Continental
Verandah	Eclectic/American

Andre's ◐ | 27 | 25 | 26 | $59 |

401 S. Sixth St. (bet. Bridge & Lewis Aves.), 702-385-5016

Andre's in the Monte Carlo ◐[S]

Monte Carlo Resort & Casino, 3770 Las Vegas Blvd. S. (bet. Harmon & Tropicana Aves.), 702-798-7151

■ "Pure Andre" is local shorthand for "simply the best", which is how smitten fans view these two "romantic and special" Classic French "gems", one a "Downtown institution", the other a "Monte Carlo surprise"; chef Rochat is the man under the toque, and he knows how to produce "great cuisine", stock his cellars with "wonderful, rare wines" and then serve it all up in "comfortable, elegant" settings loaded with "European charm."

Aqua [S] | 28 | 25 | 26 | $62 |

Bellagio Hotel, 3600 Las Vegas Blvd. S. (Flamingo Rd.), 702-693-7111

■ "Neptune would be proud" of this Bellagio branch of an acclaimed San Francisco seafood house, where admirers are hooked on "the best fish in the desert", including "to-die-for lobster pot pie" and other "flawless" fin fare, as well as "anything with foie gras"; its "beautiful, modern setting" in the Conservatory and "top-class service" tip the scales to make this a "fabulous" experience, and though some mutineers mutter it's "too pricey", others opine "it's worth every penny."

Aureole [S] | 24 | 27 | 23 | $66 |

Mandalay Bay Hotel, 3950 Las Vegas Blvd. S. (Hacienda Ave.), 702-632-7401

■ The four-story "glass-walled Tower of Wine" is a "vision", as are the cable-powered "glitzy 'angels'" who retrieve your bottle from over 3,000 choices at this Mandalay Bay New American, a flashier sibling of Charlie Palmer's NYC original; most hail the "highest-caliber" cuisine that's "successfully inventive" and swoon for the Swan Court (a separate room that overlooks a lake), but the disgruntled deem it "overrated" with prices that "soar as high as the architecture."

Border Grill [S] | 20 | 20 | 20 | $30 |

Mandalay Bay Hotel, 3950 Las Vegas Blvd. S. (Hacienda Ave.), 702-632-7403

◪ "Go, ladies!" cheer champions of this "incomparable upscale Mexican", a Mandalay Bay offspring of Mary Sue Milliken and Susan Feniger, the Food Network's *Too Hot Tamales*; "great margaritas" douse "spicy, fantastic" fare that includes "sublime chips and salsa" and "phenomenal seviche", and a "funky" setting with "poolside" patio also elicits *olés*; some hotheads, however, roast it as "overpriced" and "watered down."

Charlie Palmer Steak [S] | 25 | 26 | 25 | $62 |

Four Seasons Hotel, 3960 Las Vegas Blvd. S. (Hacienda Ave.), 702-632-5120

■ "Tucked away in the blissfully quiet Four Seasons", this steakhouse is a "popular" "oasis" with a "luxurious" ambiance; Aureole's Charlie Palmer puts his special spin on "absolutely exquisite" beef and "outstanding side dishes" and offers a "great" (though "pricey") wine list; the "superior service" in this "classy setting" makes for an evening of "pure comfort."

Cili §　　　　　　　– | – | – | VE |

*Bali Hai Golf Club, 5160 Las Vegas Blvd. S. (Russell Rd.),
702-856-1000*

Bali Hai Golf Club on the Strip called, and Wolfgang Puck answered
with a new Pan-Asian–American honeybun that'll provide you with
some enchanted evenings (or brunches or lunches) as you dine
on tandoori lamb chops, Thai chicken salad and the like, while
the tropical decor indoors and view of the greens from the patio
will inspire lots of happy talk; its name derives from the Balinese
word for 'prosperity and good health', a grace note from the
cockeyed optimist chef.

Commander's Palace §　　　　25 | 25 | 26 | $52 |

*Desert Passage at Aladdin, 3663 Las Vegas Blvd. S. (Harmon Ave.),
702-892-8272*

■ "Y'all will find Southern hospitality" at this "elegant" Cajun-
Creole newcomer in the Aladdin's Desert Passage; loyal subjects
say it's "as good or better than the New Orleans original", and
portions of "excellent stone-ground grits" with goat cheese, "must-
try turtle soup" and "extremely fresh fish" are big, but not easy on
the wallet (it's "pricey"); Dixieland jazz at Sunday brunch, the "best"
complimentary pralines and the presence of Brad Brennan (of
the famed N'Awlins restaurant dynasty) add to the authenticity.

Delmonico §　　　　　26 | 24 | 25 | $59 |

*Venetian Hotel, 3355 Las Vegas Blvd. S. (bet. Flamingo &
Spring Mountain Rds.), 702-414-3737*

■ Essentially, it's "the very best of Emeril" at chef Lagasse's
"gourmet" steakhouse in the Venetian Hotel, where you can dine
à la bam on "excellent garlic mashed potatoes" and other favorites,
washed down by wines from a list "longer than most novels";
service is the "tops in town", "friendly but with a high degree
of professionalism", and though a few beef about the decor,
calling it "too severe", it doesn't stop the stampedes, so "book
months in advance."

Eiffel Tower §　　　　　22 | 26 | 22 | $71 |

*Paris Las Vegas, 3655 Las Vegas Blvd. S. (bet. Flamingo Rd. & Harmon Ave.),
702-948-6937*

■ The "incredible view of the Strip and Bellagio fountains" is
an eyeful at this literally "haute French" at the Paris, where the
"marvelous food", including "superb foie gras" and "just-right
lamb", is also to-sigh-for; even those who find the "way expensive"
l'addition in-Seine admit it's an "unbelievable experience."

8-0-8 §　　　　　　　– | – | – | VE |

*Caesars Palace, 3570 Las Vegas Blvd. S. (Flamingo Rd.),
702-731-7110*

Chef Jean-Marie Josselin hulas into town with this new Pacific
Rim fusion seafood house (with a French accent) in Caesars
Palace; it's named for Hawaii's area code, and, appropriately,
the phones are ringing off the hook as diners dial for a table in
the island-themed room; as for the food prepared under the
toqueship of Wesley Coffel, the Deconstruction Ahi Roll – tuna
tartare, avocado, white truffle dressing – is splendid proof of how
well this creative cuisine can work.

Emeril's New Orleans Fish House S 　25 | 22 | 25 | $49

MGM Grand Hotel, 3799 Las Vegas Blvd. S. (Tropicana Ave.), 702-891-7374
☑ Starstruck surveyors say the "absolutely fabulous" Big Easy eats "really kick it up a notch" at this MGM Grand Cajun-Creole seafood house where the "sparkling fresh fish" is followed by "the best banana cream pie", ensuring that "everybody here is having a great time"; critics carping "there's something fishy" about "overhyped" fare and "sloppy service" wish the telechef would "check up on his establishment" and offer more 'bam' "for the buck."

Hugo's Cellar S 　　　　　25 | 23 | 25 | $44

Four Queens Hotel, 202 Fremont St. (Casino Center Blvd.), 702-385-4011
■ "Elegant and timeless", this "Downtown institution" provides a "delightful dining experience" starting with "a rose for every lady"; the "classic" Continental steakhouse dinners include an "unbelievable salad cart" and "exceptional entrees" and end with "special chocolate-dipped fruit" after dessert, all served by a "charming" staff; though antagonists abase it as "past its prime", most maintain this 25-year-old is "still a winner."

Le Cirque S 　　　　　　27 | 26 | 26 | $74

Bellagio Hotel, 3600 Las Vegas Blvd. S. (Flamingo Rd.), 702-693-8100
■ "As good as the NYC original", this "fabulous" French at the Bellagio is "luxury defined" ("but not at all pretentious"), offering "impeccable service" in a "gorgeous" setting overlooking the lake; the "extraordinarily flavorful" fare is "elevated to art", "perfectly complemented by exquisite wines", with "delightful desserts" as epilogue; epicureans agree "it's a joyous place to eat, drink and be merry" despite "eye-popping prices"; N.B. jacket and tie required.

Mayflower Cuisinier 　　　　26 | 20 | 23 | $34

Sahara Pavilion, 4750 W. Sahara Ave. (Decatur Blvd.), 702-870-8432
■ Pilgrims give thanks for this "unsurpassed" West Side Chinese "with French flair" where "incredible chef Ming See Woo" wows 'em with "the best noodles", "great fish" and "delicate sauces" that create "unusual flavors"; the "delightful decor" includes "outstanding artwork", and the "personal service" helps make this a "must-visit."

Michael's S 　　　　　　26 | 22 | 26 | $64

Barbary Coast Hotel, 3595 Las Vegas Blvd. S. (Flamingo Rd.), 702-737-7111
■ "The staff fawns over you as you fawn over the food" at this Barbary Coast vet where VIPs have "every whim attended to" as they dine on "ultimate gourmet" American fare like "the best stone crabs" and "divine shrimp scampi", preceded by a complimentary "relish tray full of delicacies"; the "classy", "quiet" setting features "lots of dark wood and red leather chairs" that produce an "old-world" feeling, but the "outrageous prices" are up-to-the-minute.

Mon Ami Gabi S 　　　　　23 | 25 | 22 | $38

Paris Las Vegas, 3655 Las Vegas Blvd. S. (bet. Flamingo Rd. & Harmon Ave.), 702-944-4224
■ Francophiles profess it's "like eating on the Champs Elysées" at this "charming French bistro" at the Paris, where the "fantastic people-watching" and "beautiful view of the Bellagio fountains" are equaled by the *très* "yummy food" and "good wines"; some shun the "slow service", but most say it's a "great experience."

Morton's of Chicago [S] 27 | 25 | 24 | $52

400 E. Flamingo Rd. (Paradise Rd.), 702-893-0703

■ In a city where steakhouses abound, this East Side chain link of a "beef-eaters' bonanza" sets the "gold standard", serving "simply the best" steak, "delicious seafood" and "decadent desserts"; a recent move elicits encomiums for "elegant surroundings" that "enhance" the experience, and though wallet-watchers warn "you'll pay a ton", weight-lifters retort it's "worth it every time."

Napa 24 | 24 | 24 | $64

Rio All-Suite Hotel, 3700 W. Flamingo Rd. (bet. I-15 & Valley View Blvd.), 702-247-7961

◪ Chef Jean-Louis Palladin is "a master at what he does", capable of producing "innovative", even "ethereal food" at his art-filled Californian with French influences in the Rio that boasts a "wonderful, relaxing atmosphere"; those who would bypass this valley caution go "only when the chef is there."

NOBHILL [S]⊄ – | – | – | E

MGM Grand Hotel, 3799 Las Vegas Blvd. S. (Tropicana Ave.), 702-891-1111

Laid-back chic and dynamite cooking courtesy of chef Michael Mina and partner Charles Condy quickly made this relaxing addition to the MGM Grand a happening spot; paying homage to San Francisco, the American offerings range from artisanal breads baked hourly (irresistible stuff) to à la carte comfort foods to desserts warm from the showcase dining room oven.

Nobu ◐[S] 27 | 25 | 22 | $58

Hard Rock Hotel, 4455 Paradise Rd. (bet. Flamingo Rd. & Harmon Ave.), 702-693-5090

■ "As good as its NYC namesake" rave the reverent of the Hard Rock's "outstanding neo-Japanese"; "sit at the sushi bar to marvel at the preparation" of "exquisite fresh fish" with a "spicy approach", or spring for the "heavenly" tasting menu consisting of a lineup of "exotic dishes with no anticlimax"; there's also "great celebrity spotting" in the "Zen-like setting", but a few dharma bums bash the minimalist portions and "way-out-there prices."

Osteria del Circo [S] 24 | 26 | 24 | $52

Bellagio Hotel, 3600 Las Vegas Blvd. S. (Flamingo Rd.), 702-693-8150

■ It's all in *la famiglia* at this Bellagio bistro managed by a son of Sirio (that's Maccioni, as in the more formal Le Cirque next door), who serves up "superb" Northern Italian fare inspired by mama Egidiana and prepared by chef de cuisine James Benson; the "whimsical" circus-themed, Adam Tihany–designed setting and "spectacular view of the fountain show" on 'Lake Como' provide a fitting overture for the "creative" yet "authentic" cooking.

Palm [S] 26 | 22 | 24 | $50

Forum Shops at Caesars, 3500 Las Vegas Blvd. S. (Flamingo Rd.), 702-732-7256

■ "Steak and lobster fit for Caesar" say those 'frond' of this "always-superb" "national chain without a missing link" at the Forum Shops; "big spenders" spring for "tremendous portions" of "excellent food" and little spenders vie for "Vegas' best $15 prix fixe lunch", all delivered in a "clubhouse setting" with "celebrity-adorned walls"; it may be "noisy as hell", but gents can retreat to the loo and dig the Elvis look-alike attendant.

Picasso S   27 | 29 | 28 | $79

Bellagio Hotel, 3600 Las Vegas Blvd. S. (Flamingo Rd.),
702-693-7223

■ There are two "awe-inspiring" artists at this "destination" in the Bellagio, the *Las Vegas Survey*'s Most Popular; the one in the kitchen is "genius" Julian Serrano, whose "innovative" tasting and prix fixe menus comprising "flawlessly served" French dishes are "spectacular from start to finish"; the "opulent" interior includes "beautiful flowers", "lake views" and, oh yeah, Picasso paintings that make you "feel like you're dining in a museum"; in fact, the only thing that's not "*magnifico*" is a "hard-to-get" reservation, so book well in advance.

Piero Selvaggio Valentino S   23 | 21 | 22 | $57
(aka Valentino)

Venetian Hotel, 3355 Las Vegas Blvd. S. (bet. Flamingo &
Spring Mountain Rds.), 702-414-3000

◪ This "elegant" Venetian Hotel Northern Italian collects valentines from the cognoscenti, who call the cuisine "superb" (particularly the "wonderful pastas"), especially as it's accompanied by a "bang-up wine list" of more than 20,000 bottles and served by a staff that treats you "like royalty"; however, antagonists argue it's "oceans away from the LA" original, adding it's "overrated."

Piero's Italian Cuisine S   24 | 22 | 23 | $52

355 Convention Center Dr. (bet. Debbie Reynolds Dr. & Paradise Rd.),
702-369-2305

■ If you're "looking for the old Vegas", you'll find it at this off-Strip bastion of "upscale Northern Italian" eats known as "the place to network with local shakers" and a "celeb hangout"; a "good Caesar", "killer osso buco" and the "best Florida stone crabs" (in season) are served in a "romantic" setting with "dark lighting", though a few sniff at the "snooty waiters" and sneer it's "overpriced."

Postrio S   24 | 24 | 23 | $48

Venetian Hotel, 3355 Las Vegas Blvd. S. (bet. Flamingo &
Spring Mountain Rds.), 702-796-1110

■ "He's done it again" assert adherents of Wolfgang Puck's Venetian Hotel New American "delight" cloned from the San Francisco original; the "interesting menu" stars "great duck pizza" capped by the "planet's best crème brûlée", and if a few find it a bit "pretentious", its regulars rejoin "sit on the plaza and enjoy" the view of St. Mark's Square.

Prime Steakhouse S   27 | 28 | 27 | $64

Bellagio Hotel, 3600 Las Vegas Blvd. S. (Flamingo Rd.),
702-693-7111

■ Jean-Georges Vongerichten is in his prime at this "transcendent" Bellagio Hotel steakhouse, about which even blasé beef lovers burble like the "breathtaking fountains" viewed windowside; beyond "perfect steaks", partisans pick "fabulous" veggies and swoon for the "splendid", "airy" interior "draped in velvety blues and browns"; the staff is "concerned and prompt", and while you'll pay primo prices, it's "well worth it."

Renoir [S] 28 | 28 | 27 | $76

Mirage Hotel, 3400 Las Vegas Blvd. S. (Spring Mountain Rd.), 702-791-7353

■ The "sublime", "Paris-quality" meal is as much "a work of art" as the eponymous painter's originals adorning the walls of chef Alessandro Stratta's "superb" New French "heaven" at the Mirage, where the "imaginative" offerings – including an "outstanding tasting menu" – were voted "the very Top" for Food in the *Las Vegas Survey*; the "expert" staff works together "like a ballet" in "plush, romantic surroundings" that make for "a calm and relaxing world away from the chaos just outside the door."

Rosemary's [S] 26 | 22 | 24 | $45

W. Sahara Promenade, 8125 W. Sahara Ave. (bet. Buffalo Dr. & Cimarron Rd.), 702-869-2251

■ This New American West Side sophomore is "the biggest hit in the desert", with husband-and-wife toque team Michael and Wendy Jordan preparing a "marvelous selection" of "innovative" fare (try the "incredible Maytag blue cheese slaw" served with the signature BBQ shrimp), and if they "kick it up a notch", it's no accident: Mike cooked under Emeril in New Orleans; the "attractive" art-filled decor and "good service" also impress, and though a few grouse the "tables are too close together", a recent expansion should take care of it.

Ruth's Chris Steak House [S] 24 | 21 | 23 | $48

Citibank Park Plaza, 3900 Paradise Rd. (bet. Flamingo Rd. & Twain Ave.), 702-791-7011

Cameron Corner Shopping Ctr., 4561 W. Flamingo Rd. (bet. Arville St. & Decatur Blvd.), 702-248-7011 ◑

◪ "Always dependable", these steakhouse chain links on the East and West Sides are known for "unbeatable slabs o' beef" and a "range of wines" as well as a "knowledgeable staff"; opponents ruthlessly reveal an overuse of "butter camouflages the meat" and they're "definitely overpriced."

Samba Brazilian Steakhouse [S] 23 | 23 | 23 | $36

Mirage Hotel, 3400 Las Vegas Blvd. S. (Spring Mountain Rd.), 702-791-7111

■ Gluttonous gourmands can go to town at this "carnivore's paradise", courtesy of the Mirage and their "Brazilian-style feast" known as rodizio (which translates loosely as "more and more and still more keeps coming"); a hip-swaying "Latin beat" accompanies the rotisserie items, making this "dining and entertainment wrapped into one" – and all at a "reasonable price."

Spago [S] 25 | 22 | 23 | $42

Forum Shops at Caesars, 3500 Las Vegas Blvd. S. (Flamingo Rd.), 702-369-0360

■ "Always a favorite", this Wolfgang Puck pioneer in the Forum Shops at Caesars continues to "set the standard" with its "still cutting-edge menu" of Californian–New American fare; the wolf pack devours the signature "succulent salmon pizza" and partakes of "great people-watching" on the patio or in the "more elegant dining room", and though service comments roam from "warm" to "disappointing", the gang agrees it "lives up to the hype."

Spiedini [S] 23 | 24 | 22 | $39

Regent Las Vegas, 221 N. Rampart Blvd. (Summerlin Pkwy.), 702-869-8500

■ "It's fun to spend an evening" at this "it" Italian at the Regent in Summerlin, where "hospitable owner" Gustav Mauler and the "modern decor" create a "cozy" setting; the food's "excellent", the wine's "reasonable" and the "only drawback is the noise" from all the delighted diners.

Steak House [S] 26 | 23 | 25 | $38

Circus Circus Hotel, 2880 Las Vegas Blvd. S. (Sahara Ave.), 702-794-3767

■ There's "no clowning around with the steaks" at this "icon" set in the Circus Circus Hotel, where promoters parade into a "romantic atmosphere" for "huge portions" of "fantastic meats" and "excellent salads" at "best-bargain" prices; "be sure to reserve" in advance – it's a hot ticket – and check out the "out-of-this-world Sunday brunch."

St. James at the London Club [S] 25 | 25 | 24 | $62

(fka The London Club)

Aladdin Resort & Casino, 3667 Las Vegas Blvd. (bet. Flamingo Rd. & Harmon Ave.), 702-785-5788

Newly rechristened, this "exclusive club" at the Aladdin that's open to everyone still attracts a "high-end, multinational crowd" with its "surprisingly diverse" International menu of "superb" dishes inspired by Europe, the Mediterranean, China, Thailand, the Middle East and India, all served by a staff that makes even commoners "feel like royalty"; the exceptional chef's table with a sweeping view of the kitchen, "elegant" atmosphere and "gorgeous bar" and lounge only add to the "stylish" experience.

Terrazza [S] 22 | 24 | 23 | $46

Caesars Palace, 3570 Las Vegas Blvd. S. (Flamingo Rd.), 702-731-7568

■ Tucked into the Garden of the Gods at Caesars Palace, this Northern Italian features "elegant, well-prepared dishes" that are "delicious to the last bite", while the dining room offers "wonderful" ambiance and "solid", "attentive" service; P.S. "go early" because it can get "crowded."

Top of the World [S] 23 | 27 | 22 | $48

Stratosphere Hotel & Tower, 2000 Las Vegas Blvd. S. (north of Sahara Ave.), 702-380-7711

■ Even the most worldly sigh for the "stunning views" at this "romantic" revolving room high atop the Stratosphere; the "gourmet" Continental menu includes many "excellent choices" to pair with the "special wine list", and "experienced servers" are tops too, but wallet-watchers warn "bring lots of money" to cover the towering tariff.

Trumpets [S] 26 | 28 | 25 | $33

Sun City Anthem Ctr., 2450 Hampton Rd. (bet. Eastern Ave. & Horizon Ridge), Henderson, 702-614-5858

■ "Spectacular views of the city" hit the right note at this New American spot located in the recently built Anthem Center in Henderson; the menu is "wonderful", with service to match, and grown-ups go for the "quiet" ambiance (enhanced by a weekend jazz quartet) and get up early for the "great Sunday brunch."

Verandah 🅂   24 | 24 | 24 | $36 |

Four Seasons Hotel, 3960 Las Vegas Blvd. S. (Hacienda Ave.),
702-632-5000

■ The "epitome of elegance", this Four Seasons Eclectic-American boasts a "charming" interior and gardenside patio dining that's "conducive to relaxing with friends" over breakfast, lunch, dinner and "very good high tea"; detractors dismiss it as "an overgrown coffee shop", but the majority maintains the "food's wonderful" and the "service is excellent."

Wild Sage Cafe 🅂   26 | 21 | 23 | $31 |

600 E. Warm Springs Rd. (Amigo St.), 702-944-7243

■ "Puck prodigies" Laurie Kendrick and Stan Carroll run this "casual", "hip" New American, widely recognized as one of "the best off-Strip restaurants in town" thanks to an "imaginative menu and decor", "gorgeous preparations", "great breads" and "reasonable prices"; in short, it's just "what this city needed."

Long Island

TOP 20 FOOD RANKING

Restaurant	Cuisine Type
28 Mill River Inn	New American
27 Mirabelle	New French
Kotobuki	Japanese
Mirepoix	International
Peter Luger	Steakhouse
Panama Hatties	New American
La Plage	Eclectic
26 Tellers Chophouse	Steakhouse
Stone Creek Inn	New French/Med.
Mirko's	Continental/Eclectic
Da Ugo	N&S Italian
Sempre Vivolo	N&S Italian
La Piccola Liguria	Northern Italian
Sen	Japanese
Polo Grill	New American
Coolfish	New American
Trattoria Diane	Northern Italian
Piccolo	N&S Italian/New American
25 Louis XVI	New French
Stresa	N&S Italian

ADDITIONAL NOTEWORTHY PLACES

American Hotel	Classic French
Barney's	New French/New American
Blake's Bistro	New American
Bryant & Cooper	Steakhouse
Casa Rustica	N&S Italian
Della Femina	New American
Focaccia Grill	New American
Harvest on Fort Pond	N. Italian/Med.
La Marmite	Classic French/N&S Italian
La Pace	Northern Italian
L'Endroit	Classic French/N. Italian
Le Soir	French Bistro
Maidstone Arms	American
Mario	Northern Italian
Mazzi	Continental
Morton's of Chicago	Steakhouse
Palm	Steakhouse/Seafood
Palm Court at the Carltun	Continental/New American
Plaza Cafe	New American
Starr Boggs	Long Island

American Hotel [S] 25 | 24 | 22 | $55

The American Hotel, 25 Main St. (Washington St.), Sag Harbor, 631-725-3535

■ The "elegant grande dame of the East End", this Sag Harbor "landmark" (circa 1846) is "the place to go for special wines" to accompany "awesome", "incomparable" Classic French dishes served by a "professional" (if a tad "pretentious") staff; its "old-world ambiance" "takes diners back to a lost era", attracting an eclectic crowd of "celebrities", the "intelligentsia" and "tourists."

Barney's [S] 25 | 22 | 23 | $51

315 Buckram Rd. (Bayville Rd.), Locust Valley, 516-671-6300

■ Like an "intimate" "country inn" with a "charming setting", this "upscale" Locust Valley "gem" is beloved for its "superb, creative" French–New American menu, "exquisitely presented" by a "terrific" staff in "warm and inviting" surroundings (try to get a "candlelit table by the fireplace"); add on a "very good wine selection that complements the food" beautifully and the result is a "perfect" "getaway with your sweetie."

Blake's Bistro [S] 25 | 18 | 22 | $49

1066 Broadway (Franklin Pl.), Woodmere, 516-569-2259

■ Adventurous palates rave about chef-owner Blake Verity's "absolute genius" at masterminding "top-flight" New American meals in which "every course is a work of art"; though the wee Woodmere digs may be "tight" enough to induce "claustrophobia" in some sensitive sorts, others find the "tiny quarters" "cozy", making this "South Shore gem" a most "welcome addition."

Bryant & Cooper Steakhouse [S] 25 | 20 | 21 | $50

2 Middle Neck Rd. (Northern Blvd.), Roslyn, 516-627-7270

■ A "moneyed crowd" descends upon this "outstanding" "classic" steakhouse in Roslyn for "wonderfully aged", "sizable slabs" of prime cuts "cooked to perfection" and paired with "delicious sides" like "great creamed spinach"; "newcomers", though, "better know someone", since "regulars get preferential" treatment ("reservations don't seem to mean a thing" and the "gruff" staff tends to "play favorites"), but if you don't mind "watching the steaks age" while you "wait" for a table, it's "worth it."

Casa Rustica [S] 25 | 21 | 23 | $45

175 W. Main St. (Edgewood Ave.), Smithtown, 631-265-9265

■ "Back at the top of its game", this "romantic" "special-occasion" destination in Smithtown has unveiled an updated Italian menu, resulting in "interesting" dishes that are even more "fabulous" than before, proffered in an "elegant", "beautifully decorated room"; regulars are "always pleased" with this "fine-dining" experience, especially if they can "sit near the fireplace."

Coolfish [S] 26 | 23 | 21 | $46

North Shore Atrium, 6800 Jericho Tpke. (Michael Dr.), Syosset, 516-921-3250

■ Despite its "hard-to-find" location in the back of a Syosset office building, this "cosmopolitan" New American "scene" is "another winner" from chef-owner Tom Schaudel; it's "worth the drive from anywhere" for his "off-the-chart-good" creations (especially what many fin fanatics vote as "the best fish on Long Island"), "gorgeously" presented in "cool" but "comfortable" digs packed with the "beautiful people"; needless to say, it's very "tough to get reservations", but keep persevering – it's "worth it."

Da Ugo   26   20   24 $42
509 Merrick Rd. (Long Beach Rd.), Rockville Centre, 516-764-1900
■ "Exceptionally high-quality" Italian cooking – zero in on "the best baked clams", "unforgettable seafood risotto" and a "wonderful veal chop" – makes this Rockville Centre standout a "class act from top to bottom", not to mention the "on-the-ball" owner and "impeccable", "tuxedoed waiters"; the only drawbacks: the "lovely" room is extremely "intimate" (read: "claustrophobic"), and they "cater first to their weekly regulars."

Della Femina S   25   24   22 $56
99 N. Main St. (bet. Cedar St. & Talmage Ln.), East Hampton, 631-329-6666
■ Some say the "see-and-be-seen show" at this "people-watching" "hot spot" in East Hampton overshadows the "superb" New American cooking, but foodies are "always pleased" with the "wonderful", "creative" dishes, if not the "expensive" tabs; "attractive", "understated" decor and "professional" service contribute to a "classy" experience (despite the "deafening" din), making it a "winner" in all respects.

Focaccia Grill S   –   –   –   E
Gateway Plaza, 2010 Wantagh Ave. (Woodward Ave.), Wantagh, 516-785-7675
Chef-owner Brian Arbesfeld wields the whisk with confidence at this Wantagh New American where his "consistently original", "NYC-quality" cooking ("love the soups" and "the tuna steak is a 10"), accompanied by "extraordinary", "unusual wine selections" and served by a "professional" staff, easily offsets an "unbearable noise level" and so-dim lighting ("could we turn up the lights?").

Harvest on Fort Pond S   25   23   22 $42
11 S. Emery St. (S. Euclid Ave.), Montauk, 631-668-5574
■ "Well worth the drive to the end of the Island", this "superior", family-style Montauk destination takes the local dining standard "up a notch" with its "phenomenal" Northern Italian and Mediterranean dishes "made for sharing" and served by a "friendly" staff in a "beautiful" (if "noisy") setting; enthusiasts can't help but exhort: "do whatever you can to get" here.

Kotobuki S   27   16   19 $32
86 Deer Park Ave. (Main St.), Babylon, 631-321-8387
377 Nesconset Hwy. (Rte. 111), Hauppauge, 631-360-3969
■ Regarded as the premier Japanese option on Long Island, this pair of "fantastic" "winners" in Babylon and Hauppauge thrills with its "innovative choices" of "sumptuously fresh sushi" ("perfection on rice"); the "long waits" ("go early or you'll wait forever"), "bright lights and tight seating aren't exactly my cup of sake, but there's nothing like" its "dynamite" way with raw fish.

La Marmite S   25   22   24 $48
234 Hillside Ave. (bet. Campbell Ave. & Mineola Blvd.), Williston Park, 516-746-1243
■ "A Cadillac among Hondas" declare devotees of this "favorite" "old-timer" nestled for more than a quarter century in a "charming Victorian house" in Williston Park; thanks to "superb" Classic French and Italian dishes turned out by a "courteous staff" in a "luxurious yet relaxing" setting, it is for many the "epitome of fine dining" – "perfect, as it should be at these prices."

La Pace S   25 | 24 | 24 | $49

51 Cedar Swamp Rd. (2nd St.), Glen Cove, 516-671-2970

■ "Artful, edible towers" of "spectacular" savory creations and a "sumptuous", "romantic setting" ("especially near the fireplace") keep loyal customers coming back to this "first-class" Glen Cove Northern Italian; "be prepared to be pampered" by "the royal treatment" from the owner ("Angelo always provides a warm welcome") and his staff at this "special-occasion" place ("one of Long Island's best") that's "worth every penny."

La Piccola Liguria S   26 | 20 | 25 | $46

47 Shore Rd. (Main St.), Port Washington, 516-767-6490

■ Establishing "the standard" in Port Washington, this "heavenly" temple of "old-world charm" wins the "best Northern Italian on Long Island" award with its "consistently superior" menu, "intimate" setting and "gracious", "immaculate" service; though it "deserves all its accolades", the "awe-inspiring" "list of nightly specials" "recited by waiters with very good memories" has even devoted worshipers praying "please write them down" lest "people fall asleep" during the "sermon."

La Plage S   27 | 21 | 24 | $48

131 Creek Rd. (Sound Rd.), Wading River, 631-744-9200

■ "Bring a map and an empty stomach" to this "out-of-the-way" Eclectic "jewel" near the beach in Wading River, where the "superb", "creative" dishes, "intimate" ambiance and "friendly", "professional" service make it "worth the hunt"; though a few killjoys carp that the "quaint", "beach-bungalow" quarters are a "poor match" for such pricey "culinary artistry", laid-back types have no problem with the concept of "black-tie food in a jeans-and-sweater setting."

L'Endroit   25 | 24 | 24 | $51

290 Glen Cove Rd. (Park Dr.), East Hills, 516-621-6630

■ "Absolutely superb in every way" croon pampered patrons of this "Long Island classic", a bastion of "gracious dining" in East Hills that endures due to its "five-star" French cuisine (chef-owner Avelino De Sousa "scores well" with Northern Italian dishes too), "elegant", "romantic" ambiance and, ahem, "interesting artwork"; consider also the "professional" staff overseen by a "concerned maitre d'" and it's easy to see why so many smitten habitués gush "*c'est magnifique!*"

Le Soir S   25 | 21 | 23 | $41

825 Montauk Hwy. (Bayport Ave.), Bayport, 631-472-9090

■ "*Cuisine vraiment française*" distinguishes this "intimate, romantic" Bayport bistro that's renowned for its "extraordinary" classic masterpieces "beautifully presented" in a "charming country inn" setting by a "caring", "dedicated" staff; as it's "too popular" on weekends, the cost-conscious cognoscenti recommend the "out-of-this-world" Sunday–Thursday prix fixe dinner as both an "excellent value" and an ideal way to avoid the crowds.

Louis XVI §   25 | 28 | 25 | $64

600 S. Ocean Ave. (Atlantic Ocean), Patchogue, 631-654-8970
■ "Marie Antoinette herself would be jealous" of the patrons who
are "treated like royalty" at this Patchogue New French "palace",
which reigns as the most "beautiful" restaurant on Long Island
thanks to its "breathtaking" decor and "fabulous" views of Great
South Bay; nearly as impressive are the "rich, savory" creations
from the kitchen, so "elegantly presented" that they're veritable
"works of art", brought to table by a "first-class" staff; "*très
cher*" prices may leave frugal sorts speechless, but this is all
that "fine dining should be."

Maidstone Arms §   25 | 25 | 24 | $51

Maidstone Arms, 207 Main St. (Mill Hill Ln.), East Hampton, 631-324-5006
■ Cherished as a "heavenly retreat in a hectic area", this "refined"
American "superstar" is the "epitome of Hamptons class" thanks
to chef William Valentine's "perfectly prepared" dishes based on
"impeccable flavor combinations", paired with "fabulous" wines
and served in a country-inn setting with a "romantic" ambiance
by an "excellent" staff practiced in "finesse"; this is the "classic"
experience that "you should expect in East Hampton."

Mario §   25 | 21 | 23 | $42

*644 Vanderbilt Motor Pkwy. (bet. Marcus Blvd. & Washington Ave.),
Hauppauge, 631-273-9407*
■ "Amazingly good year in and year out", this "classy" Hauppauge
Northern Italian standout is renowned for its "fantastic" traditional
fare ("you really get an authentic piece of Italy here") offered at
"ridiculously reasonable prices"; backers boast that you "can't
beat" the "simple elegance" of the room or the "attentive" service
and come away confident that "it'll always be excellent."

Mazzi   25 | 22 | 23 | $48

*493 E. Jericho Tpke./Rte. 25 (bet. Depot & Melville Rds.), Huntington Station,
631-421-3390*
■ The "all-time favorite" of many Huntington Station residents, this
"top-quality" Continental (the younger sibling of the renowned
Piccolo) delivers "delicious" dishes that "leave the taste buds
dancing", complemented by an "exceptional", "offbeat" wine list
and "superb" service; set in a "quaint" old house, its "warm,
inviting" ambiance pleases most comers, though a few spoilsports
fuss that it's "so dark you can't read the menu."

Mill River Inn §   28 | 23 | 26 | $57

160 Mill River Rd. (bet. Lexington Ave. & Rte. 25A), Oyster Bay, 516-922-7768
■ Once again rated No. 1 for Food on Long Island, this perennial
"favorite" housed in an unassuming little building in Oyster Bay
didn't miss a beat after the departure of chef Henry Barone; new
top toque Nick Molfetta maintains this "gem's" stellar standards
by executing "elegant", "outrageously creative New American"
dishes, proffered by a staff that "treats you like royalty"; it's "tiny"
but "romantic", "especially by the fireplace in wintertime", and
without doubt among the "best overall dining experiences" around.

Mirabelle S   27   24   26 $60
404 N. Country Rd. (Edgewood Ave.), St. James, 631-584-5999
■ The "best French restaurant east of NYC", this St. James "destination" thrills adventurous palates with master chef-owner Guy Reuge's "ambitious" menu of "superlative", "flawlessly executed" contemporary dishes, served by an "absolutely" "professional" staff in a "charming" farmhouse setting; while a few grousers wish they'd "double the portions or halve the prices", most promise it's "worth every dollar" for an "amazing" experience that's not just "a meal but a trip" to Paris.

Mirepoix   27   20   24 $55
70 Glen Head Rd. (Railroad Ave.), Glen Head, 516-671-2498
■ "You don't have to know how to pronounce the name" to indulge in the "superb", "innovative" International cooking at this "romantic" "little place" near the Glen Head train station that's so "intimate it's like eating in someone's dining room"; chef Michael Maroni turns "luxe ingredients" into "absolutely delicious" "creations" that are "heaven in your mouth"; it's all "presented beautifully" by "superb servers", so even though it's "expensive", it's "worth every penny."

Mirko's S   26   22   24 $54
Water Mill Sq., 670 Montauk Hwy. (bet. Old Mill & Station Rds.), Water Mill, 631-726-4444
■ A "steady clientele keeps returning year after year" to this "hidden jewel" in Water Mill for "fabulous" Continental-Eclectic fare served in a "quiet", "charming" locale "away from the madding crowd" by a "knowledgeable", "professional" staff; though a few down-to-earth types protest that it "caters to the 'in' crowd", habitués need no convincing that it's "wonderful in every way."

Morton's of Chicago S   25   24   23 $57
777 Northern Blvd. (bet. Community Dr. & Lakeville Rd.), Great Neck, 516-498-2950
■ The newest addition to Great Neck's famed "beef belt" and already one of the "best on Long Island", this palatial chophouse showcases "huge" slabs of "phenomenal", "tender steaks" "that almost melt in your mouth", delivered by a "courteous" staff in a "men's club" arena; a few squeamish sorts prefer not to "see the meat before it's cooked" and cry ouch! "my wallet" when the bill comes, but this "hot spot's" popularity seems secure.

Palm S   25   20   22 $56
Huntting Inn, 94 Main St. (Huntting Ln.), East Hampton, 631-324-0411
■ "Good luck getting a reservation during the summer on a Saturday night", but keep trying anyway because this "posh" "scene" set in the "beautiful" 300-year-old Huntting Inn in East Hampton is a "packed" "favorite", and it "can't be beat" for its "succulent" steaks, "famous" four-pound lobsters and "superb" blue cheese salad dressing, served by a "courteous" staff; though a few bluebloods gripe that it's "full of the nouveau riche", fans are too busy "checking out who's at the next table" to notice.

Palm Court at the Carltun S   24 | 27 | 23 | $51
Eisenhower Park (Merrick Ave.), East Meadow, 516-542-0700
■ "Elegant" surroundings, a "romantic" atmosphere and "superb" Continental–New American dishes make this "palace" in East Meadow's Eisenhower Park the "place to bring guests you want to impress" and "perfect" for "special occasions", with "live jazz in the courtyard" in the summer as a bonus; though Miss Manners types "could do without the attitude" from the staff and frugal foes cry foul over "ridiculous" prices, the enchanted feel as if they've "walked into a dream."

Panama Hatties S   27 | 25 | 24 | $61
Post Plaza, 872 E. Jericho Tpke./Rte. 25 (bet. Beverly & Pidgeon Hill Rds.), Huntington Station, 631-351-1727
■ Chef Matthew Hisiger proves that he's at the top of his game at this "exquisite" Huntington Station gem where he masterminds "stupendous" New American dishes that are "out of this world", "magnificently" presented in "picture-perfect" arrangements by a "knowledgeable" (if "snooty") staff; its strip-mall location belies the "suave" ambiance of its "elegant" room, though gourmands feel that dinner would be "worth it even if you sat in the parking lot"; yes, it's very "high-priced", but it's "also very high-class."

Peter Luger S⧧   27 | 18 | 21 | $54
255 Northern Blvd. (bet. Lakeville Rd. & Little Neck Pkwy.), Great Neck, 516-487-8800
■ Yet again voted the Most Popular restaurant on Long Island, this legendary "institution" on Great Neck's beef belt is "in a class by itself", providing a "carnivorous experience" that "outshines all the competition" with "succulent mouthfuls" of "exquisite" porterhouse teamed with "unbelievably fresh and tasty side dishes"; the decor may be "dull", it's "always" "loud, loud, loud" and the servers are "cranky" (though they "add character"), but in the end, legions will attest that "it's by far the best steakhouse this side of heaven."

Piccolo S   26 | 21 | 23 | $48
Southdown Shopping Ctr., 215 Wall St. (bet. Mill Ln. & Southdown Rd.), Huntington, 631-424-5592
■ "Still the one" for "truly divine" dining in the eyes of loyalists, this perennial pride of Huntington is a "classy establishment" legendary for "incredible" Italian–New American fare (chef Mark Sorrentino "has a perfect sense of seasoning") served in a "romantic" setting by a "top-notch" staff; reservations glitches and long "waits" for a somewhat "cramped" table notwithstanding, it gives virtually "all Long Island Italian restaurants something to aspire to."

Plaza Cafe S   25 | 22 | 25 | $51
61 Hill St. (bet. Breese & Windmill Lns.), Southampton, 631-283-9323
■ "It's about time that this community by the sea has a chef who really knows how to cook a fish" say appreciative admirers of this "tasteful" Southampton hideaway where Douglas Gulija prepares "absolutely delectable" New American dishes (his signature seafood shepherd's pie is "heavenly"); equally "phenomenal" is the service – "warm, friendly" and "caring" – so rest assured that you'll be "made to feel welcome and not rushed."

Polo Grill [S] 26 | 26 | 25 | $53

Garden City Hotel, 45 Seventh St. (Franklin Ave.), Garden City, 516-877-9353

■ "The perfect place to impress a stuffy client" gush besotted boosters of this "luxurious" New American "haven" housed in the Garden City Hotel, which promises to dazzle with "heavenly, luscious" "creative combinations" that are "gorgeously presented" amid "elegant" surroundings; of course it's "expensive", but it offers "Manhattan poshness on Long Island", and you'll be "pampered" by "real professionals" from beginning to end.

Sempre Vivolo 26 | 23 | 24 | $47

696 Motor Pkwy. (Old Willets Path), Hauppauge, 631-435-1737

■ "Consistently classy", this "elegant", "sophisticated" Hauppauge Italian is "a real winner", "a grown-up place that's not stuffy" and "just the right size to be cozy"; it's a "good family operation and it shows" – the owners "know how to run a restaurant" and they're "always trying to please", as does the "impeccable but not overbearing" staff; "relax" and indulge in "outstanding" fare proffered in a "civilized" ambiance while being made to "feel special" – this is "romantic" "fine dining" that's "worth the high price tag"; N.B. jacket required on Saturdays.

Sen [S] 26 | 20 | 21 | $44

23 Main St. (bet. Bay & Madison Sts.), Sag Harbor, 631-725-1774

◪ Splurge on just about the "best" sushi on Long Island at this "excellent" Japanese "favorite" in Sag Harbor, which is renowned for its "delicious, fresh and properly prepared" raw fish and "classic" cooked dishes; of course, it's "always crowded" and it doesn't take reservations except for parties of 10 or more, so it can seem "impossible to get into in the summer", but consider "going early or taking it out"; critics, on the other hand, carp that it's "now overpriced" and "overrated" and frown that its once "serene environment has been ruined by its popularity."

Starr Boggs [S] 25 | 23 | 22 | $55

Dune Deck Hotel, 379 Dune Rd. (bet. Harbor Rd. & Jessup Ln.), Westhampton Beach, 631-288-5250

■ "Fine dining on the water" reels in plenty of "glitzy" gourmands to this "foodie heaven" set in the Dune Deck Hotel in Westhampton Beach, where the eponymous chef-owner turns out "inventive", "top-of-the-line" Long Island dishes (based on "local ingredients") that are "never boring" (the "Monday night lobster bake can't be beat"); it may be a bit "snooty", but it's "worth putting up with the service" to dine on food that's almost "perfect", plus the midweek "prix fixe dinners are a great bargain" – "what a treat!"

Stone Creek Inn [S] 26 | 25 | 24 | $49

405 Montauk Hwy. (bet. Carter Ln. & Wedgewood Harbor), East Quogue, 631-653-6770

■ "Hurrah and kudos to the chef!" cheer the "hip" devotees of this "romantic hideaway" quartered in a "beautiful" Victorian-era former speakeasy in East Quogue that's appointed with "old-world" details; it's a "handsome", "inviting" backdrop for Christian Mir's "unbelievable" French-Mediterranean dishes prepared with "panache" ("don't expect the usual menu, but it's nothing weird" either) using the "freshest high-quality ingredients" and "elegantly presented" by an "outstanding" staff; "a perfect celebration restaurant", "everything is first-rate here – except the noise level."

Stresa S   25 | 22 | 22 | $49 |
1524 Northern Blvd. (east of Shelter Rock Rd.), Manhasset, 516-365-6956

■ Like a "NYC spot in Nassau", this "elegant" Manhasset Italian pulls in the "beautiful people" with "superb" "classics" paired with an "eclectic" wine list and complemented by a "beautiful" room adorned with "amazing floral displays" and "divine" service; critics, though, croon "to know, know, know you is to love, love, love you", warning that unless you're a "favored regular" you may as well be "invisible" to the staff.

Tellers Chophouse S   26 | 27 | 24 | $52 |
605 Main St. (Veterans Memorial Park), Islip, 631-277-7070

■ "Deposit this one under delicious" rave gourmands about this "spectacular", "big-time" chophouse set in a "beautiful old bank building" (circa 1926) in Islip, where "the best steaks this side of Peter Luger" are paired with an "inspirational, award-winning wine list" (the vault now houses the wine cellar and humidor); equally "breathtaking" are the "dramatic" dining room and "gorgeously designed bar", so even if you have to "see the loan officer on the way in", it's "worth it" to live this "steak-lover's dream."

Trattoria Diane S   26 | 22 | 22 | $46 |
21 Bryant Ave. (Northern Blvd.), Roslyn, 516-621-2591

■ "Sophisticated" and "stylish", this Roslyn standout has "quietly emerged as one of the North Shore's best" thanks to chef (and co-owner) John Durkin's "superb", "sumptuous" Northern Italian dishes (make sure you "leave room for the fabulous desserts" made by wife Diane); the culinary works of art are served in "bright, attractive" quarters with an "elegant" ambiance by a "capable", "professional" staff; it's "a real treat", so of course "long waits" can be expected on weekends.

Los Angeles

TOP 20 FOOD RANKING

Restaurant	Cuisine Type
28 Matsuhisa	Japanese
Sushi Nozawa	Japanese
27 Chinois on Main	Asian/New French
Belvedere, The	Californian/Eclectic
Water Grill	Seafood
L'Orangerie	New French
Spago	Californian/Eclectic
Patina	Californian/New French
Shiro	Californian/Asian
Mélisse	New American
Nobu Malibu	Japanese
Bel-Air Hotel	Californian/Classic French
Joe's	Californian/Classic French
Valentino	N&S Italian
26 R-23	Japanese
Campanile	Mediterranean
Diaghilev	Franco-Russian
Ruth's Chris	Steakhouse
Devon	Californian/New French
La Cachette	Classic French

ADDITIONAL NOTEWORTHY PLACES

Bistro 45	Californian/French Bistro
Brent's Deli	Deli
Café Bizou	Californian
Cafe Blanc	Californian/Asian
Capo	N&S Italian
Chaya Brasserie	Asian/Eclectic
Depot	Eclectic
Frenchy's Bistro	French Bistro
Grill	Steakhouse
JiRaffe	Californian
Josie's	New American
Jozu	Pacific Rim
Lawry's	Steakhouse
Locanda Veneta	Northern Italian
Michael's	New American
Mimosa	French Bistro
Palm	Steakhouse
Parkway Grill	Californian
Saddle Peak Lodge	New American
Yujean Kang's	Chinese

Bel-Air Hotel ⓢ   27 | 29 | 27 | $55
Bel-Air Hotel, 701 Stone Canyon Rd. (north of Sunset Blvd.), LA, 310-472-1211
■ Acclaimed as having the most beautiful dining room in LA, this highly rated Cal-French is lauded as an "unrushed", "quiet and wonderful place far from the real world" with a "gorgeous setting" that "looks like paradise" and "fabulous" food to match; diners can "pamper themselves" indoors, outdoors or in the private room in the kitchen called Table One, a glass bubble where "your wish is their command"; truth be told, "you'll feel famous just showing up", even if you're not one of its many "movers and shakers."

Belvedere, The ⓢ   27 | 27 | 27 | $55
Peninsula Beverly Hills Hotel, 9882 Little Santa Monica Blvd. (Wilshire Blvd.), Beverly Hills, 310-788-2306
■ The Bel-Air is the top hotel when it comes to decor, but this "classy", "elegant" Cal-French-Asian "oasis" in Beverly Hills is tops in terms of hotel food, delivering "marvelous, creative" meals in a "fabled old-style dining room" attended by "faultless" servers who "make everyone feel special"; a "wonderful guy place for lunch or dinner", it's "simply the best" for "special occasions", proffering "heaven at unearthly prices"; P.S. "the potato-crusted sea bass is not to be missed."

Bistro 45 ⓢ   26 | 23 | 24 | $43
45 S. Mentor Ave. (bet. Colorado Blvd. & Green St.), Pasadena, 626-795-2478
■ This well-loved "art deco" Cal-French bistro is an "oasis" of "classy elegance", beginning with a greeting from "perfect host Robert Simon" and extending to the "outstanding" cooking ("we've never had a bad meal here"), "divine wine list", "first-class service" and patio that's ideal for "special occasions"; overall, a "great place for memories that last a lifetime."

Brent's Deli ⓢ   26 | 14 | 21 | $15
19565 Parthenia St. (bet. Corbin & Tampa Aves.), Northridge, 818-886-5679
■ There's nary a word of dissent from those who beat a path to this "great place to go and schmooze" in a San Fernando Valley mini-mall; vox populi agrees the goods are "as close to Jewish soul food as you get in LA" and cites a plethora of "bests": cabbage soup, corned beef, chopped liver, pastrami, blintzes, mushroom-barley soup; moreover, if you "come hungry", you're guaranteed to "leave stuffed" ("a huge slice of cake, seemingly for four, turned out to be just for me!"); P.S. "there's always a wait, but it's worth it."

Café Bizou ⓢ   24 | 20 | 22 | $27
91 N. Raymond Ave. (Holly St.), Pasadena, 626-792-9923
Watergarden, 2450 Colorado Blvd. (bet. Cloverfield Blvd. & 26th St.), Santa Monica, 310-582-8203
14016 Ventura Blvd. (bet. Hazeltine & Woodman Aves.), Sherman Oaks, 818-788-3536
■ Once again ranked the Most Popular restaurant in town, this Culinary Concept That Ate Los Angeles proves its staying power with a third branch in Santa Monica that follows in the footsteps of its forebears as "a bit of heaven with down-to-earth prices" (including the "cheapest corkage fee" around); since "anything you order" from the Californian menu "is excellent" and the waiters are "refreshingly polite", it's a "totally pleasing experience for both the taste buds and the wallet"; of course, all three locations are "always packed."

Cafe Blanc
25 | 15 | 22 | $43

9777 Little Santa Monica Blvd. (Wilshire Blvd.), Beverly Hills, 310-888-0108
■ "Talented, creative" chef Tomi Harase continues his exercise in the "zen" of dining at this Cal-Asian entry in a "spare" "white room" "across from CAA in Beverly Hills"; expect "small portions" of "exquisitely presented" cuisine "so divine" that "serious foodies" "return again and again."

Campanile 🖬
26 | 24 | 23 | $44

624 S. La Brea Ave. (bet. 6th St. & Wilshire Blvd.), LA, 323-938-1447
■ "Still at the top" is the verdict on this beloved Mediterranean situated in a "beautiful" historic space built for Charlie Chaplin; voters say it's "always a treat" for everything from "incredible" breads from the adjacent La Brea Bakery to "superb" herbed and olive-oiled dishes and "desserts alone worth a visit"; orchestrated by "master chef Mark Peel", it's versatile enough for a "Monday evening family-style meal", "fabulous" grilled cheese on Thursday's sandwich night or a "romantic" "special occasion."

Capo
23 | 24 | 22 | $57

1810 Ocean Ave. (Pico Blvd.), Santa Monica, 310-394-5550
■ Chef Bruce Marder "hits the ball out of the park" at this "heavily atmospheric", beach-adjacent Santa Monica Italian known for its "use of seasonal produce", much of which comes from his own garden; the "dreamy food" will have you "loosening your belt" and marveling at the "quality", which is why some devotees say damn the cost – "even at these prices, I'll go again."

Chinois on Main 🖬
27 | 22 | 23 | $48

2709 Main St. (bet. Ocean Park Blvd. & Rose Ave.), Santa Monica, 310-392-9025
■ The highest-rated restaurant in the Wolfgang Puck empire, this "amazing" Asian-inspired New French trendsetter in Santa Monica is an "eye- and palate-opener" that "attracts foodies from around the world"; enthusiasts gush that the cooking is "so good it's hard to wait for a special occasion to return" for "original dishes" that make for a "heavenly" experience.

Chaya Brasserie ◐🖬
25 | 24 | 22 | $41

8741 Alden Dr. (bet. Beverly Blvd. & 3rd St.), LA, 310-859-8833
■ One of the best "reasons to rejoice when leaving Cedars" Hospital is the proximity of this West Hollywood "hot spot" that's "still hip after all these years"; a "cool, cooler and coolest" "movie/TV power crowd" shows up for the "best martinis in town" ("the raspberry one makes green apple seem so five months ago!") and a "creative, tasty" Asian-Eclectic "fusion" menu; for scenesters, this is an "eye treat" where there's "always a trend" in the making.

Depot
24 | 21 | 23 | $34

1250 Cabrillo Ave. (Torrance Ave.), Torrance, 310-787-7501
■ Acolytes are "all aboard" chef Michael Shafer's Eclectic set in an "old" "Torrance train station"; "dedicated" to making "every meal exceptional", this "remarkable" kitchen whiz ("the South Bay's answer to Emeril") is "a master at blending spices and cuisines", and his "always creative" food, coupled with a "quiet, elegant" ambiance, makes this the "power-lunch hangout" for execs from the nearby Toyota sales headquarters.

Devon [S] 26 | 21 | 24 | $43

109 E. Lemon Ave. (Myrtle Ave.), Monrovia, 626-305-0013

■ "By far the best restaurant in Monrovia", this "temple" of "terrific cooking" is "well worth the drive" to its "out-of-the-way location" according to dazzled devotees who "worship" its "great wine list" and "exquisite" Cal–New French cuisine; the chef "is a master with sauces" who creates "unusual entrees like boar ravioli" and other "wild game" that make for an "adventure in food", while "owners with taste" "who care about the dining experience" ensure that the place "runs like a fine watch."

Diaghilev 26 | 28 | 27 | $57

Wyndham Bel Age Hotel, 1020 N. San Vicente Blvd. (Sunset Blvd.), W. Hollywood, 310-854-1111

■ A "throwback to the czars", this "special-occasion" Franco-Russian in West Hollywood offers an "exciting, romantic evening"; not only will you "be treated like royalty" with "much bowing and scraping" courtesy of maitre d' "Dmitri [Dmitrov] and his attentive staff", but you'll also eat "like a prince or princess" sampling blini, "caviar and more caviar" to the strains of "delightful harp music" at this bastion of "heavenly civility."

Frenchy's Bistro [S] 26 | 17 | 22 | $33

4137 E. Anaheim St. (bet. Termino & Ximeno Aves.), 562-494-8787

■ "Head-and-shoulders above anything else" in Long Beach, this "inviting" French bistro offers "creative chef" Andre Angles' "outstanding" cooking; sure "he loves to work with foie gras and pâté", but "you must also try the sand dabs and soufflé" and sample a bottle from the "reasonably priced" cellar.

Grill [S] 25 | 22 | 24 | $43

9560 Dayton Way (Wilshire Blvd.), Beverly Hills, 310-276-0615

■ "An old reliable", this "man's restaurant" offers a taste of "Manhattan for the Hollywood biggies" that's as "close to a NYC steakhouse" as they're likely to find; "superb" cuts, some of the "best martinis in Lalaland" and "professional, welcoming" service from "waiters who have been there forever" make this booth-and-brass venue "in a Beverly Hills alley" a "big treat anytime."

JiRaffe [S] 26 | 22 | 23 | $43

502 Santa Monica Blvd. (5th St.), Santa Monica, 310-917-6671

■ "Grand dining without the snobbery" is what awaits at this "world-class" Californian "taste treat" in Santa Monica that's "better than ever"; the "intimate, warm" surroundings set the stage for "brilliant" chef Raphael Lunetta's "beautifully presented", "exceptional" "creations"; "expect flawless everything", including "supreme" service that's as "stylish as the food."

Joe's [S] 27 | 19 | 23 | $40

1023 Abbot Kinney Blvd. (bet. Main St. & Westminster Ave.), Venice, 310-399-5811

■ For "an enchanting evening in Venice", legions of "foodies" head to this "big deal" "island of calm and good manners" that put "funky" Abbot Kinney on the culinary map; "a marriage of true gourmet and homestyle comfort", chef-owner Joe Miller's "first-class" Cal-French dishes are marked by "flavor and adventure" and he always tempts with "something new", so despite tables that are "packed in too tight", fans revel in this "delightful" experience.

Josie's S   26 25 25 $51
2424 Pico Blvd. (25th St.), Santa Monica, 310-581-9888
■ "Hurray! – she finally opened" her own "beautiful place" in Santa Monica rejoice fans of Josie Le Balch who, after honing her skills at the Saddle Peak Lodge, is now putting her "innovative" stamp on the hottest newbie in town; a "rising star" "destined" for fame, she "shines" with "fabulously creative", "inspired" New American cooking, brought to table by a "top-notch" staff in a setting that exudes "quiet elegance."

Jozu S   26 23 24 $46
8360 Melrose Ave. (La Cienega Blvd.), W. Hollywood, 323-655-5600
■ "Gentleman of the first order" "Andy Nakano and his entire staff should be kissed on a daily basis" for delivering this "ethereal" "New Wave" Pacific Rim "winner" to West Hollywood; simply "impeccable all around", it crafts "mouth-teasing" dishes that are "too exciting and exotic to be called merely food", turned out in an "elegantly" minimalist room with a "Zen tranquility"; just sit back, breathe deep and "inhale the creativity."

La Cachette S   26 25 24 $48
10506 Little Santa Monica Blvd. (bet. Beverly Glen Blvd. & Overland Ave.), Century City, 310-470-4992
■ "Talented chef Jean-François Meteigner has hit his stride" at this "first-rate" French in Century City, where "everything tastes exquisite", from the "gotta-have-it pâté" to the chocolate soufflé, and the "beautiful room" with "lovely flowers" produces a "great special-occasion" atmosphere; *bien sûr*, it's "pricey", but those who are "hooked" uphold it as "fantastic all around."

Lawry's The Prime Rib S   25 23 25 $38
100 N. La Cienega Blvd. (Wilshire Blvd.), Beverly Hills, 310-652-2827
■ "I went there for Valentine's Day and fell in love with prime rib" sigh surveyors smitten with this "perennial favorite" chain link in Beverly Hills; besides the namesake dish, there's "scrumptious salad", "crème de la crème" creamed corn and "fantastic Yorkshire pudding"; the "well-choreographed service" and "charming, dark-wood" decor also delight devotees, whose only beefs are the "long waits", perhaps due to "busloads of tourists."

Locanda Veneta S   25 18 21 $40
8638 W. Third St. (bet. Robertson & San Vicente Blvds.), LA, 310-274-1893
■ "They make you feel special", be you "star or nobody", at this "friendly" "favorite" where the Northern Italian fare is "always excellent", from "amazing salads" to "fabulous pastas" to "superb seafood"; though the room is decidedly "tiny", it's recently been remodeled to provide more comfort for "celebs" and the rest of us.

L'Orangerie S   27 28 26 VE
903 N. La Cienega Blvd. (bet. Melrose Ave. & Santa Monica Blvd.), W. Hollywood, 310-652-9770
■ A visit to this "definitive" New French in West Hollywood is "heaven for all the senses", starting with the "gigantic flowers" that fill its "beautiful", "opulent" dining room and add to the "peaceful" ambiance; chef Ludovic Lefebvre's "extraordinary" way with "unusual ingredients" yields "stellar dishes", which are paired with "phenomenal wines" and "served magnificently" by a "discreet" staff; though it's "*très* expensive", it's worth "every $100 bill."

Matsuhisa 🅂   28 | 19 | 24 | $56
129 N. La Cienega Blvd. (Wilshire Blvd.), Beverly Hills, 310-659-9639
■ Before there were branches of Nobu in the capitals of the world, there was this "low-key" Japanese seafood cafe in Beverly Hills that's once again No. 1 for Food in LA thanks to a "great variety" of "continually innovative", "visually stunning" sushi that "bursts with flavor" (and well it should at roughly "$3 a bite"), along with "incredible" cooked items like the "wonderful black cod in miso"; insiders say "try the hidden omakase room."

Mélisse 🅂   27 | 25 | 24 | $58
1104 Wilshire Blvd. (11th St.), Santa Monica, 310-395-0881
■ Chef Josiah Citrin's French-influenced New American in Santa Monica is lauded as "a foodie's dream" for its "spectacular tasting menus", "decadent cheese course" and unexpected "treats" from the kitchen; factor in "classy" service and an "elegant" multi-room setting and it's clear why it's "worth the big bucks" and is one of the "hottest", "special-occasion" places in town.

Michael's   25 | 26 | 25 | $52
1147 Third St. (Wilshire Blvd.), Santa Monica, 310-451-0843
■ "Still excellent" after all these years, this groundbreaking New American (with Cal-French undertones) has become an "old friend" whose "amazingly romantic", "lush" "green" patio ("the prettiest garden spot of all") continues to be "a must" place to return to for "inventive cuisine" that's "worth every dollar"; moreover, note voters, owner Michael McCarty "sincerely communicates the message that your presence is appreciated."

Mimosa 🄿   22 | 19 | 20 | $37
8009 Beverly Blvd. (Crescent Heights Blvd.), LA, 323-655-8895
■ "Serious", "correct" "true French bistro" food like olives marinated in-house, "the best foie gras in town", "fantastic salad Lyonnaise" and redoubtable cassoulet, monkfish and bouillabaisse are why this warm, photograph-filled entry remains a "very popular" "touch of France"; the one menu deviation: "addictive macaroni and cheese."

Nobu Malibu 🅂   27 | 21 | 23 | $50
3835 Crosscreek Rd. (PCH), Malibu, 310-317-9140
■ Nobu Matsuhisa hits the beach in Malibu with this "terminally hip" Japanese shrine, wowing scores of supporters who simply swoon over his "out-of-this-world" sushi and other "signature" fare (don't miss the "rock shrimp – so good you almost cry when it's gone"); a "doting" staff oversees the über-"cool" "scene" packed with bold-face names – ooh, there's Steven Spielberg, and there's Gwyneth Paltrow – but there is one problem: "you'll never be happy with a $5 California roll again."

Palm 🅂   25 | 21 | 22 | $49
9001 Santa Monica Blvd. (bet. Doheny Dr. & Robertson Blvd.),
W. Hollywood, 310-550-8811
■ For those in the Biz, this "loud, obnoxious" ("in a fun kind of way") "NY steakhouse" in West Hollywood is "the place" to meet, greet and become part of the "boys' club" over "strong cocktails", "humongous lobsters" and "big steaks at a big price"; "it never changes, which is a good thing."

Parkway Grill S
25 | 24 | 24 | $39

510 S. Arroyo Pkwy. (bet. California & Del Mar Blvds.), Pasadena, 626-795-1001

■ Often referred to as "Spago East", this "Pasadena jewel", the keystone of the Smith brothers' restaurants (Arroyo Chop House, Ducz, Crocodile Cafe), is where "incredible, creative" Californian fare, a "beautiful setting" and "outstanding" servers who "really know the menu" add up to "pure bliss from beginning to end"; it's "worth the drive from anywhere" sigh satisfied surveyors.

Patina S
27 | 25 | 26 | $60

5955 Melrose Ave. (bet. Highland Ave. & Vine St.), LA, 323-467-1108

■ Joachim Splichal's "beautifully redone" Hollywood flagship continues to rate raves as an "always exciting", "exquisite dining experience"; voters swear it's "better than ever", citing "creative, bold, exquisitely presented" Cal–New French food, "absolutely the best wine list in LA" and "superb service" as a few of the many reasons a "splurge" here is "worth every last penny"; P.S. "the tasting menu is the way to go."

R-23
26 | 22 | 21 | $39

923 E. Third St. (bet. Alameda St. & Santa Fe Ave.), Downtown LA, 213-687-7178

■ In an effort to secure a seat, devotees "don't really want to tell anyone" about this "jewel" of a Japanese "hidden away" in a "run-down neighborhood" next to Downtown's SoHo equivalent; "if you can find it, you deserve" to dine on the "sublime sushi and sashimi" amid decor that's as "hip" and "minimalist" as the name, including "eccentric" cardboard chairs designed by Frank Gehry.

Ruth's Chris Steak House S
26 | 22 | 24 | $45

224 S. Beverly Dr. (bet. Olympic & Wilshire Blvds.), Beverly Hills, 310-859-8744

■ "Huge, well-poured martinis" start the meal off right at this "pricey" beefhouse chain that's "still the standard by which others are judged" for "fabulous", "buttery steaks" and serious sides ("excellent creamed spinach", "perfect mashed potatoes"); a "fine", "quick" staff is another feather in its cap – just remember to "wear elastic pants" and plan to "go to the gym the next day."

Saddle Peak Lodge S
26 | 27 | 25 | $49

419 Cold Canyon Rd. (Piuma Rd.), Calabasas, 818-222-3888

■ "Always a 'peak' place to go for that special occasion", this "unique" New American "escape" high in the mountains of Malibu takes you "away from it all" with its "romantic hunting lodge decor" (complete with "animal heads" on the walls) and "incredibly prepared" game like venison, wild boar and elk ("no point in ordering chicken"); pampered patrons say it's "excellent in every respect" and well "worth the ride."

Shiro S
27 | 18 | 23 | $41

1505 Mission St. (Fair Oaks Ave.), S. Pasadena, 626-799-4774

■ You'd never know there was more than one dish on the menu at this "stark" South Pasadena Cal-Asian seafood house, since most comments insist "you must try the catfish in ponzu sauce"; that's fine, though that might mean missing out on other "delicious rewards" (like the Chinese ravioli or lobster spring rolls) that await in this bento box of a room that "deserves its reputation for food and service."

Spago S
27 | 26 | 25 | $54

176 N. Cañon Dr. (Wilshire Blvd.), Beverly Hills, 310-385-0880

■ Though it may not have the highest ratings, Wolfgang Puck's "celebratory" Beverly Hills flagship Cal-Eclectic is "still the place to be seen" and the one SoCal restaurant that everyone (from "tremendous celebs" to "out-of-towners") wants to dine at; expect "beautiful surroundings", "amazing", "heady" combinations from chef Lee Hefter and attentive service at this destination that put LA on the culinary map and helps keep it there.

Sushi Nozawa
28 | 10 | 16 | $40

11288 Ventura Blvd. (Vineland Ave.), Studio City, 818-508-7017

■ Despite a "boring", "no-frills" setting, "hovering hordes" and "overeager servers" that have been known to say "'you go now, we need the chairs'", as well as a "strict", "imperious" chef who "chooses the menu" and expects you to "be respectful of the rules" ("I love it when he throws someone out"), this Studio City Japanese is a destination for raw-fish purists; the reason: sushi so "spectacular" – "the albacore is a seminal experience", "I live for the crab roll" – it will "bring a tear to your eye."

Valentino
27 | 24 | 26 | $57

3115 Pico Blvd. (bet. 31st & 32nd Sts.), Santa Monica, 310-829-4313

■ "Always No. 1" for Italian in SoCal, this "truly elegant" "hideaway on Pico" is a "class act all the way" and a "place to brag about" to out-of-towners thanks to "amazing" authentic cooking ("the pasta sampler will blow you away"), an "awesome wine list" that may be the most "encyclopedic" in the city and "impeccable service", led by "personable" owner Piero Selvaggio ("its strongest asset"); N.B. lunch is served Fridays only.

Water Grill S
27 | 25 | 25 | $47

544 S. Grand Ave. (bet. 5th & 6th Sts.), Downtown LA, 213-891-0900

■ Hailed as a "reason in itself to go Downtown" and a "superb pre- or post-theater" choice, this flagship of the King's Seafood chain dazzles surveyors with "incredibly fresh oysters", the "best clam chowder on earth", "amazing diver scallops" and "mouthwatering fish"; factor in a "very attentive" staff that "treats you like royalty" and a "stylish", "beautiful" setting, and you have a restaurant at "the pinnacle" of its category ("nothing even comes close").

Yujean Kang's S
25 | 21 | 23 | $37

67 N. Raymond Ave. (bet. Colorado Blvd. & Walnut St.), Pasadena, 626-585-0855
8826 Melrose Ave. (Robertson Blvd.), W. Hollywood, 310-288-0806

■ Chef Yujean Kang's "cutting-edge", "meticulously prepared" "original" "Westernized" Chinese "fusion" cuisine "scores big points" with surveyors ("the place never ceases to amaze me") who've dined at this "classy", "upscale", "minimalist" duo; since "very accommodating" "waiters abound", "ask them what to order", including the "appropriate beers and wines"; P.S. "lunch is a bargain."

Miami

TOP 20 FOOD RANKING

Restaurant	Cuisine Type
27 Chef Allen's	New World
Romeo's Cafe	Northern Italian
Palm	Steakhouse
Norman's	New World
26 Osteria del Teatro	N&S Italian
Joe's Stone Crab	Seafood
La Palme d'Or	Classic/New French
Tropical Chinese	Chinese
Toni's Sushi Bar	Japanese
Ortanique on the Mile	Caribbean
Pacific Time	Pan-Asian/Seafood
Escopazzo	N&S Italian
Mark's South Beach	New American
Hy-Vong	Vietnamese
Astor Place	New American
Crystal Cafe	Continental
Pascal's on Ponce	New French
Grazie Cafe	Northern Italian
25 Miss Saigon Bistro	Vietnamese
Morton's of Chicago	Steakhouse

ADDITIONAL NOTEWORTHY PLACES

Azul	New French/Asian
Baleen	Seafood/Pacific Rim
Bambú	Pan-Asian
Blue Door	New French
Cafe Prima Pasta	Northern Italian
Caffé Abbracci	N&S Italian
Carpaccio	Northern Italian
Casa Juancho	Spanish
Cheesecake Factory	Eclectic
Forge	Steakhouse
Garcia's	Seafood
Liaison	New American/Cajun
Nemo	New World
Nobu Miami Beach	Japanese/Peruvian
Pit Bar-B-Q	Barbecue
Porcao	Brazilian
Tantra	Med./New French
Touch	New American
Versailles	Cuban
Wolfie Cohen's	Jewish/Deli

Astor Place [S] 26 | 25 | 23 | $49
Hotel Astor, 956 Washington Ave. (10th St.), Miami Beach, 305-672-7217
■ Chef Johnny Vinczencz is "better than ever" at this "deco-decadent" destination in the "trendy" Hotel Astor; "sophisticated, sexy" New American dishes "show Florida's influence on the food" while the "upbeat", "good-looking" crowd reflects South Beach's effect on the "scene"; though it's not quite "the hot spot" it once was, it's still "the place to go with someone who enjoys a good meal", particularly during the "amazing Sunday gospel brunch."

Azul 25 | 27 | 25 | $63
Mandarin Oriental, 500 Brickell Key Dr. (SE 8th St.), 305-913-8358
■ Miami's "latest must-try" is this top-rated newcomer in the Mandarin Oriental hotel on Biscayne Bay where chef Michelle Bernstein, formerly of Tantra and the Strand, "seldom falls" from the "high wire" of her "stellar" "Asian-Caribbean-French fusion"; the "bare sophistication of the decor" and the "food mood" are so "Zen" that, despite "catastrophic prices", "from door to table to door it's a soothing experience."

Baleen [S] 25 | 27 | 22 | $54
Grove Isle Hotel, 4 Grove Isle Dr. (Bayshore Dr.), Coconut Grove, 305-858-8300
■ For "the most beautiful view in all of Miami", "get a table outside and dine under the stars" on "breezy Biscayne Bay" at this "dazzling" "Pacific Rim–inspired" seafood house in the Grove; the "breathtaking setting" is as "magical" as chef Robin Haas' "sumptuous" "touch", though perhaps the decor's "whimsical" simian touches influence the staff to "monkey around" too much.

Bambú ◐[S] 23 | 25 | 20 | $57
1665 Meridian Ave. (Lincoln Rd.), Miami Beach, 305-531-4800
◪ "You won't see [co-owner] Cameron Diaz here", but there's "nice people-watching" nonetheless in the "cool interior" of this "fashionable" Pan-Asian off lively Lincoln Road; "a kitchen with a passion for ingredients" turns out "insanely decadent, delicious" sushi, foie gras, caviar and other food "with a 'tude" to a "chaotic crowd that digs it", though diners less dazzled by the "happening ambiance" pooh-pooh "small portions" at "over-the-top prices."

Blue Door ◐[S] 24 | 27 | 21 | $59
Delano Hotel, 1685 Collins Ave. (17th St.), Miami Beach, 305-674-6400
◪ Philippe Starck has draped the Delano's dining "dream" in "breezy, long, white curtains from the ceiling to the floor", and the "celebrities galore" make this New French "gem" feel like a "luxurious movie set"; the "scene" shouldn't "distract you from the excellent" "seafood-heavy menu", though common folk who don't "kiss up or scream at their waiter" might "never be served", and "fantasy meets reality" when the big bill comes.

Cafe Prima Pasta ◐[S] 24 | 18 | 21 | $27
414 71st St. (Collins Ave.), Miami Beach, 305-867-0106
◪ Where else would you find "Northern Italian food with a Latin beat" but in Miami Beach?; "off-the-beaten-path for tourists", this "favorite" "break from that SoBe triple headache – parking, pricing and attitude" – has "expanded" to accommodate locals who flock here for Argentine steak and "the best" "fresh-made pasta" "bargains" "in a lively setting", though some "old-timers" gripe that it was "better" when it was more "intimate."

Caffé Abbracci ◐ [S] 25 | 22 | 24 | $41

318 Aragon Ave. (bet. Le Jeune Rd. & Ponce de Leon Blvd.), Coral Gables, 305-441-0700

■ You're bound to "see some of the beautiful society people schmoozing" and, true to the name of the place, hugging at this "warm" and "wonderful" Gables Italian; owner Nino Pernetti "manages to balance the highest levels of quality, service, decor and atmosphere", though the "excellence" is matched by an equally extravagant degree of "noise" in a place "alive" with "flashy big shots" feeding on "strong standards and specials."

Carpaccio ◐ [S] 24 | 20 | 22 | $33

Shops of Bal Harbour, 9700 Collins Ave. (97th St.), Bal Harbour, 305-867-7777

■ "Even a bowl of soup is special here" claims the couture crowd at this "great break from shopping" at Bal Harbour; sit on the patio at the "winning" Northern Italian and "gorge your eyes" on the "beautiful people" and "poodles in Gucci strolling by" as you feast on "excellent fresh pastas" and a dozen varieties of carpaccio at prices that leave "enough money left over for Prada or Tiffany."

Casa Juancho ◐ [S] 22 | 22 | 21 | $35

2436 SW Eighth St. (bet. 24th & 25th Sts.), 305-642-2452

■ "Take out-of-town guests" for "a jumping evening" at this "authentic" Spanish *taverna* in Little Havana where "superior" tapas and paella, a vast and varied Iberian wine list and a "lively bar scene with dancing" make "a great combination"; if "the musicians and singers are annoying at times", "forget about the hams strung up around the place" as well as the ones strolling with guitars and "just enjoy the repast."

Cheesecake Factory [S] 21 | 19 | 19 | $24

Aventura Mall, 19501 Biscayne Blvd. (195th St.), Aventura, 305-792-9696 ◐
CocoWalk, 3015 Grand Ave. (Virginia St.), Coconut Grove, 305-447-9898 ◐
Dadeland Mall, 7497 N. Kendall Dr. (88th St.), Kendall, 305-665-5400

◪ These Eclectic "upscale chains" are "factories for sure", serving "tasty" "industrial-size portions" in "such a variety" that you might "never know what to eat"; though "the wait for a table is agony" and the "noise level" and "huge crowds" make it feel "like a visit to the zoo", the cheesecakes are "sinfully delicious."

Chef Allen's [S] 27 | 23 | 25 | $53

19088 NE 29th Ave. (191st St.), Aventura, 305-935-2900

■ No. 1 for Food in the *Miami Survey,* this New World "favorite" in Aventura "deserves the accolades" for "tropical fusion flavors at their best"; "always evolving" yet "always superb", busy chef-owner Allen Sasser is "the reigning king" of "Florida cuisine", and though he "travels a lot", when he's in-house he "visits each table, making everyone feel special"; "if price is no object and you wish to impress or propose, this is the place."

Crystal Cafe [S] 26 | 20 | 25 | $38

726 41st St. (bet. Chase & Prairie Aves.), Miami Beach, 305-673-8266

■ "Sophisticates" "satisfy all the senses" at this "superb", almost-"secret" "spot" sired by "super-talented" chef-owner Klime Kovaceski; "extraordinary European-style creativity from the kitchen" meets "intimate", "formal ambiance" and "excellent service" in the dining room for a "wonderful" Continental meal that's got in-the-know fans saying "hats off."

Escopazzo ◐ [S] 26 | 22 | 24 | $50

1311 Washington Ave. (bet. 13th & 14th Sts.), Miami Beach, 305-674-9450

■ The "native Italians know what they're doing" at this "romantic, vest-pocket"-size bistro; the "delicate and delicious" "cuisine is delivered with tender-loving care" and the "warm, courteous" staff "accommodates all whims" so that, even though this "wonderful place" isn't part of the "South Beach scene", "you feel like a celebrity" nonetheless here.

Forge ◐ [S] 25 | 26 | 24 | $55

432 Arthur Godfrey Rd. (Royal Palm Ave.), Miami Beach, 305-538-8533

◪ The "'60s Miami Beach" vibe of this "classic" chophouse "splurge" is as real as can be; for over three decades, the stained-glass palace has forged its role as the "traditional place" for "old-fashioned, high-end dining" where "Caesar salad and prime rib are stars", the "museum" of a wine cellar houses the "Mona Lisas" of vintages and there's "no counting calories" or change.

Garcia's [S] ▽ 23 | 15 | 18 | $20

398 NW North River Dr. (4th St. Bridge), 305-375-0765

■ Locals "love to go by boat up the Miami River" to catch a "delish fish sandwich" at this "funky" waterfront seafood market near Downtown; "if you don't mind eating next to a bustling canal" amid a school of midday feeders, this "unpretentious", "great value" meal is "South Florida at its casual best"; N.B. it's now open for dinner Thursday through Sunday.

Grazie Cafe [S] 26 | 19 | 25 | $32

Suniland Plaza, 11523 S. Dixie Hwy. (bet. 114th & 115th Sts.), Pinecrest, 305-232-5533

■ Go figure – "nobody is Italian" at this "cozy" "storefront" in "residential Pinecrest", but you'll "*mangia, mangia, mangia*" on "delicious" dishes from the Northern tip of The Boot nonetheless while the "zealous" "waiters sing"; the "chef will prepare anything you have a craving for", so you "feel welcome" to "go back again and again" with "your requests" for "call-ahead", "mouthwatering filet mignon ravioli" and other "favorites."

Hy-Vong [S] 26 | 9 | 13 | $24

3458 SW Eighth St. (34th Ave.), 305-446-3674

■ The "room's the size of the head of a pin", but the "superb Vietnamese is worth the long wait" for one of the few tables at this "no-frills" "gem in Little Havana"; as long as you realize "it's all about" eating, you won't be too bothered by the "abysmal decor and service" that a fiercely loyal "cult following" vows are part of the "charm" of a "grubby hole-in-the-wall with fantastic food."

Joe's Stone Crab [S] 26 | 21 | 23 | $51

11 Washington Ave. (1st St.), Miami Beach, 305-673-0365

◪ "Celebs, tourists and those spending other people's money" get their "annual fix" of "melt-in-your-mouth stone crabs" and "world-class sides" at South Beach's Most Popular restaurant; "bring someone who's never been and they'll be your friend for life", though you might want to "opt for the carry-out next door" and "make a mess at home", 'cause those cooling their jets in the bar'll tell you "you have to know God to get in"; N.B. it's stone-cold closed from mid-May through mid-October.

La Palme d'Or

26 | 27 | 25 | $61

Biltmore Hotel, 1200 Anastasia Ave. (Granada Blvd.), Coral Gables, 305-445-1926

■ "Maybe the most grown-up, romantic" dining in Coral Gables is at this "grande dame of French cuisine" at the Biltmore Hotel; "gorgeous" frescoes and "flawless service" enhance the "drama" of "epicurean delights" that include "quintessential Sunday brunch" and "samplers" by visiting Michelin-starred chefs "on the first week of each month"; though every "pricey" "star" has its critics, "celebrants" say "*l'ultra de l'ultra*" is "worth every penny."

Liaison ●S

25 | 21 | 23 | $38

1436 Drexel Ave. (Española Way), Miami Beach, 305-538-1055

■ As the name implies, this "hidden treasure" on South Beach is a "good place for a date", not only because of its "romantic", "French Quarter" feel but because its New American–Cajun cuisine is "superbly creative", "fresh and healthy" at "reasonable prices"; sit at the "hip" bar and sample from the "killer martini menu" as you wait for that special someone to arrive.

Mark's South Beach

26 | 23 | 24 | $57

Nash Hotel, 1120 Collins Ave. (11th St.), Miami Beach, 305-604-9050

■ For "trendy" fans of the 'Mango Gang', the culinary "zenith" of South Beach just might be Mark Militello's "upscale original" in the "stylish" Nash Hotel; fashionable foodies feast on "crisp, clean, pure" New American "flavors blended perfectly" "with a Caribbean touch" that "satisfies" "chic" "palates" dining "alfresco" "around the pool" or in a "dining room that resembles a ship's" galley.

Miss Saigon Bistro S

25 | 17 | 24 | $25

148 Giralda Ave. (Ponce de Leon Blvd.), Coral Gables, 305-446-8006

■ "Mama does it right" with her "fantastic creations" at this "all-in-the-family, homestyle" Vietnamese while, "if you're lucky", her "wonderful" waiters/children "sing some opera" for your supper; the "spicy" "treats" are "deservedly popular", so expect a "long wait", quickly "turned tables" and "noise" at this recently expanded, "inexpensive" "oasis on Coral Gables'" restaurant row.

Morton's of Chicago S

25 | 24 | 24 | $53

1200 Brickell Ave. (Coral Way), 305-400-9990
17399 Biscayne Blvd. (NE 173rd St.), North Miami Beach, 305-945-3131

◪ At these "carnivore heavens" Downtown and in North Miami Beach, the "showing of the flesh" doesn't have the usual sun-worshiper's connotation; here it means that "delicious red meat" is "presented raw" to each "entertained" table before orders are placed (the "very good seafood" is worth considering too); some critics find the cigar-friendly chainster's "pomp" and prices to be "major turnoffs."

Nemo ●S

24 | 23 | 21 | $46

100 Collins Ave. (1st St.), Miami Beach, 305-532-4550

■ "Mmm, yum" – for "delicious food and delicious people", "a must-stop on the SoBe circuit" is this "all-around" "interesting" New World "favorite" with multicultural accents; when you dine on a "nearly flawless" dinner followed by "heavenly dessert" or "gorge on Sunday brunch" here, it's all about "location, location, location", so "sit outside in the courtyard" "under the trees" and maybe you'll see "beautiful" folk like "Calvin Klein at the next table."

Nobu Miami Beach ◐[S] – | – | – | E

1901 Collins Ave. (20th St.), Miami Beach, 305-695-3232

Since its pre-season debut in late 2001, the trendy Shore Club's Nouvelle Japanese has shaken and stirred the South Beach scene with a dash of Peru and lots of hype thanks to co-owner Nobu Matsuhisa, who has opened outposts in several cities; the near impossibility of getting a reservation leaves non-celebs clawing and conniving their way in for a taste of signature black cod with miso and other delectable, pricey tidbits.

Norman's 27 | 25 | 26 | $58

21 Almeria Ave. (Douglas Rd.), Coral Gables, 305-446-6767

◪ "One of the best restaurants in the country" "lives up to its reputation"; "passionate" chef-owner Norman Van Aken is "still on top of his form", turning out "original" New World "dishes fit for a queen" in a "quietly sophisticated" atmosphere with "perfectly attentive" service that makes diners "feel like royalty"; hungry peasants pout the "cutting-edge culinary masterpieces" are miniatures, "leaving you literally asking for more."

Ortanique on the Mile [S] 26 | 23 | 23 | $45

278 Miracle Mile (Le Jeune Rd.), Coral Gables, 305-446-7710

■ It's "Jamaica in the Gables" at this "wonderful" "addition to the "Miami dining scene"; the "tropical atmosphere" "puts you on a Caribbean island immediately", and French-"inspired" "flavor explosions" "make that feeling linger"; the crowd is "festive", "young" and "noisy", but even adults who "don't like Florida" "would make a trip back just to eat" here – after all, "where else can you get a great glass of wine to go with your jerk foie gras?"

Osteria del Teatro 26 | 18 | 24 | $48

1443 Washington Ave. (Española Way), Miami Beach, 305-538-7850

■ Obsessive diners "can't be in South Beach without eating" at this "tiny little place" where the "pastas are phenomenal" and the other "elegant" showstoppers are "seasoned to perfection"; it may be "in need of an interior decorator", but even "wealthy Italians" are "impressed" by the "sublime" fare.

Pacific Time [S] 26 | 22 | 23 | $50

915 Lincoln Rd. (bet. Jefferson & Michigan Aves.), Miami Beach, 305-534-5979

■ "Talk about fusion!" – "everything and the kitchen sink" shows up on the menu at chef-owner Jonathan Eismann's South Beach Pan-Asian where "very fresh fish" practically "jumps off the plate", "sauces are sublime" and desserts like the chocolate bomb are, you guessed it, "dynamite"; it's "tight" inside, so if you're not down with the din and "people bumping into your chair", a table "outside on Lincoln Road is a nice option."

Palm [S] 27 | 20 | 25 | $54

9650 E. Bay Harbor Dr. (Kane Concourse), Bay Harbor Island, 305-868-7256

◪ "The power" of the "ultimate steak" "keeps pulling" "junkies" "back into" this "New York landmark transported to Miami"; as befits a "place that's not for pecking at your food", everything here is outsized: "larger-than-life portions" come with "price tags to match" in a "big, barn-like space that's not conducive to conversation"; despite the "raves" of well-treated "regulars", some diners read too much "snobbery" in this Palm.

Pascal's on Ponce
26 | 19 | 22 | $44

2611 Ponce de Leon Blvd. (bet. Almeria & Valencia Aves.), Coral Gables, 305-444-2024

■ Francophiles figure this "awesome little" "rising star" is "the best newcomer to the Gables"; "light", "sophisticated" New French fare makes it worth the "squeeze" at "tables that are on top of each other" in this "intimate" slice of "Provence" that visitors "hope doesn't become spoiled by success."

Pit Bar-B-Q S
22 | 14 | 15 | $14

16400 SW Eighth St. (Krome Ave.), 305-226-2272

■ "Whoa, amazing!" say families who "board the kids in the van" and head for this "Deep South" "institution" near the Everglades; in a quarter century of serving "the best ribs", "fresh local gator, catfish and frogs' legs", the "trailer park"–fabulous "place hasn't changed" and "neither have its prices"; you'll get "BBQ sauce on your hands", but you'll be too busy "pigging out" "to care about what you learned from Miss Manners."

Porcao ●S
23 | 18 | 21 | $39

801 Brickell Bay Dr. (SE 8th St.), 305-373-2777

■ Rodizio experts suggest you "fast for a week beforehand" and line up "someone to drive you home afterward", 'cause chances are this Downtown Brazilian "bacchanalia" will land you in a "meat coma"; the "amazing" "salad bar just won't quit", but "save room" to "try every cut you can think of" at this "noisy", "fill-'er-up" fleshfest clamoring with carnivores.

Romeo's Cafe S
27 | 20 | 26 | $51

2257 Coral Way (bet. 22nd & 23rd Aves.), Coral Gables, 305-859-2228

■ With Romeo as your "own private chef", you will feel like a "pampered" Juliet at this "romantic" Coral Gables Northern Italian that offers "a unique dining experience"; the owner "individually tailors a six-course meal" to the "liking" of each of the nine tables in the "tiny", "pretty" place where "you can go 50 times and never receive the same" dish twice, though "each one will be excellent."

Tantra ●S
22 | 26 | 17 | $58

1445 Pennsylvania Ave. (Española Way), Miami Beach, 305-672-4765

☑ It's "more of a party scene than a restaurant" say supplicants of this "very, very expensive" South Beach "adult date place" with its "dark and sultry" surroundings and "grass on the floor"; it's not that the "aphrodisiac" Mediterranean–New French fare isn't "unbelievably good", it's just that with everyone "smoking hookah pipes", dancing to "blaring trance music" and "lounging" beneath an endless loop of the movie *The Kama Sutra*, it's too "distracting to eat."

Toni's Sushi Bar ●S
26 | 22 | 23 | $30

1208 Washington Ave. (12th St.), Miami Beach, 305-673-9368

■ "Seasoned fish eaters" hook "the freshest and best presented" "huge portions" around for a "great price" at South Beach's most senior sushi bar; the "mixed crowd" in this "laid-back" fin den is great for "people-watching", but you might get tired of ogling your neighbors when the "friendly" service gets "slow" here on busy weekends.

Touch ◑ [S] | 21 | 24 | 18 | $55

910 Lincoln Rd. (Jefferson Ave.), Miami Beach, 305-532-8003

◪ "Ooh-la-la!" – it's "like the circus" at this "trendsetting" Lincoln Road "dine-and-disco"-rama where, if you don't mind "smoke and noise with your salad", the New American eats are as "exciting" and "delicious" as late-night acts like "fire-twirling gymnasts, sax players and belly dancers"; the "funky" fete lures a touch too many "tourists" for local tastes, and the caress becomes a pinch – "ouch! – when you get the check."

Tropical Chinese [S] | 26 | 18 | 22 | $29

Tropical Park Plaza, 7991 SW 40th St. (79th Ave.), 305-262-7576

■ "Dim sum!, dim sum!, dim sum!" are the three top reasons it's "worth the drive" to Southwest Dade's "Hong Kong–style" strip-mall hall; "large crowds" of Sunday Sinophiles "wait in line" "to watch the preparations" through the "huge glass window into the kitchen" and to flag down "carts" loaded with a "massive array" of "alluring interpretations on the traditional" choices at what is "Miami's best Chinese."

Versailles ◑ [S] | 19 | 15 | 18 | $19

3555 SW Eighth St. (35th Ave.), 305-445-7614

■ Folks with their heritage in the island-nation south of us say having a "satisfying" and "totally authentic" meal at this Little Havana "landmark" is "like lunch at my family's home on a Sunday afternoon"; it's "as Cuban as it gets" in this diner where the decor is pseudo–Louis XIV, i.e. "overdone", but the "history, politics and characters are exceptional."

Wolfie Cohen's Rascal House ◑ [S] | 20 | 12 | 16 | $20

17190 Collins Ave. (172nd St.), Sunny Isles, 305-947-4581

◪ The "average age at breakfast is no less than 67" and the "surly" servers and "Members Only"–clad customers "provide a late-night floor show", so a "nostalgia-filled" nosh at this grungy Miami Beach "institution" is "a cultural experience" around the clock; some say it's "still the gold standard" for "the best" "Jewish soul food" "this side of New York", but others opine it "ain't what it used to be" since its corporate takeover in the late '90s.

Minneapolis/St. Paul

TOP 10 FOOD RANKING

	Restaurant	Cuisine Type
27	Goodfellow's	New American
	La Belle Vie	New French/Med.
26	Bayport Cookery	Eclectic
	D'Amico Cucina	N&S Italian
	Lucia's	New American
	Manny's	Steakhouse
25	Ristorante Luci	Southern Italian
	Punch Neapolitan Pizza	Pizza
	128 Cafe	New American
	Oceanaire	Seafood

ADDITIONAL NOTEWORTHY PLACES

Aquavit	Swedish
Cafe Brenda	Health Food
Dakota Bar & Grill	Midwestern
Gardens of Salonica	Greek
Kincaid's	Seafood/Steakhouse
Loring Café	New American
Origami	Japanese
Restaurant Alma	New American
St. Paul Grill	American
Zander Cafe	New American

	F	D	S	C
Aquavit	24	25	23	$56

IDS Ctr., 80 S. Eighth St. (Nicollet Mall), Minneapolis, 612-343-3333

■ Nothing of the "mythically dour Scandinavian" about this place – "the first thing that comes to mind" when you enter is how the "sleek", "sophisticated" space is so "light and airy"; it makes for a "chic" background for Marcus Samuelsson's "minimalist but fabulous" "Nouvelle" Swedish menu, presented by an "excellent" staff; it's "fun to receive the little gifts from the chef between each course", which means that this Downtown "splurge" is "really an event" rather than a mere meal.

	F	D	S	C
Bayport Cookery [S]	26	17	23	$48

328 Fifth Ave. N. (Rte. 95), Bayport, 651-430-1066

■ "Definitely a quintessential foodie experience", this "charming", "romantic" "getaway" in the river town of Bayport near the state line has "yet to disappoint" gourmands with its five-course prix fixe Eclectic "culinary excursions", which change weekly but are always "imaginatively created and presented" (don't miss the "fabulous morel-fest" in the springtime); though a few impatient types find the very "leisurely" pace "quite a long ordeal", admirers are adamant that this is "a worth-the-drive restaurant if ever there was one"; N.B. one seating nightly at 7 PM.

Cafe Brenda
23 | 19 | 21 | $30

300 First Ave. N. (3rd St.), Minneapolis, 612-342-9203

■ "Top-quality ingredients and a little imagination make all the difference" at this Warehouse District "jewel", a health food cafe that "pleases even the non-veggie crowd"; chef-owner "Brenda creates dishes that look as beautiful as they taste", and paired with "fabulous house wines", they're served by a "patient", "eccentric" staff in a "simple yet refined" setting.

Dakota Bar & Grill
20 | 19 | 18 | $34

Bandana Sq., 1021 E. Bandana Blvd. (Lexington Pkwy.), St. Paul, 651-642-1442

■ It's so "refreshing to have the same owner, chef and passions after all these years" say regulars of this "fun, hip club with lots of atmosphere"; uniquely set in a rehabbed railroad roundhouse in suburban St. Paul, it features a "satisfying" menu of Midwestern "regional specialties" enhanced by a "creative" wine list; garnering even more applause is the "best jazz in the Twin Cities, bar none", leading plenty of fans to enthuse "good food, good music" – this "combo is hard to beat."

D'Amico Cucina
26 | 24 | 25 | $55

Butler Sq., 100 N. Sixth St. (bet. 1st & 2nd Aves.), Minneapolis, 612-338-2401

■ "Impress out-of-town food snobs" or "make up with your wife over almost anything" by visiting this "upscale" "special-occasion" destination "somewhat hidden" in the Warehouse District, where the "heavenly" Italian dishes not only "never disappoint" but will also "push the boundaries of what you thought you liked to eat"; equally "refined" are the "palatial" surroundings and "incredibly knowledgeable" staff; the only drawback: "ouch, the price."

Gardens of Salonica
23 | 14 | 15 | $17

19 NE Fifth St. (Hennepin Ave.), Minneapolis, 612-378-0611

■ "In a city lacking for good Greek food", this Northeast "gem" is "definitely the pinnacle"; providing an experience that's "like a slice of the islands", it thrills the palate with "fantastic" cooking that yields "special flavors" ("must have: the skordalia appetizer"); though the "wait is annoying" and it can get "a bit noisy" (and "service tends to be on the slow side"), "it's worth tolerating for the quality" of the dishes, not to mention the "1970s prices."

Goodfellow's
27 | 25 | 25 | $59

City Ctr., 40 S. Seventh St. (bet. Hennepin & Nicollet Aves.), Minneapolis, 612-332-4800

■ "There's nothing like sipping a dry martini and gazing" at "stunning" "art deco" decor while dining on chef Kevin Cullen's ("the king of Minneapolis") "divine", contemporary "twists on American standards" at this Downtown standard bearer, voted No. 1 for Food in the Twin Cities; his "flavor combinations are wonderful" and the "impeccable" staff provides "a pampering experience", making it a "good place to take high-maintenance clients"; though a few sniff that it's a bit too "uppity", loyalists can't wait to return to "escape the mundane and pretend they're Zelda or F. Scott."

Kincaid's [S] 22 | 22 | 22 | $41

8400 Normandale Lake Blvd. (84th St.), Bloomington, 952-921-2255
380 St. Peter St. (6th St.), St. Paul, 651-602-9000

◪ Despite its mass popularity, this "bustling" pair of American surf 'n' turf "institutions" is a "solid performer but a far cry from fine cuisine", which makes it "dependable, if a bit predictable"; nevertheless, legions of business suits feel it offers "the best power lunch around", so it's "often hard to get a reservation", both at the flagship in "suburban" Bloomington and the "newer hot spot in Downtown St. Paul."

La Belle Vie [S] 27 | 23 | 26 | $57

312 S. Main St. (Nelson St.), Stillwater, 651-430-3545

■ Take a "beautiful drive to Stillwater" and discover this "oh-so-romantic" "hidden gem along the St. Croix River", "a total joy from the moment you walk in the door"; in a "lovely", "unpretentious environment", a "knowledgeable" staff delivers "superb" New French–Mediterranean dishes (executed by co-chefs Josh Thoma and Tim McKee) that are "grounded in classical techniques yet always include surprising twists", while a sommelier expertly advises on the "wonderful wine selection"; the "aromas, tastes, sights and sounds all contribute to the marvelous experience" – "*La Belle Vie* indeed!"

Loring Café [S] 20 | 24 | 16 | $38

1624 Harmon Pl. (Hennepin Ave.), Minneapolis, 612-332-1617

◪ The "brilliant" decor translates to "serious visual and theatrical fun" at this "eclectic", "bohemian" hang bordering Loring Park, where an "arty crowd" swarms around for "cool" "people-watching"; curious appetites praise the "ultra-creative" New American kitchen's "witty collaborations", but grouches grumble "they try to do too much with too many ingredients", resulting in concoctions that are overly "avant-garde", and warn about service that "ranges from mildly petulant to aggressively surly."

Lucia's [S] 26 | 20 | 24 | $35

1432 W. 31st St. (Hennepin Ave.), Minneapolis, 612-825-1572

■ True, the "limited" New American lunch and dinner menus at this "chef-driven" Uptown "landmark" include "only four" entree items (only three or four appetizers too), but "genius" Lucia Watson's roster "changes weekly" and always stars "incredibly fresh, top-quality" "heartland ingredients" turned into "simple, pure preparations" with "amazing depths of flavor"; though the digs are "sardine-can" "cozy", the space is made comfortable by a "calm" atmosphere and "attentive yet relaxed" service, leading the "enchanted" to regard this "gem" as "the Chez Panisse of Minneapolis"; only one question: "can we clone this one?"

Manny's Steakhouse [S] 26 | 19 | 25 | $56

Hyatt Regency, 1300 Nicollet Mall (Grant St.), Minneapolis, 612-339-9900

◪ "Everything is super-size" at this Downtown "steakhouse of steakhouses", a "classic boys' club" that provides "big food and big drinks for big shots" in a "big room"; though the "loud, bright" quarters have "all the charm of a meat locker" and the staff is "as well-aged as the beef" (but with "a great sense of humor"), meat lovers are convinced that they've reached "carnivore heaven."

Oceanaire [S] 25 24 25 $52

Hyatt Regency, 1300 Nicollet Mall (Grant St.), Minneapolis, 612-333-2277

■ Ranked the Most Popular restaurant in the Twin Cities, this "cosmopolitan" send-up of a vintage supper club that's styled after a '40s-era luxury ocean liner is appointed with cherrywood and red-leather booths and infused with a "clubby, old-money atmosphere"; the seafood "counterpart" of Manny's Steakhouse across the hall in Downtown's Hyatt Regency, its daily changing menu showcases "intelligently" prepared fish dishes (notably a "spectacular" Chilean sea bass) that "recall an earlier time of elegant" dining; what's more, "nothing" is "snobbish here except the prices"; P.S. "the oyster bar is fantastic."

128 Cafe [S] 25 12 20 $32

128 Cleveland Ave. N. (Laurel Ave.), St. Paul, 651-645-4128

■ "Don't miss this gem" urge followers about this "cool" "diamond-in-the-rough" near the University of St. Thomas, even though it's "weirdly" set in the "basement of an apartment building"; you'll forget all about the humble digs once you tuck into Brock and Natalie Obee's "fabulous" New American "interpretations" (justly renowned are their "zippy" BBQ babyback ribs), delivered by a "very caring" staff; romantic types laud it as a "great place to bring a date", though a few wags quip they're "always expecting a washing machine to overflow."

Origami 23 17 18 $35

30 N. First St. (1st Ave.), Minneapolis, 612-333-8430

■ "Even Japanese businessmen are impressed" by this "trendy" spot near the river in the Warehouse District, where "young locals" also congregate to bask in the "urban atmosphere"; the sushi is so "fresh" it'll "knock your socks off" and the staff is "attentive and unobtrusive" (if "overworked"), but be forewarned that the "no-reservations policy" often leads to a "horrible wait" and the joint can get as packed as a Tokyo commuter train at rush hour.

Punch Neapolitan Pizza 25 18 18 $19

(aka Punch Woodfire Pizza)

704 Cleveland Ave. S. (Highland Pkwy.), St. Paul, 651-696-1066

■ Discover "the deal of the century" at this "family-owned" "neighborhood spot" in Highland Park, where the "interesting flavors and great prices" make it "a religious experience" among the faithful; there are "very few items on the menu, but what they do have is perfect" – namely "wood-fired" "pizza for adults", made with a "smoky" crust, "the sexiest tomato sauce in the city" and "delectable" toppings – which amply explains why a "diverse crowd" puts up with "long waits", "hard chairs, a cramped space" and a "deafening" "noise level."

Restaurant Alma [S] 25 20 20 $42

528 University Ave. SE (6th Ave.), Minneapolis, 612-379-4909

■ A "little" "jewel" in SE Minneapolis near the University of Minnesota, this "exciting" New American is a "dream come true" thanks to chef-owner Alex Roberts' "terrific homegrown menu" of "contemporary" dishes (based on local, organic products) that leave fans "licking the plate clean"; accompanied by a "great", eclectic wine list, it's all turned out by a "helpful" staff in a "casual, urban atmosphere"; "these people know what they're doing."

Ristorante Luci [S] 25 | 14 | 23 | $35

470 Cleveland Ave. S. (Randolph Ave.), St. Paul, 651-699-8258

■ "Don't be turned off by the low-key storefront" environs of this "definitive" "neighborhood" "hole-in-the-wall" in Highland Park because its "true" Southern Italian cooking is "excellent – no other way to put it"; the "personable" family owners don't "try to pull your palate into submission" but instead feed you "normal-size portions" of "flavorful" food, including "homemade mozzarella", "delightful" pastas and "marvelous" seafood ("order the tasting menu and you won't be disappointed"); though it's "well worth the cost", note that there are only 36 seats, so "book way in advance."

St. Paul Grill [S] 22 | 24 | 24 | $44

St. Paul Hotel, 350 Market St. (5th St.), St. Paul, 651-224-7455

■ Ever a "consistent standby for the scotch-and-cigar crowd", this "clubby", "classy" "tradition" in Downtown St. Paul has secured a place for itself as a premier "old boys' place" for "power dining"; quartered in the "historic" St. Paul Hotel, it boasts a "fabulous view of Rice Park" and an "elegant" backdrop for all-American fare ("it may not be inventive, but you know you're going to have a good meal") proffered by a "formal, knowledgeable" staff; furthermore, it gets plenty of votes for having the "best bar in town – period."

Zander Cafe [S] 25 | 17 | 20 | $35

525 Selby Ave. (Dale St.), St. Paul, 651-222-5224

■ Though "they clearly didn't spend a lot of money on the decor" at this "hip" storefront in Cathedral Hill, most patrons don't mind when they're rewarded with "brilliant" chef-owner Alexander Dixon's "inventive but always balanced" dishes; his New American menu is "limited", but it changes frequently and it's presented in a "buzzing" atmosphere that gets livelier still on nights when there's "great live jazz"; no wonder many first-timers "aspire to be habitués" – "the overall package is so welcoming and satisfying that I could eat here every week."

New Jersey

TOP 20 FOOD RANKING

Restaurant	Cuisine Type
28 Ryland Inn	New French
Daniel's on Broadway	New American
27 Cafe Panache	New French
Sagami	Japanese
Saddle River Inn	New American/Classic French
Scalini Fedeli	Northern Italian
Café Matisse	Eclectic
Washington Inn	American
Moonstruck	Mediterranean
Serenäde	New French
Ebbitt Room	New American
410 Bank Street*	Cajun/Caribbean
Le Rendez-Vous	French Bistro/Med.
Union Park	New American
26 Jocelyne's	New French
Dining Room	New American
Jeffrey's	New American
Fromagerie	Classic French
Siri's	Classic French/Thai
Bobby Chez	Seafood

ADDITIONAL NOTEWORTHY PLACES

Acacia	New American
Bernards Inn	New American
DeLorenzo's Tomato Pies	Pizza
Doris & Ed's	Seafood
Esty Street	New American
Frog & The Peach	New American
Harvest Moon Inn	New American
Heatwave at Windows	New American
Highlawn Pavilion	New American
Karen & Rei's	New American
Little Cafe	International
Madeleine's Petit Paris	Classic French
Manor	American
Park & Orchard	Eclectic/Vegetarian
Rat's	New French
River Palm Terrace	Steakhouse
Shumi	Japanese
Stage House Inn	New French
Waters Edge	New American
Zarolé	New French/American

---

* Tied with the restaurant listed directly above it

Acacia 🅂　　　25　21　23　$42
2637 Main St. (bet. Craven Ln. & Phillips Ave.), Lawrenceville, 609-895-9885
■ Shutterbugs "want to take a picture of the plate" at this "smart" Lawrenceville New American that presents "pretty" dishes that are "executed flawlessly" in a "lovely", "lively" but sometimes "loud" setting; nitpickers grumble it's "a bit precious", but "civilized dining" fans deem it the "best in the Princeton area" "bar none" and note that its BYO policy makes this "sublime" spot "almost affordable."

Bernards Inn　　　25　26　24　$53
The Bernards Inn, 27 Mine Brook Rd. (Quimbey St.), Bernardsville, 908-766-0002
■ Chef Edward Stone's "marvelous" cuisine paired with "one of the best wine lists in New Jersey" sets a "tony" tone at this "luxurious" New American in Bernardsville that's the epitome of "classic hunt-country sophistication"; indeed, it's such a "romantic getaway" that it's almost "guaranteed to get a husband out of the doghouse"; P.S. "a stay at the inn after dinner is a must to complete the experience."

Bobby Chez　　　26　11　18　$18
Southgate Plaza, 1225 Rte. 561 (bet. Franklin Ave. & Laurel Rd.), Voorhees, 856-768-6660
The Village Walk, 1990 Rte. 70 (Rte. 29), Cherry Hill, 856-751-7373
■ "Heavenly", "chock-full-of-crab" cakes that just might be the "best in the universe" are the house specialty at these Voorhees and Cherry Hill seafood houses offering limited seating but a roaring "take-out" trade; even though crab is king here, the lobster mashed potatoes and "spicy shrimp are to die for" too, so expect "long lines all day."

Café Matisse 🅂　　　27　23　25　$49
167 Park Ave. (bet. E. Park Pl. & Highland Cross), Rutherford, 201-935-2995
■ "Who needs NYC" when there's "flawless, original" Eclectic cooking in Rutherford that's "as artful as its name"?; chef-owner Peter Loria's BYO, located in a former fire station, offers an ambiance so romantic it can "turn a sparring couple into Romeo and Juliet"; N.B. they've renovated recently and added a wine shop next door.

Cafe Panache　　　27　21　25　$49
130 E. Main St. (Rte. 17), Ramsey, 201-934-0030
■ Chef-owner Kevin Kohler just "keeps getting better" at this Ramsey BYO where each of the frequently changing New French menus "proves to be more spectacular than the last" thanks to the "innovative use of herbs and sauces"; the "tiny, country-cottage" setting is "unpretentious" yet "posh", and the "thoughtful staff" helps keep this one on everyone's "celebration favorite" list.

Daniel's on Broadway 🅂　　　28　27　25　$46
416 S. Broadway (4th Ave.), West Cape May, 609-898-8770
■ Chef/co-owner Harry Gleason creates some of New Jersey's "most imaginative food" at this New American BYO in West Cape May where "innovative" dishes are "prepared with a creative flair" (their "signature dish, grouper Charleston, is fantastic"); set in a "charming" "converted Victorian home", it features "first-class" service down to the "well-spaced course timing" and is "perfect for a special occasion" – "they care about everything" here.

DeLorenzo's Tomato Pies 🅂⌀   26   11   18 $15
530 Hudson St. (bet. Mott & Swann Sts.), Trenton, 609-695-9534
■ "Tomato fans" insist that this "Trenton institution for thin-crust pies" serves the "best pizza in the tri-state area" "bar none"; even if there's "no salad, no pasta, no bathroom" and "nothing fancy" going on decor-wise, few care when they "wake in the middle of the night with cravings" for what this "popular" BYO does best.

Dining Room   26   28   27 $64
Hilton Short Hills, 41 JFK Pkwy. (Rte. 24), Short Hills, 973-379-0100
■ "The staff has sharp antennae" at this "flawless" New American in the Short Hills Hilton that reeks of "class, class, class", from the more-than-"capable kitchen" to the "exquisite", flower-laden dining room that comes complete with "live harp music"; owing to its "consistent high standards", you should expect correspondingly "top-of-the-line pricing", but hey, "you get what you pay for" – and "everything's perfect" here.

Doris & Ed's 🅂   26   20   23 $46
348 Shore Dr. (Waterwich Ave.), Highlands, 732-872-1565
■ "Mouthwatering seafood" whets appetites at this Highlands James Beard Award winner where you can expect a "whale of a meal, and that's no fish story"; besides the stunning "art on a plate" presentations, count on an "impressive wine list", "pleasant, knowledgeable servers" and "lovely" "ocean views" – plus the inevitable "big summer crowds" and "waits that can exceed the meal time."

Ebbitt Room 🅂   27   26   25 $49
Virginia Hotel, 25 Jackson St. (bet. Beach Dr. & Carpenter Ln.), Cape May, 609-884-5310
■ "Beyond the beyond" is how foodies regard chef Michael Merlo's meals at this New American "gem in Cape May" that's a "yardstick for all others"; set in a boutique hotel and festooned with "breathtaking floral arrangements", this "romantic" spot is a "throwback to the elegance of the '50s", with service that's "Swiss level", so you're virtually guaranteed a "perfect evening."

Esty Street   26   20   22 $47
86 Spring Valley Rd. (Fremont Ave.), Park Ridge, 201-307-1515
■ "Passaic Valley's best" is this "aristocratic" New American in Park Ridge where "innovative", "eclectic dishes that change seasonally" and "sublime presentation" are the "equal of any in NYC"; granted, it may be "noisy", with "tables much too close together", but owing to its "knowledgeable staff", "wonderful wine list" and "sophisticated atmosphere", it's "always a joy."

410 Bank Street 🅂   27   21   23 $46
410 Bank St. (bet. Broad St. & Lafayette Ave.), Cape May, 609-884-2127
■ Putting Cape May "on the culinary map" is this Cajun-Caribbean BYO "tropical retreat" set in Victorian digs, where fans continue to "explore the menu and find dishes to fall in love with"; they have their own smokehouse for meats and seafood (the fish is "heaven"), but whatever you select, be prepared for "taste-bud explosions" – "after all these years, it still has what it takes."

Frog and The Peach [S] 26 | 23 | 24 | $51

29 Dennis St. (Hiram Sq.), New Brunswick, 732-846-3216

■ "A pioneer that doesn't age", this "landmark" New Brunswick "dream" continues to put together "magnificent presentations" of "inspired", "inventive" New American cuisine that keeps it on the "cutting edge"; from its "chic", "industrial" setting to the "impeccable service", devotees "can't say enough about the old girl" – just "be prepared to drop some mad loot."

Fromagerie [S] 26 | 25 | 25 | $55

26 Ridge Rd. (Ave. of Two Rivers), Rumson, 732-842-8088

◪ *Le* big cheese in Rumson for *"magnifique"* meals, this "cozy" French is "perfect for a special occasion", given its "excellent" cooking, "terrific" decor, "perfect" service and "NY wine list" (albeit at "NY prices"); the majority says dining here is "a grand night out", though a minority frets it's "just not as inspiring as it used to be."

Harvest Moon Inn [S] 26 | 24 | 23 | $49

1039 Old York Rd. (Rte. 202), Ringoes, 908-806-6020

■ The "old world meets the 21st century" at this "historic" building-turned-inn where chef-owner Stanley Novak presents cutting-edge New American cooking to a "crowd that's not quite NY, though the food certainly is"; granted, it's a "bit of a ride" to Ringoes, but "more than worth it", since most are willing to "eat from the time the moon rises till it sets" at this "perfect getaway."

Heatwave at Windows [S] – | – | – | E

White Sands Hotel, 1205 Ocean Ave. (Philadelphia Ave.), Point Pleasant Beach, 732-714-2030

Nestled in the serene, multi-windowed dining room of a resort/spa, this sophisticated New American satisfies fine-dining dreams with hazelnut-crusted Chilean sea bass, tuna tartare with a ponzu drizzle and the kind of skilled service rarely seen in casual, rollicking Point Pleasant Beach.

Highlawn Pavilion [S] 24 | 28 | 24 | $51

Eagle Rock Reservation, Eagle Rock Ave. (Prospect Ave.), West Orange, 973-731-3463

■ "Knockout", "magical" vistas of Manhattan "wow" diners at this West Orange bit of "heaven" where the New American "food holds its own" so well that some sigh the "view is gravy"; granted, you should "be prepared to spend a bundle" for the chance to experience "how the better half lives", but for "imaginative, lush dining", this "celebration" spot is hard to beat.

Jeffrey's 26 | 20 | 25 | $45

73 Main St. (Washington St.), Toms River, 732-914-9544

■ "Out-of-this-world delicious" cooking is the calling card of this New American BYO, a "wonderful surprise in Toms River", where chef Jeffrey Schneekloth's menu features the "finest, freshest ingredients"; though some say the decor "could use a little sprucing up" and others feel "they've lost their touch since they got famous", most sigh this dining experience is simply "what an evening should be."

Jocelyne's S   26 | 21 | 24 | $42
168 Maplewood Ave. (Baker St.), Maplewood, 973-763-4460
■ "Ooh-la-la!" – such "charm", such "fabulous" food, such a "darling" staff trill the many admirers of this New French BYO in Maplewood where chef Mitchell Altholz turns out exquisitely "delicate" dishes, "never serving an average meal"; wife Jocelyne works the front of the house, offering a "warm welcome" that makes "all guests feel special" at this "tiny suburban jewel."

Karen & Rei's S⌐   ▽ 27 | 18 | 24 | $39
1882 Rte. 9 N. (south of Rte. 83), Clermont, 609-967-4488
■ "How can one woman cook so well for so many?" wonder fans of this New American BYO, where chef/co-owner Karen Nelson "must work around the clock to make everything taste so superb"; to experience the "innovative preparations using fruits and spices" and the "fantastic desserts", "you practically have to book the summer before – but it's totally worth it"; N.B. a press-time move to Clermont outdates the decor score.

Le Rendez-Vous S   27 | 20 | 24 | $44
520 Boulevard (N. 21st St.), Kenilworth, 908-931-0888
■ "You won't believe you're in Kenilworth" after a taste of the "innovative", "slice-of-France" cooking at this "sweet" French-Mediterranean BYO that's "one of NJ's undiscovered gems"; though the "really tight" quarters guarantee you'll "rub elbows" with fellow diners, the "food makes you forget you're a sardine."

Little Cafe   26 | 19 | 23 | $35
Plaza Shoppes, 118 White Horse Rd. (Burnt Mill Rd.), Voorhees, 856-784-3344
■ "Big-city food" makes the scene in Voorhees at this "teeny-tiny" International BYO that proves you "can't judge a place by its size"; the "storefront atmosphere" may be "lacking in ambiance" and the "limited" "space is a problem" for claustrophobes, but it compensates with "unbeatable early-birds" and service that's "attentive without being pushy."

Madeleine's Petit Paris S   26 | 21 | 24 | $46
(fka Chez Madeleine)
416 Tappan Rd. (Paris Ave.), Northvale, 201-767-0063
■ Finally, "atmosphere to match the fabulous cooking" at this Northvale Classic French that's in a "spacious new home", where "elegant" dishes continue to dazzle diners; the owners' "warm hospitality" helps keep this "winner" squarely in the "crème de la crème" league; P.S. don't miss the crêpe Madeleine or the soufflés.

Manor S   24 | 26 | 24 | $52
111 Prospect Ave. (Eagle Rock Ave.), West Orange, 973-731-2360
■ They "treat you like a king" at this "glitz-to-the-hilt" West Orange American, aka the "Tavern on the Green of New Jersey", where "more people than Grand Central Station" gather to dig into its "fresh seafood buffet"; though some dismiss it as "Jurassic dining", it's still a "must for special occasions" and "delivers the whole nine yards" – you can "present that engagement ring", then book the wedding here.

Moonstruck [S] 27 | 21 | 23 | $39

57 Main Ave. (bet. Ocean Ave. & Rte. 71), Ocean Grove, 732-988-0123

■ "Get on line with your wine" at this fine Ocean Grove Med BYO that "never disappoints" owing to "fab", "lovingly prepared" creations from a "consistently talented chef" and "exceptional service"; the "no-reservations" policy, though, can make entry a "real hassle."

Park & Orchard [S] 24 | 15 | 20 | $34

240 Hackensack St. (Union Ave.), East Rutherford, 201-939-9292

■ "The most creative [red] meatless menu I've ever seen" sums up the eating scene at this Eclectic-Vegetarian "institution" in East Rutherford where "chicken, fish and pasta dishes abound"; "come hungry" ("huge portions") and "get there early" ("no reservations"), but while waiting, peruse the "glorious wine list" – with 2,000 bottles, it's about "the size of a legal brief."

Rat's [S] 24 | 28 | 23 | $60

16 Fairgrounds Rd. (Ward Ave.), Hamilton, 609-584-7800

■ "Beautiful doesn't begin to describe" this "fantasyland" set on Hamilton's Grounds for Sculpture; it's "magnificent on all counts", from chef Eric Martin's "out-of-this-world" New French cooking to its "spectacularly decorated" rooms and "unbelievable" gardens; though its name refers to the creature in the kids' classic *The Wind in the Willows*, its existence comes courtesy of J. Seward Johnson Jr. and is testimony to "what you can create if you're a billionaire."

River Palm Terrace [S] 25 | 19 | 21 | $49

1416 River Rd. (Palisade Terrace), Edgewater, 201-224-2013

41-11 Rte. 4 W. (bet. Paramus & Saddle River Rds.), Fair Lawn, 201-703-3500

209 Ramapo Valley Rd. (Rte. 17), Mahwah, 201-529-1111

■ "Here's the beef": for "prime meat in a prime restaurant", these "sophisticated", "upscale" North Jersey landmarks are "worth it no matter the price"; look for "tender", "tasty" cuts that set the "standard for all steakhouses" and a staff that's "amazingly patient", given the "high volume on Fridays and Saturdays."

Ryland Inn [S] 28 | 28 | 27 | $69

Rte. 22 W. (Rte. 523), Whitehouse, 908-534-4011

■ "Mere mortals may not fully appreciate the complexity" of "culinary god" Craig Shelton's cooking at this "magical" place in Hunterdon County that's voted both No. 1 for Food and Most Popular; "classy and gracious" from top to bottom, it also boasts a "beautiful" setting and an impressively "deep wine list", leaving the smitten to sigh that a meal at this New French "food heaven" is simply "perfection" – even if a few find it "overpriced."

Saddle River Inn 27 | 26 | 26 | $55

2 Barnstable Ct. (bet. E. Allendale Ave. & W. Saddle River Rd.), Saddle River, 201-825-4016

■ "Dream-making grand dining" and "European charm" are the calling cards of this New American–French in Saddle River that has produced "masterful meals in a country setting" for two decades; chef-owner "Hans Egg's hand has never lost its skill", turning out "excellent", "inventive" dishes, while "immaculate service" and a cost-cutting BYO policy are "bonuses" – just make sure to "plan ahead and reserve a table."

Sagami [S] 27 | 17 | 22 | $34

37 Crescent Blvd. (Haddon Ave.), Collingswood, 856-854-9773

■ Just "ask the execs at Subaru of America" – they'll tell you about the "melt-in-your-mouth" "precision sushi" sliced by chef Shigeru Fukuyoshi and his crew at this Collingswood BYO that's "worth the price" for a taste of the "zenith in Japanese cuisine"; you may have to wait your turn for a seat in the "dark-wooded, low-ceilinged" room, but the "charming, efficient staff" will make the meal pleasurable.

Scalini Fedeli 27 | 26 | 26 | $60

63 Main St. (Parrot Mill Rd.), Chatham, 973-701-9200

■ Chatham has its own "masterpiece" of "pure perfection" in this "superbly flavorful" Northern Italian BYO where "heavenly and ultimately romantic" evenings are the norm; chef Michael Cetrulo may be spending time at its NYC sibling, but that hasn't interfered with the "off-the-scale" "pleasure" of the fare or the "marvelous atmosphere"; yes, it's "expensive", but the lengthy wait for a reservation is, by most accounts, well "worth it."

Serenäde 27 | 25 | 25 | $59

6 Roosevelt Ave. (Main St.), Chatham, 973-701-0303

■ It's not only music lovers who "bliss out" over the "ingenious elegance" of the New French tasting menu at this Chatham "CEO dining capital of New Jersey", where chef/co-owner James Laird employs the "highest-quality ingredients" and scores "straight A's"; credit the "sensational" but "serene" atmosphere for devoted diners being "always surprised at how special they make you feel."

Shumi [S] 24 | 12 | 18 | $34

30 S. Doughty Ave. (Veterans Memorial Dr.), Somerville, 908-526-8596

■ Some of "the best sushi in New Jersey" turns up in this "Somerville strip mall", where the "fish is so fresh, you'd think it was caught out back"; so ignore this BYO's "hospital cafeteria" decor, settle in for "civilized service" and "let Ike (chef-owner Kunihiko Aikasa) do his magic for you."

Siri's [S] 26 | 23 | 24 | $36

Track Town Shopping Ctr., 2117 Rte. 70 W. (Haddonfield Rd.), Cherry Hill, 856-663-6781

■ "French elegance and sophistication" combine with "exotic" Thai flavors at this Cherry Hill venue that's the "best of both worlds" and earns unanimous praise for its "gorgeous, creative food" ("each dish is better than the last"); all the other elements at this BYO are in perfect harmony too, from the "attractive decor" to the "well-trained, attentive servers" and "reasonable" tabs.

Stage House Inn [S] 26 | 24 | 23 | $53

366 Park Ave. (Front St.), Scotch Plains, 908-322-4224

■ "From the *amuse-bouche* to the petit fours", you can anticipate "incredible culinary extravagance" via "awesome chef" David Drake's "masterful" cooking at this New French in Scotch Plains; the food's a cunning counterpoint to its "colonial setting" (in a 1737 historic building), the "wine list is loaded with exceptional vineyards at wonderful prices" and "they do all the little things that most places don't" – so it promises to be a "longtime superstar."

Union Park [S] 27 | 27 | 27 | $47

Hotel Macomber, 727 Beach Ave. (Howard St.), Cape May, 609-884-8811

■ "Park yourself" in a "beautiful room" and get ready for a "thrilling experience" at this New American BYO in Cape May that "has it all": "superb" cooking with "unique flavors" and "delicious combinations", plus service renowned for its "meticulous attention to detail"; it all unfolds in such a "lovely atmosphere" that it's a "must-stop for fine dining" in these parts.

Washington Inn [S] 27 | 27 | 26 | $49

801 Washington St. (Jefferson St.), Cape May, 609-884-5697

■ "Everything's first-class" at this "perfect" American in Cape May that remains the epitome of "civilized, elegant dining", offering "traditional food prepared with finesse", an "unbelievable wine cellar" and "extremely professional service"; its 1840s plantation house setting is "gorgeous, especially at Christmas", prompting fans to gush "the whole package is fabulous."

Waters Edge [S] 26 | 23 | 23 | $45

1317 Beach Dr. (Pittsburgh Ave.), Cape May, 609-884-1717

■ If you're dining at this Cape May New American on a "summer evening", try a "gin and tonic and a plate of veal" or one of the "highly imaginative seafood entrees with Asian and Caribbean touches" – you can be certain of a "tempting" and "eclectic" repast; in addition, its "exceptionally beautiful" "waterfront setting" makes it one of the "trendiest places at the Shore", leaving fans convinced that it "deserves its reputation in every way."

Zarolé [S] ▽ 26 | 27 | 19 | $45

20 E. Ridgewood Ave. (S. Broad St.), Ridgewood, 201-670-5701

■ "Your companion will look great in the lighting" at this French-American BYO in Ridgewood that's quite possibly the "most innovative new restaurant" in the area; though the "different and delicious" fusion cuisine pairs easily with the "breathtaking", "dramatic" decor, service is "a little off" – when it catches up, this "upscale" spot will be truly "tops."

New Orleans

TOP 20 FOOD RANKING

Restaurant	Cuisine Type
27 Bayona	New American
Brigtsen's	Louisiana
Gabrielle	Lousiana/Creole
Grill Room	New American
Artesia	New French
Ruth's Chris	Steakhouse
Commander's Palace	Creole
26 Galatoire's	Creole
Sal & Judy's	Creole/S. Italian
Clancy's	Creole
Upperline	Creole/Eclectic
Emeril's	Creole
25 Irene's Cuisine	N&S Italian
Gautreau's	Creole
Louis XVI	Classic French
Mosca's	N&S Italian
Kim Son	Vietnamese
La Provence	Classic French
Pelican Club	Louisiana
Mr. B's Bistro	Creole

ADDITIONAL NOTEWORTHY PLACES

Antoine's	Creole/Classic French
Arnaud's	Creole
Basil Leaf	Thai
Bistro at Maison de Ville	French Bistro
Brennan's	Creole
Cafe Giovanni	N&S Italian
Christian's	Creole/Classic French
Dakota	New American
Emeril's Delmonico	Creole
Gamay	Creole
Gerard's Downtown	New French
Herbsaint	New French/New American
La Crêpe Nanou	French Bistro
Le Parvenu	Creole
Muriel's	New Orleans
Nine Roses	Vietnamese
NOLA	New Orleans
Peristyle	Louisiana/Classic French
Rib Room	Continental/Steakhouse
RioMar	Spanish/Med.

Antoine's
22 | 24 | 23 | $48

713 St. Louis St. (bet. Bourbon & Royal Sts.), 504-581-4422

◪ Exuding "great old-world charm", this "venerable New Orleans institution" is an arena-size Creole–Classic French in the Quarter that has remained a "grand tradition" since 1840; despite its "reputation", however, even veterans concede that for a "fine" meal here you must land "the right waiter and order the right food": "any oyster dish – Rockefeller, Thermidor, Foch" – and for the entree, "stick to the fillet."

Arnaud's S
22 | 24 | 24 | $45

813 Bienville St. (bet. Bourbon & Dauphine Sts.), 504-523-5433

◪ "Romantic and festive", this French Quarter Creole "landmark" is regarded by its followers as the "best of the old guard", with a "superb" staff proffering "perpetual favorites" like "sensational" shrimp rémoulade and trout meunière in "elegant" surroundings (insiders recommend the "brilliant main room"); though some are "disappointed" that it's "not what it used to be", many feel it's still a "wonderful special-occasion treat", despite "too many tourists."

Artesia S
27 | 25 | 24 | $40

21516 Hwy. 36 (Hwy. 59), Abita Springs, 504-892-1662

■ "Heaven in the country" is promised at this "first-class" Abita Springs New French housed in a "beautifully" restored Victorian-era mansion where a "marvelous" chef turns out "exquisitely tasty and appealing food"; it may be "out of the way" and a bit "hard to find", but admirers are convinced that it's "well worth the drive" to the North Shore for a "memorable" experience.

Basil Leaf S
24 | – | 21 | $26

1438 S. Carrollton Ave. (bet. Jeannette & Willow Sts.), 504-862-9001

■ A move from Metairie brought this "upscale", "clean and original" nouvelle Thai to adoring Carrollton admirers; "wonderful presentations" of "fabulous fresh food", along with "great service", make this "healthy gourmet" spot one where diners are "treated like a friend of the family."

Bayona
27 | 26 | 25 | $45

430 Dauphine St. (bet. Conti & St. Louis Sts.), 504-525-4455

■ Reviewers love the "consistently sublime", "absolutely superb" cuisine (voted No. 1 for Food in the *New Orleans Survey*) at this French Quarter New American, whose "chef, Susan Spicer, just gets better"; the "romantic", "lush" and "sophisticated" setting (including "beautiful patio dining in nice weather") and "attentive service" round out an "always exceptional experience."

Bistro at Maison de Ville S
25 | 24 | 23 | $44

Maison de Ville, 727 Toulouse St. (bet. Bourbon & Royal Sts.), 504-528-9206

■ This "authentic bistro" is not only "small and chic", it's also "wonderfully charming and romantic", making it a "tried-and-true" French Quarter "favorite"; it may be a "little pricey", but admirers opine that, with "delicious" Gallic food and a maitre d' who's a most "gracious host", it's "one of the best of its kind in the country."

Brennan's [S] — 23 | 26 | 24 | $47

417 Royal St. (bet. Conti & St. Louis Sts.), 504-525-9711

◪ Fans feel that this French Quarter "high Creole" "classic" with a "great atmosphere", a "beautiful patio" and an "excellent wine list" is a "must-visit landmark" and a "favorite" destination for "special occasions", "expense-account dinners" and "wonderful breakfasts"; but a vocal contingent of critics contends that it's "pricey", with "too many tourists."

Brigtsen's — 27 | 21 | 25 | $40

723 Dante St. (bet. Maple St. & River Rd.), 504-861-7610

■ It may be a bit "crowded and noisy", but its many devotees dismiss the decibels here because chef Frank Brigtsen is a "culinary genius" whose modern Louisiana cooking is some of the "best anywhere"; "wonderful, caring service" and a "cozy", "quaint setting" also add to the appeal of this "hidden gem" in the lower-Carrollton neighborhood – "thank goodness, it's still not on the tourist map."

Cafe Giovanni [S] — 24 | 23 | 23 | $37

117 Decatur St. (bet. Canal & Iberville Sts.), 504-529-2154

◪ Supporters say that this "excellent", "imaginative" French Quarter Italian is a "cut above most", but the less enthused shrug that the food is "solid but unremarkable"; still, the pleasant space makes a comfortable venue for opera nights (Wednesday, Friday and Saturday) and its "engaging singers" (aka your servers).

Christian's — 24 | 25 | 23 | $38

3835 Iberville St. (N. Scott St.), 504-482-4924

■ It's a "religious experience" and a "place to worship great food" declare devotees of this charming Mid-City restaurant set in a "beautiful" "old converted church" and featuring Creole-French fare that's a "delight to the taste and eyes"; since it's already "crowded and noisy", no wonder locals lament "please don't tell the tourists"; N.B. jacket required.

Clancy's — 26 | 20 | 23 | $38

6100 Annunciation St. (Webster St.), 504-895-1111

■ This "comfortable", "familiar" "insiders'" "hangout" Uptown pleases with "excellent" Creole-inspired dishes like oysters with brie and spinach and "the best soft shells and sweetbreads in town"; people-watching is part of the pleasure at this very N'Awlins "social scene" that's a "favorite of many locals."

Commander's Palace [S] — 27 | 28 | 27 | $47

1403 Washington Ave. (Coliseum St.), 504-899-8221

■ "Feel the magic" say more than 1,000 reviewers about the *New Orleans Survey*'s Most Popular restaurant; "first-class in every way", this Garden District haute Creole "shining star" is "always fabulous, festive and delicious", and that's because chef "Jamie Shannon and the Brennans know what true dining is", making it "perfect for a special occasion", as well as the "best for [weekend] jazz brunch."

Dakota
25 | 22 | 23 | $36

629 N. Hwy. 190 (¼ mi. off I-12), Covington, 504-892-3712
■ A "consistently good" North Shore "asset", this "innovative" Louisiana-inspired New American boasts a "crab-meat-and-brie soup that alone is worth the drive"; the "first-class staff" and charming surroundings are more reasons it's "worth the trip", even if it is "a bit expensive."

Emeril's
26 | 21 | 24 | $51

800 Tchoupitoulas St. (Julia St.), 504-528-9393
■ "Creative, innovative and oh-so-noisy" is the consensus on this contemporary Creole "jewel of the Warehouse District", the flagship of celebrity chef Emeril Lagasse that draws the "hip, young and cool" (plus plenty of tourists) with its "amazing food" and "energy level"; but even a few admirers complain that stardom has led to sometimes "haughty service" and that the kitchen "suffers" when the "bam man" is out of town – "Emeril, please phone home."

Emeril's Delmonico S
23 | 27 | 24 | $57

(fka Delmonico)
1300 St. Charles Ave. (Erato St.), 504-525-4937
◪ Though everyone raves over the decor at this "luxurious" Lower Garden District star in chef Emeril Lagasse's crown (some even hail it as the "most wonderful, elegant restaurant ever"), the majority is less enthused about the Creole food that's "good" but "doesn't meet expectations" ("too rich", "overblown") in light of the "outrageously expensive" prices; locals still "go for that special night", but warn "take out a loan" first.

Gabrielle
27 | 20 | 24 | $43

3201 Esplanade Ave. (bet. Maurepas & Mystery Sts.), 504-948-6233
■ While this "great little jewel" near the New Orleans Museum of Art can feel "cramped", its very size reminds devotees of "a French country restaurant", as does its "superior and creative" contemporary Louisiana and haute Creole cooking; "hooray for Greg and Mary Sonnier" say the enchanted about "one of the city's most talented culinary couples."

Galatoire's S
26 | 24 | 26 | $42

209 Bourbon St. (Iberville St.), 504-525-2021
■ "A New Orleans original" (since 1905), this French Quarter "institution" boasts "great old ambiance", plus a renovated second floor; locals are pleased that "despite the changes, it remains constant", turning out "delicious" haute Creole dishes that are "never a disappointment" and are served by experienced waiters who know not only your name, but also your drink – it's "worth any wait."

Gamay
25 | 24 | 23 | $42

Bienville House Hotel, 320 Decatur St. (additional entrance at 321 N. Peters St.), 504-299-8800
■ In the French Quarter, "a star is born" and it's "off to a great start" enthuse admirers of this second venue by top restaurateurs Mary and Greg Sonnier; a "worthy sister to Gabrielle", it boasts a "busy, fashionable atmosphere", not to mention "very good" contemporary Creole cooking.

Gautreau's 25 | 22 | 24 | $42

1728 Soniat St. (Danneel St.), 504-899-7397

■ "Fabulous, innovative Creole food" and "wonderful service in charming surroundings" add up to a "true classic hidden in Uptown New Orleans"; despite efforts to lower the decibels (carpeting, table padding, sound baffles), many say it's "still too noisy", but that doesn't stop anyone from enjoying the "fine dining" in this beautifully remodeled "old pharmacy with a pressed-tin ceiling"; it's unanimous: an "extraordinary" "local gem."

Gerard's Downtown 24 | 22 | 22 | $38

Parc St. Charles, 500 St. Charles Ave. (Poydras St.), 504-592-0200

■ "Impressive" say reviewers of chef Gerard Marais' return to New Orleans with this "elegant" New French cafe, one of the "best upscale" spots in the Central Business District; his "great attention to detail" translates into "well-prepared" "new and classic" dishes (some based on fresh ingredients from his own farm), "good service", a "comfortable setting" and valet parking that is much appreciated – in sum, a "real comer", so "get in while you can."

Grill Room [S] 27 | 29 | 27 | $58

Windsor Court Hotel, 300 Gravier St. (bet. S. Peters & Tchoupitoulas Sts.), 504-522-1992

■ "Beautiful", "classy", "elegant" are just a few of the accolades showered upon this dining room in the world-class Windsor Court Hotel, where the "outstanding" New American cuisine with French flair and "impeccable service" make it "a wonderful place to celebrate"; a few gripe that it's "too formal" and "not a happening place", but for the majority it's "well worth" any expense, so "mortgage the farm and eat here."

Herbsaint – | – | – | E

701 St. Charles Ave. (Girod St.), 504-524-4114

Susan Spicer, Bayona's queen of the kitchen, and partner-chef Donald Link are the powers that be behind this new hot spot on the edge of the Warehouse District; a simple but comfortable setting is the backdrop for New French–American cuisine (extraordinary gumbos, along with bistro favorites); though it's named after an obscure apéritif (which turns up in some signature dishes and drinks at the bar), this instantly popular place is strictly high profile.

Irene's Cuisine [S] 25 | 22 | 22 | $33

539 St. Philip St. (Chartres St.), 504-529-8811

■ "Please don't tell the tourists" beg locals about this "great hidden restaurant" at the far end of the Quarter, a "cozy" Italian with a reputation for "robust", "lusty" cooking; even though the "ridiculous no-reservations policy" results in "long waits", admirers agree the "challenge to get in is worth it."

Kim Son 25 | 13 | 18 | $18

349 Whitney Ave. (Westbank Expwy.), Gretna, 504-366-2489

■ Devotees of Vietnamese "dream about" the "incredibly tasty food" ("love that salt-baked stuff!") at this West Bank venue where the fare's "astonishing quality and complexity" come at a "very reasonable price"; in spite of swipes at the service, it's still "worth crossing the river" for this town's "best Viet."

La Crêpe Nanou S   24 | 22 | 20 | $26

1410 Robert St. (Prytania St.), 504-899-2670

■ In the eyes of its *amis*, "a trip to France is all that beats this bistro"; "a little loud" and always "crowded", it's an "Uptown favorite" for "delicious", "simple Gallic fare" ("best steamed mussels around") enhanced by a "romantic", "very European atmosphere"; P.S. there's no reserving, so "expect to wait" – "it's worth it."

La Provence S   25 | 25 | 24 | $45

25020 Hwy. 190 E. (bet. Lacombe & Mandeville), Lacombe, 504-626-7662

☑ "Inviting and welcoming", this "lovely country" inn in Lacombe matches a "beautiful setting" with "fantastic" Classic French cooking for some of the "best fine dining on the North Shore"; romantics from both sides of the lake are drawn to the "Provençal atmosphere", and if a few worry it's "overrated", by consensus it's "still worth the trip."

Le Parvenu S   25 | 22 | 21 | $33

509 Williams Blvd. (bet. Kenner Ave. & Short St.), Kenner, 504-471-0534

■ Cognoscenti consider this "quiet, charming" cottage a "best bet in Kenner" due to Dennis Hutley's "delicious" Creole-accented dishes; "lovely decor" and "attentive service" also ensure this "standout" stays "on top."

Louis XVI S   25 | 26 | 25 | $52

St. Louis Hotel, 730 Bienville St. (bet. Bourbon & Royal Sts.), 504-581-7000

■ An "old favorite that's still going strong", this "elegant special-occasion" stalwart in the French Quarter sets a "romantic" tone with a "*magnifique*", "old-style French" setting and "fantastic" food; it's a certified "classic", though a few Jacobins warn it's "dated" and "stuffy."

Mosca's ⊅   25 | 12 | 18 | $33

4137 US Hwy. 90W (bet. Butler St. & Live Oak Rd.), Avondale, 504-436-9942

■ This "great" "old-fashioned New Orleans Italian" "mecca for garlic and olive oil" still offers the "best oyster dish in the world", "unmatched BBQ shrimp" and "definitive baked chicken"; it may be "cholesterol central" and "cash only", but it's a "one-of-a-kind roadside inn" that's a "favorite" for a "food frenzy."

Mr. B's Bistro S   25 | 24 | 24 | $34

201 Royal St. (bet. Bienville & Iberville Sts.), 504-523-2078

■ "Everyone loves" this "day-in-and-day-out consistent" and "clubby" French Quarter haute Creole bistro serving "gumbo ya-ya to die for" and "ethereal BBQ shrimp"; a few feel it's "too noisy and crowded", but most maintain that it's "still the best of the more casual Brennan-owned restaurants."

Muriel's S   – | – | – | E

Jackson Sq., 801 Chartres St. (St. Anne St.), 504-568-1885

A prime location overlooking Jackson Square is but one reason to visit this romantic newcomer set in a building that was once one of the French Quarter's most elegant private residences; equally appealing is Devlin Roussell's progressive menu, which emphasizes contemporary New Orleans fare based on local ingredients, served in a formal upstairs room appointed with Victorian-inspired decor, fine crystal and silver, and in a rustic first-floor bistro with a charming courtyard bar.

Nine Roses   23 | 15 | 19 | $15

1116 Tulane Ave. (Loyola Ave.), 504-566-0950
1100 Stephen St. (Westbank Expwy.), Gretna, 504-366-7665 S

■ Asian food aficionados enthuse that this remodeled and renovated "really good Vietnamese" with a "large selection" of "addictive", "fresh" and "light" dishes ("try the quail" and spring rolls) at "great prices" is "the best reason to go to the West Bank"; P.S. the simple Central Business District "express location is quick, easy, cheap and delicious."

NOLA S   24 | 22 | 23 | $37

534 St. Louis St. (bet. Chartres & Decatur Sts.), 504-522-6652

◪ "Bam!" – star chef Emeril Lagasse's other "hit" is "more casual and lighthearted" than his namesake spots, and it features "tasty" contemporary New Orleans cuisine served in a "funky, jumpin' three-story" French Quarter space; but the "cramped" ("tables so close you might be dining *en famille*") and "touristy" ambiance irks others who complain about "inconsistent", "showy" food and "intrusive service."

Pelican Club S   25 | 24 | 23 | $40

312 Exchange Alley (bet. Bienville & Chartres Sts.), 504-523-1504

■ If you're looking for a "sophisticated" spot in the French Quarter to "impress a date", this is it; fusion fans favor its "innovative" contemporary Louisiana menu that merges Asian and International cuisines, while wallet-watchers opt for the "early-bird prix fixe"; in fact, "noise is the only knock in an otherwise fabulous evening."

Peristyle   – | – | – | E

1041 Dumaine St. (N. Rampart St.), 504-593-9535

"Brilliant", "delicious" contemporary Louisiana-French cuisine that's as "good as it gets" is the word on Anne Kearney's small, esteemed French Quarter bistro, now fully recovered from a fire two years ago; surveyors say her creative use of local seafood and meat is better than ever, while a series of mirrors dotting the pale lavendar walls makes the interior feel even more spacious; since power insiders take up most of the tables, however, plan to reserve way ahead.

Rib Room S   24 | 24 | 23 | $41

Omni Royal Orleans Hotel, 621 St. Louis St. (bet. Chartres & Royal Sts.), 504-529-7046

■ "Consistently good and fashionable", this Continental steakhouse is a "French Quarter stalwart" that's "classy in every way", whether for a "two-martini" "power lunch" or a "very elegant" supper (though penny-pinchers protest it's "much too expensive at dinner"); habitués hint it's "best for prime rib" and recommend a "table by the window" for some dandy people-watching.

RioMar   – | – | – | E

800 S. Peters St. (Julia St.), 504-525-3474

If you're a finatic, you'll be in the swim at this year-old, seafood-centric Warehouse Districter that's a skip and a jump from the Convention Center; chef Adolfo Garcia and attentive co-owner Nick Bazan oversee a Spanish-Mediterranean menu that ranges from *bacalaitos* (cod fritters) to crawfish *croquetas*; meat eaters have nothing to moan about either, since they say the Argentine *chimichurri* steak is *maravilloso!*

Ruth's Chris Steak House S
27 | 21 | 25 | $44

711 N. Broad St. (Orleans Ave.), 504-486-0810
3633 Veterans Memorial Blvd. (N. Causeway Blvd.), Metairie, 504-888-3600
■ "If you must have steak", look no further than these "reigning champions", links of the national chain that was hatched in New Orleans; fans rave there's "nobody better" (despite the "pricey" tabs) and tout the original North Broad Street outpost for "power lunching" amid "movers and shakers."

Sal & Judy's S
26 | 16 | 21 | $28

Hwy. 190 (14th St.), Lacombe, 504-882-7167
■ "Gargantuan portions" of "delectable" Creole–Southern Italian cooking, "bargain" pricing and "can't-be-beat" quality make this "North Shore favorite" a "don't-miss" destination; regulars report "reservations are a must" (and even then, there's "always a wait"), but it's unquestionably "worth the drive" for one of "the best" dining experiences around.

Upperline S
26 | 23 | 24 | $38

1413 Upperline St. (bet. Perrier & Prytania Sts.), 504-891-9822
■ "Always a treat" sigh supporters of this haute Creole–Eclectic where the "excellent" eating is complemented by "classy" fine-art decor and "personal" attention courtesy of owner and "gracious hostess" JoAnn Clevenger; "comfortable and innovative", it's "a true original" that Uptowners insist is "much more pleasant" than its French Quarter competitors.

New York City

TOP 20 FOOD RANKING

Restaurant	Cuisine Type
28 Daniel	Classic French
Chanterelle	Classic/New French
Le Bernardin	Classic French/Seafood
Nobu	Japanese/Peruvian
Jean Georges	New French
27 Gramercy Tavern	New American
Aureole	New American
Peter Luger	Steakhouse
Gotham Bar & Grill	New American
Il Mulino	Northern Italian
Lespinasse	Classic French
La Grenouille	Classic French
Kuruma Zushi	Japanese
Bouley Bakery	New French
Union Square Cafe	New American
Oceana	Seafood
Four Seasons	Continental
Tomoe Sushi	Japanese
Café Boulud	Classic French/Eclectic
Sushi Yasuda	Japanese

ADDITIONAL NOTEWORTHY PLACES

Alain Ducasse	Classic French
Aquavit	Scandinavian
Babbo	N&S Italian
Balthazar	French Bistro
Café des Artistes	Classic French
Carnegie Deli	Deli
Craft	New American
Danube	Austrian
db Bistro Moderne	French Bistro
Eleven Madison Park	New American
Felidia	N&S Italian
Ilo	New American
La Caravelle	Classic French
La Côte Basque	Classic French
Le Cirque 2000	Classic French
Lutèce	Classic French
March	New American
Milos, Estiatorio	Greek
Montrachet	Classic French/French Bistro
Park Avenue Cafe	New American
Picholine	Mediterranean
River Cafe	New American
Russian Tea Room	Russian
Shun Lee Palace	Chinese
Smith & Wollensky	Steakhouse
Sparks	Steakhouse
Sylvia's	Southern/Soul
Tabla	New American/Indian
Tavern on the Green	New American
Town	New American
'21' Club	American
Union Pacific	New American

Alain Ducasse 26 | 25 | 27 | $162

Essex House, 155 W. 58th St. (bet. 6th & 7th Aves.), 212-265-7300

◪ After a bumpy start, Michelin eight-star chef Alain Ducasse has turned what threatened to be a "bomb into fireworks" with "superb" French cuisine, "elegant" decor and "impeccable" service, all of which make it the *NYC Survey*'s highest-rated newcomer; despite top-of-the-market prices (the dinner prix fixe menus start at $160, though as a sign of the times, it now offers a $65 lunch), fans report it's "extraordinary in every way" and thus "acknowledge perfection and pay up."

Aquavit [S] 26 | 25 | 25 | $61

13 W. 54th St. (bet. 5th & 6th Aves.), 212-307-7311

■ From its "sublime" Scandinavian specialties to its "therapeutic" waterfall, this "flawless" Midtown "modernist classic" from "culinary magician" Marcus Samuelsson celebrates the "joys of salmon" and "just gets better" with time; though the prices are "as high as the [atrium] ceiling", its "wonderful selection of aquavits" numbs the sting, and the casual upstairs "cafe remains a bargain."

Aureole 27 | 26 | 26 | $73

34 E. 61st St. (bet. Madison & Park Aves.), 212-319-1660

■ Gerry Hayden is the new chef at this "fine-dining" "benchmark" owned by Charlie Palmer that still remains a "last-meal-of-your-life" kind of place, featuring "precise" New American cuisine and desserts resembling "MoMA's sculpture garden"; Romeos report that its "timeless" duplex townhouse (complete with "perfect flowers" and "better lighting than Barbara Walters gets") will "sweep your lady away."

Babbo ◐[S] 26 | 23 | 24 | $63

110 Waverly Pl. (bet. MacDougal St. & 6th Ave.), 212-777-0303

■ "Everything you've heard is true" about this "mind-boggling" Village "crowd-pleaser" from the Batali-Bastianich team, where the "lusty" "modern Italian" cooking and "beautiful bi-level" townhouse setting are equally "fabbo"; even though this "red-hot" celeb spot is "crazy busy", it still "runs like a Swiss watch" – except for a "reservation hassle" that may leave you with a "blister from hitting redial."

Balthazar ◐[S] 23 | 23 | 20 | $50

80 Spring St. (bet. B'way & Crosby St.), 212-965-1414

■ Keith McNally's "archetypal French brasserie" in SoHo is "as close to Paris as you can get" without paying airfare; "bustling, noisy and crowded", it's a "real happening" with "consistently good food" and "surprisingly good service", and rather than fight for a reservation at night, go for a more laid-back lunch or after 10 PM; if not everyone is a fan ("overpriced", "overhyped", "overrated"), they're a distinct minority.

Bouley Bakery ◐[S] 27 | 23 | 25 | $66

120 W. Broadway (Duane St.), 212-964-2525

■ For repasts that "transcend expectations", foodies cheer David Bouley's TriBeCa New French where "heaven on a plate" awaits either in its "relaxing", vaulted dining room or the "more casual" cafe, backed up by "polished", "not stuffy" service; if "no match for the original" Bouley, it's "excellent" by any other standard, and the $35 prix fixe lunch is a "steal."

Café Boulud [S] 27 | 24 | 26 | $68

Surrey Hotel, 20 E. 76th St. (bet. 5th & Madison Aves.), 212-772-2600

■ "Everyone wears black" but the "food is in Technicolor" at Daniel Boulud's "less formal" yet still "divine" East Side French-Eclectic where "dynamite" cuisine and "lovely service" are "on a par" with that of his eponymous flagship; though seating may be "close" and tabs indubitably "pricey", "nobody does it better" when it comes to "sophisticated, comfortable" dining.

Café des Artistes ◐[S] 24 | 27 | 23 | $60

1 W. 67th St. (bet. Columbus Ave. & CPW), 212-877-3500

■ "Everything glows" at this "famously romantic" Lincoln Center–area "grande dame" via George and Jenifer Lang, where "glorious" French fare, "truly courteous" service, bowers of flowers and lovely Howard Christy Chandler murals combine to produce an incredibly "seductive" experience that "makes one thankful to be a NYer"; though a meal here can be "expensive", the prix fixe menus are bona fide "deals."

Carnegie Deli ◐[S]≠ 21 | 10 | 13 | $24

854 Seventh Ave. (55th St.), 212-757-2245

■ This "bustling", "crowded" Midtown deli is an "institution" that "even jaded NYers enjoy"; plan to sit elbow-to-elbow at communal tables, eat "impossibly large" sandwiches followed by "mountains" of cheesecake and try to forget what your cardiologist would say; besides the tourists, diners are a cast of characters right out of *Broadway Danny Rose* (which was filmed here).

Chanterelle 28 | 27 | 27 | VE

2 Harrison St. (Hudson St.), 212-966-6960

■ "Beyond cloud nine and past seventh heaven" floats David and Karen Waltuck's TriBeCa French "classic that continues to impress" after more than two decades; since this "sustained champion's" "sumptuous" cuisine is enhanced by a "beautifully appointed dining room" and "divine service", "it's about the total experience, not just one element"; "if you can afford it", it's "absolutely essential" for any serious food lover; N.B. dinner is $84, prix fixe only.

Craft [S] 25 | 26 | 23 | $67

43 E. 19th St. (bet. B'way & Park Ave. S.), 212-780-0880

■ "A la carte" dining rises to the next level at this handsome, "groundbreaking" Flatiron New American from Gramercy Tavern's "crafty" Tom Colicchio, whose "design-your-own-meal" concept features a menu emphasizing "purity" and broken down by food type and cooking method; sure, it "gets pricey fast" and a few find the process of ordering "too much work", but fervent foodies say it's "worth the extra thought."

Daniel 28 | 28 | 27 | $87

60 E. 65th St. (bet. Madison & Park Aves.), 212-288-0033

■ "Oh, to be rich" sigh wanna-be regulars "swooning" over "main man" Daniel Boulud's "truly deserving" East Side French "stunner", a "heavenly" "feast for the eyes and palate" featuring "flawless" food (rated No. 1 in the *NYC Survey*) and "exquisite wines", "impeccably" decanted in ultra-"luxe", colonnaded quarters; though a tad "haughty", it's a "sensual", "crème de la crème" experience – so long as you don't forget to "bring at least *one* Amex."

Danube ●S
26 | 28 | 26 | $80

30 Hudson St. (bet. Duane & Reade Sts.), 212-791-3771

■ A Tyrolean "feather in the cap" for David Bouley, this "amazing" TriBeCa "dreamworld" transports diners with "heavenly, not heavy" Austrian cooking showcasing "spectacular" takes on schnitzel and other Viennese "classics"; set in a "gorgeous" "temple to Klimt" ("vat a room!") with "exemplary service" worthy of the "Hapsburg dynasty", it's way über the top but "hits every note" in Straussian style – "*ach, du liebe!*"

db Bistro Moderne S
– | – | – | E

City Club Hotel, 55 W. 44th St. (bet. 5th & 6th Aves.), 212-391-2400

Star chef Daniel Boulud has just opened this new Midtown French eatery offering refined, modern bistro cooking that includes an already famous $27 burger; it's divided into two sections: the fiery-red space up front is livelier, while the banquette-lined back room is somewhat more formal – either way, the prices are lower than at Boulud's other outlets.

Eleven Madison Park S
25 | 26 | 25 | $61

11 Madison Ave. (24th St.), 212-889-0905

■ "Danny Meyer does it again" at this Madison Park New American where "grand", "airy" deco-rations, pleasing private party rooms and "superb" hospitality are backdrops to an "exciting menu" from "top chef" Kerry Heffernan that's accompanied by a well-balanced, well-priced wine list; in sum, "everything works" here – "modern" "sophistication" "never felt so sexy", nor so "warm and friendly."

Felidia
25 | 22 | 23 | $64

243 E. 58th St. (bet. 2nd & 3rd Aves.), 212-758-1479

■ PBS cooking show host Lidia Bastianich "excels on TV and in person" at her East Midtown Italian namesake, a temple of "innovative" "culinary delights", effortlessly matched by an "elegant" "townhouse" setting, seamless black-tie service and "adventurous" "high-end" wines; fans say forget the expense and "just go."

Four Seasons
27 | 28 | 27 | $76

99 E. 52nd St. (bet. Lexington & Park Aves.), 212-754-9494

■ "Oh to be a regular" at this "classic" "for all seasons", a Midtown "experience" that "still lives up to its reputation" for "consistently glorious" Continental dining framed by "sensational service" and the "grandeur" of Philip Johnson's "timeless" design; from "fabulous" lunching among the bold-faced "elite" in the Grill Room to the "sheer elegance" of the Pool Room, it's "tops" among the city's "best places to splurge."

Gotham Bar & Grill S
27 | 25 | 26 | $63

12 E. 12th St. (bet. 5th Ave. & University Pl.), 212-620-4020

■ "Quintessential NYC dining" finds a "benchmark" at this "resplendent" Village New American that generates enough "electricity" to light up all of Gotham; Alfred Portale's "exquisite" "architectural food" still "towers above most", while the "elegant", "soaring space" and "impeccable service" "hit the mark" too, whether the occasion is a "lovely evening" out or the "bargain" $20 prix fixe lunch.

Gramercy Tavern [S] | 27 | 26 | 27 | $66 |

42 E. 20th St. (bet. B'way & Park Ave. S.), 212-477-0777

■ Still "as good as it gets", Danny Meyer's "brilliant" Flatiron/ Gramercy "tavern for our time" continues to amaze" with Tom Colicchio's "intensely delicious" American cuisine and "out-of-this-world" desserts from pastry chef Claudia Fleming; the "tasteful" "modern colonial" decor and "wonderful service" are a "sheer delight", and while it's a "so-civilized" way to "blow the budget", the "front tavern room" is "more relaxed" (no reservations necessary) and easier on the wallet.

Il Mulino ◐ | 27 | 20 | 24 | $68 |

86 W. Third St. (bet. Sullivan & Thompson Sts.), 212-673-3783

■ This "dark", "crowded" Villager serves "huge amounts" of "gutsy", "garlicky" Northern Italian food that's so good it "makes you feel you died and went to *Sopranos* heaven"; though owner/ maitre d' Fernando and his family "run a tight ship", enormous popularity can mean "waiting even with reservations" – to beat the lines, go for lunch or at off-hours.

Ilo ◐[S] | – | – | – | VE |

Bryant Park Hotel, 40 W. 40th St. (bet. 5th & 6th Aves.), 212-642-2255

Only the name of this Midtown newcomer (meaning "joyous" in Finnish) reflects chef-owner Rick Laakkonen's Scandinavian roots, since his ambitious menu is entirely New American; set in a slick yet serene space, this is serious destination dining, from the cheese and wine selections to the table settings to the skillful servers; naturally, the price tags are just as serious.

Jean Georges [S] | 28 | 26 | 27 | $86 |

Trump Int'l Hotel, 1 Central Park W. (bet. 60th & 61st Sts.), 212-299-3900

■ "As good as it gets", "A-plus", "food as good as sex", "better each time" typify the reactions to "innovative" chef Jean-Georges Vongerichten's New French flagship on the north side of Columbus Circle; with a choice of eating in the more formal (and more expensive) dining room, the more casual Nougatine Room or on the terrace in summer, there's something for everyone – and the regularly changing $20.01 three-course lunch may be "NY's best dining buy."

Kuruma Zushi | 27 | 17 | 23 | $77 |

7 E. 47th St., 2nd fl. (bet. 5th & Madison Aves.), 212-317-2802

■ What may be NY's "ultimate sushi" turns up at this "hidden", second-floor Japanese Midtowner that takes you to a "whole other level" with "phenomenal" "fish prepared to perfection"; the only catch is the cost, which can be "staggering", but in the end it's "worth every yen."

La Caravelle | 26 | 25 | 26 | $75 |

33 W. 55th St. (bet. 5th & 6th Aves.), 212-586-4252

■ "One of the last bastions of civilization", André and Rita Jammet's "elegant" Midtown French, after 40 years, continues to set the "gold standard" for "luxury dining"; credit the "flawless cuisine" of new chef Troy Dupuy, a setting that melds "luxury and comfort" seamlessly and service more "gracious" than "the average 'La Restaurant'"; though not inexpensive (prix fixe only, $68 dinner, $38 lunch), an "extraordinary" meal is the payoff – "if only real life could be this good."

La Côte Basque [S] | 26 | 26 | 26 | $74 |

60 W. 55th St. (bet. 5th & 6th Aves.), 212-688-6525

■ An "age-old favorite that never ages", this "perennial" French Midtown "star" still "twinkles" thanks to Jean-Jacques Rachou's "heavenly" creations, service that's "formal yet friendly" and a "glamorous" setting highlighted by murals of the Basque coast; be prepared for "upper-crusty" tabs (prix fixe $36 lunch, $68 dinner), but then again it'll save you the "bother of going to France."

La Grenouille ◐ | 27 | 28 | 27 | VE |

3 E. 52nd St. (bet. 5th & Madison Aves.), 212-752-1495

■ "A perennial favorite", this dressy East Side French "classic" combines "elegance" and "glamour" with "great food and service"; many consider it "NY's most beautiful restaurant" given its "breathtaking flowers" and "*magnifique*" atelier private room; for an affordable intro, try the $45 prix fixe lunch and sit with Henry Kissinger; for dinner, you have the choice of wearing your jewels or pawning them.

Le Bernardin | 28 | 27 | 27 | $84 |

155 W. 51st St. (bet. 6th & 7th Aves.), 212-489-1515

■ "Superlatives do not suffice" to describe Maguy LeCoze's French "seafood extravaganza", yet "hooked" fans try anyway, lauding chef Eric Ripert's "flawless" food, a "sumptuous" setting offering that "most precious NY commodity – space" – and service that's "attentive but non-intrusive"; granted, pricing is equally "extravagant" but worth it for the "*ne plus ultra*" of fine "dining from start to finish" (prix fixe only: $45 lunch, $77 dinner).

Le Cirque 2000 [S] | 26 | 27 | 26 | $82 |

NY Palace Hotel, 455 Madison Ave. (bet. 50th & 51st Sts.), 212-303-7788

■ "In a class by itself", "over the top in every way", a "Manhattan happening" – all apply to ringmaster Sirio Maccioni's Midtown French "landmark"; it's a "high-wire act" that balances a kitchen "at the top of its game" with a "clairvoyant" staff and enough colorful "circus wonderland" decor to create "sensory overload"; despite all the tourists here, it's still the place for NYers to flash "their Harry Winston jewels" and "impress" the hell out of someone.

Lespinasse | 27 | 28 | 27 | $90 |

St. Regis Hotel, 2 E. 55th St. (bet. 5th & Madison Aves.), 212-339-6719

■ "Well near perfect" "in every regard", this "magnificent" Midtown French "treat for the senses" provides "elegance and grandeur like no place else", from the "gilded", "luxurious" Louis XV dining room to "top-of-his-game" chef Christian Delouvrier's "sublime" cuisine to the "discreet", "cosseting" formal service; but just "be prepared" to "mortgage the house" because such a "memorable experience" doesn't come cheap.

Lutèce | 25 | 24 | 25 | $78 |

249 E. 50th St. (bet. 2nd & 3rd Aves.), 212-752-2225

■ No one will ever fill the shoes of André Soltner, but David Féau is producing his own "more contemporary" brand of "delicious food" that's "right up there with the best"; thanks to a successful rehab and continuing "excellent service", this "lovely" East Midtown townhouse deserves another try, especially for the $38 "best-value" lunch; for those diners who lament that "it's not the same as in the old days", think of it as Mantle replacing DiMaggio in center field.

March ▫️   26 | 25 | 26 | $83
405 E. 58th St. (bet. 1st Ave. & Sutton Pl.), 212-754-6272
■ For "unforgettable splurging", this "flawless" New American in an "elegant" Sutton Place townhouse "marches to a higher culinary beat" thanks to a tasteful revamping and expansion and a $72 tasting menu from chef Wayne Nish; while most agree the meals are "heavenly", "heaven ain't cheap", so bring along an angel with "deep pockets."

Milos, Estiatorio ❶▫️   26 | 24 | 23 | $65
125 W. 55th St. (bet. 6th & 7th Aves.), 212-245-7400
■ Offering fish "fresh from the ocean to the table with a short kitchen detour", this "dramatic", high-ceilinged grill is the top "high-class Greek eatery in town"; always fun with a group, it's a good value if you share appetizers or go for the $32 lunch or pre-theater prix fixe, but it can get "deceptively expensive" if you order the main-course fish that's subject to "per-pound pricing."

Montrachet   26 | 21 | 25 | $66
239 W. Broadway (bet. Walker & White Sts.), 212-219-2777
■ Ever a "model" for "gracious dining", this French "pioneer" in TriBeCa is a "total pleasure", showcasing "superior", "carefully orchestrated cuisine", a "terrific wine list" and "marvelous service"; the Friday $20 prix fixe lunch remains a "great deal", and despite hints that the "'80s" decor "needs sprucing up", most agree Drew Nieporent's beloved "baby never grows old."

Nobu ▫️   28 | 25 | 25 | $70
105 Hudson St. (Franklin St.), 212-219-0500
■ It's next to impossible to get a seat (they don't always bother to pick up the phone) at Nobu Matsuhisa's Japanese-Peruvian "classic" in TriBeCa, where the "incredible" offerings prove "some things are worth the wait"; expect "dining as theater" in a "richly atmospheric" David Rockwell–designed setting "packed with celebs", but be prepared for "car payment"-worthy prices; P.S. those who "can't plan two months ahead" opt for Nobu's "gorgeous" Next Door sibling offering equally "brilliant food" for a "little less", without reservations.

Oceana   27 | 25 | 26 | $69
55 E. 54th St. (bet. Madison & Park Aves.), 212-759-5941
■ "Phenomenal phish" "leagues above the rest" defines this "opulent yacht" moored in landlocked Midtown that rises to the surface with "slick" "nautical decor" and "flawless service" directed by the "best captain in the city"; though priced way above the water (prix fixe only: $40 lunch, $65 dinner), this deep-sea "shrine" is "worth every last dime" – "you'll never want to go back on shore again."

Park Avenue Cafe ▫️   25 | 23 | 23 | $60
100 E. 63rd St. (bet. Lexington & Park Aves.), 212-644-1900
■ "All-American cooking goes Uptown" at this "top-rate" Eastsider where Neil Murphy's "clever" cooking is as much a "work of art" as the "folk art" decorating the room; ok, it's "*très* spendy", but from the "splendid bread basket to the opulent desserts", there are "no disappointments here."

Peter Luger Steak House S≠ 27 | 15 | 20 | $59
178 Broadway (Driggs Ave.), Brooklyn, 718-387-7400
■ "No one argues about" this one: "steak doesn't get any better" than at Williamsburg's "cash-only" "landmark"; "carnivores" consider it a "nostalgic" "pleasure to be mistreated by gruff, old-time waiters" and note its basic German beer-hall decor makes it all the better for "concentrating on" the main event: porterhouse "like buttah" served in "cow-and-a-half"-per-person portions – and "don't forget" the "oh-my-god" sides.

Picholine S 27 | 24 | 25 | $69
35 W. 64th St. (bet. B'way & CPW), 212-724-8585
■ Proving that a "wonderful" restaurant can indeed make it on the Upper West Side, Terry Brennan's "inventive", "comfortable" Lincoln Center Mediterranean "just keeps getting better", at least according to those who don't already consider it "impeccable"; if you can't get reservations at night, try it for the bargain prix fixe lunch, but at any meal make sure to leave room for the cheese course – unquestionably among "NYC's best" – and let *fromager* Max McCalman explain them all to you.

River Cafe S 25 | 27 | 24 | $70
1 Water St. (bet. Furman & Old Fulton Sts.), Brooklyn, 718-522-5200
■ "All occasions are special ones" at this beautiful, barge-based Brooklyn waterside "escape", a "fabulous date place (even with your husband)" thanks to that "priceless view" that you "pay dearly for" (dinner, $70, is prix fixe only); the more-than-"memorable" American dishes are now prepared by chef Brad Steelman, who joins an illustrious list of celebrity alumni – notably David Burke, Larry Forgione, Rick Laakkonen and Charlie Palmer – who all earned their stripes here.

Russian Tea Room ●S 19 | 25 | 21 | $62
150 W. 57th St. (bet. 6th & 7th Aves.), 212-974-2111
◪ The "comeback of the century" and a "dream come true" for some, "all smoke and mirrors" to others, this "gaudy" Midtown "red, red, red" Russian revived by the late, great Warner LeRoy splits voters: fans say the borscht and blintzes and "glittery", "Christmas"-like decor are "fit for a tsar", but foes insist the cooking's strictly "for rubes with rubles", ditto the "overdone" trimmings; granted, it's "as pricey as it looks", but the huge "glass bear aquarium" and "fine private dining" floors have most saying they're "glad it's back"; N.B. for a bargain taste of excess, try the $32 prix fixe.

Shun Lee Palace ●S 24 | 22 | 22 | $50
155 E. 55th St. (bet. Lexington & 3rd Aves.), 212-371-8844
■ Restaurateur Michael Tong's "superior" East Midtown "grande dame" continues to set the NY "gold standard" for "sophisticated" Chinese dining; backed up by a clever, colorful Adam Tihany interior design and professional service that "never wavers" ("let them order for you"), it has a lock on the Sinophile market, since "one bite" transports patrons "worlds away."

Smith & Wollensky ⏺🅂   23 | 18 | 20 | $58
797 Third Ave. (49th St.), 212-753-1530
■ "Carnivores in their element" hail Alan Stillman's "classic" Midtown steakhouse, a "tradition" for "tremendous" cuts of "mouthwatering" red meat consumed among "real men" (and "man-watching" women); the "hedonistic" duplex scene comes complete with "great wines", a "professional" staff, "lotsa noise and commotion" and tabs that encourage "meals on the client"; in sum, this is everything a great steakhouse should be, and a quintessential NY experience in the bargain.

Sparks Steak House   25 | 20 | 22 | $62
210 E. 46th St. (bet. 2nd & 3rd Aves.), 212-687-4855
■ Always a "cut above", this "cavernous" Midtown cow palace "makes life simple" with "massive", "melt-in-your-mouth" prime steaks and an "unbelievable wine list" that result in "extremely satisfying" "macho meals" for free-spending "financiers"; throw in "classic" "Diamond Jim Brady decor" and "no-nonsense professional" service, and even Luger loyalists wonder "why travel to Brooklyn?"

Sushi Yasuda   27 | 23 | 23 | $61
204 E. 43rd St. (bet. 2nd & 3rd Aves.), 212-972-1001
■ "Melt-in-your-mouth" sushi and a "stylish", blond wood–lined interior make for "exquisite" (albeit "Tokyo-priced") dining at this UN-area Japanese "class act"; with "gracious" chef Maomichi Yasuda offering commentary, this is a "unique experience", no matter how you slice it.

Sylvia's 🅂   18 | 14 | 17 | $31
328 Lenox Ave. (bet. 126th & 127th Sts.), 212-996-0660
☑ Harlem's "queen of Soul Food" dishes out "lips-to-hips" "Deep South cooking" that attracts "cholesterol" lovers from far and wide ("where's Bill?"); its weekend jazz and gospel brunches are "lots of fun", though some rue the first coming of the "tour buses."

Tabla 🅂   25 | 26 | 25 | $61
11 Madison Ave. (25th St.), 212-889-0667
■ "East meets West with delicious consequences" at Danny Meyer's "memorable" Madison Square New American where chef Floyd Cardoz's Indian-accented menu keeps your "imagination engaged" with "seriously subtle flavors", while "impeccable service" and a "gilded setting" also curry favor; if the $54 prix fixe dinner is too rich for your blood, lunch and the handsome ground-floor Bread Bar are more affordable.

Tavern on the Green 🅂   17 | 25 | 18 | $57
Central Park W. (bet. 66th & 67th Sts.), 212-873-3200
☑ The late Warner LeRoy's "breathtaking", "over-the-top" "glitz" "fantasyland" attracts tourists and locals alike with a choice of lovely rooms (especially the multi-chandeliered Crystal Room) and spacious gardens "perfect for parties"; while some find the American food "just average", far more say it's "improved" and "surprisingly good", especially for an alfresco meal.

Tomoe Sushi

F	D	S	C
27	10	16	$35

172 Thompson St. (bet. Bleecker & Houston Sts.), 212-777-9346

◪ "Something fishy" is going on at this West Villager: "mind-boggling" "pristine sushi at bargain prices" that's among the "city's best"; the trade-off is a "rinky-dink", "postage stamp–size" setting translating into "long lines" that look like "open casting calls", making the "need to expand *urgent*."

Town [S]

F	D	S	C
25	26	22	$63

Chambers Hotel, 15 W. 56th St. (bet. 5th & 6th Aves.), 212-582-4445

■ "Look out, gourmands" – this New American newcomer with a sexy upstairs bar scene in Midtown's Chambers Hotel is a "serious" destination for "inventive yet recognizable" cuisine from standout chef Geoffrey Zakarian (ex 44, Patroon); with a well-edited, almost minimalist menu enhanced by a "wonderful", "soaring" space, this "bright star" is pretty near "perfection", except perhaps for the price.

'21' Club

F	D	S	C
22	23	23	$65

21 W. 52nd St. (bet. 5th & 6th Aves.), 212-582-7200

■ "A timeless NY classic that's still going strong", this Midtown townhouse "landmark" has only "improved with age", offering "handsome" men's club quarters, seamless black-tie service, a "happening" "see-and-be-seen" power scene and "better-than-ever" American food from chef Erik Blauberg; in addition, there are numerous private party rooms – don't miss the wine cellar – and bargain prix fixe menus at lunch ($29) and pre-theater ($33) that allow you to "feel like a master of the universe" for a day-trader tab; N.B. jackets and ties are required, of course.

Union Pacific

F	D	S	C
26	26	25	$70

111 E. 22nd St. (bet. Lexington Ave. & Park Ave. S.), 212-995-8500

■ "Knockout dining" leaves fans breathless at this Gramercy New American "paragon" where "rock star" chef Rocco DiSpirito produces "sublime", "synergistic" dishes that more than "meet expectations"; service is nearly as "flawless", while the setting replete with a "waterfall" is virtually "therapeutic", so though the "bottom line" is "platinum card"–worthy, it's hard to put a price on a "guaranteed magical evening."

Union Square Cafe [S]

F	D	S	C
27	24	26	$60

21 E. 16th St. (bet. 5th Ave. & Union Sq. W.), 212-243-4020

■ What alchemy keeps Danny Meyer's original cafe NYC's Most Popular restaurant for the sixth year in a row?; the answer is an "appealing amalgam of three different, muraled dining areas, an "urbane", "comfortably casual" ambiance, genuinely "friendly" service and "good value" for chef Michael Romano's "always fresh, wonderfully prepared" "regular American food"; other restaurants may beat it in specific areas, but no one "makes it seem so easy."

Orange County, CA

TOP 10 FOOD RANKING

	Restaurant	Cuisine Type
28	Pavilion	Californian/Med.
	Pinot Provence	Classic French
	Napa Rose	Californian
27	Ritz	Continental
	Aubergine	Californian/Classic French
	Hobbit	Classic French/Continental
	Troquet	New French
	Gustaf Anders	Swedish
26	Ritz-Carlton Lag. Niguel	Classic French
	Back Pocket	Swedish

ADDITIONAL NOTEWORTHY PLACES

California Pizza Kitchen	Pizza
Cheesecake Factory	Eclectic
El Cholo	Mexican
Five Crowns	English
Houston's	American
Il Fornaio	N&S Italian
McCormick & Schmick's	Seafood
P.F. Chang's	Chinese
Roy's	Hawaiian/Fusion
Ruth's Chris	Steakhouse

	F	D	S	C
Aubergine [S]	27	24	25	$64

508 29th St. (Newport Blvd.), Newport Beach, 949-723-4150

■ "A culinary masterpiece on every level" rave acolytes about this "high-end" Newport destination where "brilliant" chef-owner Tim Goodell flexes his Cal-French culinary muscle with "inspirational" prix fixe dinners ("not for the un-adventurous") enhanced by "flawless service"; "exquisite" dining in this "gorgeous little beach cottage" strikes most as a "phenomenal" "splurge", though a minority is turned off by a "punitive corkage fee."

	F	D	S	C
Back Pocket [S]	26	22	24	$32

South Coast Plaza Village, 3851 S. Bear St. (Sunflower Ave.), Santa Ana, 714-668-1737

■ "Swedish comfort food" attracts astute admirers to this "best-kept secret" in Santa Ana, a "cozy bistro" adjunct within the upscale Gustaf Anders; "save the airfare" to the land of the midnight sun and revel in "the best Swedish meatballs" and sea bass from the crackling wood oven, "served with care" in a "laid-back room"; fans feel it's "just as good" as its pricier consort, and better yet, it's "less expensive."

California Pizza Kitchen   18 | 15 | 17 | $17 |

2957 Michelson Dr. (Jamboree Dr.), Irvine, 949-975-1585 ⊭
Laguna Hills Mall, 24155 Laguna Hills Mall (bet. El Toro Rd. & Regional Ct.),
Laguna Hills, 949-458-9600 S
25513 Marguerite Pkwy. (La Paz Rd.), Mission Viejo, 949-951-5026 S
1511 Newport Center Dr. (bet. Corporate Plaza & Farallon Drs.),
Newport Beach, 949-759-5543 S
2800 N. Main St. (Town & Country Rd.), Santa Ana, 714-479-0604 S
■ Hordes of surveyors claim they "always need a periodic fix" of this chain's "encyclopedic" variety of "crazy designer pizzas" like the BBQ, Thai and tandoori chicken versions; while the novelty may have worn off ("a cliché by now"), it's still a "reliable" "family favorite" "in a pinch."

Cheesecake Factory S   21 | 18 | 18 | $21 |

Irvine Spectrum Ctr., 71 Fortune Dr. (Pacifica), Irvine, 949-788-9998
42 The Shops at Mission Viejo (I-5, Crown Valley Pkwy. exit), Mission Viejo,
949-364-6200
Fashion Island, 1141 Newport Center Dr. (Santa Barbara Dr.), Newport
Beach, 949-720-8333
☑ Acolytes routinely brave "perennially long waits" to choose from a "dizzying", "something-for-everyone" menu of Eclectic eats at this "moderately priced", "kid-friendly" chain, voted the most popular restaurant in Orange County; but bird-like appetites beware: everything from the "unusual" avocado egg rolls to the "sinfully delicious" cheesecakes comes in "monster portions."

El Cholo S   19 | 19 | 19 | $19 |

5465 Alton Pkwy. (Jeffrey Rd.), Irvine, 949-451-0044
■ Mention Mexican cooking in Irvine, and this "legendary" chain link always comes to mind, a "classic LA experience" turning out "strong margaritas", "divine green-corn tamales", "exceptional guac" and other "tried-and-true recipes" that date back three quarters of a century.

Five Crowns S   24 | 25 | 25 | $39 |

3801 E. PCH (Poppy St.), Corona del Mar, 949-760-0331
☑ At this "nice piece of déjà vu in Corona del Mar", "Anglophile" eats like "perfect prime rib and Yorkshire pudding" are served in an "authentic replica" of an "Olde English manor" (add your own "fog and rain") by "wenches in push-up bras" who proffer "first-class service"; though legions insist this "Orange County cousin of Lawry's" is "perfection in every respect", cynics sniff "it's cute, but you can't eat atmosphere"; best bet: "go at Christmas, when it's decorated to the nines", making you "feel like you're in a Dickens novel."

Gustaf Anders S   27 | 24 | 25 | $45 |

South Coast Plaza Village, 3851 S. Bear St. (Sunflower Ave.), Santa Ana,
714-668-1737
■ In Santa Ana's South Coast Plaza Village, this "class act for all eternity" has urbane types jonesing for a "Swedish fix" by making a beeline for crawfish, "the best cured salmon in the universe" and a "truly memorable" "mile-long holiday season buffet" ("don't forget the aquavit"); "perfectly balanced service" complements the "cool, reserved" decor (so expect "purity of food and mood"); all told, "if you're serious about what you eat, you must visit this gastronomic temple."

Hobbit 🅂   27 | 24 | 26 | $60 |
2932 E. Chapman Ave. (Malena St.), Orange, 714-997-1972

■ A "special-occasion spot if ever there was one" weigh in worshipers who find the "restored hacienda" "charming and magical"; it's truly a "legend in Orange" for "special" prix fixe dinners that begin with "bubbly and appetizers in the wine cellar" and proceed upstairs for "creatively prepared" Continental and French dishes; though "reservations are hard to get", fans insist "everyone should try this place once."

Houston's 🅂   20 | 19 | 20 | $26 |
2991 Michelson Dr. (Jamboree Rd.), Irvine, 949-833-0977

■ "Some of the better corporate food going" is at this "upmarket" Irvine American where everyone "starts with the spinach artichoke dip" then moves on to "to-die-for BBQ chicken" and "melt-in-your-mouth" babyback ribs; since it's "always busy" and "reservations aren't accepted", kill time at the "buzzing bar."

Il Fornaio 🅂   21 | 20 | 19 | $27 |
18051 Von Karnan Ave. (bet. Main St. & Michelson Dr.), Costa Mesa, 949-261-1444

■ "Wonderful bread" from a "fantastic bakery" is the specialty of this "bright, cheery" upscale Italian chain, which also keeps patrons coming back with "creative pastas", rotisserie chicken, lots of daily specials and monthly supplemental menus featuring dishes and wines from different regions of The Boot.

McCormick & Schmick's 🅂   20 | 20 | 20 | $31 |
2000 Main St. (MacArthur Blvd.), Irvine, 949-756-0505

■ "One of the best fish chains" in SoCal, this "solid" performer offers a winning combination of handsome, "interesting", "wood-and-brass" decor and "high-quality" seafood; it's also a "fun place to meet after work" for tremendous "happy-hour deals", though a few underwhelmed diners find it "pleasant but unremarkable."

Napa Rose 🅂   28 | 28 | 26 | $46 |
Grand Californian Hotel, 1600 S. Disneyland Dr. (Katella Dr.), Anaheim, 714-300-7170

■ "You'll love Disney's California Adventure just for" this "amazing", "elegant" hotel dining room (it's definitely "not Mickey Mouse") wrapped in vineyard murals and soaring windows with a "surprise view of Grizzly Peak"; gourmands adore chef Andrew Sutton's "fresh, innovative" wine-country cuisine that's "as good as you'll find in Napa", supported by an "incredible wine list" (over 900 entries) and a "friendly" staff that "meets high standards"; it all leaves admirers wondering "is this really in a theme park resort?"

Pavilion 🅂   28 | 29 | 28 | $49 |
Four Seasons Hotel, 690 Newport Center Dr. (Santa Cruz Dr.), Newport Beach, 949-760-4920

■ "Outstanding in all respects" rave reviewers who ranked this "fabulous" Newport Beach "gem" No. 1 in Orange County for Food; "flawless from appetizers to dessert", it "dispels the hotel dining myth" by supplying "elegant presentations" of Cal-Med creations "that don't require a bank loan" served in a "luxurious" room adorned with "beautiful flowers"; the "elegant" experience is bolstered by an "impeccable staff" that "doesn't miss a beat."

P.F. Chang's China Bistro [S] | 20 | 20 | 19 | $23 |

Irvine Spectrum Ctr., 61 Fortune Dr. (Irvine Center Dr.), Irvine, 949-453-1211
1145 Newport Center Dr. (Santa Barbara St.), Newport Beach, 949-759-9007

■ No reservations means there's "always a long wait" at this upscale "contemporary" Chinese chain where "lettuce wraps done right" and "crab won tons to die for" are complemented by "very cool" Asian decor ("replicas of warriors"), a California-focused wine list and trendy martinis; sure, "it's a formula, but a nice one."

Pinot Provence [S] | 28 | 27 | 25 | $45 |

Westin South Coast Plaza, 686 Anton Blvd. (Bristol St.), Costa Mesa, 714-444-5900

■ "Anyone who loves Provence will love Pinot" coo converts to this "elegant, not stuffy" "Classic French" destination in Costa Mesa that's "perfect" "before the Performing Arts Center" or "for special occasions", especially when "you want to impress"; disciples declare that the changing menu of "great and different" dishes with "abundant flavor" is "flat-out poetry", though a few warn that "some nights can be rather ordinary"; all said, this is "mellow food in a pretty room" and "another great" offering from Joachim Splichal.

Ritz | 27 | 27 | 27 | $49 |

Fashion Island, 880 Newport Center Dr. (Santa Barbara Ave.), Newport Beach, 949-720-1800

■ "As good as it gets" agree admirers of this "primo" "favorite forever" Continental, where "elegance is the watchword"; "special celebration" diners bask in a "country club setting" that "oozes old money" while indulging in culinary classics like "fabulous tartare" and "almost perfect" Châteaubriand and soufflés; it's the "unbeatable" "cosseting" from "longtime servers" that really allows each guest to "feel like a king", just one more "great reason to drive to Newport Beach."

Ritz-Carlton Laguna Niguel | 26 | 28 | 27 | $54 |

Ritz-Carlton Laguna Niguel, 1 Ritz-Carlton Dr. (PCH), Dana Point, 949-240-5008

■ "Bring your wallet – and someone else's" – if you want to experience "fine dining at its highest level" at this "breathtaking" Laguna Niguel cliff-top resort "club room"; "it's the very definition of luxury" gasp gastronomes who "like to spend hours in heaven" feasting on "flawless" French fare "prepared with precision and flair" in a "formal", "class-act" setting enhanced by "immaculate" service; P.S. "afternoon tea is lovely at sunset", and the popular Sunday brunch is like a "dream" come true.

Roy's [S] | 24 | 22 | 22 | $42 |

Fashion Island, 453 Newport Center Dr. (San Miguel Dr.), Newport Beach, 949-640-7697

◪ "Hoopla galore" surrounds this "hip" Fashion Island "franchise" outpost featuring celeb chef Roy Yamaguchi's "cutting-edge" Hawaiian fusion cuisine "prepared with gusto" and served by an "attentive", "friendly staff" in an island setting; detractors say the "bloom is off the rose, Roy can't live off his reputation anymore", but they're outvoted by those who assert "when it's on, it's great" and "cheaper than a flight to Maui."

Ruth's Chris Steak House S   26 | 22 | 24 | $45

2961 Michaelson Dr. (Carlson Ave.), Irvine, 949-252-8848

■ "Huge, well-poured martinis" start the meal off right at Irvine's "pricey" beefhouse chain outpost that's "still the standard by which others are judged" for "fabulous", "buttery steaks" and serious sides ("excellent creamed spinach", "perfect mashed potatoes"); a "fine", "quick" staff is another feather in its cap – just remember to "wear elastic pants" and plan to "go to the gym the next day."

Troquet S   27 | 23 | 24 | $47

South Coast Plaza, 3333 Bristol St. (Town Center Dr.), Costa Mesa, 714-708-6865

■ Wow – such "magnificence in a mall" rave reviewers who crown Tim and Liza Goodell's South Coast Plaza bistro a "winner" for "magical" New French cuisine that could "turn any mood positive"; it's "the next best thing to Paris", in a "lovely" setting" complete with a "delightful" "rooftop patio"; a handful complains about "cool and indifferent service" and deems the kitchen performance "hit or miss", but many insist it exudes "less attitude than Aubergine" – in fact, it "doesn't get any better than this."

Orlando

TOP 20 FOOD RANKING

Restaurant	Cuisine Type
29 La Coquina	International
Louis' Downtown	Southern
28 Victoria & Albert's	American
Le Coq au Vin	French Bistro
Del Frisco's	Steakhouse
Flying Fish Café	Seafood
Chatham's Place	Continental
27 Maison et Jardin	Continental
California Grill	Californian
Café de France	French Bistro/Continental
Christini's*	Northern Italian
26 Arthur's 27	International
Yachtsman Steakhouse	Steakhouse
Citricos	New French
Ruth's Chris	Steakhouse
Emeril's	Cajun/Creole
Thai House	Thai
Antonio's La Fiamma	N&S Italian
Manuel's on the 28th	International
Cafe Allegre	Mediterranean

ADDITIONAL NOTEWORTHY PLACES

Artist Point	Northwest
Bahama Breeze	Caribbean
Brio Tuscan Grille	N&S Italian
Cafe D'Antonio	N&S Italian
California Cafe Bar & Grill	Californian/Fusion
Charley's Steak House	Steakhouse
Delfino Riviera	Northern Italian
Dux	New French/New American
Enzo's on the Lake	Northern Italian
Haifeng	Chinese
Harvey's Bistro	New American
Houston's	Seafood/Steakhouse
La Boheme	Steakhouse/American
Les Chefs de France	French Bistro
Narcoossee's	Seafood
Outback	Steakhouse
Peter Scott's	Continental
Rolando's	Cuban
Thai Place	Thai
Vito's Chop House	Steakhouse

---

* Tied with the restaurant listed directly above it

Antonio's La Fiamma 26 | 22 | 23 | $29

611 S. Orlando Ave. (Maitland Ave.), Maitland, 407-645-1035

■ "Superb" Italian food makes this "upscale" favorite overlooking Maitland's Lake Lily "as close to Italy as can be found in Central Florida"; the "fabulous" menu features dishes both "innovative" and "traditional", the wine list boasts more than 500 labels and the service is "friendly" yet "elegant"; too bad the "horrible acoustics" mean that the "lovely", "contemporary" room is often "much too noisy", but then that only adds to the "big-city" "party" atmosphere.

Arthur's 27 [S] 26 | 27 | 27 | $56

Wyndham Palace Resort & Spa, 1900 Buena Vista Dr. (Hotel Plaza Blvd.), Lake Buena Vista, 407-827-3450

■ "The best view at Disney" may well be from this super "posh" International on the 27th floor of the Wyndham Palace, where "perfectly orchestrated" meals amount to "the ultimate in fine dining"; the "creative" dishes are "elegantly" presented by a "superb", pampering staff, but by all counts the crowning glory of this "very special place" is its "beautiful" panoramic park vista – especially if you can get a "late reservation by a window to enjoy the fireworks."

Artist Point [S] 24 | 25 | 24 | $40

Disney's Wilderness Lodge, 901 Timberline Dr. (World Dr.), Lake Buena Vista, 407-824-1081

■ "Forget you're in Florida" at this Pacific Northwestern retreat in Disney's Wilderness Lodge, where the Arts and Crafts interior feels like a "hunting lodge" in the "North woods"; a recently installed chef brings "new ideas" to the "fantastic" menu that's heavy on "wild game" and fish and backed by "great wines" from Oregon and Washington State; P.S. Sunday brunches where "Disney characters" "mingle with the diners" are "delightful", if often "punctuated by screams" from excited "young patrons."

Bahama Breeze ◐ [S] 22 | 24 | 20 | $20

8849 International Dr. (1 mi. south of Sand Lake Rd.), 407-248-2499
8735 Vineland Rd. (State Rd. 535), 407-938-9010
Altamonte Mall, 499 E. Altamonte Dr. (Palm Springs Blvd. & State Rd. 436), Altamonte Springs, 407-831-2929

■ Why take a "tropical vacation" when this "extremely fun" Caribbean chain "makes you feel like you're in the Bahamas"?; the fare's "surprisingly good" for a "meet market" (though a small minority advises "stick with the drinks" at the "great bar"), but "be prepared to wait for a table" because it turns into "a major scene" on weekends.

Brio Tuscan Grille [S] – | – | – | M

Winter Park Village, 480 N. Orlando Ave. (Canton Ave.), Winter Park, 407-622-5611

A "trendy newcomer" to Winter Park Village's thriving dining district, this "lively" Italian grill "makes you feel like you're Uptown" thanks to its "sophisticated" menu; "the beautiful people" have claimed it as "the place to see and be seen", so no surprise it gets "crowded" and "noisy."

Cafe Allegre
26 | 22 | 22 | $29

2401 Edgewater Dr. (Vassar St.), 407-872-2332

■ "Small and sophisticated", this "real neighborhood jewel" in College Park radiates "charm" while showcasing an "exceptional" Mediterranean menu of "unusual" yet "honest" dishes that make it "worth going off any diet"; the staff "tries hard" to please and helps make "every meal such a delight" that the enchanted "want to return again and again."

Cafe D'Antonio S
23 | 22 | 20 | $25

691 Front St. (Market St.), Celebration, 407-566-2233

■ Boasting a "wonderful view of Downtown Celebration", the patio at this popular Italian is a "people-watcher's paradise"; as the "casual", family-friendly offshoot of Antonio's La Fiamma, it "does the original proud" with "very good" food (try the *zuppa di pesce*) prepared in an open kitchen with a wood-burning grill and rotisserie.

Café de France
27 | 23 | 23 | $32

526 S. Park Ave. (Fairbanks Ave.), Winter Park, 407-647-1869

■ "Lots of locals" frequent the "best" French-Continental bistro in Winter Park to savor seasonal gourmet menus of "consistently outstanding" fare ("try any soup or fish dish"); the "small and cozy" space is more "charming" than ever, and the staff remains as "personable" as can be, which means it's "great for a special celebration" or just when you want to "feel like you're in France."

California Cafe Bar & Grill S
22 | 23 | 20 | $27

Florida Mall, 8001 S. Orange Blossom Trail (August Ln.), 407-816-5555

■ A "totally unexpected" "find" in Florida Mall, this newcomer tempts shoppers with its "lovely" contemporary decor and "imaginative" Californian fusion fare (think sushi spreads, flatbread pizzas), all "creatively presented" and served by a "pro" staff; while not cheap, this link of a national chain is more affordable than the California Grill, with which it's oft confused.

California Grill S
27 | 26 | 25 | $41

Disney's Contemporary Resort, 4600 N. World Dr., Lake Buena Vista, 407-824-1576

☑ "The Mouse can cook, baby!"; this Californian on "top of the world" (or on the 15th floor of Disney's Contemporary Resort, anyway) is again voted Orlando's Most Popular restaurant; "gifted" chef Clifford Pleau continually reinvents his "unique seasonal menus", creating "divine" dishes paired with an "equally eloquent wine list"; add "impeccable" service and "spectacular" views of the park and its fireworks, and the result is truly "great dining" – "tourists" in "shorts and Mickey Mouse ears" notwithstanding.

Charley's Steak House S
25 | 22 | 22 | $36

6107 S. Orange Blossom Trail (1 mi. north of Sand Lake Rd.), 407-851-7130
Goodings Plaza, 8255 International Dr. (Sand Lake Rd.), 407-363-0228
Parkway Pavilion, 2901 Parkway Blvd. (Hwy. 192), Kissimmee, 407-396-6055

■ Steaks so tender you can "cut them with a fork" are the province of this steakhouse mini-chain where "incredible slabs of meat" are "cooked to perfection" over a "hardwood" fire, emerging "thick, juicy" and "exceptionally flavorful" ("the best filet mignon I've ever had!"); add a "great martini" or a bottle from the "extensive wine list" and you're in "beef-lover's paradise."

Chatham's Place [S]

28 | 24 | 26 | $39

7575 Dr. Phillips Blvd. (Sand Lake Rd.), 407-345-2992

■ Founder "Louis Chatham has left and opened a new restaurant" (Louis' Downtown), but the current owners of this "top-grade" Continental in the Dr. Phillips area of South Orlando continue to maintain its tradition of gustatory "excellence"; respondents rhapsodize about the "sublime" cuisine "exquisitely prepared", "elegant service" and an atmosphere both "romantic" and "convivial"; the makings are all there for a "perfect evening."

Christini's [S]

27 | 24 | 25 | $52

Bay Hill Mktpl., 7600 Dr. Phillips Blvd. (Sand Lake Rd.), 407-345-8770

■ "A treasure among restaurants", this "buttoned-up" Northern Italian "standby" in the Dr. Phillips area of South Orlando produces "feasts" of near-"perfect" execution, complemented by a 450-label wine list; among its many "charms" are "exquisite service", ornate, "beautiful" decor and "strolling musicians" who complete the "romantic" picture; just bear in mind that such "very special" dining doesn't come cheap – the prices are "high" even by "expense-account" standards.

Citricos [S]

26 | 28 | 26 | $48

Disney's Grand Floridian Resort & Spa, 4401 Grand Floridian Way, Lake Buena Vista, 407-939-3463

■ Chef Gray Byrum's "magnificent" creations are "rivaled only by the unique decor" at this "incredible" French "jewel" that boasts an impressive view of the Grand Floridian Resort – perfect for "enjoying the fireworks" – and an "elegant" modern interior with an exhibition kitchen; the "innovative", "always delicious" dishes are "nicely executed and finely served" and are backed by a "superb wine list", making this "great celebration place" "one of Disney's best."

Delfino Riviera

▽ 24 | 27 | 22 | $51

Portofino Bay Hotel, 5601 Universal Blvd. (I-4, exit 29B), Lake Buena Vista, 407-503-1415

◪ "Elegant, beautiful" surroundings with a "superb ambiance" define this upscale hotel Italian overlooking Portofino Bay at Universal Studios Escape; the "excellent" menu offers "fabulous" specialties from Liguria, including handmade pastas and striped bass with capers and olives, and the "romantic" mood is made even more so by the "wandering musicians"; still, grouches say it's "just not quite worth the price."

Del Frisco's Double Eagle Steak House

28 | 22 | 27 | $45

729 Lee Rd. (1½ blocks west of I-4), 407-645-4443

■ "Don't dare ask for a knife" – a fork is all you need to tackle "the best steaks in town" and "oh those side dishes" at this "dark, clubby" "treat"; even if the decor could stand a "redo", the "fabulous flavors" combine with an "excellent wine list" and "superb" service to add up to "cow heaven"; yes, this is "expense-account" territory, but for such "huge portions" of "consistently" "top-quality" fare, the prices are "very fair"; N.B. there's a new cigar-friendly piano lounge.

Dux
25 | 25 | 25 | $53

Peabody Orlando Hotel, 9801 International Dr. (opp. Orange County Convention Ctr.), 407-345-4550

■ "For that special person you want to impress", this "epitome of class" at the Peabody Orlando is "very expensive but worth it" for its "first-rate" haute New French–American menu, opulent surroundings and attentive service; while a few find it "imposing" and "a bit stuffy", the majority lauds it as "fine dining at its best"; P.S. make sure that you take the time to "see the ducks in the lobby's" marble fountain.

Emeril's Restaurant Orlando S
26 | 23 | 24 | $50

Universal Studios Escape, Universal CityWalk, 407-224-2424

■ "Bam! – you can't take it a notch higher than the fabulous food and locale of this hot spot" rave fans of Emeril Lagasse's "splendiferous" Cajun-Creole centerpiece of Universal CityWalk, where the celebrity chef himself sometimes makes a surprise appearance in the show kitchen; rest assured the cuisine is "not just TV fluff" – it's "exhilarating", and though it's "expensive", most insist it's "all it's cracked up to be"; P.S. "plan way ahead" because it's very "hard to get in."

Enzo's on the Lake
25 | 23 | 23 | $40

1130 S. Hwy. 17-92 (State Rd. 434), Longwood, 407-834-9872

■ To fully enjoy the "enchanting" atmosphere at this "pretty" Longwood Northern Italian, "ask for a table with a view" of Lake Fairy and savor a "consistently excellent" "special dinner"; though insiders report being "treated like family", first-timers detect a "caste system" that favors some customers over others ("we're still trying to figure out the password to get good service here") and warn about the "terrible acoustics"; still, the food is so "extraordinary" that it's "worth putting up with the pretensions."

Flying Fish Café S
28 | 28 | 26 | $43

Disney's BoardWalk Inn, 2101 N. Epcot Resorts Blvd. (Buena Vista Dr.), Lake Buena Vista, 407-939-3463

■ "Scrum-dittily-umptious!" exclaim enthusiasts of this seafood cafe at Disney's Boardwalk that soars with "memorably" "well-prepared" catches "fresh off the boat"; its "fanciful" decor "beautifully" evokes Atlantic City's golden age of roller coasters, and it provides some of the "best service" around, all of which makes very effective "date bait"; P.S. insiders say get a seat "near the open kitchen."

Haifeng S
∇ 27 | 24 | 25 | $36

Renaissance Orlando Resort, 6677 Sea Harbor Dr. (International Dr.), 407-351-5555

■ Considered among "the best Asian restaurants" in the area, this International Drive hotel Chinese turns out impressive Peking duck, orange beef and sushi in an upscale room with a sharp black color scheme and a 30-foot dragon hand-painted on a glass wall; N.B. regulars are given their own set of personalized chopsticks, kept on premises.

Harvey's Bistro
24 | 23 | 22 | $28

*Bank of America Bldg., 390 N. Orange Ave. (Livingston St.),
407-246-6560*

■ "Always dependable" for "upscale comfort food" (like Yankee
pot roast and seared calf's liver), this "fashionable" but "reasonably
priced" European-influenced American bistro Downtown bears lots
of stained wood and brass appointments; "especially convenient
for a business meeting or pre- or post-theater" meal, it's considered
an overall "solid" choice.

Houston's S
24 | 24 | 21 | $25

*215 S. Orlando Ave. (bet. Fairbanks Ave. & Lee Rd.), Winter Park,
407-740-4005*

■ "Long waits" for a table seem "not so bad" when taking in the "best
lake view" in all of Orlando at this "bustling" Winter Park branch of
the surf 'n' turf chain where a "young, sophisticated crowd" enjoys
"heaping portions" of "great food", an upscale lodge motif and
"courteous", "attentive" service; it's also "a meet market galore."

La Boheme S
– | – | – | E

*Westin Grand Bohemian, 325 S. Orange Ave. (bet. Jackson & South Sts.),
407-313-9000*

Instantly establishing itself as the most upscale chophouse
Downtown, this swanky American newcomer tempts locals
and visitors alike with chef Robert Mason's modern renditions of
prime steaks (such as a New York strip encrusted with roasted
garlic) and fresh seafood (like seared sea bass with champagne
vinaigrette); expect plush surroundings appointed with art from
the private collection of hotelier Richard Kessler and echoes of
Gershwin from an Imperial Grand Bösendorfer concert piano
(one of only two in the world) in the adjoining cocktail lounge.

La Coquina S
29 | 28 | 27 | $51

*Hyatt Regency Grand Cypress, 1 Grand Cypress Blvd. (State Rd. 535),
407-239-1234*

■ Voted No. 1 for Food in Orlando, this "exquisite" "special-
occasion" destination housed in the Hyatt Regency Grand Cypress
is "a feast for the eyes and palate"; the contemporary International
menu is "superb", showcasing a "great choice" of "expertly
prepared" dishes that are served in a "stunning setting" by a very
"fine" staff; of course it's "expensive", but you'll be "treated like
royalty" and know that "you've had a real gourmet meal"; P.S. don't
miss the "incredible" Sunday brunch.

Le Coq au Vin S
28 | 21 | 25 | $34

4800 S. Orange Ave. (Holden Ave.), 407-851-6980

■ "Quaint, intimate and charming", this South Orlando French
bistro is a "perennial favorite that's holding up well" and continues
to prove that "fine things come in small packages"; so devoted is
chef-owner Louis Perrotte's following that regulars claim to have
the "phone number programmed on their cell phones", and why
not? – the "simply excellent" menu "caters to the connoisseur" by
"changing seasonally, so each visit is a delicious new experience"
(but always "finish with a soufflé").

Les Chefs de France [S] 25 25 22 $37

Epcot Ctr., French Pavilion, Lake Buena Vista, 407-939-3463

■ "Like being in the heart of Paris" (except for the folks at the next table wearing "shorts, sneakers and baseball caps"), this upscale Epcot French (owned by famed chefs Paul Bocuse, Gaston Lenôtre and Roger Vergé) is a "beautiful" recreation of a traditional Gallic bistro; "excellent" duck à l'orange and other classics are delivered by "pampering" servers imported "from France", making for a "special dining experience" that's further enhanced by the "great" view of the park's fireworks.

Louis' Downtown 29 29 26 $42

135 N. Lucerne Circle (bet. Anderson St. & Orange Ave.), 407-648-4688

■ Much to the delight of his followers, chef-owner Louis Chatham is back in town and every table is a hot, hot ticket at his "gourmet" Southern charmer; at press time, it was set to move to the heart of Downtown, the better to reach the power set that raves about his truly "amazing" "creations"; so though it's "pricey", "everything is just right" promise supporters who insist that "if you have time for only one dinner in the area, this is the place to go."

Maison et Jardin 27 27 27 $46

430 S. Wymore Rd. (½ mi. south of I-4 & State Rd. 436), Altamonte Springs, 407-862-4410

■ "When we win the lottery, we'll eat here once a week" vow acolytes of this "romantic" Altamonte Springs Continental, an "elegant" "class act" with an "absolutely gorgeous" interior overlooking "a beautiful grove of oaks"; the "exceptional" menu (think blinis filled with caviar, beef Wellington) is executed with "old-school finesse" and paired with a "fantastic" wine list; despite some grumbles about "pretentious" service, most feel that this "cream of fine restaurants" "sets the standard" in the Orlando area.

Manuel's on the 28th 26 28 27 $54

Bank of America Bldg., 390 N. Orange Ave. (Livingston St.), 407-246-6580

■ Boasting a "breathtaking skyline view" from the 28th floor of a Downtown skyscraper, this "sophisticated" International is "as good as it gets locally" rave boosters; it's "a terrific place to take someone you want to impress" because the "eclectic, creative" dishes are simply "exquisite" and proffered by a "superb" staff that's "knowledgeable and professional without being snooty"; this experience is "memorable", but prepare for expense-account tabs.

Narcoossee's [S] 25 26 25 $37

Disney's Grand Floridian Resort & Spa, 4401 Grand Floridian Way, Lake Buena Vista, 407-939-3463

■ "What a view!" exclaim visitors to this "memorable" seafood house in Disney's Grand Floridian, where the "fabulous" panoramic vista encompasses the Seven Seas Lagoon and the Magic Kingdom beyond; add chef Ron Rupert's "unusual" culinary touch, a "great wine list" and "friendly, attentive service" and voters conclude "first-rate, from drinks to desserts to fireworks"; P.S. while on the "pricey" side, it's "perfect for special evenings."

Outback S

24 20 21 $24

4845 S. Kirkman Rd. (Conroy Rd.), 407-292-5111
Florida Mall, 1301 Florida Mall Ave. (Orange Blossom Trail & Sand Lake Rd.), 407-240-6857
Shops at Lake Brantley, 990 N. State Rd. 434 (Jamestown Blvd.), Altamonta Springs, 407-862-1050
Formosa Gardens, 7804 W. Irlo Bronson Memorial Hwy. (Formosa Gardens Blvd.), Kissimmee, 407-396-0017
3109 W. Vine St. (Dyer Blvd.), Kissimmee, 407-931-0033
Wyndham Palace Resort & Spa, 1900 Buena Vista Dr. (Hotel Plaza Blvd.), Lake Buena Vista, 407-827-3430
180 Hickman Dr. (State Rd. 46), Sanford, 407-321-5881
1927 Aloma Ave. (Lakemont Ave.), Winter Park, 407-679-1050
Albertson's Shopping Ctr., 5891 Red Bug Lake Rd. (Tuskawilla Rd.), Winter Springs, 407-699-0900

■ "Wallaby darned" – this may be "the best steakhouse around" enthuse adherents of this "fun", "friendly" franchise that has crowds enduring "ridiculous waiting times" for the chance to chow down on "consistently" "tender, flavorful" beef and "who-could-resist bloomin' onions"; on the other end of the spectrum, grouches grumble that this "Australian fraud" is little more than a "dime-a-dozen" "theme" joint, and a "noisy" one at that.

Peter Scott's

24 24 25 $47

Longwood Village, 1811 W. State Rd. 434 (I-4), Longwood, 407-834-4477
◪ "Dust off your dancing shoes" and traipse over to this "romantic" Longwood Continental, a "real supper club" "in the classic style"; showcasing a variety of lounge acts and a spacious dance floor, as well as "great Dover sole" and a 500-bottle wine list, this "pricey" ("overpriced"?) haunt is ideal for a "very, very special night."

Rolando's S

24 13 20 $15

870 E. State Rd. 436 (Red Bug Lake Rd.), Casselberry, 407-767-9677
■ After many years in business, this Casselberry Cuban favorite was bought out by its longtime chef, whom fans "hope will keep up" the high standards because this is "*the* place to go" for "authentic" food at "fantastic values"; "very friendly" service adds to the appeal for a mostly "local" clientele (you'll find "very few tourists" here).

Ruth's Chris Steak House S

26 24 25 $49

Winter Park Village, 610 N. Orlando Ave. (Webster Ave.), Winter Park, 407-622-2444
■ "When it absolutely, positively has to be a great meal", seek out this "sooo good" chophouse chain that "lives up to its reputation" for "almost orgasmic" beef ("if tastier steaks exist, I've certainly never had one"); "everything here is first-class", from the "elegant dining room" to the "extremely professional" service that thankfully is "not of the stuffed-shirt variety"; just keep in mind that such "wonderful experiences" don't come cheap.

Thai House S

26 17 23 $15

2117 E. Colonial Dr. (Bumby Ave.), 407-898-0820
◪ Recently relocated a few doors down from its original site on East Colonial Drive (not reflected in the decor rating), this Thai "favorite" remains among "Orlando's best" thanks to its "varied menu" of "flavorful", "excellent" options (curries, satays, etc.).

Thai Place
25 | 17 | 19 | $18

501 N. Orlando Ave. (bet. Hwy. 17-92 & Lee Rd.), Winter Park, 407-644-8449

■ "If grandma were Thai" she'd cook up "tasty" classics like the "excellent", "quick and inexpensive" renditions offered at this "good neighborhood stop" in Winter Park, where regulars "love the complimentary salad" and recommend the crispy fish or one of the "great red curries"; the "newly remodeled" room has doubled in size, while service remains as "fast and courteous" as ever.

Victoria & Albert's S
28 | 28 | 29 | $81

Disney's Grand Floridian Resort & Spa, 4401 Grand Floridian Way, Lake Buena Vista, 407-824-1089

■ "Proof that Disney can amaze adults as well as children", this "ultimate" Grand Floridian American achieves near-"perfection from start to finish": chef Scott Hunnel masterminds "glorious" prix fixe extravaganzas (especially at the "chef's table in the kitchen", where the meals are personalized), and "you couldn't possibly get better service", given that each table is pampered by a "maid-and-butler" team that apparently attends to "you and you only"; of course, as "the pinnacle of fine dining", it's "very expensive."

Vito's Chop House S
▽ 28 | 25 | 26 | $33

8633 International Dr. (Austrian Ct.), 407-354-2467

■ "Classy without being stuffy", this upscale International Drive spot has already become a favorite steaks-and-chops choice for carnivores who rave they're "the best I've had in a long time"; the "high-quality" beef is "cooked exactly as requested" and presented by "attentive servers" who can also recommend "excellent" selections from the ambitious 900-plus bottle wine list.

Yachtsman Steakhouse S
26 | 25 | 26 | $42

Disney's Yacht Club Resort, 1700 Epcot Resorts Blvd., Lake Buena Vista, 407-939-3463

■ "Morton's for the Disney set", this upscale steakhouse in the Yacht Club Resort is renowned for "succulent" beef that may be the "best" on Mouse property; this "favorite" truly "has all the elements" – from "mouthwatering" dishes to dark, "clubby decor" to "top-notch" service – leading fanatics to venture "if I had to pick a last meal", this would be the place.

Palm Beach

TOP 10 FOOD RANKING

Restaurant	Cuisine Type
29 Chez Jean-Pierre	French Bistro
27 Cafe L'Europe	Continental
La Vieille Maison	New French
New York Prime	Steakhouse
Four Seasons	Caribbean/New American
Kathy's Gazebo Cafe	Continental
26 Renato's	N&S Italian
Maison Janeiro	New French
Cafe Chardonnay	New American
25 John G's	American

ADDITIONAL NOTEWORTHY PLACES

Cheesecake Factory	Eclectic
11 Maple Street	New American
La Belle Epoque	New French
Le Mistral	New French
Le Mont	Continental
L'Escalier	New American
Marcello's La Sirena	N&S Italian
Roy's	Hawaiian/Fusion
32 East	New American
Zemi	New American

F	D	S	C

Cafe Chardonnay S
26	23	24	$45

Garden Square Shoppes, 4533 PGA Blvd. (Military Trail), Palm Beach Gardens, 561-627-2662
■ "Year after year after year", "you can count on" the "solidly" "superb" New American eats and "exciting wines" at this perennial Palm Beach "favorite"; given the "gourmet gem's" "inventive appetizers" and "delicious" "fresh fish", design mavens concede that the "reasonably priced" place has "panache" despite its "Ikea going-out-of-business-sale decor"; "hey, it's fun, like upscale but casual", you know?

Cafe L'Europe S
27	28	26	$60

331 S. County Rd. (Brazilian Ave.), Palm Beach, 561-655-4020
■ For the "ultimate chic", you "must" try this "magnificently well-run Continental establishment" with its "unbeatable caviar bar"; Palm Beach's Most Popular place "delights all the senses" with "fabulous food", "lovely decor" and the "smell of fresh-cut roses" in the "lush dining room", plus "beautiful people"-watching and "lively" piano jazz in the "bustling bistro"; the "rich and famous" say that "every celebration should be here."

Cheesecake Factory ●🅂   21 | 19 | 19 | $24
5530 Glades Rd. (Butts Rd.), Boca Raton, 561-393-0344
City Pl., 701 S. Rosemary Ave. (bet. Hibiscus & Irish Sts.), West Palm Beach,
561-802-3838
■ "Super-size portions", "phenomenal selection" and consistent "quality and value" are the ingredients in this "cookie-cutter recipe that works every time"; these Eclectic franchises are "very popular", so "if you wait less than 45 minutes" for a table, consider yourself "lucky"; to avoid the "deadly lines", regulars suggest "get takeout" and make sure you order a "sinfully tasty" slice of the eponymous sweet stuff.

Chez Jean-Pierre   29 | 24 | 26 | $56
132 N. County Rd. (bet. Sunrise & Sunset Aves.), 561-833-1171
■ "Far and away the best" meals are served at this "authentic French" "charmer", rated No. 1 for Food in the *Palm Beach Survey*; "sophisticated" "locals love" "consistently excellent" dishes such as "really fresh Dover sole" and "exquisite sea bass" served by a "friendly, expert" staff at this "quaint" "family-run" "favorite"; despite trompe l'oeil wall paintings, there's "little glitz" here – "just quality" that's "not to be believed."

11 Maple Street 🅂   – | – | – | M
3224 NE Maple Ave. (11th Ave.), Jensen Beach, 561-334-7714
Tucked away on a tiny, sandy alley "up in Jensen Beach" is this 1909 picket-fenced place where "creative" chef-owners Mike and Margie Perrin "really know their way around the kitchen", dishing up New American eats with an emphasis on organic and natural ingredients; the "wonderful", tropical-themed dining room and porch are open just four nights a week, though when you "dine in the beautiful house with the twinkle lights" you may "wish it was an inn so you could spend the weekend."

Four Seasons 🅂   27 | 28 | 27 | $59
Four Seasons, 2800 S. Ocean Blvd. (Lake Ave. Bridge),
561-582-2800
■ "If you need pampering and attention", sink into a seat at this "elegant showstopper" in a "lovely" beachfront hotel; "gorgeous" ocean views and hand-painted Chinese murals set the stage for "heaven-on-a-plate" Caribbean–New American cuisine by chef Hubert Des Marais, followed by Tom Worhach's "wondrous" desserts delivered by "pure professionals" who attend to details as exacting as "lint-preventing black napkins [for diners wearing] darker clothes"; supplicants swoon that "the Greek gods must have built this place."

John G's 🅂⌷   25 | 15 | 22 | $18
10 S. Ocean Blvd. (Lake Ave.), Lake Worth, 561-585-9860
■ "You need to loosen your belt" after what regulars rave are "the best breakfasts and lunches in South Florida" at this "great-value" traditional American eatery open daily till 3 PM; don't mind the "long lines" – while you cool your jets with the other devotees of the "family-owned" "local legend's" "outstanding French toast" and "memorable fish 'n' chips", you can enjoy the "beach view and salty air" of its oceanside location.

Kathy's Gazebo Cafe S
27 | 24 | 25 | $53

4199 N. Federal Hwy. (Spanish River Rd.), Boca Raton, 561-395-6033
☑ "Dover sole to die for" and other "exquisitely prepared" "classic Continental" dishes "please even the most finicky diner" at this "traditional" Boca cafe where an "older, well-heeled crowd" "treats itself to an elegant evening"; the staff in the "beautiful little room" "is extremely attentive", though it can "still keep patrons with reservations waiting" for a table.

La Belle Epoque S
26 | 26 | 25 | $48

253 SE Fifth Ave. (Atlantic Ave.), Delray Beach, 561-272-5800
■ Few surveyors have discovered this "[New] French find" "off the beaten track", but those who have say the "wonderful" newcomer is ushering in a beautiful epoch of dining for Delray Beach with "exquisite food combined with a charming staff"; patrons may want to pitch pennies in the fountain at the center of the "clean and stylish interior" and make a wish for a speedy return trip.

La Vieille Maison S
27 | 27 | 26 | $57

770 E. Palmetto Park Rd. (bet. Olive Way & Spanish Trail), Boca Raton, 561-737-5677
■ The "grande dame of Boca" gets "kudos" galore, as diners gush over "the best captain in the USA" and his "French-speaking" staff who serve "consistently divine" New French fare in a "beautifully furnished old house"; "private small rooms" make it the "place to come and not be seen" when you want to get *très romantique.*"

Le Mistral S
25 | 21 | 23 | $46

Northbeach Plaza, 12189 Hwy. 1 (PGA Blvd.), North Palm Beach, 561-622-3009
■ "Appearances are deceiving" in South Florida – "if you're looking for an authentic New French restaurant", an ordinary North Palm Beach strip mall houses this "top-notch" place where "everything is extraordinary"; an "outstanding" bouillabaise and numerous other "wonderful gourmet" treats make the "cozy charmer" an "overall favorite for a special evening."

Le Mont
▽ 23 | 26 | 23 | $51

Northbridge Ctr., 515 N. Flagler Dr. (bet. 4th & 5th Sts.), West Palm Beach, 561-820-2442
☑ High in the sky on the 20th floor of a Downtown bank tower, this "very glitzy" new Pittsburgh import is "good if you need la-di-da" "bordello decor" and a "spectacular view of Lake Worth and Palm Beach" to seduce your date; some say the Floribbean-influenced Continental cuisine is "delicious", but foodies who've 'been there, eaten that' crave "more selection" from the "overpriced" menu.

L'Escalier S
– | – | – | VE

The Breakers Hotel, 1 S. County Rd. (Royal Palm Way), Palm Beach, 561-659-8480
The Breakers in Palm Beach has renovated its Florentine Room and renamed it after the stairway; an open kitchen doesn't detract from the intimacy of silky banquettes and flower-adorned tables, while "pampering" service presents "outstanding" New American cuisine with French accents, including an unusual cheese selection and a winning wine list; just be forewarned that a meal in this "elegant" hotel can be a bank breaker.

Maison Janeiro S   26 | 25 | 25 | $61

191 Bradley Pl. (bet. Oleander & Seminole Aves.), 561-659-5223

■ "A certain crowd" with a flare for the "dramatic" "hangs" out at this "colorful" Palm Beach house where the New French fare served on "knock-your-socks-off" Versace-designed china is as "original and creatively presented" as the room's "funky and sophisticated" "mix of Morrocan, European and Brazilian" styles; highlighted by a "never-ending wine list" and a choice of many "different soufflés for dessert", a meal here is an "experience" that "really rocks."

Marcello's La Sirena S   25 | 19 | 23 | $46

6316 S. Dixie Hwy. (bet. Forest Hill & Southern Blvds.), West Palm Beach, 561-585-3128

☑ In a "small but charming" A-frame south of Downtown West Palm Beach is an Italian that's "a cut above" most others for its "fresh, simple, perfectly prepared" dishes with an emphasis on seafood, including a signature roasted yellowtail snapper for two; married with "one of the best wine lists ever", the "wonderful" fare is presented "without pretense" – but , alas, with an "expensive" price tag.

New York Prime S   27 | 23 | 24 | $56

2350 Executive Center Dr. (Glades Rd.), Boca Raton, 561-998-3881

■ "Fuhgeddabout New York" – the "mack daddy of steakhouses" is in Boca Raton; every night is "boys' night out" at this beef bacchanalia where "huge", "delicious" cuts can result in "Great Dane–size doggy bags" and non-meat treats like lobsters are equally "leviathan" in size; just be warned that a "clubby" "attitude" means if you're not one of the "boisterous" "regulars", you may find it "hard to get a reservation in season" at the "popular" "glutton"-fest.

Renato's S   26 | 25 | 24 | $55

87 Via Mizner (Cocoanut Row), 561-655-9752

■ "Romantic" "Palm Beachers who want to eat well" dine with their dates amid this "stylish Italian's" "spectacular mix of wood and fresh flowers" or "eat outside on a nice night" in its "lovely" courtyard; with "wonderful" meals plated on "beautiful Limoges china" and served with a "courteous all-around manner" in a space that's "charming in and out", this bistro "off Worth Avenue" simply "oozes atmosphere."

Roy's S   23 | 22 | 22 | $48

1901 N. Military Trail (19th St.), Boca Raton, 561-620-9401

■ For a culinary "aloha" from Hawaii, try "the daily changing menu of fresh seafood" at peripatetic superstar chef Roy Yamaguchi's "extremely promising" chain-link newcomer in east Boca; the Hawaiian "fusion" fare is "strange" but "fabulous", the "room is lovely with very high ceilings" and, though they're still "working out the bugs", "the staff can't do enough to please you"; reviewers deem this "different and delicious" dining experience "expensive but fun."

32 East [S] | 23 | 20 | 21 | $42 |

32 E. Atlantic Ave. (bet. 1st & Swinton Aves.), Delray Beach, 561-276-7868

■ A "creative, daily changing menu" based on "simple, perfect ingredients" "keeps the locals" and the far-flung "coming back" "again and again" to "Delray's fun place for grown-up" gourmands; though the "noisy, busy" bar scene "feels like Manhattan", it's "genius" chef Nick Morfogen's "plentiful" New American "fusion dishes" that really take this "upscale joint" "beyond South Florida."

Zemi [S] | 25 | 24 | 23 | $49 |

Boca Ctr., 5050 Town Center Circle (Military Trail), Boca Raton, 561-391-7177

◪ The "Modern American" menu has "a bit of an Asian influence" here at chef John Belleme's "chic" east Boca "be-seen"-ery; a "noisy", "trendy" crowd "loves the lobster wonton soup" and other "exquisite", "exotic dishes" "beautifully presented" in this "sophisticated" shopping-center "hot spot" where "even the bathroom is pretty"; introverts should "avoid weekends", when "they sure do pack 'em in here."

Philadelphia

TOP 20 FOOD RANKING

Restaurant	Cuisine Type
29 Le Bec-Fin	Classic French
Fountain	New French/New American
28 Le Bar Lyonnais	Classic French
27 Swann Lounge	American/French Bistro
Susanna Foo	Chinese
Deux Cheminées	Classic French
Jake's	New American
Dilworthtown Inn	New American
Vetri	N&S Italian
Striped Bass	Seafood
26 Dmitri's	Mediterranean
Brasserie Perrier	New French
Prime Rib	Steakhouse
La Famiglia	N&S Italian
La Bonne Auberge	Classic French
Mainland Inn	New American
Monte Carlo Living Room	N&S Italian
Tacconelli's Pizzeria	Pizza
Buddakan	Asian
25 Evermay on the Delaware	New American

ADDITIONAL NOTEWORTHY PLACES

Alma de Cuba	Cuban
Audrey Clair	Mediterranean
Bistro St. Tropez	French Bistro
Blue Angel	French Bistro
DiPalma	N&S Italian
Fork	New American
Nan	Thai/Classic French
Opus 251	New American
Overtures	New French/Med.
¡Pasion!	Nuevo Latino
Passerelle	New French/New American
Rouge	New French/Asian
Saloon	N&S Italian
Sansom St. Oyster House	Seafood
Savona	N.Italian/Seafood
Tangerine	Moroccan/New French
333 Belrose	New American
20 Manning	New American
White Dog Cafe	Eclectic
Yangming	Chinese

Alma de Cuba [S] – | – | – | E

1623 Walnut St. (bet. 16th & 17th Sts.), 215-988-1799

The godfather of Nuevo Latino cuisine, NY chef Douglas Rodriguez, has partnered with über-restaurateur Stephen Starr to open the eatery of the moment: a good-looking, three-level Cuban on Restaurant Row; the downstairs lounge brims with beautiful people sipping mojitos, and the bright upper floors are full of foodies savoring octopus, duck and other sophisticated tastes.

Audrey Claire [S]⊄ 22 | 17 | 19 | $28

276 S. 20th St. (Spruce St.), 215-731-1222

■ Reservations are available Tuesday–Thursday and on Sunday, but at other times it pays to "go early" to snare a table at this Center City Mediterranean BYO; admirers know it as an "airy", "minimalist" corner storefront where the "creative", "beautifully presented" food is "as delicious" as the crowd is "hip."

Bistro St. Tropez 23 | 20 | 20 | $34

2400 Market St., 4th fl. (23rd St.), 215-569-9269

■ Though newcomers may "need a guide" to find this "delightful" French treasure "buried" in the Marketplace Design Center, the "magnificent" Schuylkill views and "head-swirling menu" are apt to make Francophiles "feel far from Philadelphia"; most sigh it's "romantic to say the least."

Blue Angel [S] 24 | 25 | 23 | $39

706 Chestnut St. (7th St.), 215-925-6889

■ "Another Starr in the heavens" sigh admirers of Stephen Starr's "smashing", "jewel-like" "Paris bistro" in the Historic District; those who suppose the "noise makes you vibrate" may be quivering in anticipation of the "sumptuous" fare, "attentive service" and prime "people-watching" – either way, the scene is "happening."

Brasserie Perrier [S] 26 | 25 | 24 | $52

1619 Walnut St. (bet. 16th & 17th Sts.), 215-568-3000

■ "Ooh-la-la" squeal surveyors over Georges Perrier's "less stuffy Le Bec-Fin sib" (aka "Le Bec-Fin Lite") on Restaurant Row; "inventive" New French food with "wonderful flavors", "attentive service", "trendy" surroundings and "gorgeous" people "at the bar" make it *très* chic and "top-notch in every category."

Buddakan [S] 26 | 27 | 22 | $46

325 Chestnut St. (bet. 3rd & 4th Sts.), 215-574-9440

■ "Lamborghini-driving divorcées" and "black-clad" "beautiful people" pack Stephen Starr's "sexy" Old City Asian powerhouse in pursuit of "out-of-this-world" "fusion" fare served in a "striking" room dominated by a "giant golden Buddha" and a running waterfall; faced with the "see-and-be-seen" atmospherics, demure diners warn of a "noisy", "intimidating" time ("bring earplugs").

Deux Cheminées 27 | 27 | 26 | VE

1221 Locust St. (bet. 12th & 13th Sts.), 215-790-0200

■ "Step back in time to a grander era" at Fritz Blank's Classic French "class act" in two "elegant" Center City rowhouses; ever a "very romantic" experience, it "exhilarates all the senses" with "fabulous food", "stunning decor" and an "attentive" staff – just beware of "attitude" and try to "forget the cost"; N.B. dinner only, $80 prix fixe.

Dilworthtown Inn S　　　27　27　26　$48
1390 Old Wilmington Pike (Brinton Bridge Rd.), West Chester, 610-399-1390

■ For "candlelit dining" "in the 'burbs", this "romantic", "button-down" West Chester New American is an acknowledged "class" act where the room's "elegance" is matched with "exquisite cuisine", a "superb wine list" and "unobtrusive" service; in sum, it's a chance to "feel special" – but be sure to "bring lots of dough"; N.B. jackets and reservations are required.

DiPalma　　　21　22　20　$44
114 Market St. (bet. Front & 2nd Sts.), 215-733-0545

◪ Chef-owner Salvatore DiPalma's "high-end" Old City Italian claims a following that finds the "sophisticated" cooking "first-rate" and the "spacious" surroundings just plain "beautiful"; hedgers cry "too expensive" and remain cautious with the kudos ("promising, but not there yet"); N.B. signature dishes include octopus carpaccio and herb-coated rack of lamb.

Dmitri's S　　　26　13　19　$25
2227 Pine St. (22nd St.), 215-985-3680
795 S. Third St. (Catharine St.), 215-625-0556 ⊟

■ To get a table in one of owner Dmitri Chimes' eponymous Mediterranean "gems" in Fitler Square and Queen Village, patrons put up with "long lines" ("get there early"), "no reservations" and "noisy", "cramped" conditions; it's deemed worth it for such "amazingly fresh seafood", including "sublime" squid and octopus and "wonderful", "unadulterated" whole fish.

Evermay on the Delaware S　　　25　27　25　VE
River Rd. (Headquarters Rd.), Erwinna, 610-294-9100

■ Since it's attached to a B&B that's a "long" "country drive" from Philly, loyalists love to "make a weekend out of" this Upper Bucks New American; a jacket-required "whisper" restaurant, it offers an "excellent" (if "limited") prix fixe menu and two "pretty", "romantic" seating options: a formal, Victorian-style dining space and a "beautiful" garden room; N.B. open Friday–Sunday only.

Fork S　　　24　23　22　$37
306 Market St. (bet. 3rd & 4th Sts.), 215-625-9425

■ This airy, banquette-lined Old City entry can claim a "cult-like following" among a "young crowd" that admires its "elegant", "snappy" decor, "delicious combinations" of "inspired" New American cuisine and "attentive", "gracious" staff; it can get "hectic" and feel "cramped", but overall it's "exciting" and "deserving of its success"; P.S. if dinner reservations are scarce, "try Sunday brunch."

Fountain S　　　29　29　29　$66
Four Seasons Hotel, 1 Logan Sq. (Benjamin Franklin Pkwy. & 18th St.), 215-963-1500

■ In Logan Square, this "special-occasion" favorite is a "dining fantasy come true" lauded for its "superb" New French–American cuisine, "flawless service" and a "luxurious" (but "not stuffy") setting that defines "simple elegance"; N.B. longtime chef de restaurant Martin Hamann assumed the top toque this past summer.

Jake's 🖻   27 | 22 | 24 | $45

4365 Main St. (bet. Grape & Levering Sts.), 215-483-0444
■ Bruce Cooper's "high-powered" storefront New American wins praise for its "beautiful presentations" of "consistently outstanding" fare ("amazing lobster mashed potatoes", "sublime" crab cakes), "conscientious" staff and "classy" art-filled dining room; the bottom line: it's *the* place to dine in Manayunk."

La Bonne Auberge 🖻   26 | 27 | 25 | $64

Village 2 Apt. Complex (Mechanic St.), New Hope, 215-862-2462
🗹 The "ultimate" "romantic hideaway", this Classic French "beauty" quartered in a New Hope farmhouse sets "the standard" for "special-occasion dining" with its "wonderful" cooking; devotees deem it "worth every penny", though those unenchanted with the "small portions" grumble it's "all fluff and no substance."

La Famiglia 🖻   26 | 23 | 24 | $54

8 S. Front St. (bet. Chestnut & Market Sts.), 215-922-2803
■ For "marvelous", "authentic" Italian cuisine matched with "great wines" in a "luxurious" room, it's hard to top the Sena clan's Old City "classic", a long-running "favorite" for "elegant", "unrushed" dining; it's a "pricey" package, but one of "the best" – this "family knows food and hospitality."

Le Bar Lyonnais ◑   28 | 25 | 26 | $50

1523 Walnut St. (bet. 15th & 16th Sts.), 215-567-1000
■ Anyone looking for a "way to enjoy Le Bec-Fin for less" can grab a "tiny table" at Georges Perrier's "cozy", "sophisticated" "grotto" in a space beneath the Restaurant Row powerhouse; here's a chance to "feel like an insider" while savoring "fabulous" Classic French food in "the lap of luxury."

Le Bec-Fin   29 | 28 | 29 | VE

1523 Walnut St. (bet. 15th & 16th Sts.), 215-567-1000
■ "It's all been said before", but it bears repeating: Georges Perrier's "world-class" Classic French "gastronomic temple" on Walnut Street remains Philly's Most Popular restaurant (and No. 1 for Food) on the strength of its "incomparable" cuisine, "gorgeous" atmospherics, "servers who anticipate your every move" and a dessert cart "to die for"; though "cheaper than flying to France for dinner (barely)", it's even more tempting "if someone else pays"; N.B. $40 lunch prix fixe, $120 dinner.

Mainland Inn 🖻   26 | 24 | 25 | $45

17 Main St. (Sumneytown Pike), Mainland, 215-256-8500
■ "Country dining with sophistication" sums up the scene at this "bucolic" New American near Lansdale that wins raves for its "superior" food ("delicious goat cheese appetizer", "amazing tulip dessert"), "great" French-California wine list, crackerjack staff and "intimate", candlelit rooms; N.B. a more casual, English-style grill recently opened downstairs.

Monte Carlo Living Room 🖻   26 | 23 | 24 | $55

150 South St. (2nd St.), 215-925-2220
🗹 "World-class" dining is alive and well at this "special-night-out" Italian on South Street, where "superb" chef Nunzio Patruno is famed for his "exquisitely flavored" fare; the "impressive" ambiance and "formal" service are "elegance in action" and come at prices to break the bank.

Nan
25 17 20 $30

4000 Chestnut St. (40th St.), 215-382-0818

■ "Long may he cook" – "hardworking" Kamol Phutlek dazzles diners with his "wonderful", "stylish" dishes and "unbelievable", "synergistic" sauces at his Thai-French BYO in University City; an amiable staff and "reasonable" tabs help offset a "minimalistic" space that can get "chaotic" on weekends (reserve ahead).

Opus 251 S
24 23 22 $45

Philadelphia Art Alliance, 251 S. 18th St. (Rittenhouse Sq.), 215-735-6787

■ Sited in a "handsome" mansion just off Rittenhouse Square whose "splendor is matched" by the "innovative" American cuisine, this "jewel" is ideal for that "romantic" "special-occasion" meal or a "wonderful" brunch; nature lovers appreciate the "delightful outdoor garden" too.

Overtures S
25 23 24 $42

609-611 Passyunk Ave. (bet. Bainbridge & South Sts.), 215-627-3455

■ "Go, Peter, go!" rave the many fans of Peter Lamlein's simply "wonderful" BYO off South Street, which features "fabulous" New French–Mediterranean food, "gracious" service from a "thoughtful" staff" and a romantic, "European atmosphere"; in sum, it's a "classy" establishment and *the* place to "bring your best wine."

¡Pasion! S
25 25 23 $46

211 S. 15th St. (bet. Locust & Walnut Sts.), 215-875-9895

■ Chef Guillermo Pernot's "melt-in-your-mouth" cuisine and a "lush", "tropical" setting ensure this Center City Nuevo Latino's status as a "must-go"; from the "outstanding seviches" to the "superb" sea bass, enthusiasts evince passion aplenty for the "unique" "gourmet" fare, calling this a "hot spot" that "lives up to the hype."

Passerelle S
25 26 24 $48

175 King of Prussia Rd. (Lancaster Ave.), Radnor, 610-293-9411

☑ "Bliss in the 'burbs" awaits at this "romantic" Radnor New French–American with a "gorgeous setting and food to match"; it's a "can't-wait" destination for "inspired" cuisine served in a "beautiful", "formal" setting ("look for the swans" in the pond), though detractors pass on the "small portions" and "uptight" airs.

Prime Rib S
26 26 25 $54

Warwick Hotel, 1701 Locust St. (17th St.), 215-772-1701

■ The "perfectly cooked meats", "impeccable" service and "lavish decor" qualify this "old-school" "manly place" in the Warwick as a "fantasy of a clubby steakhouse"; a link of the DC-based chain, it claims legions of loyalists who relish the "sophisticated" style and "enormous quantities" of "outstanding" food, though a few say it "overdoes it."

Rouge ◐S
23 24 19 $39

Rittenhouse Claridge Apt. Bldg., 205 S. 18th St. (bet. Locust & Walnut Sts.), 215-732-6622

☑ With its "electric" mood and "delicious" New French–Asian food, Neil Stein's "chic", "crowded" "jewel box" on Rittenhouse Square is a magnet for the "cell phone" and "Rolex" set; it's the "place to be seen", though foes oppose the "dieter's" portions and service that "defines the word 'attitude.'"

Saloon   24 | 22 | 22 | $53
750 S. Seventh St. (bet. Catharine & Fitzwater Sts.), 215-627-1811
◪ "Fat cats" drop "big bucks" for "hearty portions" of "excellent" Italian ("best veal chops") at this "classy" South Philadelphia "oldie but goodie" where a "good-natured" staff works the "dark" room; a post-*Survey* chef change may address gripes that they're "resting on their laurels"; P.S. "oops, they only take Amex."

Sansom Street Oyster House   21 | 16 | 19 | $28
1516 Sansom St. (bet. 15th & 16th Sts.), 215-567-7683
■ Over the past few years it's seen a chef-owner change and a remodeling, but this "old-fashioned", family-owned Center City "pearl" continues to be a "mainstay for fresh, well-prepared" "comfort seafood" at "reasonable prices"; it's a local favorite for happy hour–priced "oysters and a glass of steely Sauvignon Blanc."

Savona 🖸   25 | 26 | 23 | $56
100 Old Gulph Rd. (Montgomery Ave.), Gulph Mills, 610-520-1200
■ "Commendably serious", this Main Line Ligurian seafood house is "full of minks" and "expense-account" types savoring "absolutely fabulous" food and a "dreamy", "elegant" setting with terra-cotta tiles, Venetian banquettes and mahogany furniture; the generally "excellent" staff comes off as "pretentious" to a laid-back few.

Striped Bass 🖸   27 | 28 | 24 | $59
1500 Walnut St. (15th St.), 215-732-4444
◪ Neil Stein's "swank", "over-the-top" Restaurant Row seafood house "lives up to its stellar reputation" for "mouthwatering", "decadent" cuisine and an "exquisite" "NYC" environment; but skeptics style it "stuffed shirt" and scold "it's just fish – get those prices under control!"

Susanna Foo 🖸   27 | 25 | 25 | $54
1512 Walnut St. (bet. 15th & 16th Sts.), 215-545-2666
■ "Culinary nirvana" sums up the sentiment on Ms. Foo's truly "awesome" Chinese fusion house on Restaurant Row, where the "Jag and Mercedes" crowd lines up for "intoxicatingly" "innovative cuisine"; each dish is a "delicate" "work of art" in keeping with the "elegant" setting (and "expense-account" prices).

Swann Lounge & Cafe ●🖸   27 | 27 | 27 | $47
Four Seasons Hotel, 1 Logan Sq. (bet. Benjamin Franklin Pkwy. & 18th St.), 215-963-1500
■ "If you don't feel like dressing for the Fountain", its "comfortable" yet "sophisticated" French-American neighbor at the Four Seasons is a "spectacular" alternative; pampered patrons "feel like royalty" at "afternoon tea" or the "amazing brunch", or when listening to jazz "by the fireplace."

Tacconelli's Pizzeria 🖸⌿   26 | 9 | 16 | $15
2604 E. Somerset St. (bet. Almond & Thompson Sts.), 215-425-4983
■ "Get your dough orders in early" at this BYO Port Richmond pizza "legend", so popular that patrons are obliged to reserve their own hunks of dough; the payoff is the "extraordinary", "crispy-crust" pies ("white pizza is better than sex") served amid "nonexistent" decor; N.B. dinner only, Wednesday–Sunday.

Tangerine S

_ _ _ M

232 Market St. (bet. 2nd & 3rd Sts.), 215-627-5116

Moor is more at Stephen Starr's slick New French–Moroccan fusion fantasy in Old City; trendsetters traipse through a dimly lit, theatrical space to enjoy adventurous food designed for sharing, making it one of Downtown's "hottest" spots.

333 Belrose S

23 20 18 $36

333 Belrose Ln. (King of Prussia Rd.), Radnor, 610-293-1000

■ Chef-owner Carlo De Marco's "super" New American set in the former Carolina's in Radnor remains a "see-and-be-seen" scene; credit "top-notch" "Cal-style" fare served in "attractive" (albeit "noisy") digs, though some bristle at "impertinent" service.

20 Manning S

_ _ _ M

261 S. 20th St. (bet. Locust & Spruce Sts.), 215-731-0900

Audrey Claire's sexy, Asian-influenced American wows the Rittenhouse Square crowd with excellent cuisine (try the tuna sashimi) and a casual, non-stuffy setting, which features gray banquettes, a glass-backed bar and a communal metal table.

Vetri

27 22 25 $54

1312 Spruce St. (bet. Broad & 13th Sts.), 215-732-3478

■ "*Bellissimo!*" cheer champions of Marc Vetri's "intimate", "romantic" Italian in the "pedigreed" former Center City digs of Le Bec-Fin and Chanterelles; the "classy atmosphere" sets the tone for "delicious" cuisine "lovingly served" by a "warm" staff, and if a few flinch at the cost, most find the "fabulous" experience "worth every penny."

White Dog Cafe S

24 21 20 $34

3420 Sansom St. (34th St.), 215-386-9224

■ "Innovative" cuisine mixes with "socially minded" (some say "hippie") values at Judy Wicks' "bustling" Eclectic "perennial" on the Penn campus; it's one of this town's "top dogs" for "trendy but tasty" "organic" cooking, and the room's usually "crowded" with "noisy" intellectuals; P.S. "check out the bar for cheap eats and a varied crowd."

Yangming S

24 22 22 $34

1051 Conestoga Rd. (Haverford Rd.), Bryn Mawr, 610-527-3200

■ "Not your strip-mall" joint, Michael Wei's "outstanding" Main Line Chinese is a "mainstay" for "creative", "delicious" food, served in a "classy space" by a "courteous", "knowledgeable" staff; the "bustling" scene makes it "a winner" worth "showing off to friends."

Phoenix/Scottsdale

TOP 10 FOOD RANKING

	Restaurant	Cuisine Type
28	Mary Elaine's	New French
27	Marquesa	Mediterranean
	Vincent Guerithault	Classic French/SW
26	T. Cook's	Mediterranean
	RoxSand	New American
	Pizzeria Bianco	Pizza
	La Hacienda	Mexican
	Coup des Tartes	Classic French/Eclectic
	Morton's of Chicago	Steakhouse
	Michael's at the Citadel	New American

ADDITIONAL NOTEWORTHY PLACES

Christopher's	French Bistro
Convivo	New American
Gregory's World Bistro	International
Lon's at the Hermosa	New American/SW
Medizona	Southwestern/Med.
Rancho Pinot Grill	New American
Razz's	International
Restaurant Hapa	New American/Asian
Roaring Fork	Western
Ruth's Chris	Steakhouse

	F	D	S	C
Christopher's Fermier Brasserie [S]	23	22	20	$36

Biltmore Fashion Park, 2584 E. Camelback Rd. (N. 24th St.), Phoenix, 602-522-2344

◪ This "exciting" Biltmore Fashion Park French brasserie from chef Christopher Gross has a "more informal" setting than his previous place, and it's punctuated by an "excellent" wine bar (100 selections by the glass, plus house-brewed beers); otherwise, expect the same "hip crowd" and such "exquisite" signature dishes as his truffle-infused sirloin; still, some say this incarnation "needs some edges polished."

Convivo	–	–	–	E

Walgreen's Shopping Ctr., 7000 N. 16th St. (E. Glendale Ave.), Phoenix, 602-997-7676

Convivial is certainly an apt description of the atmosphere at this Phoenix New American that gracefully transcends its strip-mall setting; new chef-owner Jeffrey Beeson tweaks his cooking with zingy Southwestern accents based on fresh herbs and veggies brought in from his own garden (resulting in dishes like lobster tamales) and crowns the meal with innovative desserts such as an ancho-chile brownie with cinnamon ice cream and cajeta sauce, easily worth its gazillion calories.

Coup des Tartes 26 20 24 $32

4626 N. 16th St. (E. Highland Ave.), Phoenix, 602-212-1082

■ "Reminiscent of grandma's house", this Midtown Phoenix cottage features a monthly changing menu of "excellent" Classic French–Eclectic fare and the "personal attention" of the owner; while the "small" space might seem "cramped" at first, by the end of the evening you'll agree that this is a "charming" "jewel" and one of the best places in the city to BYO.

Gregory's World Bistro – – – E

Village at Hayden, 8120 N. Hayden Rd. (Via De Ventura), Scottsdale, 480-946-8700

When chef-owner Gregory Casale moved his eatery to roomier digs in McCormick Ranch, he changed his restaurant's name (formerly Gregory's Grill) to better reflect his progressive International menu, which is even more eclectic than before; nowadays, diners can satisfy their wanderlust with diminutively portioned dishes inspired by France, Japan, Thailand, India, Morocco and Mexico, all prepared with classical techniques.

La Hacienda [S] 26 24 22 $39

Fairmont Scottsdale Princess, 7575 E. Princess Dr. (bet. Pima & N. Scottsdale Rds.), Scottsdale, 480-585-4848

■ "They do things right" at this "elegant but comfortable" hotel Mexican in Scottsdale, whose beamed ceilings, tiled floors and crooning mariachi trio transport diners south of the border; foodwise, the "authentic" offerings include a signature roast suckling pig that's simply a showstopper.

Lon's at the Hermosa Inn [S] 25 26 23 $38

Hermosa Inn, 5532 N. Palo Cristi Rd. (E. Stanford Dr.), Paradise Valley, 602-955-7878

■ Set in a "beautiful" adobe hacienda built by artist Lon Megargee in the '30s, this "romantic" retreat oozes an "authentic old Arizona" feel right down to its "great patio" with a commanding view of Camelback Mountain; as the "last of the small resorts", with "great" service and "superior" Southwestern-influenced New American combos, it's no surprise that it was voted Phoenix/Scottsdale's Most Popular restaurant.

Marquesa [S] 27 27 27 $47

Fairmont Scottsdale Princess, 7575 E. Princess Dr. (bet. Pima & N. Scottsdale Rds.), Scottsdale, 480-585-4848

■ Housed in one of Scottsdale's plushest resorts, this "world-class" Mediterranean showcases an "imaginative" menu ranging from paella and pan-flashed loup de mer to "creative desserts"; moreover, as the name implies, guests are "treated royally", and the "elegant setting" – replete with paintings of princesses – is sure to impress.

Mary Elaine's 28 29 27 $57

The Phoenician, 6000 E. Camelback Rd. (N. 60th St.), Scottsdale, 480-423-2530

■ "Everything is superb" at this "special-occasion" destination quartered in The Phoenician – from James Boyce's "incredible" New French creations (voted No. 1 for Food in Phoenix/Scottsdale) and the "great wine list" to the "outstanding valley views" to the "impeccable" service; bring your jacket and your "expense account" and indulge in a "five-star" experience.

Medizona   _ _ _ E

7217 E. Fourth Ave. (Winfield Scott Plaza), Scottsdale, 480-947-9500
This cozy little gem tucked away amid the office buildings of
Downtown Scottsdale is well worth tracking down for chef-owner
Lenny Rubin's knockout Southwestern cooking spun with a creative
Mediterranean twist; look for dishes like rabbit baklava, eggplant
tacos and blackened shrimp that are strictly swoon material.

Michael's at the Citadel S   26 25 24 $39

*The Citadel, 8700 E. Pinnacle Peak Rd. (Pima Rd.), Scottsdale,
480-515-2575*
☑ "As comfortable as being at home with much better food" is
the high praise surveyors bestow upon Michael DeMaria's
"plush" Scottsdale New American, a "grown-up" spot with an
indoor waterfall, "inventive" dishes, "good wines by the glass"
and "seductive desserts"; P.S. try to reserve the "great" chef's
table overlooking the kitchen.

Morton's of Chicago S   26 23 23 $49

*Camelback Esplanade, 2501 E. Camelback Rd. (N. 24th St.), Phoenix,
602-955-9577*
15233 N. Kierland Blvd. (N. Scottsdale Rd.), Scottsdale, 480-951-4440
■ Suspender-wearing "manly men" flock to these top-tier chain
steakhouses for their "woody" environs, "large portions" of
"excellent" beef (notably the "best porterhouse for two") and
solid sides; more delicate sensibilities, however, could do without
"the smell of cigars" and find it "hard to justify the prices" if you're
not on an expense account.

Pizzeria Bianco S   26 23 21 $19

Heritage Sq., 623 E. Adams St. (N. 7th St.), Phoenix, 602-258-8300
■ When it comes to "the best wood-fired pizza in Phoenix, maybe
anywhere", "nobody does it better" than Chris Bianco and his
"wonderful staff", who use only the finest ingredients to achieve
their "awesome" results; handily located Downtown, it draws a
"great crowd" that can't get enough of the transcendent tastes
and "big-city" decor.

Rancho Pinot Grill   25 22 24 $36

*Lincoln Village, 6208 N. Scottsdale Rd. (E. Lincoln Dr.), Scottsdale,
480-443-0680*
■ Given decor that's sort of a cross between "funky cowboy"
and "rancher chic", it's hard not to "love" this Scottsdale New
American, which also features an "excellent" menu of "creative"
"comfort food" (from a wood-burning oven and mesquite grill),
delicious desserts, a "great" 5,000-bottle wine list and a "pleasant
staff"; truth be told, it's "what a restaurant should be" and "the
Valley is lucky to have it."

Razz's   25 19 24 $35

10315 N. Scottsdale Rd. (E. Shea Blvd.), Scottsdale, 480-905-1308
■ Popular chef Razz Kamnitzer "cooks with pizzazz" and "comes
around to schmooze" too at this North Scottsdale International
where loyalists lap up the "welcoming" service and "very creative"
combos (think cashew-encrusted salmon with hibiscus-and-lime
sauce); though a few don't warm to his "strange recipes", the
majority finds this a "happy place."

Restaurant Hapa   25   21   24 $38

Lincoln Village, 6204 N. Scottsdale Rd. (E. Lincoln Dr.), Scottsdale, 480-998-8220

■ "Exciting" Asian-influenced New American fare served on "beautiful" Japanese-style plates, along with a minimalist dining room and a sushi lounge appointed with rattan furniture, generates high praise for James and Stacey McDevitt's "great little" spot in Scottsdale; their signature dishes include caramelized beef tenderloin with Chinese mustard and prawn tempura.

Roaring Fork   22   22   21 $35

7243 E. Camelback Rd. (east of N. Scottsdale Rd.), Scottsdale, 480-947-0795

☑ Rugged, charming chef-owner Robert McGrath's rustic yet elegant mountain lodge–like Western retreat in Central Scottsdale features not only a patio with a stone fireplace and a palomino-brown dining room with paintings done by locals but also a bar filled with boisterous patrons at happy hour, an all-American wine list and "interesting" "macho" dishes like campfire salmon fillet; in sum, you should be roaring to try it.

RoxSand S   26   24   24 $36

Biltmore Fashion Park, 2594 E. Camelback Rd. (N. 24th St.), Phoenix, 602-381-0444

■ This "hip", "bi-level", global-accented New American is "a true cut above" the competition thanks to chef-owner RoxSand Scocos' "wonderful" cooking, served in a "sophisticated", "stark" setting that's "the closest thing to NYC in Phoenix"; P.S. don't leave without ordering a "wonderful" dessert (the display case features probably "the most chocolate choices in the Southwest").

Ruth's Chris Steak House S   26   23   25 $42

2201 E. Camelback Rd. (N. 24th St.), Phoenix, 602-957-9600
Scottsdale Seville, 7001 N. Scottsdale Rd. (E. Indian Bend Rd.), Scottsdale, 480-991-5988

■ The No. 2 steakhouse in Arizona, this top-tier chain is praised for its "big-city ambiance" and "melt-in-your-mouth steaks" (especially the "best filet mignon ever"), served sizzling hot in butter (it's known as "the widow-maker"); while many customers are "businessmen" on "expense accounts", if you're paying your own way, "share and the price drops dramatically."

T. Cook's S   26   28   25 $43

Royal Palms Hotel & Casitas, 5200 E. Camelback Rd. (bet. N. Arcadia Dr. & N. 56th St.), Phoenix, 602-808-0766

■ Housed in a "beautiful" Phoenix hotel, this "spectacular" Med destination boasts "excellent" rustic dishes and inviting quarters replete with a lodge fireplace and a "fantastic", romantic bar appointed with antiques, overstuffed chairs and a leather-floor cigar room; in short it merits a "wow from beginning to end."

Vincent Guerithault on Camelback   27   24   25 $45

3930 E. Camelback Rd. (N. 40th St.), Phoenix, 602-224-0225

■ Chef-owner Vincent Guerithault pairs classic Gallic technique with "Southwestern ingredients" to produce "exceptional" dishes at this candlelit "old-time favorite" reminiscent of a French country inn; despite an occasional gripe that this former trendsetter on Camelback Road "needs some new tricks", the majority says it's "still one of the best."

Portland, OR

TOP 10 FOOD RANKING

	Restaurant	Cuisine Type
28	Genoa	N&S Italian
	Paley's Place	Northwest/French Bistro
	Tina's	Northwest/Classic French
27	Joel Palmer House	Northwest
	Cafe des Amis	Classic French
	Couvron	New French
	Wildwood	Northwest
26	Saburo's	Japanese
	Castagna	N. Italian/New French
	Winterborne	Seafood

ADDITIONAL NOTEWORTHY PLACES

Bluehour	Mediterranean
Cafe Azul	Mexican
Caffe Mingo	Northern Italian
El Gaucho	Steakhouse
Heathman	Northwest/Classic French
Higgins	Northwest
Mint	Latin American
Pazzo Ristorante	Northern Italian
Sungari	Chinese
Zinc Bistrot	French Bistro

Bluehour [S]

F	D	S	C
24	27	22	$42

250 NW 13th Ave. (Everett St.), 503-226-3394

■ "Wear black and you'll fit in" at this "instant hit" in the Pearl, serving "inventive" but "surprisingly unpretentious" Mediterranean cuisine; the dishes are "elegant from start to finish", ranging from "celestial salmon tartare" and seasonal "pumpkin ravioli that's a taste of fall" to "unforgettable chocolate pudding", all "superbly served" in "lovely surroundings" with high ceilings and drapes that create intimate areas; P.S. it's red-"hot, hot, hot", so reserve ahead.

Cafe Azul

F	D	S	C
25	21	22	$33

112 NW Ninth Ave. (bet. Couch & Davis Sts.), 503-525-4422

◪ "Haute Mexican" that would make "Diane Kennedy proud" transforms this Pearl spot into a "sophisticated" experience; "homemade chips and salsa" are hard to resist, and the "vibrantly flavored" "mole is darn close to what you'd find in Oaxaca"; though the "service is impeccable" and the "ambiance lovely", a few gringos gripe it's "too expensive" and "overly noisy."

Cafe des Amis
27   23   26 $40

1987 NW Kearney St. (20th Ave.), 503-295-6487

■ A "long-standing favorite" of Francophiles, this Gallic "classic" in the Northwest District features a "charming setting" that's the backdrop for "intimate dining"; its many friends say *encore* to "satiny soups", the "duck with blackberry sauce" and an "excellent wine list" but save loud cheers for the "superior service"; N.B. they've added a new franc-friendly bistro menu.

Caffe Mingo 🅂
25   21   22 $29

807 NW 21st Ave. (bet. Johnson & Kearney Sts.), 503-226-4646

■ "A tiny room full of Tuscan sunshine" keeps the *famiglia* growing at this trattoria in Northwest that's a "crowded" pleaser; the chef's "maniacal passion for fine food" produces "fabulous risotto" and the "best pasta around"; *paesani* appreciate the "jolly, 'peasanty' atmosphere" and "good value", but even regulars regard the "no-reservations policy" for parties under six as "a real problem."

Castagna
26   22   25 $41

1752 SE Hawthorne Blvd. (18th Ave.), 503-231-7373

■ This Hawthorne French-Italian is an embodiment of the "clear vision" of husband-and-wife owners Kevin Gibson ("former Genoa chef") and Monique Siu (ex Zefiro), where the kitchen "artistically" creates "spectacular scallops, duck and rack of lamb" using "clean, pure flavors [that] echo the minimalist decor" (though a few find it "sterile"); with a "varied, affordable wine list" and "gracious service", it's a "chic place for clients" and out-of-towners.

Couvron
27   22   25 $66

1126 SW 18th Ave. (bet. Madison & Salmon Sts.), 503-225-1844

■ "Every bite is truly delicious" at this "elegant" Downtown New French – the crème de la crème in local "haute cuisine", famed for its "fanatical devotion" to "world-class" flavors, "architectural presentations" and "personalized service"; featuring "amazing" seven- and nine-course prix fixe meals only (the "vegetarian offering brings tears" to some eyes), it's an "expensive splurge", but go ahead – "sell the family jewels and enjoy."

El Gaucho ●🅂
23   24   24 $52

Benson Hotel, 319 SW Broadway (bet. Oak & Stark Sts.), 503-227-8794

■ Bypass the pampas and go Downtown to "the new kid on the block" in the Benson Hotel where visiting Presidents bunk and buckaroos bet on "big portions" of "fabulous steaks", including "excellent" classics such as Châteaubriand followed by "bananas Foster to rival Brennan's", served by a staff that "bends over backward to make you happy"; however, a number of el grouchos grumble it's "overpriced."

Genoa
28   24   28 $63

2832 SE Belmont St. (bet. 28th & 29th Aves.), 503-238-1464

■ Portland's No. 1 for Food as well as Most Popular, this 31-year-old "world-class" Belmont Italian "is a sublime experience", whether for the "gastronomic euphoria" of the seven-course prix fixe dinner or the service where "no detail is overlooked" or a setting that's "opulent without being stuffy"; three-hour meals and a "hugely expensive" tab put off a few who say "if not the best, easily the longest experience in town", but most concur: "it's worth every penny" and minute.

Heathman [S] 26 | 24 | 24 | $41

Heathman Hotel, 1001 SW Broadway (Salmon St.), 503-790-7752

■ Normandy-born Philippe Boulot is the "outstanding" presiding force at this "dependably excellent" Downtown Northwest-French landmark where "elegance and class" define setting, service, food and wine; added attractions include "power breakfast and lunch", afternoon tea or a rendezvous by the bar's fireplace for "heavenly crab cakes and Irish coffee"; N.B. under new management, the menu now offers a wider price range.

Higgins [S] 26 | 24 | 25 | $39

1239 SW Broadway (Jefferson St.), 503-222-9070

■ Local, organic "ingredients combined with imagination" are the hallmark of this Downtown "foodies' paradise", notable for "Mr. Natural" (chef Greg Higgins), whose "flawless execution" of Northwest cuisine elicits repeat visits from carnivores and vegheads alike, not to mention fans of the 400-bottle wine list; the busy bar serves a "great hamburger", and the Broadway "location, location, location" makes it a magnet for theater- or concert-goers.

Joel Palmer House 27 | 25 | 24 | $42

600 Ferry St. (6th St.), Dayton, 503-864-2995

■ It's "worth the drive to Dayton" in wine country to dine at this "remodeled historic house" that's known for "classic, chef-run gourmet" Northwest cuisine; "mushroom mavens" pop in for "fabulous" fungi appearing in everything from salad to cheesecake, but the "zingy grilled meats" and "rich coq au vin" are also good picks; the "lovely setting", a "happy" staff and "caring" owners cap the experience, though it costs a little morel than some would like.

Mint ◐ – | – | – | M

816 N. Russell St. (bet. Albina & Mississippi Aves.), 503-284-5518

Fashionistas are flocking to this tropically hot scene in North Portland, where comfy banquettes and a cozy, chat-space–filled bar offer an inviting ambiance in which to sip fruity cocktails in giant glasses; the vibrant Latin cuisine stars such goodies as prawns with purple potatoes, jerked pork and the house's own banana-rum ice cream.

Paley's Place Bistro & Bar [S] 28 | 23 | 26 | $43

1204 NW 21st Ave. (Northrup St.), 503-243-2403

■ For a "perfect experience", most places pale next to this "touch-of-class" Northwest-French bistro in a "charming" "converted house" in the Northwest District, where the "superior" cuisine "never misses"; "gracious" owners and a "knowledgeable staff" serve "sweetbreads to die for" and other "exceptional entrees" with "well-chosen wines"; while treasure-hunters dig the "superb complimentary goodies" before and after your meal, wallet-watchers wail "you need to be William Paley to afford it."

Pazzo Ristorante [S] 23 | 23 | 22 | $33

Hotel Vintage Plaza, 627 SW Washington St. (Broadway), 503-228-1515

■ The "classic" yet "imaginative" Italian fare at this Downtown "perennial pleaser" in the Hotel Vintage Plaza takes an upswing with chef Nathan Logan in the *cucina* cooking "yummy Piedmont beef", "orgasmic" filled pastas and "excellent desserts"; stylish touches like the "lively bar", open kitchen and "special-occasion wine room" make it "a good place to entertain" as well.

Saburo's Sushi House S

26 | 11 | 14 | $22

1667 SE Bybee Blvd. (bet. 16th & 17th Aves.), 503-236-4237

■ This Westmoreland "Tokyo-style phone booth of a restaurant" calls converts with "unbelievably fresh sushi" in "huge portions" as well as "good green-tea ice cream and plum wine"; be warned the decor is "humble" and seating limited; still, connoisseurs continue to redial, saying it's "worth it all."

Sungari

25 | 21 | 22 | $25

735 SW First Ave. (Yamhill St.), 503-224-0800

■ "At last, outstanding Chinese" cheer fans of this "upscale" Downtown recent arrival; "everyone raves" about the "subtly seasoned" Szechuan fare, including "the best moo shu pork" and other "high-style" dishes, served in an "elegant atmosphere"; N.B. check out adventurous choices from the wine list: Alsatian, German and Californian.

Tina's S

28 | 22 | 25 | $40

760 Hwy. 99 W. (opp. fire station), Dundee, 503-538-8880

■ "Perennial wine-country star" that sparkles with Northwest-French fare in Dundee; the "sophisticated" "ingredients shine through" in "super sautéed oysters" and "fab beef tenderloin", all "well matched" by "superb" *vins d'*Oregon and warmed by "friendly" service; though some whine about the "city prices", most "find excuses to make the trip."

Wildwood S

27 | 23 | 24 | $39

1221 NW 21st Ave. (Overton St.), 503-248-9663

■ Homegrown chef and best-selling author "Cory Schreiber gave Portland a gift when he opened" this "wildly popular" "Northwest cuisine icon" in the Northwest District that "does justice to local provender" and pays "attention to sustainable farming" and "boutique wines"; loyalists "love watching the open kitchen" turn out "incredible duck", "excellent Washington mussels" and "fresh desserts" served in an "intriguing milieu" (where "cheek-to-jowl" dining can produce "thunderous noise").

Winterborne

26 | 21 | 24 | $36

3520 NE 42nd Ave. (Fremont St.), 503-249-8486

■ Turning "meat-and-potatoes girls" into born-again fish freaks, this seafood-only old-timer speaks with both Northwest and French accents in a "small, cozy" Northeast setting; "whatever they suggest, order it" is one school of thought, but consider the "unique crab juniper" and "terrific sautéed oysters", remembering that "every entree is special" and so are you with "personal attention from the staff" (that strikes a few as "interfering").

Zinc Bistrot S

– | – | – | M

500 NW 21st Ave. (Glisan St.), 503-223-9696

Long wood tables, a mirror and a bar topped with the namesake metal dominate the light-infused room of this Parisian-style bistro buzzing with spirit – and the sound of politicos, trendy Northwest locals and Francophiles digging into traditional plates of steak frites, coq au vin and seasonal fruit crêpes with homemade ice cream; N. B. *naturellement*, there's sidewalk seating in summer.

Salt Lake City & Mountain Resorts

TOP 10 FOOD RANKING

Restaurant	Cuisine Type
27 Seafood Buffet	Seafood
Fresco Italian Cafe	Northern Italian
Metropolitan	New American
Mariposa	New American
Tree Room	American/Western
26 Cafe Diablo	Southwestern
New Yorker Club	American
Center Cafe	Californian
Shallow Shaft	Southwestern
Mandarin	Asian

ADDITIONAL NOTEWORTHY PLACES

Bambara	New American
Blue Boar Inn	Continental
Cafe Madrid	Spanish
Foundry Grill	American
Glitretind	New American
Log Haven	New American
Lugano	Northern Italian
Snake Creek Grill	American
Tuscany	Northern Italian
Wahso	Asian/Classic French

F	D	S	C

Bambara S
	24	25	22	$35

Hotel Monaco, 202 S. Main St. (W. 200 South), 801-363-5454

■ "A delightful addition to Salt Lake City dining" crow customers who consider this "chic" New American bistro inside the Monaco "a breath of fresh air"; it's a "delectable experience" with service that makes guests feel "taken care of" and some of the "most consistently interesting food in town" including "imaginative" specials; aesthetes adore the "zippy decor" in this former bank, a "grand setting" replete with "marble and ornamental iron"; a few find it a "little frou-frou", but most agree it's "top-notch."

Blue Boar Inn S
	26	26	26	$37

1235 Warm Springs Rd. (Snake Creek Canyon Rd.), Midway, 435-654-1400

■ What was once a well-kept "secret in Wasatch County" now stands revealed, thanks to the "outstanding" Continental cuisine, "incredible service" and "European feel" of this small destination inn set in "charming", "peaceful" country surroundings on the edge of Heber Valley; the "wonderfully romantic" atmosphere, maximized by "exquisitely furnished interiors", blankets Boar boosters with a feeling of "complete happiness", and so does chef Jesse Layman's "amazingly creative", "out-of-this-world food."

Cafe Diablo S
26 20 23 $26
599 W. Main St. (N. Center St.), Torrey, 435-425-3070

■ Southwestern "favorites like trout, lamb and rattlesnake" and "pecan-crusted chicken – yee-haw!" – are "great finds" at this "middle of nowhere" "oasis of excellence" in "tiny Torrey", near the gate of Capital Reef National Park; "the chef is big on vertical presentations" (you'll find "towers galore"), and the "fabulous" dishes are presented in a "must-see" desert "setting that can't be beat"; N.B. open April–November.

Cafe Madrid
25 20 23 $27
2080 E. 3900 South, Holladay, 801-273-0837

■ If you "feel like a mini-European vacation", head to this "authentic" Iberian "charmer", a "great find off-the-beaten-track" in Holladay, run by a "friendly" owner who's "eager to please" and flanked by "enthusiastic servers"; it's a "transporting" "gustatory experience" rave reviewers, who rally 'round for "the true flavors of Spain", which include a trip to "tapas heaven", "unparalleled paella" and "unique wines"; "lively" paintings from local artist Pilar Pobil fill a room that most find "cozy and intimate", but a handful chide the digs for being "crowded" and "chaotic."

Center Cafe S
26 19 23 $33
92 E. Center St. (Main St.), Moab, 435-259-4295

■ It's a "not-to-be-missed Moab stop" say adventurous diners who seek out the globally inspired modern Californian eats offered by a "CIA-trained chef in the middle of red rock country", "the land of 4x4s and mountain bikers"; the "absolutely incredible" "variety of creative entrees" "delights the palate", and "great service" helps make it a "real gem" that "would be a hit anywhere"; N.B. a new location (summer 2001) greatly expands charm and seating capacity, but may impact the decor rating.

Foundry Grill S
25 25 22 $26
Sundance Resort, Rural Rte. 3 (North Fork, Provo Canyon), Sundance, 801-223-4220

■ "The food is so good it doesn't matter if Robert Redford shows up or not" declare devotees of this "down-to-earth" American, a "favorite place for a getaway meal" inside Provo's Sundance Resort; the "excellent variety" of "fresh, wonderful", "innovative" fare, including "brunches to die for", is "served up in a tasteful" alpine "setting that's beyond exceptional", with a "gorgeous", "breathtaking view" of the 12,000-ft. Mt. Timpanogos.

Fresco Italian Cafe S
27 24 25 $33
1513 S. 1500 East (bet. Emerson & Kensington Aves.), 801-486-1300

■ "Bravo" applaud admirers who "can't say enough good" things about this "consistently delightful Northern Italian" Eastside "neighborhood bistro"; "everything comes together seamlessly for a perfect evening on the beautiful patio" with "imaginative dishes that are always fresh" and "service that's friendly and knowledgeable"; while most dub the "romantic setting" "intimate" and "quaint", a handful say "maybe it's too cozy", since it's "tightly packed and hard to converse"; P.S. "don't go on a whim" because "reservations are a must."

Glitretind S
26 | 26 | 24 | $48

Stein Eriksen Lodge, 7700 Stein Way (Royal St.), Deer Valley, 435-645-6455

■ A formidable new culinary team recently stepped up to the plate, which may propel this "top-notch" New American in Deer Valley's "exquisite" "Austrian-style" Stein Eriksen Lodge even higher into the stratosphere; "it's worth the drive up the mountain" because "you know you're going to eat well" say surveyors who savor the "outstanding wine list", "fantastic Sunday brunch", "great buffets" and "beautiful presentations" of "true gourmet" fare with Norwegian and European flourishes, all served "without attitude."

Log Haven S
25 | 28 | 23 | $38

6451 E. 3800 South (Wasatch Blvd., 4 mi. up Millcreek Canyon), 801-272-8255

■ It's "the perfect place on a blustery winter evening" laud loyalists who love this "lavish" New American "mountain hideaway just outside of Salt Lake City" in the Wasatch National Forest; set in a "sprawling" log cabin built in 1920, its atmosphere is "rustic and charming", but there's "nothing backwoodsy" about chef David Jones' "creative mixes" of "superlative" fare that's "full of depth"; gripers grumble that the "food's a little too nouvelle and pricey", but most say "take a date" and enjoy the "beautiful canyon setting" with a "gorgeous" waterfall view.

Lugano S
24 | 20 | 22 | $29

3364 S. 2300 East (3300 South), Holladay, 801-412-9994

☑ "Finally, good food in Holladay" say diners who've discovered the "delicious" "homestyle Northern Italian" fare at chef-owner Greg Neville's "wonderful" Eastside neighborhood addition; the "fresh ingredients", "consistently" "innovative" cooking" and "reasonable prices" add up to an "unexpected treat" that's prepared in the "cool open kitchen" and "splendidly served"; "we feel like family here" say supporters, who find it "warm, comfortable" and a "bit loud", but a few grumblers gripe "oh, the noise! – you can't hear your dinner companions."

Mandarin
26 | 21 | 22 | $20

348 E. 900 North, Bountiful, 801-298-2406

■ "Greek hospitality" (reflecting the owners' heritage) combined with "spectacular Chinese flavors" ("the chefs are from Hong Kong" and San Francisco) and an "incredible dessert menu" add up to a "consistently wonderful" Bountiful experience at this suburban shopping-center site; it's definitely "not the same old" Asian – "you want to savor every bite" of the "distinctly different" dishes; a no-reservations policy means it's "always crowded", with "a ridiculous wait" – a "hassle" to be sure, but most say it's "well worth it."

Mariposa S
27 | 25 | 25 | $53

Silver Lake Lodge, Deer Valley Resort, 7600 Royal St., Deer Valley, 435-645-6715

☑ "Restaurant heaven" in an "Alpine setting" enthuse enamored epicureans who head to Deer Valley Resort's "quaint" Silver Lake Lodge for "innovative" New American fare; the "excellent" game, "solid entrees", "great wine list" and "polished service" are the big draws here, but it's the "unpretentious" cozy ski lodge ambiance (yes, there's a fireplace) that really wins romantics over; N.B. open December–April.

Metropolitan   27 | 27 | 25 | $51

173 W. Broadway (300 South, bet. 200 West & W. Temple St.), 801-364-3472

▨ It's "still the pinnacle of sophistication" say soigné surveyors who head Downtown for New American "artistic creations in an artfully re-created warehouse"; the "exquisitely prepared meals" (including the "creative", "dreamy" tasting menu) are "a little extravagant" but "worth the money", bolstered by "excellent service"; dissenters, however, find the flavor combinations "extreme" and claim the "humorless" staff is high on "attitude."

New Yorker Club   26 | 26 | 25 | $42

60 W. Market St. (Main St., bet. 300 & 400 South), 801-363-0166

■ "This is where we take clients" and "impress friends" say acolytes who voted this "kiss-kiss", "see-and-be-seen" traditional American "fine dining" "favorite" the Most Popular restaurant in Utah; the "fantastic fare matches the shimmering elegance" of the "classic, clubby" surroundings in this historic building, plus there's "terrific service" that makes you "feel pampered"; nitpickers proclaim "pretension is served with every wonderful meal" at this "faded lady" that's "nothing like New York", but the smitten counter "they succeed on all fronts"; N.B. there's a membership fee at this private club.

Seafood Buffet   27 | 21 | 22 | $51

Snow Park Lodge, Deer Valley, 435-645-6632

■ "Come hungry, leave satiated" say insiders who rank this Deer Valley "favorite" No. 1 for Food in Utah; fans flock to this "rustic mountain setting" each ski season for an "incredible spread" of sushi and shellfish, advising "survey the extensive food stations before embarking on the wonderful culinary odyssey"; it's a veritable wintertime "treat", making worshipers only wish "they were open all year"; N.B. call to check its schedule during the Winter Olympic Games 2002.

Shallow Shaft S   26 | 22 | 24 | $41

Alta Ski Resort, Little Cottonwood Canyon Rd., Alta, 801-742-2177

■ "The view is to die for and the food is to live for" at this "Alta tradition", a "wonderful discovery" in Little Cottonwood Canyon for "excellent" Southwestern fare; the "unique" "unexpected combinations" of flavors make this a "complex experience" say foodies who "dream about the lamb"; the "beautiful setting" with high-mountain ambiance is "more casual than the food would suggest", attracting skiers and non-skiers alike.

Snake Creek Grill S   25 | 20 | 22 | $32

650 W. 100 South, Heber City, 435-654-2133

■ "Bold American comfort foods" and a "charming" roadhouse ambiance, complete with "nostalgic photos" and retro "jazz sounds", attract admirers to this "friendly, welcoming" frontier-themed turn-of-the-century-style building in "beautiful" Heber Old Town; chef-owner Barb Hill serves "unpretentious and delicious" "modern takes on the classics" and "terrific grill selections" that make this Snake "charmer" "well worth the drive"; loyal locals say "if it were closer to Salt Lake City it would be standing room only."

Tree Room S   27 | 27 | 24 | $41
Sundance Resort, 6 mi. up Provo Canyon (North Fork Canyon Rd.),
Sundance, 801-223-4200

■ "Can a restaurant be sexy?"; oh yeah, say fans who fawn over
the American "Western fare, game and desserts that'll make you
weep" at "Bob's classy", "romantic" "destination dining" spot in
the posh Sundance Resort ("we sat next to Redford – my wife loved
that!"); the "scrumptious food" is "consistently excellent" – "it
was the peak of our fantasy luxury getaway" – plus the "beautiful
Native American art", "rustic decor" and "truly special" mountain
views fill guests with "immediate serenity and warmth"; P.S. a tree
grows in this Sundance Room.

Tuscany S   23 | 27 | 23 | $35
2832 E. 6200 South (Holladay Blvd.), Holladay, 801-277-9919

☑ "One of the best in the west", this Northern Italian "European
delight" in Holladay, co-owned by former Jazz basketball player
Mark Eaton, is high on "old-world opulence", with "dynamite
decor", "incredible outdoor dining" and a "gorgeous garden";
enthusiastic diners say the "ambrosial" fare is a "gastronomic
extravaganza" that "continues to wow" (try the chocolate cake –
it's a "slam dunk"), with a wine selection that's one of "the best in
Salt Lake City"; however, cynics sniff the "amazing atmosphere"
outshines the "so-so" food, imploring "get a chef who can
rebound and score."

Wahso S   24 | 28 | 24 | $45
577 Main St. (5th St.), Park City, 435-615-0300

■ "Absolutely gorgeous" ooh and aah aesthetes who wing over to
this Park City "Asian with a French twist", the latest from "wonder
kid" Bill White; it's a "rare bird", with curtained booths and a
dramatic "Shanghai feeling" that evokes a "Hollywood set"; while a
handful find the "cool interior" "a bit contrived, all is forgiven" once
the "creative" fare arrives, including sea bass "so good it's like
sex on a plate"; N.B. 'wahso' is the phonetic spelling of *oiseux*,
the Gallic word for "birds."

San Diego

TOP 10 FOOD RANKING

Restaurant	Cuisine Type
27 Sushi Ota	Japanese
El Bizcocho	Classic/New French
WineSellar & Brasserie	New French
Pamplemousse Grille	New American/New French
26 George's at the Cove	Californian
Mille Fleurs	New French
Azzura Point	Californian/New French
Tapenade	New French
Vincent's Sirino's	Classic/New French
Rancho Valencia	Californian

ADDITIONAL NOTEWORTHY PLACES

Bertrand at Mr. A's	New American
Cafe Japengo	Asian
Cafe Pacifica	Californian/Seafood
Kemo Sabe	Pacific Rim
Laurel	New French
Marine Room	New French/Californian
Morton's of Chicago	Steakhouse
NINE-TEN	Californian
Roppongi	Asian/Fusion
Roy's La Jolla	Hawaiian/Fusion

F	D	S	C

Azzura Point S — 26 | 26 | 24 | $53

Loews Coronado Bay Resort, 4000 Coronado Bay Rd. (Silver Strand Blvd.), Coronado, 619-424-4477

■ At this "special-occasion delight" in the Loews Coronado Bay Resort, an "indulgent staff" proffers "delectable" Cal-French dishes (to truly indulge, opt for one of the "outstanding tasting menus"); of course it's "expensive", but it's "worth it" for such a "romantic" dinner that's made even more "special" by the live piano music on weekends and the "elegant" waterside setting with "magnificent views."

Bertrand at Mr. A's S — 24 | 25 | 22 | $59

2550 Fifth Ave. (Laurel St.), 619-239-1377

◪ Highly anticipated, this notable newcomer (created by Bertrand Hug of the renowned Mille Fleurs) near Balboa Park boasts "spectacular views" that "go on forever" and a "classy room" that provides a fitting backdrop for the kitchen's very "fine" New American fare tweaked with French and Mediterranean accents; even if some feel it's "outrageously expensive" and caution that "service is the weak link", early devotees proclaim this "special-occasion" spot "an instant classic."

Cafe Japengo [S] 25 24 20 $35

Hyatt Regency at The Aventine, 8960 University Center Ln. (bet. La Jolla Village & Lebon Drs.), 858-450-3355

■ Without a doubt the leading "beautiful-people hang" in the Golden Triangle, this "chichi" Asian is renowned for "fabulous" sushi "so fresh it practically moves" and "neat fusion" creations that "imaginatively" marry Japanese and Western flavors; a "too hip" staff serves an equally "trendy" clientele in a "busy, noisy" setting so buzzing with energy that groupies predict this "dating magnet" could even "succeed in NYC or San Francisco."

Cafe Pacifica [S] 24 21 22 $36

2414 San Diego Ave. (bet. Horney & Old Town Aves.), 619-291-6666

■ "Year in, year out", this "upbeat" Old Town "favorite" is lauded as a "heavenly" spot for "honest, fresh seafood" beautifully paired with hard-to-find California wines, not to mention "the best crème brûlée in the U.S."; though a new owner now runs the place, its legions of followers expect him to maintain this landmark's high standards for "creative" cooking, "casually upscale" dining and "wonderful" service.

El Bizcocho 27 26 27 $53

Rancho Bernardo Inn, 17550 Bernardo Oaks Dr. (Rancho Bernardo Rd.), Rancho Bernardo, 858-675-8550

■ This "romantic" stunner housed in the suburban Rancho Bernardo Inn is "elegance personified", dazzling "epicureans" with "exciting" French interpretations accompanied by an "extensive wine list" that's a "special treat"; "go to celebrate" any excuse and be "divinely" pampered by a "perfect" staff amid "spectacular" surroundings ("the pianist provides just the right background touch"); of course it's "expensive", but a dinner here is "like being in heaven."

George's at the Cove [S] 26 26 25 $44

1250 Prospect St. (bet. Cave & Ivanhoe Sts.), La Jolla, 858-454-4244

■ For a "must-do meal in La Jolla", head straight to this "romantic" "all-time winner" that's perennially voted the Most Popular restaurant in San Diego; no wonder, given the "absolutely superb" Californian dishes masterminded by "imaginative" Trey Foshee, decor that "oozes class" and the "top-notch" staff overseen by "great" owner-host George Hauer; sure, it's "oh-so-expensive", but rest assured that "you get your money's worth" at this "special-occasion" "splurge" – and the "wow" of a view of the cove is free.

Kemo Sabe [S] 23 22 22 $31

3958 Fifth Ave. (bet. University Ave. & Washington St.), 619-220-6802

◪ All "hail chef Deborah Scott" for the "bold", "daring" Pacific Rim "creations" – they pack "plenty of heat" – prepared at this "trendy" Hillcrest "destination" that's as "hot" as her signature dish, the "out-of-this-world 'skirts on fire'" (a chile-seasoned steak); "hip" guests "love" the dramatic "vertical presentations" and "slick" setting, which allows for prime "people-watching", but fuddy-duddies who don't get the fuss whine that the "strange food" is "a little far-fetched."

Laurel [S] 26 | 25 | 23 | $45

505 Laurel St. (5th Ave.), 619-239-2222

■ "Always outstanding", this "class act" near Balboa Park is likely "as close as San Diego gets to Manhattan"; a "big-city" haunt that showcases a "cosmopolitan", "inventive" menu of "delicious" Southern French dishes masterminded by talented new chef Alex Espiritu, it features seasonally changing Provençal renditions paired with a "spectacular wine list" and served in a "chic" room populated by the local "elite"; factor in polished, "unobtrusive service" and the result is a simply "sublime experience."

Marine Room [S] 23 | 27 | 23 | $47

2000 Spindrift Dr. (Torrey Pines Rd.), La Jolla, 858-459-7222

■ "Catch a sunset here" right on the sands of La Jolla Shores, where the "breathtaking" experience of watching the ocean "waves splash against the windows" (brunch at "high tide is not to be missed") is nearly matched by chef Bernard Guillas' "dramatically presented" New French–Californian creations, delivered by a staff that "exceeds all expectations"; better bring a "large wallet", though.

Mille Fleurs [S] 26 | 25 | 25 | $58

Country Squire Courtyard, 6009 Paseo Delicias (Avenida de Acacias), Rancho Santa Fe, 858-756-3085

■ "A jewel nestled in the gilt village" of "lovely" Rancho Santa Fe, this "very special-occasion" New French is a "beautiful" place to indulge in equally "beautiful flavors", "artistically" choreographed by "dazzling" chef Martin Woesle (his menu changes daily); the service is just as "outstanding", so despite a "slightly stiff" ambiance, legions attest that this dining experience is "close to perfection – but even the wealthy might gasp at the prices."

Morton's of Chicago [S] 26 | 23 | 23 | $53

285 J St. (bet. 2nd & 3rd Aves.), 619-696-3369

■ Be sure to "bring lots of dough" to this "superb" Downtown all-American steakery, "a carnivore's delight" where the "perfect" "beef doesn't get any better" and the portions are famously obscene; the "dark" setting ("looks like money") is "like a private men's club" and attracts lots of "beautiful people", which, of course, can make it "too crowded and noisy"; the major complaint: "we could do without the showing of the raw meat" before placing our order.

Nine-Ten [S] – | – | – | E

Grande Colonial, 910 Prospect St. (Main St.), La Jolla, 858-454-2181

On the site where Gregory Peck once served sodas at the counter of his father's drugstore, chef Michael Stebner brings a healthy understanding of Californian cooking inspired by the wine country to this spanking new addition at La Jolla's historic, extravagantly renovated Grande Colonial hotel; his brief but pleasing daily menu focuses on thoughtfully prepared seafood and meat dishes, as well as ultra-high-quality local produce, proffered in a low-key setting by a young staff that strives mightily to please.

Pamplemousse Grille [S] | 27 | 24 | 25 | $51

514 Via de la Valle (Jimmy Durante Blvd.), Solana Beach, 858-792-9090

■ "Amazingly good cooking" from "shining star" Jeffrey Strauss wows the "moneyed clientele" that flocks (especially during racing season) to this "first-class" New American–New French located across the road from the Del Mar Fairgrounds; devotees "love" the "casually sophisticated" ambiance, murals of rustic life and highly "attentive" service, and even if a less-enchanted few grouse "pretentious", the majority cheers "outstanding."

Rancho Valencia [S] | 26 | 27 | 25 | $52

Rancho Valencia Resort, 5921 Valencia Circle (Rancho Diegueno Rd.), Rancho Sante Fe, 858-759-6216

■ This "gorgeous" "retreat" is "a special place", an "intriguing hideout in the hills" of horsey Rancho Santa Fe that's situated in a "beautiful resort", which makes it a "paradise within paradise"; it attracts a "chic, sophisticated" clientele with its "old money" ambiance, "extraordinary" contemporary Californian menu and "excellent" service, so wallet-stretching prices notwithstanding, it's "worth the drive" to experience this "refined" indulgence.

Roppongi [S] | 25 | 25 | 23 | $37

875 Prospect St. (Fay Ave.), La Jolla, 858-551-5252

■ Anticipate "exciting", "exotic" Asian "fusion cuisine" at this "fabulously" "unique" "hip scene" for the "beautiful people" in La Jolla; "go with friends", "share" a "variety" of "original" tapas and other "wonderfully avant-garde" specialties and experience "perfect harmony in dining" (the interior design was determined by feng shui); P.S. "don't forget to leave room for some of the city's most spectacular desserts – the caramelized bananas over vanilla ice cream with almond brittle is an orgasm on a plate."

Roy's La Jolla [S] | – | – | – | E

Costa Verde, 8670 Genesee Ave. (bet. La Jolla Village & Nobel Drs.), La Jolla, 858-455-1616

Opened recently in the Golden Triangle, the latest venture by international chef-restaurateur Roy Yamaguchi showcases the distinctive Hawaiian fusion cuisine that he first developed on Oahu, an island memorialized in the decor by such details as a tiki torch–lined patio; indoors, expect appointments like bamboo flooring, hanging light fixtures that resemble tropical flowers and an exhibition kitchen that turns out dishes including charred butterfish, blackened ahi and Mongolian grilled pork pot roast.

Sushi Ota [S] | 27 | 12 | 18 | $30

4529 Mission Bay Dr. (Balboa Ave.), 858-270-5670

■ "Absolutely awesome" is the unanimous verdict on the menu at this Pacific Beach Japanese retreat, rated No. 1 for Food in San Diego; despite a "spartan" setting in a "nondescript" strip mall and "brusque" service, it's "always crowded" because the eponymous Ota-san prepares the "best sushi in town, hands down" ("fish willingly sacrifice themselves to be turned into his incredible delicacies"), and he's a "licensed *fugu* chef" (not to mention "a wealth of fish information"); even "people visiting from Japan know to come here."

Tapenade [S] 26 21 23 $47

7612 Fay Ave. (bet. Kline & Pearl Sts.), La Jolla, 858-551-7500

■ Francophiles gratefully tip their berets to the "inspired", "world-class" dining with a "sunny" Provençal accent at this La Jolla "gem" where "talented chef-owner" Jean Michel Diot and his wife Sylvie know a thing or *deux* about creating an "elegant" environment with a "courtly" ambiance (even if a few deride the "somewhat arrogant service"); though it helps to be "financially flush", at least the "prix fixe meals are a bargain."

Vincent's Sirino's 26 18 21 $34

113 W. Grand Ave. (Broadway), Escondido, 760-745-3835

■ To savor a "great culinary experience in Escondido", head straight to this "classy" "sleeper" where "genius" chef-owner Vincent Grumel "goes out of his way" to be "creative" and "cooks to order" "generous portions" of "consistently superb" French-Californian dishes; what's more, the room is nearly as "warm and inviting" as the "fine" staff, and its proximity to the California Center for the Arts makes it an ideal choice for pre-concert dining.

WineSellar & Brasserie 27 20 25 $48

9550 Waples St. (bet. Mira Mesa Blvd. & Steadman St.), 858-450-9557

■ Dionysians simply delight in this "classy", "special-occasion" New French tucked away in high-tech Sorrento Mesa, which has "stayed great since it opened in '89"; new executive chef Alex Espiritu masterfully uncorks "creative, fresh, focused flavors" that are only fortified by the "fantastic wine list" (2,500 selections), while the dining experience is enhanced by the "lovely" decor and "attentive" staff; it may be saddled with a "difficult location" in a business park, but "it's worth every inch of the drive."

San Francisco Bay Area*

TOP 20 FOOD RANKING

Restaurant	Cuisine Type
29 French Laundry/N	New American
28 Gary Danko	New French/New American
Ritz-Carlton Din. Rm.	New French
Le Papillon/SV	New French
Chez Panisse/E	Californian/Med.
La Fôret/SV	Classic French
Terra/N	New French/N. Italian
La Folie	New French
27 Fleur de Lys	New French
Chez Panisse Café/E	Californian
Boulevard	American
Aqua	Seafood
Masa's	New French
Bistro Jeanty/N	French Bistro
Sushi Ran/N	Japanese
Emile's/SV	Classic French
Fresh Cream/S	Classic French
26 La Toque/N	New French
Jardinière	Californian/Classic French
Slanted Door	Vietnamese/Californian

ADDITIONAL NOTEWORTHY PLACES

Acquerello	Northern Italian
Auberge du Soleil/N	Provençal
bacar	New American
Bɪx	American
Campton Place	Classic French
Chez Nous	Mediterranean
Delfina	N&S Italian
Elisabeth Daniel	New French
Farallon	Seafood
Fifth Floor	New French
Fringale	French Bistro
Globe	New American
Greens	Vegetarian
Hawthorne Lane	Asian/Californian
Lark Creek Inn/N	American
Oliveto/E	Northern Italian
Postrio	New American
Rubicon	Californian/New French
Tra Vigne/N	N&S Italian
Zuni Cafe	N. Italian/Med.

---

* E=East of San Francisco; N=North of San Francisco; S=South of San Francisco; and SV=Silicon Valley/Peninsula

Acquerello 26 | 23 | 26 | $53

1722 Sacramento St. (bet. Polk St. & Van Ness Ave.), 415-567-5432

■ For "special occasions", this Van Ness/Polk "diner's dream" "never disappoints", "setting the standard" with "heavenly", "incredibly imaginative Northern Italian food", a "world-class wine list" boasting over 750 vintages "presented in beautiful decanters", "impeccably" "gracious service" and a "posh", "polished" setting; though a paucity of patrons pooh-poohs the place as "a tad stiff by San Francisco standards", most deem dining at this "former church" a "spiritual experience."

Aqua 27 | 26 | 24 | $59

252 California St. (bet. Battery & Front Sts.), 415-956-9662

■ San Francisco's ultimate "power restaurant", this top-dollar Downtowner reels in "beautiful people", "expense-accounters" looking to "impress clients" and "debonair" "seafood freaks" who all celebrate chef Michael Mina's "fabulous" "foie-gras'd", "fueled-with-flavor fish" fare that's "even richer than the clientele" and "astoundingly presented" amid "gorgeous" minimalist decor; though a fin-icky few carp about the "deafening din" and "chilly" service, Aqua-lytes say it's "worth robbing a bank" for.

Auberge du Soleil [S] 24 | 28 | 25 | $61

Auberge du Soleil Inn, 180 Rutherford Hill Rd. (Silverado Trail), Rutherford, 707-967-3111

■ "Overlooking the Valley floor and the gentle hills beyond", this "rustic" "romantic" Rutherford resort is about as "close to heaven as you can get"; "new chef" Richard Reddington's Provençal fare is "simply sublime", the "wine wonderful" and the service "knowledgeable"; "you'll have to cash in some of your stock options (if they're still worth anything) to pay", but where else can you "feel like royalty" and "yet dress informally"?; P.S. the budget-minded can "enjoy classy snacks [and drinks] on the deck."

bacar ◐ [S] 21 | 24 | 20 | $47

448 Brannan St. (bet. 3rd & 4th Sts.), 415-904-4100

◪ "You could get lost for days" in this "sprawling", "dazzling" SoMa "work in progress" that's "three stories tall, a thousand wines rich" and fast becoming a "trendy" favorite of the "Gen X" "dot-commie crowd"; the variety of vintages at this "by-the-glass mecca" generates much "hype", but many say chef Arnold Eric "Wong is Right" on track with his "innovative" New American "nibbles" as well; almost all agree the place "still needs to smooth some kinks" in service and sound levels.

Bistro Jeanty [S] 27 | 23 | 24 | $42

6510 Washington St. (Mulberry St.), Yountville, 707-944-0103

■ Chef-owner "Philippe Jeanty's second act" in Yountville is "the *ne plus ultra* of French bistros", offering "a virtual vacation" to "rural France" sans "the jet lag" or "the airs"; the Gallic "garage-sale decor is a perfect match for the rustic", "perfectly executed" "comfort food" at comparatively "affordable prices"; an "authentic bonhomie" is palpable in the "hectic and loud" dining rooms, which extends from the staff to "the community table" (accommodating walk-ins).

Bix S 22 | 25 | 21 | $42
56 Gold St. (Montgomery St.), 415-433-6300

■ "Secreted" like a "speakeasy" in a dark Downtown "alley", this "swank", "still-happening" supper club so drips with "1940s Hollywood" "glamour" that you'll "picture Ginger Rogers and Fred Astaire at the bar" as waiters in "spiffy" "white dinner jackets" "armed with the best martinis" around serve "great" Traditional American fare; it's the "live jazz singer and piano player", though, who "make it truly memorable."

Boulevard S 27 | 26 | 25 | $52
1 Mission St. (Steuart St.), 415-543-6084

■ "A feast for the palate and the eyes", this "bustling" "top-drawer" Embarcadero American known for its "impeccable everything" is the Most Popular restaurant for the fifth consecutive *San Francisco Survey*; it's "sure to impress" with chef Nancy Oakes' "mouthwatering" "extravagant food" (is the "fish flown in from heaven"?), a "fabulous wine selection", designer Pat Kuleto's "knockout" "belle epoque decor" and "first-rate" service; it's "the consummate dining experience – hard to get in, expensive, worth every penny."

Campton Place S 26 | 26 | 26 | $57
Campton Place Hotel, 340 Stockton St. (bet. Post & Sutter Sts.), 415-955-5555

■ "Camp yourself here" fawn fans of this Downtown boutique-hotel haven "epitomizing fine dining"; expect a "superb experience in all respects", from chef Laurent Manrique's "magical" French feasts to the "uncluttered elegance" of the "civilized surroundings" to the "absolutely stellar service"; it's "worth refinancing the home" for "scrumptious" "power breakfasts", "romantic dinners" and "upper-crust" "special occasions."

Chez Nous S 24 | 17 | 20 | $29
1911 Fillmore St. (bet. Bush & Pine Sts.), 415-441-8044

■ Folks are making a "big fuss" over the "amazing small plates" of "inventive" Med meze at this "happening" "grazer's paradise" on Upper Fillmore; a staff that's "(gasp) friendly, helpful and polite" adds to the "great atmosphere", but "hellish waits" and a "jammed", "noisy" dining room have some saying "please", can't you "make it bigger and take reservations"? N.B. the food rating may not reflect a post-*Survey* chef change.

Chez Panisse 28 | 25 | 26 | $66
1517 Shattuck Ave. (bet. Cedar & Vine Sts.), Berkeley, 510-548-5525

■ "Alice for President" chant constituents of the owner of this Berkeley landmark where "excellence meets enterprise and ethics"; the "daily changing menu" of "revolutionary Cal-Med cuisine" is "cooked perfectly in a manner that allows its best qualities to shine" and doled out at a "civilized pace" by the "unpretentious" staff in a "cozy, intimate" setting; a few inevitably just "do not get it", but the only real downside is the "Russian roulette reservations" game, which locks you in to an unknown fixed menu in advance.

Chez Panisse Café 27 | 23 | 25 | $41

1517 Shattuck Ave. (bet. Cedar & Vine Sts.), Berkeley, 510-548-5049

■ "If you can't afford" Alice Waters' "famous kitchen" downstairs, keep climbing to her "casual" upstairs; the "California-on-the-plate" menu (with Med touches) is "essentially the same quality seasonal food" "but with a wider choice"; in fact, many Berkeley folk "prefer" this sibling for its more "low-key" ambiance and "unpretentious" yet "impeccable service" and delight that "now that they take reservations", you can "enjoy it more often."

Delfina [S] 25 | 18 | 22 | $37

3621 18th St. (bet. Dolores & Guerrero Sts.), 415-552-4055

■ Craig Stoll and Anne Spencer's "rockin'", "trendy" Mission "trattoria" continues to surprise and delight "hip"-sters with a one-two punch of "deceivingly" simple, "masterful" "melt-in-your-mouth" Italian dishes and "exceptional", "energetic service"; while it now "has more breathing room" and a new "buzzing" bar, it's as "noisy" as ever, and reservations are still "darn hard to get."

Elisabeth Daniel 26 | 24 | 26 | $75

550 Washington St. (bet. Montgomery & Sansome Sts.), 415-397-6129

■ Dining at this "elegant", "understated", "serene oasis" amid the Downtown "bustle" is a "superlative" experience thanks to chef Daniel Patterson's "imaginative", "incredibly delicious" (if "excruciatingly expensive") New French prix fixe meals, as well as his "terrific tasting menus" balanced "to symphonic perfection" with "matching wines"; co-proprietor Elisabeth Ramsay and her "superb" staff make it "all the more pleasurable."

Emile's 27 | 22 | 25 | $56

545 S. Second St. (bet. Reed & William Sts.), San Jose, 408-289-1960

■ "The first upscale restaurant in San Jose" remains an "old faithful" French, "nurturing longtime patrons with its atmosphere and delightful menus"; "no frills or pretense" here, "just perfect ingredients impeccably prepared" (don't miss "one of the world's finest" dessert soufflés); owner Emile Mooser, "as enthusiastic as ever", oversees the "outstanding service"; though "prices have escalated", the only question most have is "when can I go again?"

Farallon [S] 24 | 27 | 23 | $52

450 Post St. (bet. Mason & Powell Sts.), 415-956-6969

■ "Fill yourself to the gills" at designer Pat Kuleto's "dazzling" Downtown "Atlantis" featuring an "over-the-top", "under-the-sea" "atmosphere that complements" chef Mark Franz's "swimmingly good" coastal cuisine; though foes deem the decor "splashy to a fault" ("I needed scuba gear") and the fare a tad "hoity-toity", they're drowned out by fans swearing it's "worth every Benjamin."

Fifth Floor 26 | 26 | 26 | $70

Hotel Palomar, 12 Fourth St. (Market St.), 415-348-1555

■ Chef "George Morrone" "is back", "chatting" up the "venture capital crowd" that "drops in" for his "wildly styled" New French dishes that "push the envelope of creativity" and are "equally matched" by an "incredibly diverse wine list"; add in the kind of "impeccable service" that "fine diners pray for and almost never get" and a "quiet", "stylish" atmosphere "that envelops you from the moment you walk in", and you have satisfied surveyors saying "liquidate your portfolio" – this Downtowner is "seventh heaven."

Fleur de Lys   27 27 27 $72
777 Sutter St. (bet. Jones & Taylor Sts.), 415-673-7779

■ When you "want to impress" "sophisticated clients" or that someone "special", head Downtown and experience Alsace-born Hubert Keller's "consistently brilliant" New French fare and the "gracious" staff's "impeccable yet unobtrusive" service; supping under the "circus"-like "tented ceiling" may be "more akin to" attending a culinary "performance than a mere dinner", but fans insist this "mercifully quiet" "cocoon" is "still the pinnacle of Bay Area romantic dining – if you're willing to pay the big bucks."

French Laundry S   29 27 28 $102
6640 Washington St. (Creek St.), Yountville, 707-944-2380

■ "If heaven exists on earth, it must reside in chef-owner Thomas Keller's" Yountville New American, San Francisco's No. 1 for Food; the enchanting "French chateau"-like building sets the stage for "over-the-top" menus that are "a revelation of whimsical presentations and sensational tastes" "from the first minute to the fourth hour"; "unerring service" rounds out a "transcendental experience" that even "jaded" folk find "worth the pilgrimage, the splurge" and the "insanity of obtaining reservations."

Fresh Cream S   27 25 26 $56
Heritage Harbor, 99 Pacific St. (bet. Artillery & Scott Sts.), Monterey, 831-375-9798

■ After more than 20 years, this formal French standby is "still the cream of Monterey restaurants" thanks to "superb food", "accommodating service" and a "great view" that can't be beat; be sure to "ask for a window table, as the lights of the squid boats in the Harbor provide an interesting backdrop to a romantic meal"; though a few fresh types find "that's a lot of money to look at the water", most merely moan "lovely, lovely, lovely."

Fringale   26 19 22 $42
570 Fourth St. (bet. Brannan & Bryant Sts.), 415-543-0573

■ "*Magnifique*" moules and steak frites are just a few of the draws at this snug SoMa French bistro that "takes you back to the Basque country"; "masterful" chef Gerald Hirigoyen's "fantastic food" ("so good we bought the cookbook") is "much better than at other places that are twice the price"; though some wonder "is it worth" "waiting among the hordes for a table" in the "cramped quarters"?, most surveyors say "*absolument!*"

Gary Danko S   28 26 27 $75
800 North Point St. (Hyde St.), 415-749-2060

■ For "people who live to eat", "Gary Danko's reputation" (both the man and his Wharf establishment) "stretches far and wide" thanks to a novel "flexibility" in ordering that lets you "mix and match" the "artfully prepared" "nouvelle" French-American cuisine to create your "own prix fixe tasting menu" (hint: "don't miss the cheese course"); "VIP" service, an "extensive" wine list and the "exquisite setting" all prompt sighs: "I'd be here weekly if I could afford it"; P.S. the full menu is available at the bar to "walk-ins."

Globe ●S
22 | 18 | 18 | $38

290 Pacific Ave. (bet. Battery & Front Sts.), 415-391-4132

☑ "For a slice of" "suave" Manhattan in Downtown San Francisco, globe-trotters gallop to Joseph Manzare's "hip hang"; though foodies feel his "fabulous" New American fare "should be enjoyed in a less frantic atmosphere", the "NYC West" formula – "spartan" digs (think "exposed brick walls", "deafening noise"), "young, snobbish servers" and a kitchen that serves until 1 AM – is a big hit among media mavens, "restaurant people" and night-crawlers.

Greens S
22 | 23 | 20 | $33

Ft. Mason Ctr., Bldg. A (Buchanan St.), 415-771-6222

☑ "Visiting vegetarians" will "think they've died and gone to the Garden of Eden" at this Marina meatless mecca; the "upscale" "Zen-like atmosphere" is happily enhanced by the "unparalleled" panorama of the Bay outside and rough-hewn "redwood tables" within, and if cynics crack that the 22-year-old greens seem a little wilted ("really slow service", "seems to be resting on its laurels"), most maintain this is "still a standard bearer for herbivores."

Hawthorne Lane S
26 | 25 | 24 | $53

22 Hawthorne St. (bet. 2nd & 3rd Sts.), 415-777-9779

■ Though founding chef "Anne's gone", the "quality lingers" on at this sophisticated "haven from the 'in' spots" of SoMa; the "creative" yet "comforting" Asian-Californian cuisine (where dumplings and pizza happily coexist) still gets "high marks", as do the "elegant dining room" (exposed beams and an open working kitchen with "magnificent" artwork and flowers) and the "polished, professional staff"; while "not for the faint of wallet", it remains one of San Francisco's "paragons of fine" business dining.

Jardinière S
26 | 26 | 25 | $57

300 Grove St. (Franklin St.), 415-861-5555

■ When "you really want to wow" someone, "take them" to this "jazzy" Hayes Valley supper club that's "the social" stop "for pre- and post-symphony" dining ("the people-watching is almost as good as the oysters"); Pat Kuleto's "magnificent surroundings" "pull you" in, then Traci des Jardins' "orgasmic" Cal-French "garden of earthly delights" "elevates [you] to royal heights"; as for the "time-sensitive" service, "you'll only find better" "in heaven."

La Folie
28 | 24 | 26 | $70

2316 Polk St. (bet. Green & Union Sts.), 415-776-5577

■ Francophiles and foodies alike lionize Lyonnaise "master chef"- owner Roland Passot's "beautiful, if a bit cozy", Polk Street bistro as "heaven on earth"; the whimsical "jester/clown theme" lends a sense of theater but "pales in comparison" to "artfully presented" "artery-clogging", "magical modern French" "concoctions"; an "accommodating" staff "seduces you" with "Gallic charm."

La Forêt S
28 | 26 | 27 | $57

21747 Bertram Rd. (Almaden Rd.), San Jose, 408-997-3458

■ "Excellent game", "outstanding service" and an "exceptional setting" on a creek bank make this "very fancy" San Jose French situated in an old boarding house "well worth the drive" for a "special celebration"; even if there's a lingering feeling that the menu is "getting pricey", this "out-of-the-way gem" remains the "absolute favorite" of many Francophiles.

Lark Creek Inn 🅂   23 | 23 | 22 | $43
234 Magnolia Ave. (Madrone Ave.), Larkspur, 415-924-7766
■ "Dining's a lark" at Bradley Ogden's "charming country house" with a "storybook setting surrounded by redwoods" in Larkspur; the "hearty" "down-home" American cuisine is laced with "little innovations" by Jeremy Sewell and matched by "great service"; "we wish it really was an inn because we didn't want to leave."

La Toque 🅂   26 | 24 | 26 | $84
1140 Rutherford Rd. (Hwy. 29), Rutherford, 707-963-9770
■ Toques off to "culinary genius Ken Frank" for offering visitors another "pinnacle of fine dining" that many frequenters feel is the "second-best wine-country restaurant" – and a "more accessible" one too; sybarites suggest "live the life of Napa" and "do the outstanding wine-pairing" option on the prix fixe–only menu that features "marvelously presented" seasonally driven New French fare; "superb service" and a "lovely room" top off the experience.

Le Papillon 🅂   28 | 26 | 28 | $57
410 Saratoga Ave. (Kiely Blvd.), San Jose, 408-296-3730
■ Since accolades such as "flawless" and "unforgettable" are apt descriptions for this "creative and modern" "standard for fine French in the South Bay", it should come as no surprise that San Jose gourmets "go here to impress"; chef Scott Cooper's food is "exceptional", "the tasting menu is a tour de force", service is "unparalleled" ("low-key yet prompt") and the wine cellar is "excellent", causing converts to sigh "I just wish I lived closer."

Masa's   27 | 24 | 26 | $82
Hotel Vintage Court, 648 Bush St. (bet. Powell & Stockton Sts.), 415-989-7154
■ San Francisco's "formal" Downtowner is one of "the best again" since the arrival of *Iron Chef* victor Ron Siegel; his "beautifully arranged and magnificently prepared" New French cuisine "revolutionizes the way you look at food", while the "stunning" remodel ("a beautiful blend of modern art and traditional toile") and the "telepathic yet unobtrusive" waiters make a visit "like going to heaven" (only "it's easier to do, especially more than once"); just be aware "financing should be offered to pay the tab."

Oliveto 🅂   24 | 22 | 21 | $47
5655 College Ave. (Shafter Ave.), Oakland, 510-547-5356
▢ "Tuscany revisited" is the theme of this highly "hyped" Oakland "destination"; boosters boast that ex Chez Panisse executive chef Paul Bertolli's "straightforward approach" is the "benchmark for rustic Northern Italian" fare (especially the "perfectly prepared" roasted meats) served in "simple, elegant surroundings"; however, pessimists can't see past the "puny portions" and "awfully expensive prices", wondering "what is the fuss?"

Postrio 🅂   26 | 26 | 24 | $54
Prescott Hotel, 545 Post St. (bet. Mason & Taylor Sts.), 415-776-7825
■ "Trendy restaurants come and go, but few can match" the longevity of owner Wolfgang Puck's Downtown "power place"; in the kitchen, the brothers Rosenthal "consistently put out" "inventive, outstanding" New American dishes that "match" "the glamorous decor"; there's also plenty of "people-watching" at the upstairs bar where you can order "great gourmet pizza" (what else?) till midnight.

Ritz-Carlton Dining Room 28 28 28 $72

Ritz-Carlton Hotel, 600 Stockton St. (bet. California & Pine Sts.), 415-773-6198

■ "It's impossible to leave" this Nob Hill "over-the-top treat" not feeling like a VIP – albeit an "overstuffed VIP" – sigh satiated surveyors; the atmosphere of "extreme elegance", the cadre of "tuxedoed waiters" delivering "incomparable service" and chef Sylvain Portay's "sublime" New French cuisine (a "perfect blend of creative flavors") are "just what you'd expect from a hotel whose first name is Ritz"; so "don't wait for a special occasion, go now!"

Rubicon 24 21 23 $50

558 Sacramento St. (bet. Montgomery & Sansome Sts.), 415-434-4100

■ "Like DeNiro" (a minority investor), this "high-power dining" spot Downtown delivers "a consistently good performance"; new chef "Denis Leary really knows how to wow his guests", offering "something for nearly everyone" on his Cal–New French menu, and the "professionally trained staff is willing to go out of its way"; though skeptics sniff at the "somewhat stuffy surroundings", this is "a good place for entertaining", especially given the "wonderful wine list" crafted by sommelier Larry Stone.

Slanted Door [S] 26 18 20 $34

584 Valencia St. (17th St.), 415-861-8032

◪ "Absolutely epic" attest epicures about this "hip minimalist" Mission spot where chef Charles Phan's "sublime" "California take" on traditional Saigon street eats ("the 'shaking beef' will leave you shaking with pleasure") is paired with a "brilliant yet unusual wine list"; the "unbelievable noise level", "arrogant service" and "legendary wait for reservations" admittedly are "drawbacks", but "hey, it was good enough for Clinton" (we bet *he* didn't have to wait two months for a table); P.S. "go for lunch", a much easier ticket.

Sushi Ran [S] 27 20 21 $38

107 Caledonia St. (bet. Pine & Turney Sts.), Sausalito, 415-332-3620

■ "Attention, sushi aficionados", this "out-of-the-way Japanese" is the "best darn place in Marin" – "maybe in the entire Bay Area" – plying patrons with "melt-in-your-mouth fish", a "great variety of daring rolls" and other "fine delicacies"; though the jaded jibe it's "too much of a reservation circus", "there's a nice little wine and sake bar to wait in", and besides, it's "a haven for locals looking to get away from the tourists plaguing Sausalito."

Terra [S] 28 25 26 $57

1345 Railroad Ave. (bet. Adams & Hunt Sts.), St. Helena, 707-963-8931

■ For husband-and-wife team Hiro Sone and Lissa Doumani, this "romantic restaurant" in St. Helena is a "labor of love", and surveyors are smitten after sampling the "exquisite" "medley of flavors" of the Southern French–Northern Italian fare ("did these people invent fusion?") served in "elegantly plain" surroundings; not only is dining here "a haze of incredible food, well-timed service" and an unusual "selection of boutique wines", it's "shockingly affordable, given the area."

Tra Vigne [S] | 25 | 26 | 22 | $45 |

1050 Charter Oak Ave. (Hwy. 29), St. Helena, 707-963-4444

■ For a taste of "Firenze in California", Italophiles make a pilgrimage to this "see-and-be-seen" "St. Helena mainstay" whose "sublime" villa-like ambiance "transports you to Tuscany" but whose "rich, flavorful seasonal" menu "epitomizes wine-country cuisine"; if you can "overlook the tourists" and "snobby waiters", travelers insist "the highlight of any Napa trip" "is to eat and drink your way through the afternoon in the courtyard."

Zuni Cafe ◐[S] | 24 | 21 | 19 | $39 |

1658 Market St. (bet. Franklin & Gough Sts.), 415-552-2522

■ Chef-owner Judy Rodgers' "notoriously hip" and "hyped" Hayes Valley spot has been the "epitome of San Francisco's restaurant scene" since opening in 1979; the "gorgeous" "overcrowded bar" – home of "outrageous [balsamic-spiked] Bloody Marys" and an amazing array of "fresh oysters" – is ground zero for "people-watching"; though the Northern Italian–Med menu "changes daily", few venture beyond the "signature roast chicken, hamburgers and Caesar salad" that are "the yardstick" by which others are judged.

Santa Fe

TOP 10 FOOD RANKING

Restaurant	Cuisine Type
27 Old House	Continental/SW
Geronimo	Eclectic/SW
26 Santacafe	Southwestern/Eclectic
Cafe Pasqual's	Southwestern
25 Ristra	Southwestern/New French
Anasazi	Southwestern
24 Julian's	N&S Italian
Bistro 315	French Bistro
Il Vicino	N&S Italian
La Casa Sena	Southwestern

ADDITIONAL NOTEWORTHY PLACES

Andiamo!	Northern Italian
Bull Ring	American
Compound	New American
Coyote Cafe	Southwestern
El Farol	Spanish/New Mexican
Guadalupe Cafe	New Mexican
Il Piatto	Northern Italian
Pink Adobe	Continental/New Mexican
Rancho de San Juan	Eclectic/International
Rociada	French Bistro

F	D	S	C

Anasazi S
| | 25 | 27 | 24 | $42 |

Inn of the Anasazi, 113 Washington Ave. (bet. Marcy St. & Palace Ave.), 505-988-3236

■ Reviewers rave about the "gorgeous presentation" of "creative" Southwestern cuisine and the "superb decor" at this Downtowner in the Inn of the Anasazi; a minority maintains it's an "overpriced hotel dining room" that "suffers from changing staffs and chefs", but they're clearly outvoted.

Andiamo! S
| | 24 | 19 | 20 | $28 |

322 Garfield St. (bet. Guadalupe & Sandoval Sts.), 505-995-9595

■ "Terrific" Northern Italian food is the hallmark of this popular little bistro near the Rail Yard, which also gets high marks for its "friendly" service and "charming" "old bungalow" setting; though some find it too "noisy" and "cramped", they're easily assuaged after one bite of the "great duck" and "best polenta."

Bistro 315
| | 24 | 19 | 21 | $37 |

315 Old Santa Fe Trail (bet. Alameda St. & Paseo de Peralta), 505-986-9190

◪ This "lovely", "intimate" French bistro near the Plaza offers an "interesting" menu of "excellent" Provençal dishes, including "delicious duck"; the patio is touted too, though some find the interior "cramped" and the service occasionally "uneven."

Bull Ring 🄂   22 | 19 | 21 | $33

Wells Fargo Plaza, 150 Washington Ave. (Lincoln St.), 505-983-3328
■ You'll "see Santa Fe's power brokers" shooting the bull over some of "the best steaks in town" at this "old-style political hangout" Downtown, with a "lively", "smoky" bar that's an ideal perch for sipping a sublime martini; wallet-watchers be warned: unless you have an "expense account", you may find the "hearty", "straightforward" traditional American fare "too expensive" ("everything is à la carte").

Cafe Pasqual's 🄂   26 | 21 | 22 | $24

121 Don Gaspar Ave. (Water St.), 505-983-9340
■ "Fantastic breakfasts" "at the common table" are "a must" for both "tourists" and "locals" at this "loud", "crowded" and "colorful" Southwestern "old reliable", a block south of the Plaza, which still produces "delicious", "unexpected combinations" more than 20 years after its debut; most "go for breakfast and lunch" rather than dinner – just remember to "get there early" to avoid the "long lines", since this "bustling favorite" is hardly a secret.

Compound 🄂   _ | _ | _ | VE

653 Canyon Rd. (bet. Delgado St. & Palace Ave.), 505-982-4353
Reopened in May, 2000 after a much-needed renovation, this Canyon Road classic has eliminated the stuffiness (jacket and tied no longer required) while retaining the original charm of its historic adobe home; chef/co-owner Mark Kiffin (ex Coyote Café) offers an updated New American menu, featuring beef tenderloin with foie gras hollandaise and a baked-to-order liquid chocolate cake; N.B. the garden patio is ideal for romantic dinners *à deux*.

Coyote Cafe 🄂   23 | 24 | 22 | $40

132 W. Water St. (bet. Don Gaspar Ave. & Galisteo St.), 505-983-1615
☑ Acclaimed chef Mark Miller's classic eatery a block off the Plaza still "lives up to its billing" thanks to endlessly "innovative", "superbly presented" Southwestern dishes sporting "super" flavors; however, many locals feel the "noisy" main dining room has become an "overpriced" "tourist cliché" and recommend eating "on the rooftop" at the "festive", lower-priced cantina instead.

El Farol 🄂   19 | 20 | 18 | $27

808 Canyon Rd. (Camino del Monte Sol), 505-983-9912
☑ This "funky" Spanish–New Mexican "hangout" in a historic adobe on Canyon Road serves "tapas from heaven" in a "fun atmosphere" that includes "great live music" and a "late-night" "people-watching" scene; but naysayers note that the bill from all those "cute little" dishes can add up.

Geronimo 🄂   27 | 28 | 25 | $46

724 Canyon Rd. (Camino del Monte Sol), 505-982-1500
■ Voted New Mexico's Most Popular restaurant, this "pricey but worth it" Eclectic-Southwestern in a "lovely", "historic" Canyon Road adobe wins applause for Eric DiStefano's "extraordinary", "innovative" cuisine; patrons also praise the "romantic", "intimate" interior and the "thoughtful" service; overall, it's a "signature of Santa Fe" and a "must."

Guadalupe Cafe 🅂   22 | 17 | 19 | $16

422 Old Santa Fe Trail (bet. Alameda St. & Paseo de Peralta), 505-982-9762

■ A "favorite" place for "breakfast with the locals", this "standby" on the Old Santa Fe Trail is a "wonderful value" for "traditional" New Mexican fare, though the "great chili (red or green)" may be a bit "too hot" for more tender palates; it's "crowded" and waits can be long, but "monster portions" and a "great outdoor patio" keep it "popular."

Il Piatto 🅂   23 | 19 | 21 | $27

95 W. Marcy St. (bet. Lincoln & Washington Aves.), 505-984-1091

■ "Consistently good" Northern Italian food and a "reasonable wine list" pack in the crowds at this "lively" Downtown trattoria that "never disappoints" and "won't break the bank"; nevertheless, "scrunched-up" surveyors say that the "close quarters" are "not for the claustrophobic."

Il Vicino 🅂   24 | 20 | 18 | $13

321 W. San Francisco St. (bet. Guadalupe & Sandoval Sts.), 505-986-8700

■ One of Downtown's most popular lunch spots for "excellent wood-fired pizza" and lasagna washed down with "awesome microbrews", this "upbeat" Italian is also reasonably priced; a "great hangout after a movie", it tends to get "mobbed."

Julian's 🅂   24 | 25 | 23 | $38

221 Shelby St. (bet. Alameda & Water Sts.), 505-988-2355

■ A Downtown adobe is the "lovely" setting for this "very romantic", "elegant" spot that some say serves the "best Italian in Santa Fe"; the "high-quality" cuisine and "attentive service" make it a "special-occasion place" that's "worth the splurge."

La Casa Sena 🅂   24 | 25 | 22 | $36

125 E. Palace Ave. (Washington Ave.), 505-988-9232

■ This Southwestern stalwart located in a historic adobe near the Plaza is noted for its "creative" menu, "consistent" cooking, "gorgeous" courtyard and "Santa Fe charm", making it a "great" place to "bring your friends to impress them"; P.S. the adjacent cantina with its "singing waiters" is also "fun."

Old House 🅂   27 | 26 | 26 | $41

Eldorado Hotel, 309 W. San Francisco St. (bet. Guadalupe & Sandoval Sts.), 505-988-4455

■ Rated No. 1 for Food in New Mexico, this Downtown Continental-Southwestern set in the Eldorado Hotel "consistently exceeds expectations" with chef Martin Rios' "exquisite attention to detail" and "wonderful" cuisine; a "warm", "intimate" atmosphere and "sophisticated service" add to the "world-class" experience; N.B. dinner only.

Pink Adobe 🅂   21 | 24 | 21 | $31

406 Old Santa Fe Trail (Alameda St.), 505-983-7712

☑ "You'll meet everyone in town" at this long-standing "landmark" that's the "essential Santa Fe experience" for enthusiasts who come for the "cozy", historic setting, "classic" Continental–New Mexican menu and "great" Dragon Room bar; naysayers insist that "it doesn't live up to the hype", but they're outvoted by fans of the "steak Dunigan" and "always-a-joy" atmosphere.

Rancho de San Juan
26 | 29 | 28 | $55

Rancho de San Juan, Hwy. 285 (mile marker 340), Española, 505-753-6818

■ This "very special" country inn lies in a "gorgeous" rural setting north of Santa Fe; the "elegant and charming" decor, "superb" Eclectic-International menu and "wonderful" staff add up to an "exceptional dining experience"; even reviewers who find it "expensive" concur that it's an "out-of-this-world" place for a "fabulous anniversary dinner."

Ristra S
25 | 22 | 24 | $41

548 Agua Fria (Guadalupe St.), 505-982-8608

■ In Sanbusco, this "favorite" fills the bill for "excellent, imaginative" cooking, a "spectacular" "blend" of Southwestern and New French cuisines (don't miss the "simply sublime" mussel appetizer); the menu may be "limited", but there's "excellent service", plus a "sophisticated" setting with a "wonderful" patio.

Rociada
– | – | – | VE

304 Johnson St. (Chapelle St.), 505-983-3800

Hidden on a Downtown side street, this sleek French is easy to miss, but it's already garnered national attention for its versions of bistro classics (like lavender crème brûlée, the signature dessert) accompanied by a vast, all-Gallic wine list; with a zinc bar, pressed-tin ceiling and adobe walls, the place acknowledges both its Parisian inspiration and its New Mexico location.

Santacafe S
26 | 26 | 24 | $40

231 Washington Ave. (bet. Marcy St. & Paseo de Peralta), 505-984-1788

◪ This "favorite special-occasion spot" near the Plaza "remains an excellent retreat" for pros who praise its "top-notch", "inventive blend" of Southwestern and Eclectic "crosscultural" dishes, served either in the "elegant" interior or on the "lovely" patio; some report occasional "disappointment", saying the food is "up and down", but the majority maintains that the experience is "always great."

Seattle

* Tied with the restaurant listed directly above it

Brasa ◐ [S] 24 | 25 | 22 | $42

2107 Third Ave. (bet. Blanchard & Lenora Sts.), 206-728-4220

■ Chef/co-owner "Tamara Murphy does it right" at this "gorgeous" Belltowner where the "inventive menu" takes you on an eclectic tour of "Mediterranean-with-a-twist" fare; "equally impressive" is the "smashingly sharp, modern look" of the "spacious yet intimate" dining room; the "service can range from perfection to perfunctory, depending on who you get and who you know", but all in all, this is one "very civilized" and "classy" place.

Cafe Campagne [S] 27 | 23 | 23 | $31

Pike Place Mkt., 1600 Post Alley (Pine St.), 206-728-2233

■ Smitten transients "want to move in", while gambling gourmets "play the lottery to be able to eat every day" at this "ooh" and "aah"–worthy "French bistro in the heart of Pike Place Market", which offers "wonderful" cassoulet, the "best pâté" and other "comfort food *à la française*"; it's also ideal for brunch, for "relaxing with a glass of Rhône wine" "on a blustery afternoon" and as an alternative when you can't get into Campagne, its upstairs sibling.

Cafe Juanita [S] 25 | 20 | 24 | $39

9702 NE 120th Pl. (97th St.), Kirkland, 425-823-1505

■ "Hurrah for chef-owner" Holly Smith, who has taken this hard-to-find "local institution to a new level" – one that's "worth searching for" if you're seeking "innovative" Northern Italian cooking, an "outstanding wine cellar" and "always excellent service", all in a "quaint", "creekside" setting in Kirkland; no wonder cosmopolites croon it's one of the "most sophisticated" venues around.

Campagne [S] 27 | 24 | 25 | $49

Pike Place Mkt., 86 Pine St. (1st Ave.), 206-728-2800

■ Owner Peter Lewis' "classic Country French" "all-star" at Pike Place Market is "still one of the best in the city" by virtue of "exquisite food that's treated as respectfully as the customers", an "excellent wine list" and a "sexy yet refined" atmosphere; romance-seeking regulars "pop into the bar", while penny-pinchers recommend the "bargain" early-evening prix fixe – but whatever route you take to the *campagne,* "a great evening is assured."

Canlis 26 | 27 | 27 | $55

2576 Aurora Ave. N. (Halladay St., south of Aurora Bridge), 206-283-3313

■ Passing its golden anniversary, this Seattle "landmark" with a "beautiful setting" overlooking Lake Union seems to get "more and more modern while staying completely timeless"; credit chef Greg Atkinson's "updated" menu of "Northwest treats", complemented by a "superb" wine list of over 1,000 selections and "impeccable" service, especially the "impressive" valet parking; granted, this "classic" is "expensive", so "it should be perfect and usually is."

Cascadia 25 | 25 | 23 | $65

2328 First Ave. (bet. Battery & Bell Sts.), 206-448-8884

■ Pushing Northwest cuisine to ever greater heights (he uses only ingredients from the Cascade Mountain Range region), chef Kerry Sear turns out "ambitious", "cutting-edge" dishes at this Belltown "original" that's further enhanced by "stunning decor" (including a "beautiful waterfall"); a few groan at the "temple-of-gastronomy attitude", but ultimately this "gift to Seattle" leaves most patrons feeling "incredibly pampered."

Chez Shea S   25 | 25 | 24 | $42
Pike Place Mkt., 94 Pike St. (1st Ave.), 206-467-9990
■ If you're in the market (Pike Place Market, that is) for a "romantic, delightful oasis", seek out this "quaint" Northwest eatery where "attentive" yet "discreet servers" deliver "inventive" fare; you "can't beat the view" of Puget Sound, nor the "candlelit" "elegance" of "one of the best, least-known restaurants in town."

Dahlia Lounge S   27 | 25 | 25 | $40
2001 Fourth Ave. (Virginia St.), 206-682-4142
■ The verdict is in: this "perennial Downtown favorite" is "as good as ever" in "great new digs" that are "much more roomy [yet] still intimate" and embellished with "fantastic red walls"; you can count on "wonderful use of seasonal Northwest foods" in "superbly presented" Eclectic dishes "with just the right amount of creativity" ("save room for the coconut cream pie"); owner "Tom Douglas is a Seattle treasure" and his lounge "a sublime experience."

El Gaucho ●S   24 | 23 | 24 | $52
2505 First Ave. (bet. Vine & Wall Sts.), 206-728-1337
■ It's "class all the way" at this "sophisticated" Belltown shrine to "superb steaks and superb service" (though "surprisingly, the fish entrees are as good"), whose worshipers include the "martini, meat and Cuban-cigar crowd"; what with watching "Caesar salad and bananas Foster prepared tableside" and spotting the "local who's who", this is a real "dinner-as-theater" experience that "takes you back to a time long ago."

Etta's Seafood S   25 | 20 | 22 | $36
2020 Western Ave. (bet. Lenora & Virginia Sts.), 206-443-6000
■ Fish fans say there's almost nothing b-etta than this "longtime favorite" (part of owner "Tom Douglas' dynasty") at the north edge of the Pike Place Market; "warm, friendly and informal", it offers an "eclectic menu" of "superbly fresh seafood" that "gets everything right" (even "the side dishes are a must"); it's a "super weekend-breakfast place" as well, ideal for fueling up before hitting the shops; an "always-pleasant staff" rounds out a supremely "satisfying" experience that even "impresses the in-laws."

Eva S   25 | 21 | 23 | $34
(fka Brie & Bordeaux)
2227 N. 56th St. (Kirkwood Pl.), 206-633-3538
■ Locals have long lavished praise on this Greenwood bistro known for its "wonderful, casual atmosphere", "well-crafted, delicious food" and "knowledgeable staff" ("with no attitude except friendly"); regulars hope that Amy McCray's (ex Chez Shea) Eclectic–New American cooking "will continue the tradition" at this "darling spot."

Flying Fish ●S   26 | 22 | 22 | $38
2234 First Ave. (Bell St.), 206-728-8595
☑ "A lot of imagination goes into" the "superb seafood" with an Asian twist that's served at this "bustling, energetic" Belltowner; fans' favorites include "out-of-this world Thai crab cakes" and a platter of salt-and-pepper Dungeness crab that's "great for a crowd" (sharing's highly encouraged here); critics carp that it gets "way too noisy" and that "while the cash register flies, the service crawls", but most feel "this is a catch you should not miss."

Fullers 26 | 25 | 25 | $49

Sheraton Seattle Hotel & Towers, 1400 Sixth Ave. (bet. Pike & Union Sts.), 206-447-5544

◪ "Always a great place for business dinners", this Downtown "class act" offers "excellent Northwest food" and regional wines served up "in a formal setting" that showcases the distinctive art collection peppering the walls; though "mixed experiences" leave malcontents muttering it's "no longer the legend" that it used to be, the full-hearted deem this vet still "one of the city's best."

Georgian Room [S] 27 | 28 | 28 | $54

Four Seasons Olympic Hotel, 411 University St. (bet. 4th & 5th Aves.), 206-621-7889

■ There's just "no more elegant" place in town than this "posh" Downtowner; but this "class act" goes beyond the opulent "carpets and chandeliers" to offer Northwest "meals fit for a king" and "luxuriant service"; "eventually all of Seattle shows up here", so "don't wait until a special occasion" – just "dress up" and "bring the credit card."

Harvest Vine 27 | 20 | 22 | $33

2701 E. Madison St. (27th Ave.), 206-320-9771

■ "Good things come in small packages" at this "shoe box–size" Basque in Madison Valley that provides an "unparalleled ethnic experience"; since there are "no reservations", "get there early" to reap a harvest of "authentic" and "exquisite tapas"; "sit at the copper-topped bar" so you can watch mustachioed chef/co-owner Joseph Jiménez de Jiménez at work; wife and pastry chef Carolin "is a wonder", so save room for dessert.

Herbfarm [S] 28 | – | 27 | $87

Willows Lodge, 14590 NE 145th St. (Woodinville-Redmond Rd.), Woodinville, 206-784-2222

■ Oh, the superlatives that devotees dole out for the "culinary adventure" that results when chef Jerry Traunfeld applies his art to the "creative uses of herbs" ("sublime", "pure alchemy", "inventive Northwest cuisine at its best"); expect a leisurely multi-course, multi-hour and multi-dollar "gastronomic feast", supplemented by "exquisite service and [table] setting", that's "worth the long wait" for reservations.

Il Terrazzo Carmine 26 | 24 | 24 | $40

411 First Ave. S. (bet. Jackson & King Sts.), 206-467-7797

■ Expect a "continuously superb" experience at this longtime favorite in Pioneer Square, an "elegant, old-school Italian" that relies on standards such as the "best carpaccio" and the signature osso buco Milanese, served in a "sophisticated" yet "comfortable" setting; the "ever-watchful eye of owner Carmine Smeraldo guarantees you" "seamless service", but it "can get loud."

JaK's Grill [S] 26 | 18 | 22 | $32

4548 California Ave. SW (bet. Alaska & Oregon Sts.), 206-937-7809
14 Front St. N. (Sunset Way), Issaquah, 425-837-8834

■ "Great steak" at a "low price" might seem an oxymoron, but this "excellent" West Seattle and Issaquah beef duo manages to be one of the "best buys in town"; "the fact that they don't take reservations is a pain", but "service that makes you feel like family" causes folks to be "weekly regulars."

Kingfish [S]≠ 25 22 21 $26
602 19th Ave. E. (Mercer St.), 206-320-8757
■ "You go, girls!" cheer fans of the Coaston sisters, who run this "buzzing" "down-home" haunt, which offers "a taste of Southern tradition" at "reasonable prices"; the "great cookin' with all the fixin's" includes "red beans, rice and cornbread to die for" and "buttermilk fried chicken worth every minute in line"; admittedly, this can amount to a lot of minutes, so "put your name down and go for a drink" or a walk around mellow Capitol Hill.

Lampreia 25 21 23 $58
2400 First Ave. (Battery St.), 206-443-3301
◪ No Emerald City establishment polarizes patrons as much as this Belltowner: the cult-like majority "would sit on an apple box in the alley to eat" chef-owner and "culinary genius" Scott Carsberg's "sublime" Italian-influenced Northwest–New American fare – though folks don't have to, given the "stylish atmosphere" and "indulgent staff"; to heretics, however, it's a "stuck-up" spot that specializes in "confrontational dining" in the form of "skimpy portions", "robotic waiters" and "austere decor."

Le Gourmand 26 21 26 $54
425 NW Market St. (6th Ave.), 206-784-3463
■ "A little off-the-beaten-path", this Ballard "oasis of comfortable elegance" offers an "escape from the trendy set" as you enjoy "top-of-the-line French fare"; Bruce Naftaly "is a delight" with his "impeccable use of Northwest ingredients"; with "exquisite fine food, romantic atmosphere and prompt quiet service, what more can you ask for?"

Le Pichet [S] 23 22 20 $30
Pike Place Mkt., 1933 First Ave. (Virginia St.), 206-256-1499
■ There's now a "little piece of Paris" at the Pike Place Market, offering the "hearty flavors" of "artful" French bistro fare on a selective (some say "limited") menu; it may be "new", but it feels "like it's been there 40 years", with such "authentic details" as the tiled floor, hefty zinc bar, earthenware *pichets* of wine and a bill with phrases *en français.*

Macrina Bakery & Cafe [S] 25 18 18 $16
2408 First Ave. (bet. Battery & Wall Sts.), 206-448-4032
■ Can't choose from among the aptly named "morning glory muffin", the addictive "orange hazelnut pinwheel" or the "best-of-the-best cinnamon monkey bread"?; then just get "one of everything" and you're guaranteed "gustatory bliss", since this "terrific Belltown bakery" purveys pastries "worth getting out of bed for"; later on, a "varied", "rustic" Med-oriented lunch and dinner menu is served.

Metropolitan Grill [S] 26 23 24 $45
820 Second Ave. (Marion St.), 206-624-3287
■ "If you need meat, it can't be beat" say supporters of this Downtowner, a "suit-oriented" oldie that's still "the best place for steak in Seattle"; expect "always-done-to-a-turn" "portions the size of Texas" served by the "bright, funny, attentive staff" and a woody "expense-account" ambiance that, when fueled by the "good happy hour", is "busy, energetic, vibrant" – and a tad "too noisy" at times; all in all, though, this is one prime beef baron.

Mistral
27 | 20 | 24 | $67

113 Blanchard St. (bet. 1st & 2nd Aves.), 206-770-7799

■ This "intriguing" place has blown into Belltown, establishing itself among "serious, *very* serious, foodies": you pick your prix fixe price point, choose "fresh ingredients" from the daily printed list, then "relax and enjoy" chef-owner William Belickis' "wonderful and daring" New French–New American preparations, "impeccably served"; though reviewers register "sticker shock" over the price, they admit that "every course is exquisite."

Monsoon [S]
25 | 19 | 20 | $30

615 19th Ave. E. (bet. Mercer & Roy Sts.), 206-325-2111

■ Tucked into a section of Capitol Hill, this "delicious Vietnamese" run by the Banh clan delights with dishes such as "incredibly fragrant soups", 10-spice flank beef and "must-try sea bass" that "combine subtle and spicy flavors" and are joined by "well-chosen wines"; just be prepared – only a monsoon could drown out the "terrible din" when the "spare, bright" room gets packed.

Nell's [S]
26 | 21 | 24 | $45

6804 E. Green Lake Way N. (bet. 2nd & 4th Aves. NE), 206-524-4044

■ Chef-owner "Philip Mihalski is clearly a rising star", and his New American with regional influences is a "great" addition to Green Lake, with "excellent service" that makes for a "friendly atmosphere" in which to enjoy "inventive, faultless food"; whether it's an "old favorite" (beef tenderloin) or a new (black cod), "each dish is a masterpiece", so some say this sophomore "will become one of the city's best."

Nishino [S]
26 | 22 | 23 | $39

3130 E. Madison St. (Lake Washington Blvd.), 206-322-5800

■ A careful balance of "inventive Japanese fare, along with the great classics", is maintained by this "elegant, serene" Madison Park hot spot; "there is no better sushi in Seattle", and the rest of the menu is pretty "divine" too, but regulars recommend "splurge on the omakase meal" (which you must reserve in advance) and "let chef-owner Tatsu Nishino feed you whatever he wants", knowing full well that it will be something "exceptional."

Palace Kitchen ◐[S]
24 | 22 | 21 | $36

2030 Fifth Ave. (Lenora St.), 206-448-2001

■ Need we say it again?; owner "Tom Douglas is the best", and folks have "nothing but kudos" for his "very hip" "hot spot" Downtown; the "imaginative", made-for-grazing menu serves up Eclectic–New American "food with real flavor", from the simmered short ribs and applewood-grilled meats to the cheese plate; add in the "great bar scene" and you've got a "festive atmosphere" that makes for hordes of "happy people."

Place Pigalle
25 | 23 | 22 | $39

Pike Place Mkt., 81 Pike St. (Pike Pl.), 206-624-1756

■ This "very Euro" and "absolutely charming place" is a "real treat if you can find it behind the Pike Place Market pig" statue; your efforts will be rewarded with a view "overlooking Puget Sound" and an "inspired", "consistently delicious" Eclectic-Northwest menu that's complemented by "one of the city's best, and most fairly priced, wine lists"; no wonder this intimate bistro has become a "perennial" "must-get-back-to" for locals and visitors alike.

Restaurant Zoë S

25 | 23 | 25 | $37

2137 Second Ave. (Blanchard St.), 206-256-2060

■ This year-old hot spot has jogged even the most jaded diners with "flavorful food", "fab cocktails", "exceptional service" and a "totally tony" interior, all "in the middle of the action" of Belltown; chef-owner Scott Staples hits the right notes with a New American menu that's concise and consistently well-executed; no wonder Zoë-goers say they "want more places like this."

Rover's

29 | 25 | 28 | $82

2808 E. Madison St. (28th Ave.), 206-325-7442

■ Once again Seattle's No. 1 for Food, this longtime "champion" in Madison Valley is truly "the tops" for its Northwest-accented New French "edible art" prepared by chef-owner Thierry Rautureau and presented in "fantastic tasting menus" (including a veggie version) that are "well worth the splurge"; a staff that's "knowledgeable without being stuffy" and a "lovely", "elegant" setting add up to an "always exceptional" experience, leaving one surveyor to sigh "I'd be a regular if I were Bill Gates."

Salumi

27 | 14 | 21 | $16

309 Third Ave. S. (bet. Jackson & Main Sts.), 206-621-8772

■ "It's like dining with friends and family, even if you go alone" to this Pioneer Square "magical lunch spot", thanks to the communal table at the back of a narrow room; owner and "master sausage maker" Armandino Batali (papa to NY chef Mario Batali) shares his "passion" for "true Italian" flavors in a way that leaves devotees "dreaming of meatball sandwiches" and other delights; N.B. book ahead – book way ahead – for the weekly group dinners.

727 Pine S

– | – | – | VE

Elliott Grand Hyatt Hotel, 727 Pine St., (8th Ave.), 206-774-6400

In the sleek new Elliott Grand Hyatt Downtown, chef Danielle Custer takes a sophisticated approach to seasonal Northwest fare; her presentations of dishes such as lobster-and-shrimp enchilada and mango-lime soufflé are as eye-catching as the lush-but-comfy dining room.

Shiro's Sushi S

26 | 17 | 20 | $35

2401 Second Ave. (Battery St.), 206-443-9844

■ If you're lucky enough to snag a spot at the sushi bar at this Belltowner (hint: be there when it opens), "ignore the menu and have Shiro order for you", because this "master chef" uses only the "highest-grade ingredients" in his "incredible" dishes and he often has "wonderful seasonal surprises" to share; it's "extremely traditional" in decor, and most maintain it's "worth every yen."

Shoalwater S

26 | 24 | 23 | $41

Shelburne Inn, 4415 Pacific Hwy. (45th St.), Seaview, 360-642-4142

■ This Long Beach Peninsula destination has provided the region with a "20-year tradition of excellent Northwest fare", including Willapa Bay oysters and Alaskan halibut, though meat dishes shine as well; the "wine selection is great" and the "service is friendly", making this a solid choice for some of the "best dining on the Washington coast."

6 • 7 S　　　　　　　　　　　– | – | – | E |
Edgewater Hotel, Pier 67, 2411 Alaskan Way (bet. Vine & Wall Sts.),
206-269-4575

What's old is new again down on the Waterfront's Pier 67, where the venerable Edgewater Hotel has updated its dining room; the colorful, mod decor, complete with bark-covered pillars and a bank of fake fireplaces behind the sushi bar, is backdrop to a Northwest–Pan-Asian menu; the new patio perched above Elliott Bay makes a welcome addition to alfresco dining options in town.

Szmania's S　　　　　　　　26 | 22 | 24 | $40 |
3321 W. McGraw St. (34th Ave.), 206-284-7305
148 Lake St. S. (Kirkland Ave.), Kirkland, 425-803-3310

■ "A great dining experience even if no one can pronounce the name" (hint: the 'z' is silent), this Magnolia "jewel" sparkles, offering "creative Northwest cuisine with German flair" and some Asian accents; chef-owner Ludger Szmania "does everything right", turning out "imaginative" dishes in a "warm and welcoming atmosphere"; N.B. Eastsiders can now enjoy an "awesome" taste of the same in Kirkland.

Waterfront S　　　　　　　25 | 26 | 23 | $49 |
Pier 70, 2801 Alaskan Way (Broad St.), 206-956-9171

■ Owner Paul Mackay (El Gaucho) has another hit with this entry, whose "wonderful view" from the posh Pier 70 perch is only the opening number; chef Vicky McCaffree (ex Yarrow Bay Grill) assures diners of seafood "cooked to perfection" ("fantastic salt-and-pepper prawns"), while the staff offers "professional, delightful service" in "beautiful surroundings"; though the waterlogged lament that the "gigantic dining room" is pretty "noisy", most declare it "does not get better than this."

Wild Ginger S　　　　　　　26 | 24 | 22 | $36 |
1401 Third Ave. (Union St.), 206-623-4450

■ Folks are just wild about this Asian (the *Seattle Survey*'s Most Popular restaurant) whose "gorgeous" new Downtown digs "don't miss a beat" in satisfying surveyors' craving for the "incredible 'fragrant duck'" and other "fabulous flavors" that make up this "culinary adventure in smells and spices"; anyone hoping that the bigger space means "more room for the throngs" will be disappointed, though, because the "hottest place in town" is still "always packed", making it "hard to get a table" ("even with reservations, expect a wait").

Southern NY State

TOP 20 FOOD RANKING

Restaurant	Cuisine Type
29 Xaviar's at Piermont	New American
Xaviar's at Garrison	New American
28 Freelance Café	New American
La Panetière	New French
27 Escoffier	Classic French
La Cremaillère	Country French
Harralds	International
American Bounty	New American
Azuma Sushi	Japanese
Buffet de la Gare	Classic French
Terrapin	New American
Arch	Eclectic/New French
26 Le Château	Classic French
Zeph's	Eclectic
Rest. X & Bully Boy Bar	New American
Auberge Maxime	New French
Calico	Eclectic/American
Equus	New French
Iron Horse Grill	New American
Crabtree's Kittle House	New American

ADDITIONAL NOTEWORTHY PLACES

American Bistro	New American
Aubergine	New American/New French
Café Meze	Mediterranean
Citrus Grille	New American
Conte's Fishmarket	Seafood
DePuy Canal House	American/Eclectic
Eastchester Fish	Seafood
Harvest on Hudson	Mediterranean
Hunan Village	Chinese
Il Cena'Colo	Northern Italian
Inn at Pound Ridge	American
L'Europe	Classic French/Continental
Lusardi's	N&S Italian
Mighty Joe Young's	Steakhouse
Mulino's	Northern Italian
Old Drovers Inn	American
121 Rest. & Bar	New American
Peter Pratt's Inn	New American
Purdys Homestead	New American
Sun, Moon & Spoon	New American

American Bistro, An S   25 | 14 | 22 | $37 |
174 Marbledale Rd. (bet. Fisher Ave. & Main St.), Tuckahoe, 914-793-0807
■ "The chef is an artist" whose "inventive" New American dishes "never miss" declare fans of this "little gem" "tucked away in Tuckahoe's" "low-rent district"; sure, there are "long waits" and "no-frills" decor, but the staff "couldn't be nicer", and after a few bites you'll see why it was all "well worth it."

American Bounty   27 | 25 | 25 | $44 |
Culinary Institute of America, 1946 Campus Dr. (Albany Post Rd.), Hyde Park, 845-471-6608
■ "A wonderful showcase for hardworking students", who operate "every facet" of it, this CIA-based Hyde Park New American "class act" features "out-of-this-world" cuisine, a "handsome room with beautiful tableware" and "sweet", "gracious" service; in sum, it's an "ideal way to finish off a day of touring wineries."

Arch S   27 | 27 | 26 | $60 |
Rte. 22N (end of I-684), Brewster, 845-279-5011
■ Patrons predict that "you'll feel like royalty" at this venerable Brewster Eclectic-French, revered for its "glamorous", "intimate" interior (try for the garden room), pleasing patio, "personal and attentive" service and "excellent wine list"; chef-owner George Seitz's "terrific" prix fixe dinner menu (à la carte at lunch) "changes with the times" but is always "a treat for the palate."

Auberge Maxime S   26 | 25 | 25 | $56 |
721 Titicus Rd. (Rtes. 116 & 121), North Salem, 914-669-5450
■ "Strictly for grown-ups", this Gallic entry in North Salem's "horse country" is lauded for "great soufflés" and "original ways of serving duck", as well as a "wonderful French country" feel, highlighted by a "heavenly" patio; a few feel that it's getting "a bit stale on ideas" but wouldn't decline an invite for a "special-occasion" dinner here.

Aubergine S   25 | 25 | 25 | $53 |
Aubergine Fine Food and Lodging, Rtes. 22 & 23, Hillsdale, 518-325-3412
■ Set in a "gorgeous", circa-1783 auberge, chef-owner David Lawson's French-American is "as good as it gets in Columbia [County]" thanks to "beautiful rooms" furnished with antiques, a "calm", "comforting" aura, "wonderful" cuisine and a "great cellar"; while "expensive", it makes "a perfect coda to a Sunday afternoon at Tanglewood (a half hour away)."

Azuma Sushi S   27 | 15 | 18 | $38 |
219 E. Hartsdale Ave. (Central Ave.), Hartsdale, 914-725-0660
■ Raw "fish doesn't get much fresher" than the "top-quality" "traditional" sushi that's crafted inside this "tiny" Hartsdale Japanese storefront whose "very high standards" attract "hordes of people from Manhattan" (it's "convenient to Metro-North"); just "don't expect any atmosphere", many cooked dishes or coddling by the "intimidating" staff.

Buffet de La Gare   27 | 22 | 24 | $54 |
155 Southside Ave. (Spring St.), Hastings-on-Hudson, 914-478-1671
■ "Excellent in all ways" exclaim enthusiasts of this French near the Hastings train station, a "special-occasion favorite" that "can compete with the best of Manhattan" thanks to "first-rate" cuisine served in "elegant" rooms; though a few interpret the "Gallic reserve" as "pretentious", most applaud the "attentive service."

Cafe Mezé [S] 23 19 21 $42

20 N. Central Ave. (Hartsdale Ave.), Hartsdale, 914-428-2400

■ "Hail to the Livanos!" boom boosters of this family that "knows how to run a restaurant" – five, in fact; "excellent chef" Mark Filippo "never misses", scoring "points for inventiveness" with his "soul-satisfying" Mediterranean cuisine; though the "rushed waiters" are sometimes "overwhelmed" by "weekend crowds", it remains a "sophisticated dining experience."

Calico [S] 26 17 23 $34

9 Mill St./Rte. 9 (Rte. 308), Rhinebeck, 845-876-2749

■ "A piece of the Parisian Left Bank in Rhinebeck" purr patrons of this "tiny" husband-and-wife Eclectic-American bistro; Leslie Balassone's "perfect" pastry leads surveyors to suggest "pick out dessert and then work backward", patching together "wonderful" selections from chef Anthony Balassone's "first-rate" menu; weave in "excellent" service and an "outstanding wine list", and the result is a "spectacular experience" at "prices cheaper than most."

Citrus Grille [S] 25 19 22 $45

430 E. Saddle River Rd. (bet. Lake St. & Rte. 59), Airmont, 845-352-5533

■ Chef-owner Steven Christianson's "creative, superior cuisine" and "interesting vertical presentations" elevate his Rockland County New American into an area favorite; "welcoming service", a "cozy atmosphere" and "friendly patrons" make it "feel like a country restaurant", and though a few find the "intimate" seating too close for private conversation, most feel it's "charming."

Conte's Fishmarket ≠ 25 12 19 $35

448 Main St. (St. Mark's Pl.), Mount Kisco, 914-666-6929

■ Despite a tiny "no-frills" setting in a Mount Kisco fish market ("on a nice night, sit outside"), this BYO seafood house is a must-reserve spot for a "limited menu" of "simply prepared" but "wonderful" tastes of the sea; N.B. dinner Thursday–Saturday.

Crabtree's Kittle House [S] 26 25 25 $49

Crabtree's Kittle House Inn, 11 Kittle Rd. (Rte. 117), Chappaqua, 914-666-8044

■ An "atmospheric old inn [circa 1790] provides the perfect backdrop" for this Chappaqua New American, one of "the yardsticks for fine dining" in Westchester, with "heavenly" cuisine, a "world-class wine cellar", "garden views" and service that "truly caters to you"; not surprising, it's also "a favorite" choice "for special occasions" – just ask Bill and Hillary, who "had their 'welcome home' party here."

DePuy Canal House [S] 25 27 24 $55

Rte. 213 (Lucas Tpke.), High Falls, 845-687-7700

■ "A must-stop" "for the adventurous palate" say fans of "food artist" John Novi's "spectacular" American-Eclectic that's now in its 33rd year of offering "creative combinations"; the "beautiful", antique-filled "1797 stone tavern" and "excellent service" make this "*the* place to take first-time Hudson Valley visitors"; while wallet-watchers find it "expensive", most feel "it's worth it."

Eastchester Fish Gourmet [S] 24 | 17 | 18 | $39

837 White Plains Rd. (Summerfield St.), Scarsdale, 914-725-3450

◪ "One of a rare breed" say afishionados of this Scarsdale spot where "heavenly seafood" is "presented with love and passion" in a "pretty" dining room; critics note that the "portions could be bigger", the "service doesn't always go swimmingly" and the limited-reservation policy can "anchor you all night" at the bar; still, most agree the "top-drawer" food "compensates" for all.

Equus [S] 26 | 29 | 25 | $59

Castle at Tarrytown, 400 Benedict Ave. (bet. Maple St. & Martling Ave.), Tarrytown, 914-631-3646

■ "Stunning!" enthuse aesthetes over the "beautifully appointed" dining rooms, "breathtaking" "views of the Hudson" and "scenic gardens" surrounding this "fairy-tale castle"–cum–haute hotel in Tarrytown; similarly "elegant in every detail" are Belgian chef Fabrizzio Salerni's "exquisitely prepared" New French creations that are "presented like Michelangelos" by "top-notch" servers; "yes, it's expensive", but it's "worth every shilling."

Escoffier 27 | 26 | 26 | $50

Culinary Institute of America, 1946 Campus Dr. (Albany Post Rd.), Hyde Park, 845-471-6608

■ "If he ate here he'd be proud of his namesake" enthuse epicures over this Classic French "treat" that offers a "superb dining experience at the Culinary Institute" in Hyde Park; the "outstanding" food makes it "a place to pamper the palate", and there's also that "wonderful setting" as well as "friendly, eager service by students" whose "instructors keep the standards high"; though "pricey, it's worth it", so "make reservations in advance."

Freelance Café & Wine Bar [S]≠ 28 | 20 | 25 | $41

506 Piermont Ave. (Ash St.), Piermont, 845-365-3250

■ Like a freelancer, this "less-expensive" "little sister to Xaviar's" in Piermont is "always reinventing itself", serving "artful" New American fare using "superb ingredients" that has some wishing they "could eat here every night"; its résumé also includes "fabulous wines by the glass", "bend-over-backward service" and an "informal-yet-sophisticated ambiance"; the only drawback in its portfolio: the "no-reservations policy."

Harralds ≠ 27 | 26 | 27 | $66

3760 Rte. 52 (bet. Durrschmidt & Mountain Rds.), Stormville, 845-878-6595

■ The "old-world charm and menu" make for "a delightful, delicious experience" at this Dutchess County International; owner-host Harrald Boerger "treats you like a favored guest" in a "lovely country setting" where you'll dine on "nonpareil" fare from the kitchen of his wife, Ava Durrschmidt; though many find the prix fixe tariff "*très cher*", most would agree "it's worth it."

Harvest On Hudson [S] 22 | 26 | 20 | $43

1 River St. (¼ mi. north of Hastings-on-Hudson RR station), Hastings-on-Hudson, 914-478-2800

◪ "Dazzling and magical at sunset", the patio of this Hastings Mediterranean affords "amazing views" of the Hudson and a "spectacular garden", while the interior offers "nicely spaced tables" and high ceilings; the "innovative food" "has come a long way", but service sometimes "blows hot and cold."

Hunan Village [S] — 25 | 18 | 21 | $29

1828 Central Park Ave. (bet. Central & Slater Aves.), Yonkers, 914-779-2272
■ "Creative cooking" that's "far above the usual Chinese" fare helps this "gourmet" Hunan in Yonkers maintain its "best-of-show" status; you "can't go wrong" with the "always outstanding and sometimes spectacular" cuisine proffered by "expert waiters"; regulars suggest you let "gracious" owner-host Paul Chou "order for you" because "when Paul takes charge, wonders follow."

Il Cena'Colo [S] — 25 | 19 | 24 | $51

228 S. Plank Rd. (Union Ave.), Newburgh, 845-564-4494
◩ Partisans agree it's "worth the drive" to this perennially top-rated Northern Italian "treasure in Orange County" that's "like a one-night trip to Tuscany" (and a lot closer) thanks to "brilliant" cooking and "drop-dead attention to service and presentation"; a few vocal dissenters declare it's all "hype" ("pricey and not worth it", "dreary decor"), but for the majority it "never disappoints."

Inn at Pound Ridge [S] — 25 | 25 | 23 | $51

258 Westchester Ave./Rte. 137 (Rte. 172), Pound Ridge, 914-764-5779
■ A visit to this "absolutely beautiful" traditional American set on "lovely grounds" in Pound Ridge is "like stepping back in time", with "superior" "country inn fare" "carefully served" in a "romantic" "New England atmosphere" that offers the "best of both worlds" – "classy" and "tasteful", yet "not too stuffy"; indeed, guests may face only one "hard decision: dine upstairs (more elegant) or downstairs (cozier)?"; either way, it's "not to be missed."

Iron Horse Grill — 26 | 21 | 23 | $47

20 Wheeler Ave. (Manville Rd.), Pleasantville, 914-741-0717
■ This "consummately professional" New American set in a "charming" "converted railway station" "remains on track" after its "brilliant start" in 1998, with chef-owner Philip McGrath creating "inspired", "scrumptious" cuisine that's "nicely presented" by a "caring" staff; some call the prices "too steep" for Pleasantville, but given that it's almost "impossible to get reservations", cost concerns "don't seem to be holding people back."

La Crémaillère [S] — 27 | 27 | 25 | $61

46 Bedford-Banksville Rd. (bet. Noah St. & Roundhouse Rd.), Banksville, 914-234-9647
■ For a "charming" "slice of France" "transported" to Banksville, "chichi" types "dress up" and head to this Country French destination where chef William Savarese prepares "superb" cuisine, bolstered by an "impressive" 14,000-plus bottle cellar and an "attentive, unobtrusive" staff; "an extravagance, but well worth it" for a "classy evening", it can also be experienced more affordably through its prix fixe lunch.

La Panetière [S] — 28 | 27 | 26 | $63

530 Milton Rd. (Oakland Beach Ave.), Rye, 914-967-8140
■ Once again voted Southern NY's Most Popular restaurant, this Provençal-themed Rye New French destination is lauded for "outstanding food" that's "a joy to behold and eat", a "great" (if "pricey") wine list and superb service led by "dignified" owner Jacques Loupiac; quibblers find it a tad "pretentious" ("women's menus don't have prices"), but they're outvoted by the many who gladly don a jacket and "take out a home-equity loan to pay" the bill.

Le Château [S] 26 | 28 | 26 | $57

Rte. 35 (Rte. 123), South Salem, 914-533-6631

■ Situated in a 1907 mansion on "beautiful grounds" that afford "sweeping views of uninterrupted forest", this "elegant" South Salem Classic French "makes you feel as if you've come home to your private château" to enjoy "sunset cocktails" and "superb" cuisine ("try all the soufflés") proffered by an "excellent" staff; P.S. you may "want to hold your daughter's wedding" here.

L'Europe [S] 26 | 21 | 24 | $54

407 Smith Ridge Rd./Rte. 123 (Tommys Ln.), South Salem, 914-533-2570

■ "Meticulous" but "friendly service" scores almost as well as the "superb food" ("great rack of lamb") at this "old-world" French-Continental hidden away in South Salem; voters also praise the "lovely atmosphere", prix fixe dinner option (on Saturdays) and "wonderful" Sunday brunch.

Lusardi's [S] 24 | 21 | 22 | $46

1885 Palmer Ave. (bet. Chatsworth Ave. & Depot Way), Larchmont, 914-834-5555

■ "Arguably" one of "the best Italians north of NYC", this sibling to the Manhattan eatery of the same name "brings a bit of polish to Larchmont" with "food fit for the fussiest palate", "gracious service" and an "elegant" setting ("in winter try to sit near the fireplace"); since it's "expensive but worth it", you'll need to "call far in advance to get reservations" on weekends.

Mighty Joe Young's [S] 20 | 22 | 19 | $37

610 W. Hartsdale Ave. (bet. Central Ave. & Dobbs Ferry Rd.), White Plains, 914-428-6868

■ "Mighty big portions, mighty big noise, mighty big check" is a mighty apt summary of this popular "jungle-themed" steakhouse in White Plains where dinner is a "fantasy safari complete with tiki torches and exotic grilled meats" like ostrich; while waiting for a table, families can enjoy the African bush–themed lounge area and singles can cozy up to the bar (a "meat market") for "killer mixed drinks."

Mulino's of Westchester ◐ 25 | 23 | 24 | $48

99 Court St. (bet. Martine Ave. & Quarropas St.), White Plains, 914-761-1818

■ "What a pleasant surprise to find this" "excellent upscale Northern Italian" "in Downtown White Plains" providing "comfort and sophistication" as well as "generous portions" of "wonderful food" presented by a "staff that will bend over backward" for you; like "its no-relation namesake in NYC", it can be "pricey", but its popularity with "power-scene" "politicos" and "romantics" alike means it "tends to book up", so "make your reservations early"; P.S. don't miss the "great Christmas decorations."

Old Drovers Inn [S] 25 | 26 | 25 | $56

Old Rte. 22 (E. Duncan Hill Rd.), Dover Plains, 845-832-9311

■ "You expect to see George and Martha at the next table" sinking wooden teeth into an "exceptional" traditional American meal at this "historic, romantic" Dover Plains inn that "deserves its stellar reputation" for "doing wonderful things" with our nation's cuisine; most agree it's "worth the drive" ("and expense"), since dining here is like "stepping back in time" to its 1750 founding, when people were shorter, so "watch your head" at the door.

121 S
▽ 24 | 19 | 20 | $36

2-4 Dingle Ridge Rd. (Rte. 121), North Salem, 914-669-0121

■ A "young crowd" "gathers for drinks" and "delicious", "well-prepared" New American fare at this yearling set in a "nice, old refurbished building" in North Salem; its "hip", "Hamptons-moved-north" ambiance is a "real surprise" considering it's in a corner of the county "lacking in restaurants"; mild-weather porch dining offers a respite from the sometimes "busy, noisy" interior.

Peter Pratt's Inn S
23 | 20 | 20 | $42

673 Croton Heights Rd. (Rte. 118), Yorktown, 914-962-4090

■ "Yorktown's restaurant jewel" may be this "charming" New American "romantically" established in a "wood-beamed" "colonial farmhouse" that's seen "a good slice of" history; it's "hard to find" but "well worth" it if you're game for "talented" chef-owner Jonathan Pratt's "creative cuisine"; however, even advocates allow that its "hip", casual approach to service and "musty" decor "need a tune-up."

Purdys Homestead S
24 | 25 | 23 | $52

100 Titicus Rd. (bet. Rtes. 22 & 116), North Salem, 914-277-2301

■ Customers coo that the "modern flair" of the "delicious and imaginative" New American menu is as bright as the "fireplaces in every room" of this "beautifully restored" 1775 North Salem homestead; though it's "especially welcoming on a snowy night", the "old colonial house's" "cozy and romantic" charm is ever-present, thanks to chef-owners Charles and Maureen Steppe, who provide a "quiet, dressy dining" "experience."

Restaurant X & Bully Boy Bar S
26 | 25 | 25 | $51

117 N. Rte. 303 (bet. Lake Rd. & Rte. 9W), Congers, 845-268-6555

■ "Wow, what a hit" the "'x'uberant" rant about this "go-to" New American "masterpiece"; enthusiasts swear owner Peter Kelly (of the Xaviar's duo) may be the "Alain Ducasse" of the Congers "boondocks" because he "does everything right" at this "divine" venture: the "cutting-edge" cuisine is "exquisitely prepared", the "ambiance is terrific" (particularly in the "garden room") and the staff has a "magical touch" that "leaves you happy."

Sun, Moon & Spoon S
24 | 23 | 21 | $45

Hudson Valley Health & Tennis Club, 100 River St.
(Hastings-on-Hudson RR station), Hastings-on-Hudson, 914-478-4481

■ The second floor of the Hudson Valley Health & Tennis Club in Hastings is the "unorthodox setting" for this "popular" yearling where foodies enjoy "imaginative" New American cuisine "with a Pacific Rim slant", as well as "winning" river views; "inventive" chef Jason Robison "strives to impress" with his creations, while wife Allison manages the "attractive room"; the fruit of their efforts is a "simply wonderful", "relaxing dining experience."

Terrapin S
27 | 19 | 26 | $42

250 Spillway Rd. (Rte. 28A), West Hurley, 845-331-3663

■ "Inventive combinations of flavors" characterize chef-owner Josh Kroner's "shockingly brilliant" New American cooking at this West Hurley "find"; his "friendly" staff runs a "cozy, woody dining room" that "shows what caring can accomplish", and the "backwoods location" near the Ashokan Reservoir allows for plenty of room for the organic garden that supplies the kitchen.

Xaviar's at Garrison 🅂⌷ 29 | 26 | 28 | VE
Highlands Country Club, Rte. 9D (Rte. 403), Garrison, 845-424-4228
■ "Always memorable", Peter Kelly's "jewel" in Garrison is
edged out of the No.1 spot for Food in Southern NY by its sibling,
but with an almost perfect score, who's counting?; the "sublime"
New American tasting menus inspire "fine-dining gluttony", with
each course "paired with perfect wines", and the Sunday brunch
buffet is a little slice of "sheer heaven"; N.B. prix fixe dinner Friday
and Saturday is $80 and includes wine; Sunday brunch is $40.

Xaviar's at Piermont 🅂⌷ 29 | 25 | 27 | VE
506 Piermont Ave. (Ash St.), Piermont, 845-359-7007
■ There may be a little sibling rivalry at Peter Kelly's "smaller,
more intimate" and younger Piermont offspring that's now No. 1
for Food in Southern NY; the "glorious" New American prix fixe
menu ($60, wine not included; Sunday brunch is $35) "makes you
glad you have something to celebrate", as do the "impeccable"
staff and "elegant", "beautiful setting"; in fact, only those who
don't have reservations are unhappy, so be sure to book early.

Zeph's 🅂 26 | 17 | 24 | $45
638 Central Ave. (bet. Depew St. & Rte. 9), Peekskill, 914-736-2159
■ Dining at this "out-of-the-way" Peekskill Eclectic hideaway
feels "like being a pampered guest in a great cook's home"; though
the "spartan-at-best" interior of this refurbished brick grist mill
could be "more inviting", the "friendly" staff and "reasonable
prices" on the "original" menu "whet one's appetite" for the
"glorious" creations to come.

St. Louis

TOP 10 FOOD RANKING

Restaurant	Cuisine Type
26 Sidney Street Cafe	New American
Trattoria Marcella	N&S Italian
25 Crossing	New American
Tony's	N&S Italian/Seafood
Zinnia	New American
24 Cafe de France	Classic French
Dominic's	Northern Italian
Pho Grand	Vietnamese
23 Kemoll's	Continental/N&S Italian
Cardwell's at the Plaza	International

ADDITIONAL NOTEWORTHY PLACES

Bar Italia Ristorante	Northern Italian
Cafe Mira	International
Frazer's	New American/Seafood
Giovanni's	N&S Italian
Harvest	New American
India Palace	Indian
Portabella	Mediterranean
Pueblo Solis	Mexican
Remy's Kitchen & Wine Bar	Mediterranean
Shiitake	Pan-Asian

F	D	S	C

Bar Italia Ristorante S   21 | 19 | 17 | $32
13 Maryland Ave. (Euclid Ave.), 314-361-7010
☑ Patrons praise this "trendy alternative" Central West Ender for its "fresh and imaginative" Northern Italian cuisine featuring "shades of the Mideast"; while the "fantastic patio" is "perfect for people-watching", "good luck getting a table there after 5:30 on a Friday"; some are bothered by "inconsistent service", but others say this place is "all about the charm" of its Eritrean owners.

Cafe de France   24 | 20 | 23 | $53
410 Olive St. (bet. Broadway & 4th St.), 314-231-2204
■ "An excellent splurge", this Downtown French with its "old-world feel" is an "elegant" choice for a "quiet, romantic dinner"; chef-owner Marcel Keraval "brings back Parisian memories" with "fabulous" creations that include what *amis* attest is "the best soufflé in town"; a few find service "stodgy", but most feel the "waiters treat you like the only customers in the place"; P.S. at press time, renovations to update the "aging" decor and add a casual bistro were slated for completion.

Cafe Mira   23 | 21 | 19 | $42 |

12 N. Meramec Ave. (bet. Forsyth Blvd. & Maryland Ave.), Clayton,
314-721-7801
■ Towers of "tall food" that "require deconstruction before eating"
characterize this Clayton International where chef-owner Mike
Johnson's "winning combinations" taste "as good as they look"
and "could hold their own anywhere in the country"; though the
"sophisticated", "always buzzing" atmosphere can get "too noisy",
a trip to this "solid performer" is "worth the ringing eardrums."

Cardwell's at the Plaza S   23 | 20 | 19 | $33 |

94 Plaza Frontenac (Lindbergh Blvd.), 314-997-8885
☑ "Chef David Owens is on the money" with his "consistently
delicious and imaginative" fare at this "trendy" International in
Frontenac Plaza that "always has something interesting" on
the menu; "vegetarians love this joint", as do "the tony ladies
who lunch"; while dissenters think "facing onto the mall (albeit
an upscale one) does detract from the atmosphere" and it can
get "noisy" and "hectic" at times, others opine this eatery is "a
treat" "during [or after] a full day of shopping."

Crossing   25 | 19 | 21 | $47 |

7823 Forsyth Blvd. (Central Ave.), Clayton, 314-721-7375
■ Two "ambitious and accomplished chef-owners", James Fiala
and Cary McDowell, design "superb dishes" (especially with "fresh
fish") at this "chic Clayton" spot where a "formal, but relaxed"
dining room and a "warm and welcoming" attitude have gourmands
gushing; while the New American fare and international wines are
"certainly pricey", most feel the place is "getting better all the time."

Dominic's   24 | 23 | 24 | $52 |

5101 Wilson Ave. (Hereford St.), 314-771-1632
■ "A longtime favorite", this "elegant" Northern Italian "icon
for special occasions" on the Hill still attracts with its "fabulous"
fare ("love their veal dishes") and "excellent service" – even if
the "calm and civil" atmosphere is "a bit stiff" for those who tire
of "hovering waiters"; "bring a fat wallet" because "prices are
steep", but "food that speaks for itself" makes all worthwhile.

Frazer's Traveling Brown Bag   22 | 14 | 19 | $28 |

1811 Pestalozzi St. (Lemp Ave.), 314-773-8646
■ Head to this "quirky", "fun" "happening place" (a "stone's throw"
from the Anheuser-Busch brewery) for "fresh seafood" dishes,
including the eponymous chef's "famous salmon", and a blackboard
of "wildly eclectic" New American specials; though fans "wish
others hadn't talked" about this once-"undiscovered wonder" –
"it's tougher to get a table" now – the "unpretentious, friendly
staff" and "groovy digs" keep them traveling here.

Giovanni's   ▽ 22 | 20 | 20 | $48 |

5201 Shaw Ave. (Marconi Ave.), 314-772-5958
☑ A "well-known landmark on the Hill", this Italian still offers an
"old-fashioned, very formal" experience; enthusiasts insist the
"traditionally rich entrees" and tuxedo-clad staff ensure "you never
go away unhappy", but while conceding it's "still a fine special-
occasion choice", critics cite "a decor of faded elegance" and
"jaded, stuffy service" as signs this vet "could use a bit of an
overhaul all around."

Harvest [S] 23 | 22 | 20 | $42

1059 S. Big Bend Blvd. (Clayton Rd.), 314-645-3522

◪ Happy harvesters say the "constantly changing" menu is "always a delight" at this Richmond Heights New American where chef-owner Steve Gontram's "fantastic use of seasonal ingredients", "a wine list out of this world" and the "best bread pudding ever" enthrall; detractors decry "overdone" dishes with "food piled on the plate like a sculpture" ("save me from their unrelenting creativity"), but most are "intrigued" and find the staff "friendly and polished"; P.S. "don't try to get in at dinnertime without a reservation."

India Palace [S] 23 | 17 | 19 | $22

Howard Johnson Hotel, 4534 N. Lindbergh Blvd. (I-70), Bridgeton, 314-731-3333

■ Devotees devour the "moist and flavorful" tandoori at this Indian "on top of a Howard Johnson's" in North County, delighting in the "great lunch buffet" where you're "in extreme danger of overeating"; while some say the Polynesian decor "makes you feel like a *Gilligan's Island* stowaway", the "spectacular views of the airport" and "courteous" service more than compensate, leading one reviewer to reveal "I could eat here seven days a week, but I'd never be size 6 again."

Kemoll's [S] 23 | 21 | 21 | $44

Metropolitan Square Bldg., 1 Metropolitan Sq. (bet. Olive & Pine Sts.), 314-421-0555

■ Owned by the same family since 1927, this "institution for special occasions" offers "upscale Continental-Italian dining Downtown"; a few old-timers still resent its move there (13 years ago!) but most only praise for "*molto*-size portions" of "rich food that's not for the diet-conscious" (e.g. "incredible cheese bread", "fantastic fried artichokes"); a "cozy, enveloping atmosphere" and "well-experienced staff" round out the "absolutely decadent" experience; P.S. "the early-bird menu is a steal."

Pho Grand [S] 24 | 17 | 21 | $14

3195 S. Grand Blvd. (Connecticut St.), 314-664-7435

■ From "great spring rolls" to the *bo luc lac* (shaking beef) to "must-have iced coffee", the "food is grand" at this "unbelievably popular" South City Vietnamese, which "continues its wonderful ways" and "super-cheap prices" in light, larger "cool new digs"; "the service is warm and efficient" too, leading surveyors to marvel "how do they do it?"

Portabella 22 | 18 | 19 | $38

15 N. Central Ave. (Forsyth Blvd.), Clayton, 314-725-6588

◪ Though no longer new, this "trendy place" remains "action central" "for Clayton movers and shakers" ("get a window table and watch Downtown go by"); but while the "well-dressed" insist the rustic Mediterranean "fusion fare still works" (especially at lunch), the "unimpressed" proletariat pouts "it's a little too chichi for my taste" – not to mention that "the noise level and racing waiters are distracting"; P.S. check out the "savvy bar scene", which "attracts a smart set."

Pueblo Solis 🅂   22   12   18 $23

5127 Hampton Ave. (Delor St.), 314-351-9000

■ "Watch the Solis family smoothly run the show" (mama Oralia's in the kitchen, son Alfredo's out front) at this "cramped South City" cantina that serves the "hands-down best Mexican [fare] in St. Louis", including "shrimp diablo that's just about the best thing you could do to a shrimp"; the "*auténtico*" food, plus "a wide variety of tequilas", ensures "you don't notice" that the "dark" "decor looks like somebody's basement rec room."

Remy's Kitchen & Wine Bar   23   20   20 $32

222 S. Bemiston Ave. (Bonhomme Ave.), Clayton, 314-726-5757

■ "What a delightful place" report reviewers on owner Tim Mallett's "hoppin'" hangout in Clayton, "always a favorite" "because there's always something new to try" on the "wide-ranging menu that leans toward Mediterranean flavors"; "tapas-like" "large and small plates to share" and "wine flights add to the fun atmosphere"; though it gets "sorta crowded", the decor (a "nice mix of casual and elegant") and "eager-to-please" staff help ease the squeeze.

Shiitake   22   23   22 $36

7927 Forsyth Blvd. (Central Ave.), Clayton, 314-725-4334

■ A "chichi" crowd comes to this Clayton creation, an avatar of "imaginative Pan-Asian fare" that ranges from "wonderful lettuce-cup appetizers" to sushi to lobster pad Thai, served amid "striking black-and-white decor"; a few fuss that the "fusion seems confused" and "earplugs are needed on weekends", but the majority rules that "eating here is as much fun as it is delicious."

Sidney Street Cafe   26   21   24 $42

2000 Sidney St. (Salena St.), 314-771-5777

■ The "storefront style and chalkboard menu belie the fine food" (rated No. 1 in St. Louis) served at this New American, "the place to go on the South Side"; surveyors "always leave stuffed", thanks to the "phenomenal lobster-filled fillet", "great beignets" and other "delicious" "food for people with a cholesterol deficiency" – served by "well-seasoned staffers"; "only downside: you can't go on impulse", since "reservations are hard to get."

Tony's   25   24   24 $63

410 Market St. (Broadway), 314-231-7007

■ Established in 1946, this "fancy" Italian seafood house remains "a landmark in Downtown St. Louis" and is "still the best on all counts" maintain many, who marvel at the "excellent" eats ("you can get anything you want, any way you want it"), "attentive staff" and "classically classy" digs; the irreverent insist its "reputation has exceeded reality", citing a "tired menu" and "overbearing service"; but pro or con, all agree that owner Vince Bommarito puts on "a big production, ending with a big check."

Trattoria Marcella　　　　　26 | 17 | 23 | $36
3600 Watson Rd. (Pernod Ave.), 314-352-7706

■ "Those Komorek brothers sure know how to run a restaurant" sing surveyors about Steve and Jamie's South City establishment, voted St. Louis' Most Popular; yes, the "stark surroundings" ("basically a lot of wall") get "crowded and noisy, but it's worth it" for "imaginative and exquisitely executed" "rustic Italian" dishes such as "sublime risotto" and "miraculous fried spinach and calamari" – dished up by a "superb staff"; best of all, it's "still a bargain", so "plan far in advance" to get a table.

Zinnia **S**　　　　　　　　25 | 20 | 23 | $38
7491 Big Bend Blvd. (Shrewsbury Ave.), Webster Groves, 314-962-0572

■ "The lilac-colored exterior lets you know you've found" this "Webster Groves gem", which long-memoried St. Louisans can't forget "used to be a gas station"; clearly, it's been the "best conversion ever", since surveyors salivate over the "creative, nuanced New American cooking" ("especially the outstanding seafood") of "David Guempel, the genius in the kitchen"; the "hosts and servers are always welcoming" too, making this flower a "perennial favorite."

Tampa Bay/Sarasota

TOP 10 FOOD RANKING

	Restaurant	Cuisine Type
29	Ritz-Carlton Din. Rm.	Classic French
28	Caffe Paradiso	Northern Italian
	Lafite at the Registry	Continental/New American
	Blue Heron	Eclectic
27	Peter's La Cuisine	Classic French
	Beach Bistro	New American/Med.
	Bern's Steak House	Steakhouse
	Mise en Place	Eclectic
	Bistro 41	New American
	Grill at Feather Sound	New American

ADDITIONAL NOTEWORTHY PLACES

Café L'Europe	Continental/New American
Euphemia Haye	Eclectic
Jasmine	Thai
Jonathan's	Continental/Eclectic
Maritana Grille	Floribbean
Michael's on East	New American
Ophelia's	Eclectic
Prawnbroker	Seafood
SideBern's	Asian/Fusion
Zoria	New American

F | D | S | C

Beach Bistro [S] 27 | 24 | 26 | $48

Resort 66, 6600 Gulf Dr. (66th St.), Holmes Beach, 941-778-6444

■ "In a word, fabulous!" gush gastronomes of this "little" New American–Med "jewel" tucked away in unassuming quarters on the "water's edge" in Holmes Beach; yes, it's "cramped", but "what it lacks in elbow room" it more than "makes up" for in its "subtle, complex" and "excellent" fare, award-winning wine list and "knowledgeable" service, not to mention its "spectacular sunset" views; it's so "marvelous all around" that the charmed sigh "when I die, I hope this is heaven."

Bern's Steak House [S] 27 | 22 | 27 | $49

1208 S. Howard Ave. (bet. Marjorie & Watrous Sts.), Tampa, 813-251-2421

■ "The best place in Florida for steaks", this "institution" has been drawing carnivores to Tampa's Hyde Park since 1957 with its "outstanding" aged cuts served by a "knowledgeable staff" in multi-roomed, "bordello"-like quarters; "it's as much a show as a meal" if you go on "the must tour" of the kitchen and the award-winning wine cellar; P.S. "don't miss the dessert room" upstairs, which boasts a new menu of decadent finales.

Bistro 41 S
27 | 21 | 25 | $33

Bell Tower Shops, 13499 S. Cleveland Ave. (Daniels Pkwy.), Ft. Myers, 941-466-4141

■ "A surprise treat" in an "upscale shopping center", this New American is a relative "newcomer" to Ft. Myers, but it has already won many hearts; the "imaginative" dishes are "very finely presented", and "top-notch, attentive service" befits the "fashionable surroundings"; P.S. there's a "nice bar area" too.

Blue Heron S
28 | 24 | 27 | $37

Shoppes at Clover Pl., 3285 Tampa Rd. (bet. Lake St. George & US 19), Palm Harbor, 727-789-5176

■ Perhaps the "best stop in North Pinellas County" for "fine upscale dining", this "romantic" Palm Harbor "gem" is justly renowned for Robert Stea's "unique" Eclectic "fusion" cuisine, prepared with ingredients that are "unsurpassed in quality"; his "exciting" "creations" are beautifully accompanied by a smallish but "well-appointed wine list" and served by a "quick and sharp" staff, resulting in a "consistently" "delightful" dinner experience.

Café L'Europe S
23 | 25 | 24 | $42

431 St. Armands Circle (Hwy. 41), Sarasota, 941-388-4415

☑ Co-owner Titus Letschert and chef Jeffrey Trefry have "changed direction" at this beloved Sarasota institution on "lively St. Armands Circle", ushering in an updated Continental–New American menu that causes "cutting-edge" types to gush "angels must be in the kitchen" but has traditionalists "missing some of the old standards"; everyone agrees, however, that it's hard to beat as a "dress-up" place for "special occasions", given its "elegant", "old-world" setting and "exceptional" service.

Caffe Paradiso
28 | 24 | 26 | $35

Colonial Shopper Shopping Ctr., 4205 S. MacDill Ave. (bet. Knight & Wallcraft Aves.), Tampa, 813-835-6622

■ "*Perfecto!*" cheer admirers of this hideaway in South Tampa that feels just "like being in Italy" thanks to its "authentic", "delicious" Northern-style dishes, "relaxing yet elegant" setting and "friendly" "personalized" service; with such "moderate prices", patrons can return often to "feel pampered."

Euphemia Haye S
26 | 23 | 24 | $45

5540 Gulf of Mexico Dr. (Gulfbay Rd.), Longboat Key, 941-383-3633

■ "Absolutely the best restaurant for roast duckling" (the house specialty), this "consistently excellent" Longboat Key treasure offers seating options in the "quirkily" decorated yet "romantic" downstairs space and upstairs in the "casual" HayeLoft piano bar; either way, expect a "superb" Eclectic dinner delivered by a staff that pays "attention to every detail"; just be sure to check out the "awesome dessert room", "the place to go" for a sweet indulgence.

Grill at Feather Sound
27 | 22 | 22 | $39

2325 Ulmerton Rd. (Egret Blvd.), Clearwater, 727-571-3400

■ "Trendy in the best sense of the word", this Clearwater New American grill manages to be *très* "chic" despite its location in a "strip mall" (with "no view of Feather Sound" to boot); its hip clientele is drawn to its "innovative" menu (think sambal-grilled ostrich tenderloin), "sophisticated" ambiance and "excellent, knowledgeable" service; the only downside: the "terrible noise."

Jasmine Thai S 26 | 22 | 24 | $24
13248 N. Dale Mabry Hwy. (Fletcher Ave.), Tampa, 813-968-1501
■ Management's assertion that the princess of Thailand ate at this Tampa Siamese on a visit to the area is wholly plausible considering its high ratings and "excellent" dishes like pad Thai and whole red snapper; the "small" space sports a purple-hued garden look.

Jonathan's – | – | – | M
West Gate Promenade Mall, 6777 Manatee Ave. W. (67th St. W.), Bradenton, 941-761-1177
Chef-owner Jonathan Shute sets the bar high at this modest Bradenton strip mall unaccustomed to white tablecloths, fresh flowers and fine dining; at his intimate charmer, he specializes in spinning fresh twists on New Orleans classics like oysters Bienville and crawfish étouffée, while also featuring sweet surprises like Asian-inspired smoked-duck spring rolls and corn-fed beef.

Lafite at the Registry Resort S 28 | 28 | 27 | $53
Registry Resort, 475 Seagate Dr. (south of Vanderbilt Beach Rd.), Naples, 941-597-3232
■ Housed in one of the tonier properties in tony Naples, this Continental–New American resplendent with crystal chandeliers is the embodiment of opulence; its sumptuous dishes are simply "excellent" and presented with "elegance", but with such "break-the-bank" prices, it may be best reserved for "special occasions."

Maritana Grille S 27 | 26 | 25 | $53
Don CeSar Beach Resort, 3400 Gulf Blvd. (Pinellas Bayway), St. Petersburg Beach, 727-360-1882
■ Living up to its designation as the signature dining room at St. Pete's historic Don CeSar Beach Resort, this "wonderful" "jewel of a restaurant" earns enthusiastic accolades for its "innovative", "delicious" Floribbean menu, "classy" environment appointed with an aquatic motif and "top"-notch service; though it may be a "little overpriced", it's "fabulous in all regards" and even boasts one of the area's few chef's tables, set up right in the kitchen.

Michael's on East 26 | 26 | 24 | $43
Midtown Plaza, 1212 East Ave. S. (bet. Bahia Vista & Prospect Sts.), Sarasota, 941-366-0007
■ You'll think you've "died and gone to NYC" at this Sarasota New American that has again been voted the Gulf Coast's Most Popular restaurant; the "sweeping neo–art deco" setting (a "sophisticated" surprise given its strip-mall location) "seduces" as much as the "outstanding" modern renditions "served with elegance", and it now features a raw bar that cements this "institution's" position as the nexus of "power lunches", glam wine-tastings and dinner experiences that are near-"perfect every time."

Mise en Place 27 | 23 | 24 | $41
442 W. Kennedy Blvd. (Grand Central St.), Tampa, 813-254-5373
■ Expect a "big-city buzz" upon entering this "comfortable", pastel-colored Eclectic in Downtown Tampa, where chef-owner Marty Blitz proffers an "innovative" weekly menu of "outstanding" dishes employing "exotic ingredients" (ostrich, purple potatoes); winning California wines, a "courteous" service team and relatively sane prices further explain why admirers "do not miss" a chance to dine here.

Ophelia's S
26 | 25 | 24 | $41

9105 Midnight Pass Rd. (south of Turtle Beach), Siesta Key, 941-349-2212

■ "Siesta Key's most romantic waterfront" eatery may well be this Eclectic "date place" where "superior chef" Mitch Rosenbaum masterminds "imaginative", "superb" fare that's enhanced by the "elegant", "beautiful" surroundings and a "can't-be-beat view" of the bay; factor in an "excellent" wine selection and "outstanding" service from a "high-class" staff, and "pricey" though it may be, the whole package is simply "tops" for a "formal special evening."

Peter's La Cuisine S
27 | 25 | 26 | $48

2224 Bay St. (Hendry St.), Ft. Myers, 941-332-2228

■ A Gulf Coast mecca for "special occasions", this "quaint little spot for exceptional dining" "in an older part of Ft. Myers" hits the mark with "outstanding" Classic French cuisine reflecting "special touches in preparation and presentation", served in an "elegant" room by an "attentive" staff; "if you want to impress, this will do it"; P.S. check out the "fun" rooftop disco bars.

Prawnbroker S
26 | 23 | 24 | $30

13451-16 McGregor Blvd. (Cypress Lake Dr.), Ft. Myers, 941-489-2226

■ It was "completely renovated" not long ago, but this Ft. Meyers "standby" (it's two decades old) continues to provide "wonderful seafood" dishes that showcase some of the "best- tasting fish" around; plus, "you can always count on" dining in comfort in the "casual" room.

Ritz-Carlton Dining Room S
29 | 29 | 28 | $56

The Ritz-Carlton Naples, 280 Vanderbilt Beach Rd. (Gulfshore Dr.), Naples, 941-598-6644

■ "What all fine restaurants should be", this "really special" (it was voted No. 1 for Food on the Gulf Coast) and beautifully appointed dining room in the Ritz-Carlton Naples provides "luxury at its best", showcasing "excellent" Classic French cuisine, accompanied by a wine selection of nearly 700 labels and proffered by an impeccable pro staff ("if you want to feel pampered, this is the place"); P.S. the eight-course blind "tasting menu is expensive but a real challenge."

SideBern's S
27 | 23 | 23 | $36

2208 W. Morrison Ave. (S. Howard Ave.), Tampa, 813-258-2233

■ "Hats off to the chef", who gets a "chance to show off" at this "excellent" SoHo "spin-off" of the revered Bern's Steak House by introducing "innovative" Asian-accented "fusion" dishes to the menu (don't miss the "unique" dim sum or exquisite desserts); factor in an "incredible wine list", "chic" atmosphere and "smooth" service, and it's easy to see why so many admirers "love this place."

Zoria S
26 | 18 | 24 | $36

1934 Hillview St. (Tamiami Trail S.), Sarasota, 941-955-4457

■ Lovers of "superb fusion cuisine" insist "it doesn't get much better than this" New American in Sarasota's trendy Southside Village, where the "inventive menu" features "excellent" dishes marked by "lovely presentations" (don't miss the "deadly" desserts); the only drawback is the room's "impossible noise", though a recent soundproofing gives ringing ears some relief.

TOP 10 FOOD RANKING

Restaurant	Cuisine Type
28 Ventana Room	New American
27 Dish	Eclectic
Janos	SW/Classic French
25 Cafe Poca Cosa	Mexican
Le Rendez-Vous	Classic French
Tack Room	Continental
Wildflower	New American
Gold Room	SW/Continental
24 Gavi	N&S Italian
¡Fuego!	Southwestern

ADDITIONAL NOTEWORTHY PLACES

Anthony's/Catalinas	Continental
Arizona Inn	Continental
Café Terra Cotta	Southwestern
Daniel's	Northern Italian
Grill at Hacienda del Sol	New American
J Bar	Mexican
Kingfisher	New American/Seafood
Le Bistro	French Bistro
McMahon's	Steakhouse
Mi Nidito	Mexican

F	D	S	C

Anthony's in the Catalinas S   22 | 26 | 23 | $41
6440 N. Campbell Ave. (E. Skyline Dr.), 520-299-1771
◪ Nestled in the Catalina foothills, this "special-occasion" spot receives a plethora of plaudits for its "million-dollar" patio and dining room views of the city lights and one of the "best wine lists in the Southwest" (over 1,400 choices); but while pros praise the "consistently good" Continental food, others opine that it's "dull."

Arizona Inn S   22 | 25 | 24 | $32
Arizona Inn, 2200 E. Elm St. (bet. N. Campbell Ave. & N. Tucson Blvd.), 520-325-1541
■ Set in a "classic" hotel where "finger bowls" and "beautiful gardens" create the kind of "lovely refined atmosphere" that captures "old Tucson", this "sedate" Continental attracts a clientele of "blue-blooded" seniors and celebrities; the "conservative" menu may not excite cutting-edge diners, but the "lovely" ambiance "reeks of class."

Cafe Poca Cosa   25 | 22 | 22 | $21

Clarion Santa Rita Hotel, 88 E. Broadway Blvd. (S. Scott Ave.), 520-622-6400

■ "Cheerful", "bustling" Downtown Tucson Mexican where the inventive menu changes twice a day and the words "unique" and "creative" apply to both the brightly colored "trendy decor", which includes Oaxacan folk art masks, and the "huge portions" of "glorious" "gourmet" cooking ("chicken mole so good you'll weep").

Café Terra Cotta S   24 | 22 | 22 | $27

3500 E. Sunrise Dr. (Campo Abierto), 520-577-8100

☑ While it's seen the birth of many imitators, this "polished", boldly colored Tucson favorite has "maintained its edge after all these years" and continues to be a "wonderful place to bring guests" for "fun selections" of "original Southwestern" cuisine, good wines by the glass and a pair of "delightful patios"; N.B. a post-*Survey* relocation may outdate the above decor score.

Daniel's S   23 | 24 | 23 | $36

St. Philip's Plaza, 4340 N. Campbell Ave. (E. River Rd.), 520-742-3200

☑ "Stately" decor, a "formal" but "restful" ambiance, "delicious" cuisine and a "good wine list" make this bi-level Northern Italian an "upscale" choice for "gracious", "special-occasion" dining; though some find it "pretentious" and "overrated", more say that it's "worth a return", especially on an "expense account."

Dish   27 | 22 | 26 | $34

3200 E. Speedway Blvd. (N. Country Club Rd.), 520-326-1714

■ So "cozy" "it feels like coming home", this "jewel box" "hidden" behind Rum Runner Wine & Cheese is lauded as a "sparkling experience" because of its "first-class" Eclectic food, "extensive wine list" (30 by the glass) and "pampering" service.

¡Fuego! S   24 | 20 | 22 | $32

Santa Fe Sq., 6958 E. Tanque Verde Rd. (N. Sabino Canyon Rd.), 520-886-1745

■ Wild game such as Rocky Mountain elk and Alaskan caribou are some of the "daring" choices on the "creative" menu of this Tucson Southwestern, which also serves "wonderful", tamer meat and seafood dishes and has a warm, comfortable setting highlighted by a large hearth; oenophiles will want to take advantage of the award-winning, California-oriented wine list.

Gavi   24 | 16 | 20 | $23

Foothills Mall, 7401 N. La Cholla Blvd. (W. Ina Rd.), 520-219-9200 S
6960 E. Sunrise Dr. (N. Kolb Rd.), 520-615-1900
7865 E. Broadway Blvd. (N. Pantano Rd.), 520-290-8380

■ Go "early" or expect a "long wait" for a table at these "casual" "family-run" Italians, which serve "big portions" of "cheap", "phenomenal" dishes ("pasta par excallence") in "lively" dining rooms, some of which are soccer-themed; signature dishes include spicy calamari and satisfying tiramisu.

Gold Room S   25 | 26 | 24 | $40

Westward Look Resort, 245 E. Ina Rd. (bet. N. 1st Ave. & N. Oracle Rd.), 520-297-1151

■ "Beautiful views" of Downtown from a "lovely" patio and brightly colored dining room attract aesthetes to this "elegant" resort dining venue where the menu is divided between Southwestern dishes using herbs from the chef's garden and Continental entrees such as filet mignon.

Grill at Hacienda del Sol [S]
– | – | – | E

Hacienda del Sol, 5601 N. Hacienda del Sol (bet. E. River Rd. & E. Sunrise Dr.), 520-529-3500

Housed in a historic resort (formerly a girl's finishing school), this beautiful, wood-beamed New American offers fine dining in a scenic foothills setting that captures the relaxed hospitality of the region; if the views and the award-winning wine list don't wow you, the simple but elegant entrees (many grilled over pecan wood) probably will.

Janos
27 | 25 | 25 | $48

Westin La Paloma, 3770 E. Sunrise Dr. (bet. N. Campbell Ave. & N. Swan Rd.), 520-615-6100

◪ Now firmly established in its "marvelous setting", "great chef" Janos Wilder's "spectacular" space in the foothills enhances his "imaginative" Southwestern–Classic French interpretations with an "outstanding view", as well as with "excellent wines" and "solicitous" service; it's an "original" that pleases the palate as much as it "hits the wallet", and if nostalgists still "miss the old location", Wilder's disciples declare he "sets the standard" no matter where he sets up shop.

J Bar
▽ 23 | 23 | 23 | $27

Westin La Paloma, 3770 E. Sunrise Dr. (bet. N. Campbell Ave. & N. Swan Rd.), 520-615-6100

■ Bright and tourist-friendly, Janos Wilder's newest operation (right next to Janos) features Mexican specialties – sometimes spiced with a Caribbean accent – that come off as a "creative take on old friends"; noting that it shares a patio overlooking the city lights with its tony neighbor, wallet-watchers ask "how can you beat Janos at half the price?"

Kingfisher Bar & Grill ◐ [S]
22 | 17 | 21 | $30

2564 E. Grant Rd. (N. Tucson Blvd.), 520-323-7739

◪ "Loved it" even though the "decor could be updated" – so says the conflicted clientele of this New American fish house, known for "super seafood" and freshly shucked "oysters to die for" served in a "barnlike room"; the "lively atmosphere" and "thoughtful wine list" make it a popular "late-night spot" among "singles" and "Gen Xers" who find the "weird" digs "cool" and "retro hip."

Le Bistro [S]
23 | 20 | 22 | $32

2574 N. Campbell Ave. (bet. E. Glenn St. & E. Grant Rd.), 520-327-3086

■ Laurent Reux is a "wonderful" "chef-owner who cares", and the proof is in the "dependable, excellent" French food and "sumptuous desserts" that make this "cozy" bistro an area "favorite"; the menu takes a seafaring slant ("best steamed mussels in town"), and insiders say it's especially "great for lunch."

Le Rendez-Vous [S]
25 | 21 | 22 | $37

3844 E. Ft. Lowell Rd. (N. Alvernon Way), 520-323-7373

■ It's "Paris in the desert" at this Classic Gallic "gem", home to the "best Dover sole in the state", a "*magnifique*" Grand Marnier soufflé and other "traditional" fare served in an atmosphere "thick" with "romantic charm"; if the sauces seem a bit "rich", that's one measure of their "real French flavor"; N.B. the five-course prix fixe menu is priced at $70 for two.

McMahon's Prime Steakhouse S | 24 | 26 | 22 | $48 |

2959 N. Swan Rd. (bet. E. Ft. Lowell Rd. & E. Glenn St.), 520-327-2333

☑ Surveyors are split on whether this "elegant" steakhouse is "just like dining in New York" or "much ado about nothing", but carnivores concur the "excellent" beef "does not disappoint"; faced with a widespread observation that it's "way overpriced", regulars advise "take friends and split orders" or get yourself an "expense account."

Mi Nidito ●S | 24 | 16 | 19 | $16 |

1813 S. Fourth Ave. (E. 29th St.), 520-622-5081

■ "President Clinton ate here", giving official credence to this "authentic", "homey" cantina's standing as "possibly the best Sonoran in town"; no doubt POTUS skipped the "long wait", but local VIPs cheerfully "stand in line" for "a great meal" amid "Mexican ambiance to the max."

Tack Room S | 25 | 25 | 26 | $49 |

7300 E. Vactor Ranch Trail (E. Tanque Verde Rd.), 520-722-2800

☑ A "longtime staple" for "top-notch food with a Western accent", this revered Continental makes patrons "feel important" with its "formal" setting, "superb service" and "excellent food and wine"; modernists dismiss the "stuffy" style as "out of date", but the many who reckon it one of "Arizona's finest" "applaud the resistance to change"; N.B. dinner only.

Ventana Room S | 28 | 28 | 28 | $47 |

Loews Ventana Canyon Resort, 7000 N. Resort Dr. (N. Kolb Rd.), 520-299-2020

■ Tucson's Most Popular restaurant is also No. 1 for Food, and its champions crown it "best in the West" for its "spectacular views" and "supreme", "beautifully presented" New American fare; defying expectations for a "hotel setting", it complements its "lovely" atmosphere with "impeccable service" (and a musician) to make for a "special occasion" "every time"; N.B. dinner only.

Wildflower S | 25 | 21 | 22 | $29 |

Casas Adobes, 7037 N. Oracle Rd. (W. Ina Rd.), 520-219-4230

☑ Even advocates admit this "busy" "NY bistro–style" source of "adventurous" New American cuisine is "noisy", but they put up with "poor acoustics" to enjoy a "good wine list" and "trendy" food that's "always tasty" and "sometimes great"; if a few contrarians contend the performance is "inconsistent", the majority simply sighs "oh, that warm lobster salad!"

Washington, DC

TOP 20 FOOD RANKING

Restaurant	Cuisine Type
29 Inn at Little Washington	New American
28 Makoto	Japanese
27 Kinkead's	New American/Seafood
Citronelle	New French
Gerard's Place	New French
Obelisk	Northern Italian
L'Auberge Chez François	Classic French
Melrose	New American
L'Auberge Provençale	Classic French
Marcel's*	New French/Belgian
26 Galileo/Il Laboratorio	N&S Italian
Vidalia	New American/Southern
Prime Rib	Steakhouse
Prince Michel	Classic French
1789	American
Seasons	New American
Nora	New American
25 Kaz Sushi Bistro	Japanese
Morton's of Chicago	Steakhouse
Rabieng	Thai

ADDITIONAL NOTEWORTHY PLACES

Bis	French Bistro
Black's Bar & Kitchen	Seafood
Bombay Club	Indian
Bread Line	Eclectic/Sandwich Shop
Cafe Atlantico	Nuevo Latino
Carlyle Grand Cafe	New American
Caucus Room	American
D.C. Coast	New American/Seafood
Equinox	New American
Etrusco	N&S Italian
Georgia Brown's	Southern/Soul Food
Jaleo	Spanish
Johnny's Half Shell	Seafood
Majestic Cafe	New American
Old Ebbitt Grill	American
Palena	New American
Pizzeria Paradiso	Pizza
Red Sage	Southwestern
Smith & Wollensky	Steakhouse
Taberna del Alabardero	Spanish

* Tied with the restaurant listed directly above it

Bis S   25 | 24 | 22 | $44

*Hotel George, 15 E St., NW (bet. New Jersey Ave. & N. Capitol St.),
202-661-2700*

■ "Political electricity" sparks this "stunning" French bistro, a
strong "vote-getter on Capitol Hill" whose "superb" American-
influenced Gallic classics (including escargots "bursting with
flavor"), "chic bar" and "seductive lighting" have made it a
"trendy" "star-watching" destination; the bottom line: "this
one's a real comer."

Black's Bar & Kitchen S   22 | 17 | 19 | $35

*7750 Woodmont Ave. (bet. Cheltenham Dr. & Old Georgetown Rd.),
Bethesda, MD, 301-652-6278*

◪ Jeff and Barbara Black "do it again" at this "energetic"
Bethesda venue with "innovative" Gulf Coast–influenced
American seafood dishes (especially the "ethereal" fish), an
"upbeat" oyster bar, a nicely appointed room and some of the
most desirable patio and deck seating around; as might be
expected of an 'in' place, it's often "crowded."

Bombay Club S   25 | 26 | 25 | $38

815 Connecticut Ave., NW (bet. H & I Sts.), 202-659-3727

■ "You don't need a sari to be treated like a rani" by the truly
"impeccable" staff at this "sophisticated" Indian near the White
House, a "quiet", "civilized" "power lunch" haunt with a "British
colonial" club feel that makes for an "elegant" backdrop for the
"wonderful" fare (the tandoori salmon is terrific).

Bread Line   21 | 12 | 14 | $12

1751 Pennsylvania Ave., NW (bet. 17th & 18th Sts.), 202-822-8900

■ Mark Furstenberg is a "perfectionist" who brings "four-star
talent" to the "$10 lunch" trade, and his "astronomically good"
breads and sandwiches have "revolutionized the White House–
area lunch scene"; yes, his Eclectic bakery is "a bit frenzied"
and "minimalist", but the "long lines are testimony" to DC's
"appreciation of quality."

Cafe Atlantico S   23 | 23 | 20 | $35

405 Eighth St., NW (bet. D & E Sts.), 202-393-0812

■ Though James Beard nominee José Ramon Andrés, the
founding chef, has moved on from this "voguish" piece of "Rio
de Janeiro on Eighth Street" to Jaleo, word is that his successor
continues to turn out "cutting-edge" Nuevo Latino creations that
are "tops"; the Penn Quarter setting is just as "dramatic" as ever,
and the bar continues to mix "wonderful" Latin cocktails; P.S. try
the "amazing dim sum brunch."

Carlyle Grand Cafe S   24 | 21 | 21 | $29

4000 S. 28th St. (Quincy St.), Shirlington, VA, 703-931-0777

■ This "classy" New American surely "put Shirlington on the
culinary map" thanks to its "consistently" "excellent" seasonal
menu, "beautiful" surroundings and "affordable" pricing; the
service is "fast-paced", but regulars warn it draws such big crowds
that there are often "long waits", so better reserve in advance.

Caucus Room – | – | – | E

401 Ninth St., NW (D St.), 202-393-1300

It would be hard to find a more stately setting for doing the nation's business than this polished mahogany Downtown haunt, with its see-and-be-seen glass-walled dining rooms, clubby booths and barroom; it's owned by pros Michael Sternberg and Larry Work (whose specialties are VIP cosseting and prime aged beef), political heavies and big business, and features a well-rounded American menu that attracts the likes of Vernon Jordan and Pat Moynihan.

Citronelle 27 | 25 | 25 | $61

(aka Michel Richard's Citronelle)

Latham Hotel, 3000 M St., NW (30th St.), 202-625-2150

■ "Michel stays – we win"; chef-owner Michel Richard's full-time dedication to his Georgetown "splurge" destination ensures that this is "everything a restaurant should be", with "exceptional", "cutting-edge" New French fare and a "superb wine list"; the "elegant yet understated" approach comes off as "cool" to some, though not to those dining stoveside at the chef's table in the spectacular glass-walled kitchen.

D.C. Coast 25 | 24 | 23 | $44

1401 K St., NW (14th St.), 202-216-5988

■ *The* "hip Downtown place" for "A-list" "young pros", this "stylish" New American makes "sophisticated dining" fun with its "wonderful", "original" seafood dishes, "great energy", "stargazing potential" and a "soaring" space with striking sight lines; it's also one of DC's toughest reservations, but be forewarned that if you don't nab a table on the "quieter" balcony, the "only way to have a conversation will be over your cell phone."

Equinox [S] 24 | 19 | 22 | $45

818 Connecticut Ave., NW (I St.), 202-331-8118

◪ "Rising star" chef-owner Todd Gray is in the kitchen at this New American in Farragut Square – a most "welcome addition" to the neighborhood – creating "exciting" but "refreshingly unpretentious" seasonal dishes, while his wife Ellen works the front of the house and attends to "Washington's power" elite.

Etrusco [S] – | – | – | E

1606 20th St., NW (bet. Connecticut Ave. & Q St.), 202-667-0047

Chef Francesco Ricchi "is back in DC where he belongs" at this soothing Dupont Circle ristorante whose "great room" (a barrel-vaulted atrium) beautifully complements his personalized take on Italian cuisine; predictions that "this could be a favorite" are borne out by all the well-known faces in attendance.

Galileo [S] 26 | 24 | 24 | $57

1110 21st St., NW (bet. L & M Sts.), 202-293-7191

Il Laboratorio

1110 21st St., NW (bet. L & M Sts.), 202-293-7191

■ "Elegant", if "a little stuffy", Roberto Donna's "power" haunt has long been considered the "best of the best for that important lunch or dinner" Downtown thanks to "outstanding" Italian fare and "top-notch" service; he's earning even more applause at hot, hot Il Laboratorio (his "spectacular" showcase restaurant within Galileo) where several nights a week he crafts a tasting menu "extravaganza", an "out-of-this-world" experience.

Georgia Brown's 🅂   23 | 23 | 21 | $35

950 15th St., NW (bet. I & K Sts.), 202-393-4499

■ "Stunning" and "sophisticated", this Downtown Southern belle entices "Washington insiders", "celebrities" and visiting firemen with its "y'all-come"-by hospitality; even if its "delectable" Soul Food "clogs some arteries", the staff's professionalism and "energy" "warm" all hearts; P.S. check out the "great jazz brunch."

Gerard's Place   27 | 23 | 25 | $59

915 15th St., NW (bet. I & K Sts.), 202-737-4445

■ "Simple elegance" distinguishes this Downtown knockout where eponymous chef Gerard Pangaud masterminds a "brilliant" New French menu; his "gourmet" innovations are proffered by a highly "knowledgeable" staff in a "quiet", "intimate" environment that's ideal for power meals and romantic rendezvous alike; of course it's "pricey", but it's "outstanding in every regard" and "well worth the splurge."

Inn at Little Washington 🅂   29 | 29 | 29 | $90

Main & Middle Sts., Washington, VA, 540-675-3800

■ "In a class of its own" and once again the *Washington, DC Survey*'s No. 1 restaurant for Food, this "national treasure" in the Virginia countryside epitomizes a "sybaritic dining experience" with "exquisite" New American cooking that's the "gastronomic equivalent of sex", an "extravagant" "gold mine of an interior" and "phenomenal" service; given its high visibility, it's a tribute to owners Patrick O'Connell and Reinhardt Lynch that so many followers "salute" this inn as "absolutely" "unforgettable."

Jaleo 🅂   23 | 20 | 19 | $28

480 Seventh St., NW (E St.), 202-628-7949
72-71 Woodmont Ave. (Elm St.), Bethesda, MD, 301-913-0003

■ The "food and atmosphere pulse with excitement" at this Penn Quarter Spanish "scene" where the "sangria's a must", as are the "scrumptious" tapas; though the limited-reservations policy and "waits" at prime times are drawbacks, the majority thinks that this is a seriously "fun" "place to gather with friends"; N.B. José Ramon Andrés' new Bethesda offshoot is a runaway hit.

Johnny's Half Shell   24 | 18 | 21 | $32

2002 P St., NW (bet. 20th & 21st Sts.), 202-296-2021

■ A "rising star" in Dupont Circle, this "hip" but "completely unpretentious" bistro is creating quite a buzz with its "sparkling" fresh, "creatively" prepared seafood dishes and "first-rate" international wine list; be warned, however, that it doesn't take reservations and it's "too small" to squeeze in all comers, so "get there early" or try to snag a seat at the white-marble bar.

Kaz Sushi Bistro   25 | 20 | 21 | $32

1915 I St., NW (bet. 18th & 20th Sts.), 202-530-5500

■ Chef-owner Kaz Okochi delights the "eye and the palate" with "fresh, creative appetizers", "terrific, imaginative" raw-fish creations ("waiter, there's a mango in my sushi") and delightful desserts (the green tea tiramisu is "to die for") at this "minimalist", "postmodern" Japanese bistro near the World Bank; it pulls in a "hip, young crowd", major "foodies" and chefs who overlook the "slow" service as they anticipate the "truly exciting choices."

Kinkead's 🅂   27 | 24 | 25 | $49

2000 Pennsylvania Ctr., 2000 Pennsylvania Ave., NW (I St., bet. 20th & 21st Sts.), 202-296-7700

■ Bob Kinkead's "original" seafood-slanted New American cooking has made this power-central spot the *Washington, DC Survey*'s Most Popular restaurant and thus one of the toughest reservations in town; its "no-kinks" perfectionism "instantly impresses" with "stylish" surroundings, a "knowledgeable" (if "arrogant") staff and "superb fish dishes" regarded as "the best" in town.

L'Auberge Chez François 🅂   27 | 27 | 27 | $55

332 Springvale Rd. (2 mi. north of Georgetown Pike), Great Falls, VA, 703-759-3800

■ "Who doesn't love this woodsy outpost of Alsatian cooking" in Great Falls with its "adorable" Provençal decor, "warm" ambiance and "romantic" garden?; the Haeringer family is to be commended for "leaving well enough alone" by continuing to offer a "glorious" five-course prix fixe Classic French menu that may be the "best fine-dining value" around; in sum, it's an "unparalleled experience."

L'Auberge Provençale 🅂   27 | 26 | 26 | $63

13630 Lord Fairfax Hwy. (Rte. 50), Boyce, VA, 540-837-1375

■ Chef-owner Alain Borel and his wife Celeste are "delightful" hosts and their antique-filled pre–Revolutionary War manor house in the Virginia Hunt Country is a "hopelessly romantic" destination for Classic French dining; whether you linger over an "absolutely fabulous" five-course prix fixe dinner in the "beautiful" garden room or on the patio, it promises to be "lovely all the way."

Majestic Cafe 🅂   – | – | – | M

911 King St. (Patrick St.), Alexandria, VA, 703-837-9117

Chef-partner Susan Lindeborg's warmhearted tribute to Old Town Alexandria's 'good eats' restaurant legacy sports a personal-size dining room that blends art deco elements with modern comforts, suitable for anything from a casual burger to a celebration; its a perfect match for her highly regarded, regionally inspired New American dishes, plus there's a spiffy bar for sipping, supping and scoping the street.

Makoto 🅂   28 | 23 | 26 | $49

4822 MacArthur Blvd., NW (Reservoir Rd.), 202-298-6866

■ "Wear respectable socks" when taking "visiting dignitaries" and guests to this top-rated, "authentic" Japanese in the Palisades, where patrons dine shoeless in a "tiny", "exquisitely simple" "traditional" room while a "charming" staff serves "outstanding" tidbits that amount to "food as art"; P.S. if "little cubes at little tables" aren't your thing, there's also a "gem" of a sushi bar.

Marcel's   27 | 24 | 24 | $58

2401 Pennsylvania Ave., NW (24th St.), 202-296-1166

■ "Talented" chef Robert Wiedmaier's "wonderful" West End French-Belgian quickly rocketed into an "elite class" shortly after it opened thanks to "hearty" and "adventurous" cooking ("the duck is a treat", and the desserts are "mouthwatering") paired with "outstanding" wine service, as well as a "romantic" (albeit sometimes "loud"), "provincial" ambiance, beckoning sidewalk cafe and "gracious maitre d'"; in sum: "a winner."

Melrose [S] 27 25 26 $51

Park Hyatt Hotel, M & 24th Sts., NW, 202-955-3899

■ Overcome your "anti–hotel" dining room bias at this "spacious", "classy" West End "refuge" that showcases "refined" New American cuisine, museum-worthy art, an "elegant" outdoor courtyard and "gracious" service; it's "a good business restaurant", a "classy spot" for celebratory weekend dining and dancing, a "standard"-setting Sunday brunch pick and a smart choice for "super" holiday dinners; truth be told, it's awfully "hard to fault."

Morton's of Chicago [S] 25 22 23 $51

Washington Sq., 1050 Connecticut Ave., NW (L St.), 202-955-5997
3251 Prospect St., NW (Wisconsin Ave.), 202-342-6258
Reston Town Ctr., 11956 Market St. (Library St.), Reston, VA, 703-796-0128
Fairfax Sq., 8075 Leesburg Pike (Aline Rd.), Tysons Corner, VA, 703-883-0800

■ "Unreconstructed beef eaters" laud the "fantastic" porterhouse and other "decadent", "gut-busting" portions of prime meats served at these "dark", clubby steakhouses; patrons also enjoy being treated like "power brokers" by the "knowledgeable" staff, but they can skip "being introduced to their entree" as part of the pre-ordering ritual.

Nora 26 24 24 $51

2132 Florida Ave., NW (bet. Connecticut & Massachusetts Aves.), 202-462-5143

■ Nora Pouillon sure knows how to make "all-organic" dining taste "so much better than it sounds" at this "exceptional" New American set in a "romantic" room above Dupont Circle; it's "very big with official Washington" and many discerning diners, even if a few quibblers call it "too politically correct" and "costly."

Obelisk 27 22 26 $57

2029 P St., NW (bet. 20th & 21st Sts.), 202-872-1180

■ For a "superb" experience that's like "eating fine food at someone's home", indulge in this "gem" off Dupont Circle that captures the Italian sensibility with its "simple, pure and satisfying" seasonal cooking; admirers urge "be open-minded" and let the chef's "creative prix fixe menus stimulate your palate"; just as "wonderful" are the wines and the "special" service.

Old Ebbitt Grill ◐ [S] 20 22 20 $31

675 15th St., NW (bet. F & G Sts.), 202-347-4801

■ DC's big, handsome, neo-Edwardian "public club" (think dark paneling and "period" gas lamps) set in a prime Downtown locale provides a highly Washingtonian backdrop for everything from "power breakfasts" to "late-night oysters"; its "bar scene" draws plenty of "politicos", as do the "classic" American food and "helpful" staff, but even if they falter, "it's the atmosphere, stupid."

Palena – – – E

3529 Connecticut Ave., NW (Porter St.), 202-537-9250

Frank Ruta and Ann Amernick, two of DC's top toque talents, are delighting foodies with his savory French- and Italian-influenced New American dishes (inventive but never strange) and her picture-perfect, melt-in-your-mouth desserts at their own Cleveland Park place; veterans of notable kitchens, their respect for ingredients is legendary, and here it's well enhanced by a velvet-glove setting and committed crew; be sure to call early, because word is out.

Pizzeria Paradiso ▣   25 | 16 | 18 | $20
2029 P St., NW (bet. 20th & 21st Sts.), 202-223-1245

■ "Perfectly" named, the "eternal winner" of Washington's top pizza honors gets it just right – a "flavorful", "crisp" "wood-smoked" crust judiciously applied with "top-notch ingredients" (some regulars think the sandwiches are "even better"); it's a "charming little place" off Dupont Circle filled with "happy clatter", though its "paramount" pies and "well-chosen" wines often lead to peak-hour "waits."

Prime Rib   26 | 25 | 25 | $53
2020 K St., NW (bet. 20th & 21st Sts.), 202-466-8811

■ Rated the top steakhouse in DC and the "classiest of the power meateries", this gilt-edged Downtown American attracts lawyers and lovelies who "dress up" to indulge in the "finest" prime rib, accompanied by a "wonderful wine list"; the elegant surroundings exude a "coat-and-tie" "dignity" that "can't be duplicated", making all diners "feel important."

Prince Michel ▣   26 | 22 | 26 | $59
Rte. 29 S. HCR4, Box 77, Leon, VA, 540-547-9720

■ High scores signal the "excellence" of this posh haute French in Leon, where the kitchen's "exquisite" updated classics and the staff's "subtle" pampering leave patrons wishing it weren't "so far out" of town; its Jefferson and Lafayette dining rooms offer prix fixe tasting menus, as well as à la carte courses, and the extravagant midday Sunday repast makes for a "fun getaway."

Rabieng ▣   25 | 17 | 20 | $24
Glen Forest Shopping Ctr., 5892 Leesburg Pike (Glen Forest Dr.), Bailey's Crossroads, VA, 703-671-4222

■ "Incredible Thai country food" earns this "reserved" Bailey's Crossroads favorite "top" honors; in a "smallish" space with a "down-to-earth" atmosphere, diners enjoy "spicy" "peasant" dishes infused with a "wonderful blend of flavors"; P.S. you "must try" the "novel" Thai-style dim sum at the weekend brunch.

Red Sage ▣   21 | 24 | 20 | $38
605 14th St., NW (F St.), 202-638-4444

◪ A big tourist attraction, this "eye-popping" Southwestern "original" also lassos Downtown lawyers and lobbyists with its "short orders" and "fantastic happy hours" in the frenetic upstairs bar; for "real food", expense-account types entertain downstairs where the kitchen, which has a "way with chiles", keeps "reinventing" its dishes; if a few feel it has "fallen off some", at least it's now easier to "get a table."

Seasons ▣   26 | 26 | 26 | $55
Four Seasons Hotel, 2800 Pennsylvania Ave., NW (28th St.), 202-944-2000

■ The morning limo lineup outside this major "breakfast player" in Georgetown attests to the "reliably elegant" pampering and near-"perfect" orchestration of "classy" special events at this "serene" New American showcase with a "gorgeous" garden terrace; overlooking the C&O canal, it's also a "first-rate" site for afternoon tea or Sunday brunch; N.B. longtime chef Doug McNeill's gone, but that shouldn't affect this highly professional operation.

1789 S   26 | 26 | 25 | $53

1226 36th St., NW (Prospect St.), 202-965-1789

■ Open the door of this historic Federal townhouse in Georgetown and "enter the world of blue blazers" and patrons celebrating a "dressy occasion", all warmed by wintertime "fires burning" in the "private"-feeling period dining room; Ris Lacoste's "wonderful" seasonal American cooking, "imaginative but not over the top", is served in "classically" "elegant" quarters, making it "a place you can take both your mother and your daughter and love yourself."

Smith & Wollensky ●S   22 | 21 | 21 | $46

1112 19th St., NW (bet. L & M Sts.), 202-466-1100

☑ "Come with clients, not a date" to this "masculine" NYC-in-DC "big meat" haven set on Dupont Circle South's premier "steak block", where its "quality" beef and extensive wine cellar face "big competition"; while many welcome the "attentive" service, critics find the room a bit "cold" and add that it's no "match" for the Manhattan "mother ship"; P.S. the adjacent grill cooks a "fabulous burger", and it's open till 2 AM.

Taberna del Alabardero   25 | 25 | 24 | $50

1776 I St., NW (18th St.), 202-429-2200

■ As "sensuous" as Spain itself, this classic Basque eatery Downtown "transports" guests to the "old world" "in grand style", with "world-class" cooking, an "exhaustive" wine list and "impeccable" service; the "extravagant" setting is apt for "entertaining clients" or "someone you really like", thus it's not hard to see why "the King of Spain" dines here when he's in town; P.S. "strolling serenaders" play classical Spanish music Friday and Saturday nights.

Vidalia S   26 | 23 | 24 | $49

1990 M St., NW (bet. 19th & 20th Sts.), 202-659-1990

■ The "luscious" Southern-accented New American comfort food turned out at this Dupont Circle South expense-account "treat" has nouveau and native Southerners alike cheering the "great" kitchen that "performs magic" with seasonal local and Dixie ingredients; though claustrophobes clamor about the "basement" digs and not everyone cottons to the staff's leisurely "Deep South" tempo, the "warm" ambiance, "nice lighting" and "personable" staff convey a "hospitality" that's "classy in every way."

Indexes

CUISINES BY AREA

Atlanta

American
Harvest

American (New)
Aria
Bacchanalia
BluePointe
Buckhead Diner
Canoe
dick & harry's
Food Studio
Mumbo Jumbo
Oscar's
Park 75
Van Gogh's
Watershed

Asian
Sia's

Continental
Babette's Cafe
103 West
Pano's & Paul's
Ritz-Carlton Buck. Café
Seeger's

French (Bistro)
Floataway Cafe

French (Classic)
Nikolai's Roof
Ritz-Carlton Buck. Din. Rm.

French (New)
Brasserie Le Coze
103 West

Fusion
Tierra

International
Babette's Cafe

Italian (N=Northern; S=Southern; N&S=Includes both)
Abruzzi (N&S)
Floataway Cafe (N&S)
La Grotta (N&S)
Sotto Sotto (N&S)

Japanese
Haru Ichiban
Hashiguchi
Kamogawa
Soto
Sushi Huku

Latin American
Tierra

Mediterranean
Eno

Provençal
Ritz-Carlton Buck. Café

Russian
Nikolai's Roof

Seafood
Atlanta Fish Market
Brasserie Le Coze
Chops/Lobster Bar
Prime

Southern
Aria

Southwestern
Nava
Sia's

Steakhouse
Bone's
Chops/Lobster Bar
Morton's of Chicago
Prime

Thai
Tamarind

Atlantic City

American
Ram's Head Inn
Renault Winery

Eclectic
Savaradio

French (New)
Le Palais

Cuisines by Area Index

French (Classic)
Maison Robert
Mantra
Mistral
Pigalle

French (New)
Ambrosia on Huntington
Clio
Federalist
Julien
L'Espalier
Lumière
Mistral
Radius

Indian
Mantra

International
Bonfire

Italian (N=Northern; S=Southern; N&S=Includes both)
Bistro 5 (N)
Centro (N&S)
Il Capriccio (N)
La Campania (N&S)
Prezza (N&S)
Saporito's (N)

Japanese
Ginza

Mediterranean
Caffe Bella
Oleana
Olives
Rialto

Middle Eastern
Oleana

New England
Rowes Wharf

Seafood
East Coast Grill & Raw Bar

Steakhouse
Bonfire
Grill 23 & Bar
Morton's of Chicago

Chicago

American
Crofton on Wells

American (New)
Blackbird
Charlie Trotter's
Courtright's
Harvest on Huron
mk
MOD.
Naha
one sixtyblue
Seasons
Spring
302 West
Twelve 12
Zealous

Asian
NOMI
Spring

French (Bistro)
D & J Bistro

French (Classic)
Le Français
Les Nomades
Le Titi de Paris
NOMI

French (New)
Ambria
Aubriot
Avenues
Carlos'
Everest
Gabriel's
Ritz-Carlton Din. Rm.
Spring
Tallgrass
Trio
TRU

Italian (N=Northern; S=Southern; N&S=Includes both)
Gabriel's (N&S)
Spiaggia (N&S)

Japanese
  Mirai Sushi
Mediterranean
  Avenues
Mexican
  Chilpancingo
  Frontera Grill
  Las Bellas Artes
  Topolobampo
Seafood
  Atlantique
  Joe's Seafood
Steakhouse
  Gibsons
  Joe's Seafood
Thai
  Arun's
Vietnamese
  Pasteur

Cincinnati

American
  Phoenix
American (New)
  Brown Dog Cafe
  JUMP Café & Bar
  Palace
  Sturkey's
Barbecue
  Montgomery Inn
Chinese
  China Gourmet
Continental
  Phoenix
Eclectic
  Daveed's at 934
Eurasion
  Beluga
French (Bistro)
  Aioli
French (Classic)
  Chez Alphonse
  Maisonette

Indian
  Ambar India
Italian (N=Northern; S=Southern; N&S=Includes both)
  Aioli (N&S)
  Nicola's (N&S)
  Primavista (N)
Mediterranean
  Palomino Euro Bistro
Pan-Asian
  Pacific Moon Cafe
Pizza
  Dewey's Pizza
Seafood
  Precinct
Steakhouse
  Jeff Ruby's
  Precinct

Cleveland

American (New)
  Lola
  Mise
  Moxie
  One Walnut
Asian
  Phnom Penh
  Weia Teia
Continental
  Baricelli Inn
  Johnny's Bar
  Johnny's Downtown
  Oz Bar & Bistro
Eclectic
  Mise
  Oz Bar & Bistro
French (Bistro)
  Johnny's Bistro
French (Classic)
  Chez François
French (New)
  Parker's

Italian (N=Northern; S=Southern; N&S=Includes both)
- Circo Zibibbo (N&S)
- Giovanni's Ristorante (N)
- Johnny's Bar (N)
- Johnny's Downtown (N)

Mediterranean
- Sans Souci

Seafood
- Blue Pointe Grille
- Century

South American
- Sergio's

Spanish
- Viva Barcelona

Columbus, OH

American
- Lindey's
- Yard Club at O'Toole's

American (New)
- Cameron's

Caribbean
- Tapatio

Continental
- Handke's Cuisine

Cuban
- Starliner Diner

Eclectic
- Alana's Food & Wine

Eurasian
- SuLan Eurasian Bistro

French (Classic)
- L'Antibes
- Refectory

French (New)
- Refectory

International
- Handke's Cuisine
- Out On Main

Irish
- Yard Club at O'Toole's

Italian (N=Northern; S=Southern; N&S=Includes both)
- La Tavola (N)
- Rigsby's (N)
- Trattoria Roma (N)

Japanese
- Restaurant Japan

Low Country
- Braddock's Grandview

Mexican
- Starliner Diner
- Tapatio

Pan-Asian
- Shoku

Provençal
- Rigsby's

Seafood
- Columbus Fish Market

Steakhouse
- Mitchell's
- Morton's of Chicago

Connecticut

American
- Elms
- Golden Lamb Buttery
- Mayflower Inn

American (New)
- Ann Howard Apricots
- Carole Peck's
- Jeffrey's
- Max Downtown
- Métro Bis
- Rebeccas
- Steve's Centerbrook
- Terra Mar Grille
- West Street Grill

Asian
- Baang Café & Bar

Californian
- Baang Café & Bar

Chinese
- Great Taste

Mediterranean
  Il Sole
  Riviera
Mexican
  Ciudad
Pan-Asian
  Citizen
  Steel
Seafood
  Al's
  Cafe Pacific
  Sea Grill
Southwestern
  Mansion on Turtle Creek
  Star Canyon
Steakhouse
  Al's
  Bob's Steak & Chop
  Capital Grille
  Chamberlain's
  Del Frisco's
  Lawry's
  Nick & Sam's
  Pappas Bros.

Denver Area & Mountain Resorts

American
  Bang!
  Briarwood Inn
American (New)
  Beano's Cabin
  Charles Court
  Conundrum
  Fourth Story
  Highlands Garden Cafe
  Hilltop Café
  Kevin Taylor
  La Petite Maison
  Mel's
  Micole
  Mizuna
  Palace Arms
  Potager
  Q's

  Renaissance
  Splendido
  Strings
  Sweet Basil
  240 Union
  Vesta Dipping Grill
  Wildflower
Continental
  Briarwood Inn
  Charles Court
  Flagstaff House
  Palace Arms
  Penrose Room
Eclectic
  John's
French (Classic)
  Left Bank
  Tante Louise
French (New)
  Papillon Café
  Penrose Room
Indian
  India's
Italian (N=Northern; S=Southern; N&S=Includes both)
  Barolo Grill (N)
  Full Moon Grill (N)
Japanese
  Domo
  Sushi Den
Mediterranean
  Mel's
  Renaissance
Rocky Mountain
  Alpenglow Stube
  Grouse Mountain Grill
  Keystone Ranch
  Piñons
Seafood
  240 Union
South American
  Cafe Brazil
Steakhouse
  Del Frisco's

Detroit

American
  Morels
  Ritz-Carlton Grill
American (New)
  Daniel's on Liberty
  Five Lakes Grill
  Opus One
  Whitney
Asian
  Tribute
Continental
  Golden Mushroom
  Ritz-Carlton Grill
Deli
  Zingerman's
Eclectic
  Common Grill
French (Classic)
  Earle
French (New)
  Cafe Bon Homme
  Emily's
  Lark
  Tribute
*Italian (N=Northern; S=Southern;
N&S=Includes both)*
  Café Cortina (N&S)
  Earle (N&S)
  Il Posto Ristorante (N&S)
Mediterranean
  Emily's
Middle Eastern
  Steve's Backroom
Pan-Asian
  Mon Jin Lau
Steakhouse
  Capital Grille
Vietnamese
  Annam

Fort Lauderdale

American (New)
  By Word of Mouth
  Darrel & Oliver's Cafe Maxx
  Mark's Las Olas

Chinese
  Silver Pond
Continental
  Black Orchid Cafe
French (Classic)
  La Ferme
French (New)
  La Ferme
*Italian (N=Northern; S=Southern;
N&S=Includes both)*
  Cafe Martorano (N&S)
  Cafe Vico (N)
  Casa D'Angelo (N&S)
  Primavera (N)
Kosher
  Baraka
Mexican
  Eduardo de San Angel
Seafood
  Charley's Crab
  Hobo's Fish Joint
  Sunfish Grill
Southwestern
  Armadillo Cafe
  Canyon
Spanish
  Cafe Seville
Steakhouse
  Outback
  Ruth's Chris

Fort Worth

American (New)
  Café Ashton
  Café on the Green
  Classic Cafe
  Rough Creek Lodge
Barbecue
  Angelo's Barbecue
  Railhead Smokehouse
Burgers
  Kincaid's
Eclectic
  Angeluna

Grape Escape
Randall's Cafe
French (Classic)
Cacharel
Escargot
Saint-Emilion
International
Angeluna
Pegasus
Italian (N=Northern; S=Southern; N&S=Includes both)
La Piazza (N&S)
Ruffino's (N&S)
Mediterranean
Bistro Louise
Pegasus
Southwestern
Cool River Cafe
Steakhouse
Del Frisco's
Western
Lonesome Dove

Honolulu

American
Palomino Euro Bistro
Prince Court
Asian
OnJin's Cafe
Chinese
Golden Dragon
Eurasian
Bali-by-the-Sea
Indigo
French (Bistro)
OnJin's Cafe
French (Classic)
La Mer
Padovani's
French (New)
Chef Mavro's
Fusion
Roy's

Hawaiian
Roy's
Sansei
Hawaiian Regional
Alan Wong's
Chef Mavro's
Pineapple Room
International
Hoku's
Orchids
Japanese
Kyo-Ya
Prince Court
Sansei
Yohei Sushi
Mediterranean
Padovani's
Palomino Euro Bistro
Pacific Rim
3660 on the Rise
Seafood
Orchids
Steakhouse
Hy's Steakhouse
Ruth's Chris

Houston

American
Rotisserie/Beef & Bird
American (New)
Anthony's
Aries
benjy's
Daily Review Cafe
Mark's
Riviera Grill
Ruggles Grill
Ruggles Grille 5115
Tony Ruppe's
Zula
Asian
Saba Blue Water Cafe
Scott's Cellar

Barbecue
Goode Co. Barbeque
Cajun
Tony Mandola's
Caribbean
Saba Blue Water Cafe
Continental
Anthony's
Scott's Cellar
Tony's
Creole
Brennan's
Eclectic
Mosquito Cafe
Ouisie's Table
French (Bistro)
Café/Pâtisserie Descours
French (Classic)
Chez Nous
La Réserve
Riviera Grill
Ruggles Grille 5115
Gulf Coast
Rainbow Lodge
Indian
Khyber North Indian Grill
Italian (N=Northern; S=Southern; N&S=Includes both)
Aldo's (N)
Amerigo's Grille (N)
Da Marco (N&S)
Damian's (N)
La Griglia (N)
La Mora (N)
Tony Mandola's (N&S)
Latin American
Américas
Cafe Red Onion
Seafood
Goode Co. Seafood
Rainbow Lodge
South American
Churrascos

Southern
Ouisie's Table
Southwestern
Brennan's
Cafe Annie
Ruggles Grill
Steakhouse
Capital Grille
Churrascos
Morton's of Chicago
Pappas Bros.
Ruth's Chris
Tex-Mex
Irma's

Kansas City

American
Stroud's
American (New)
American Restaurant
Cafe Allegro
Café Sebastienne
Grille on Broadway
Metropolis
Starker's Reserve
Stolen Grill
zin
Barbecue
Fiorella's Jack Stack
Eclectic
Grand St. Cafe
French (Bistro)
Le Fou Frog
French (Classic)
Tatsu's
Italian (N=Northern; S=Southern; N&S=Includes both)
Garozzo's (N&S)
Lidia's (N)
Pizza
D'Bronx
Sandwich Shop
D'Bronx

American (New)
Barney's
Blake's Bistro
Coolfish
Della Femina
Focaccia Grill
Mill River Inn
Palm Court at the Carltun
Panama Hatties
Piccolo
Plaza Cafe
Polo Grill

Continental
Mazzi
Mirko's
Palm Court at the Carltun

Eclectic
La Plage
Mirko's

French (Bistro)
Le Soir

French (Classic)
American Hotel
La Marmite
L'Endroit

French (New)
Barney's
Louis XVI
Mirabelle
Stone Creek Inn

International
Mirepoix

Italian (N=Northern; S=Southern; N&S=Includes both)
Casa Rustica (N&S)
Da Ugo (N&S)
Harvest on Fort Pond (N)
La Marmite (N&S)
La Pace (N)
La Piccola Liguria (N)
L'Endroit (N)
Mario (N)
Piccolo (N&S)
Sempre Vivolo (N&S)

Stresa (N&S)
Trattoria Diane (N)

Japanese
Kotobuki
Sen

Long Island
Starr Boggs

Mediterranean
Harvest on Fort Pond
Stone Creek Inn

Seafood
Palm

Steakhouse
Bryant & Cooper
Morton's of Chicago
Palm
Peter Luger
Tellers Chophouse

Los Angeles

American (New)
Josie's
Mélisse
Michael's
Saddle Peak Lodge

Asian
Cafe Blanc
Chaya Brasserie
Chinois on Main
Shiro

Californian
Bel-Air Hotel
Belvedere
Bistro 45
Cafe Blanc
Café Bizou
Devon
Joe's
JiRaffe
Parkway Grill
Patina
Shiro
Spago

Chinese
  Yujean Kang's
Deli
  Brent's Deli
Eclectic
  Belvedere
  Chaya Brasserie
  Depot
  Spago
Franco-Russian
  Diaghilev
French (Bistro)
  Bistro 45
  Frenchy's Bistro
  Mimosa
French (Classic)
  Bel-Air Hotel
  Joe's
  La Cachette
French (New)
  Chinois on Main
  Devon
  L'Orangerie
  Patina
Italian (N=Northern; S=Southern; N&S=Includes both)
  Capo (N&S)
  Locanda Veneta (N)
  Valentino (N&S)
Japanese
  Matsuhisa
  Nobu Malibu
  R-23
  Sushi Nozawa
Mediterranean
  Campanile
Pacific Rim
  Jozu
Peruvian
  Nobu Malibu
Seafood
  Water Grill
Steakhouse
  Grill
  Lawry's

  Palm
  Ruth's Chris

Miami

American (New)
  Astor Place
  Liaison
  Mark's South Beach
  Touch
Asian
  Azul
Barbecue
  Pit Bar-B-Q
Brazilian
  Porcao
Cajun
  Liaison
Caribbean
  Ortanique on the Mile
Chinese
  Tropical Chinese
Continental
  Crystal Cafe
Cuban
  Versailles
Deli
  Wolfie Cohen's
Eclectic
  Cheesecake Factory
French (Classic)
  La Palme d'Or
French (New)
  Azul
  Blue Door
  La Palme d'Or
  Pascal's on Ponce
  Tantra
Italian (N=Northern; S=Southern; N&S=Includes both)
  Cafe Prima Pasta (N)
  Caffé Abbracci (N&S)
  Carpaccio (N)
  Escopazzo (N&S)

Grazie Cafe (N)
Osteria de Teatro (N&S)
Romeo's Cafe (N)
Japanese
  Nobu Miami Beach
  Toni's Sushi Bar
Jewish
  Wolfie Cohen's
Mediterranean
  Tantra
New World
  Chef Allen's
  Nemo
  Norman's
Pacific Rim
  Baleen
Pan-Asian
  Bambù
  Pacific Time
Peruvian
  Nobu Miami Beach
Seafood
  Baleen
  Garcia's
  Joe's Stone Crab
  Pacific Time
Spanish
  Casa Juancho
Steakhouse
  Forge
  Morton's of Chicago
  Palm
Vietnamese
  Hy-Vong
  Miss Saigon Bistro

Minneapolis/St. Paul

American
  St. Paul Grill
American (New)
  Goodfellow's
  Loring Café
  Lucia's
  128 Cafe

Restaurant Alma
Zander Cafe
Eclectic
  Bayport Cookery
French (New)
  La Belle Vie
Greek
  Gardens of Salonica
Health Food
  Cafe Brenda
Italian (N=Northern; S=Southern;
N&S=Includes both)
  D'Amico Cucina (N&S)
  Ristorante Luci (S)
Japanese
  Origami
Mediterranean
  La Belle Vie
Midwestern
  Dakota Bar & Grill
Pizza
  Punch Neapolitan Pizza
Seafood
  Kincaid's
  Oceanaire
Steakhouse
  Kincaid's
  Manny's
Swedish
  Aquavit

New Jersey

American
  Manor
  Washington Inn
  Zarolé
American (New)
  Acacia
  Bernards Inn
  Daniel's on Broadway
  Dining Room
  Ebbitt Room
  Esty Street
  Frog & The Peach
  Harvest Moon Inn

Heatwave at Windows
Highlawn Pavilion
Jeffrey's
Karen & Rei's
Saddle River Inn
Union Park
Waters Edge
Cajun
410 Bank Street
Caribbean
410 Bank Street
Eclectic
Café Matisse
Park & Orchard
French (Bistro)
Le Rendez-Vous
French (Classic)
Fromagerie
Madeleine's Petit Paris
Saddle River Inn
Siri's
French (New)
Cafe Panache
Jocelyne's
Rat's
Ryland Inn
Serenäde
Stage House Inn
Zarolé
International
Little Cafe
Italian (N=Northern; S=Southern; N&S=Includes both)
Scalini Fedeli (N)
Japanese
Sagami
Shumi
Mediterranean
Le Rendez-Vous
Moonstruck
Pizza
DeLorenzo's Tomato Pies
Seafood
Bobby Chez
Doris & Ed's

Steakhouse
River Palm Terrace
Thai
Siri's
Vegetarian
Park & Orchard

New Orleans

American (New)
Bayona
Dakota
Grill Room
Herbsaint
Continental
Rib Room
Creole
Antoine's
Arnaud's
Brennan's
Christian's
Clancy's
Commander's Palace
Emeril's
Emeril's Delmonico
Gabrielle
Galatoire's
Gamay
Gautreau's
Le Parvenu
Mr. B's Bistro
Sal & Judy's
Upperline
Eclectic
Upperline
French (Bistro)
Bistro at Maison de Ville
La Crêpe Nanou
French (Classic)
Antoine's
Christian's
La Provence
Louis XVI
Peristyle

Italian (N=Northern; S=Southern; N&S=Includes both)
- Babbo (N&S)
- Felidia (N&S)
- Il Mulino (N)

Japanese
- Kuruma Zushi
- Nobu
- Sushi Yasuda
- Tomoe Sushi

Mediterranean
- Picholine

Peruvian
- Nobu

Russian
- Russian Tea Room

Scandinavian
- Aquavit

Seafood
- Le Bernardin
- Oceana

Soul
- Sylvia's

Southern
- Sylvia's

Steakhouse
- Peter Luger
- Smith & Wollensky
- Sparks

Orange County, CA

American
- Houston's

Californian
- Aubergine
- Napa Rose
- Pavilion

Chinese
- P.F. Chang's

Continental
- Hobbit
- Ritz

Eclectic
- Cheesecake Factory

English
- Five Crowns

French (Classic)
- Aubergine
- Hobbit
- Pinot Provence
- Ritz-Carlton Lag. Niguel

French (New)
- Troquet

Fusion
- Roy's

Hawaiian
- Roy's

Italian (N=Northern; S=Southern; N&S=Includes both)
- Il Fornaio (N&S)

Mediterranean
- Pavilion

Mexican
- El Cholo

Pizza
- California Pizza Kitchen

Seafood
- McCormick & Schmick's

Steakhouse
- Ruth's Chris

Swedish
- Back Pocket
- Gustaf Anders

Orlando

American
- La Boheme
- Victoria & Albert's

American (New)
- Dux
- Harvey's Bistro

Cajun
- Emeril's

Californian
- California Cafe Bar & Grill
- California Grill

Caribbean
- Bahama Breeze

Chinese
   Haifeng
Continental
   Café de France
   Chatham's Place
   Maison et Jardin
   Peter Scott's
Creole
   Emeril's
Cuban
   Rolando's
French (Bistro)
   Café de France
   Le Coq au Vin
   Les Chefs de France
French (New)
   Citricos
   Dux
Fusion
   California Cafe Bar & Grill
International
   Arthur's 27
   La Coquina
   Manuel's on the 28th
Italian (N=Northern; S=Southern; N&S=Includes both)
   Antonio's La Fiamma (N&S)
   Brio Tuscan Grille (N&S)
   Cafe D'Antonio (N&S)
   Christini's (N)
   Delfino Riviera (N)
   Enzo's on the Lake (N)
Mediterranean
   Cafe Allegre
Northwest
   Artist Point
Seafood
   Flying Fish Café
   Houston's
   Narcoossee's
Southern
   Louis' Downtown
Steakhouse
   Charley's Steak House
   Del Frisco's

Houston's
Outback
Ruth's Chris
Vito's Chop House
Yachtsman Steakhouse
Thai
   Thai House
   Thai Place

Palm Beach

American
   John G's
American (New)
   Cafe Chardonnay
   11 Maple Street
   Four Seasons
   L'Escalier
   32 East
   Zemi
Caribbean
   Four Seasons
Continental
   Cafe L'Europe
   Kathy's Gazebo Cafe
   Le Mont
Eclectic
   Cheesecake Factory
French (Bistro)
   Chez Jean-Pierre
French (New)
   La Belle Epoque
   La Vieille Maison
   Le Mistral
   Maison Janeiro
Fusion
   Roy's
Hawaiian
   Roy's
Italian (N=Northern; S=Southern; N&S=Includes both)
   Marcello's La Sirena (N&S)
   Renato's (N&S)
Steakhouse
   New York Prime

Philadelphia

American
  Swann Lounge
American (New)
  Dilworthtown Inn
  Evermay on the Delaware
  Fork
  Fountain
  Jake's
  Mainland Inn
  Opus 251
  Passerelle
  333 Belrose
  20 Manning
Asian
  Buddakan
  Rouge
Chinese
  Susanna Foo
  Yangming
Cuban
  Alma de Cuba
Eclectic
  White Dog Cafe
French (Bistro)
  Bistro St. Tropez
  Blue Angel
  Swann Lounge
French (Classic)
  Deux Cheminées
  La Bonne Auberge
  Le Bar Lyonnais
  Le Bec-Fin
  Nan
French (New)
  Brasserie Perrier
  Fountain
  Overtures
  Passerelle
  Rouge
  Tangerine
Italian (N=Northern; S=Southern; N&S=Includes both)
  DiPalma (N&S)
  La Famiglia (N&S)

  Monte Carlo Living Rm. (N&S)
  Saloon (N&S)
  Savona (N)
  Vetri (N&S)
Mediterranean
  Audrey Clair
  Dmitri's
  Overtures
Moroccan
  Tangerine
Nuevo Latino
  ¡Pasion!
Pizza
  Tacconelli's Pizzeria
Seafood
  Sansom St. Oyster House
  Savona
  Striped Bass
Steakhouse
  Prime Rib
Thai
  Nan

Phoenix/Scottsdale

American (New)
  Convivo
  Lon's at the Hermosa
  Michael's at the Citadel
  Rancho Pinot Grill
  Restaurant Hapa
  RoxSand
Asian
  Restaurant Hapa
Eclectic
  Coup des Tartes
French (Bistro)
  Christopher's
French (Classic)
  Coup des Tartes
  Vincent Guerithault
French (New)
  Mary Elaine's

International
Gregory's World Bistro
Razz's
Mediterranean
Marquesa
Medizona
T. Cook's
Mexican
La Hacienda
Pizza
Pizzeria Bianco
Southwestern
Lon's at the Hermosa
Medizona
Vincent Guerithault
Steakhouse
Morton's of Chicago
Ruth's Chris
Western
Roaring Fork

Portland, OR

Chinese
Sungari
French (Bistro)
Paley's Place
Zinc Bistrot
French (Classic)
Cafe des Amis
Heathman
Tina's
French (New)
Castagna
Couvron
Italian (N=Northern; S=Southern; N&S=Includes both)
Caffe Mingo (N)
Castagna (N)
Genoa (N&S)
Pazzo Ristorante (N)
Japanese
Saburo's
Latin American
Mint

Mediterranean
Bluehour
Mexican
Cafe Azul
Northwest
Heathman
Higgins
Joel Palmer House
Paley's Place
Tina's
Wildwood
Seafood
Winterborne
Steakhouse
El Gaucho

Salt Lake City & Mountain Resorts

American
Bambara
Foundry Grill
New Yorker Club
Snake Creek Grill
Sundance Tree Rm.
American (New)
Glitretind
Log Haven
Mariposa
Metropolitan
Asian
Mandarin
Wahso
Californian
Center Cafe
Continental
Blue Boar Inn
French (Classic)
Wahso
Italian (N=Northern; S=Southern; N&S=Includes both)
Fresco Italian Cafe (N)
Lugano (N)
Tuscany (N)

Masa's
Ritz-Carlton Din. Rm.
Rubicon
Terra

Italian (N=Northern; S=Southern; N&S=Includes both)
Acquerello (N)
Delfina (N&S)
Oliveto (N)
Terra (N)
Tra Vigne (N&S)
Zuni Cafe (N)

Japanese
Sushi Ran

Mediterranean
Chez Nous
Chez Panisse
Zuni Cafe

Provençal
Auberge du Soleil

Seafood
Aqua
Farallon

Vegetarian
Greens

Vietnamese
Slanted Door

Santa Fe

American
Bull Ring

American (New)
Compound

Continental
Old House
Pink Adobe

Eclectic
Geronimo
Rancho de San Juan
Santacafe

French (Bistro)
Bistro 315
Rociada

French (New)
Ristra

International
Rancho de San Juan

Italian (N=Northern; S=Southern; N&S=Includes both)
Andiamo! (N)
Il Piatto (N)
Il Vicino (N&S)
Julian's (N&S)

New Mexican
El Farol
Guadalupe Cafe
Pink Adobe

Southwestern
Anasazi
Cafe Pasqual's
Coyote Cafe
Geronimo
La Casa Sena
Old House
Ristra
Santacafe

Spanish
El Farol

Seattle

American (New)
Eva
Lampreia
Mistral
Nell's
Palace Kitchen
Restaurant Zoë

Asian
Flying Fish
Wild Ginger

Bakery
Macrina Bakery & Cafe

Eclectic
Dahlia Lounge
Eva
Palace Kitchen
Place Pigalle

French (Country)
Le Cremaillère
French (New)
Arch
Auberge Maxime
Aubergine
Equus
La Panetière
International
Harralds
Italian (N=Northern; S=Southern; N&S=Includes both)
Il Cena'colo (N)
Lusardi's (N&S)
Mulino's (N)
Japanese
Azuma Sushi
Mediterranean
Café Meze
Harvest on Hudson
Seafood
Conte's Fishmarket
Eastchester Fish
Steakhouse
Mighty Joe Young's

St. Louis

American (New)
Crossing
Frazer's
Harvest
Sidney Street Cafe
Zinnia
Continental
Kemoll's
French (Classic)
Cafe de France
Indian
India Palace
International
Cafe Mira
Cardwell's at the Plaza

Italian (N=Northern; S=Southern; N&S=Includes both)
Bar Italia Ristorante (N)
Dominic's (N)
Giovanni's (N&S)
Kemoll's (N&S)
Tony's (N&S)
Trattoria Marcella (N&S)
Mediterranean
Portabella
Remy's Kitchen & Wine Bar
Mexican
Pueblo Solis
Pan-Asian
Shiitake
Seafood
Frazer's
Tony's
Vietnamese
Pho Grand

Tampa Bay/Sarasota

American (New)
Beach Bistro
Bistro 41
Café L'Europe
Grill at Feather Sound
Lafite at the Registry
Michael's on East
Zoria
Asian
SideBern's
Continental
Café L'Europe
Jonathan's
Lafite at the Registry
Eclectic
Blue Heron
Euphemia Haye
Jonathan's
Mise en Place
Ophelia's
Floribbean
Maritana Grille

French (Classic)
Peter's La Cuisine
Ritz-Carlton Din. Rm.
Fusion
SideBern's
Italian (N=Northern; S=Southern;
N&S=Includes both)
Caffe Paradiso (N)
Mediterranean
Beach Bistro
Seafood
Prawnbroker
Steakhouse
Bern's Steak House
Thai
Jasmine

Tucson

American (New)
Grill at Hacienda del Sol
Kingfisher
Ventana Room
Wildflower
Continental
Anthony's/Catalinas
Arizona Inn
Gold Room
Tack Room
Eclectic
Dish
French (Bistro)
Le Bistro
French (Classic)
Janos
Le Rendez-Vous
Italian (N=Northern; S=Southern;
N&S=Includes both)
Daniel's (N)
Gavi (N&S)
Mexican
Cafe Poca Cosa
J Bar
Mi Nidito

Seafood
Kingfisher
Southwestern
Café Terra Cotta
¡Fuego!
Gold Room
Janos
Steakhouse
McMahon's

Washington, DC

American
Caucus Room
Old Ebbitt Grill
1789
American (New)
Carlyle Grand Room
D.C. Coast
Equinox
Inn at Little Washington
Kinkead's
Majestic Cafe
Melrose
Nora
Palena
Seasons
Vidalia
Belgian
Marcel's
Eclectic
Bread Line
French (Bistro)
Bis
French (Classic)
L'Auberge Chez François
L'Auberge Provençale
Prince Michel
French (New)
Citronelle
Gerard's Place
Marcel's
Indian
Bombay Club

Cuisines by Area Index

ALPHABETICAL PAGE INDEX

Alphabetical Page Index

Alphabetical Page Index

Alphabetical Page Index

Alphabetical Page Index

Alphabetical Page Index

Alphabetical Page Index

Alphabetical Page Index

Alphabetical Page Index

Alphabetical Page Index

Alphabetical Page Index

Alphabetical Page Index

Wine Vintage Chart 1985–2000

This chart is designed to help you select wine to go with your meal. It is based on the same 0 to 30 scale used throughout this *Survey*. The ratings (prepared by our friend **Howard Stravitz**, a law professor at the University of South Carolina) reflect both the quality of the vintage and the wine's readiness for present consumption. Thus, if a wine is not fully mature or is over the hill, its rating has been reduced. We do not include 1987, 1991–1993 vintages because they are not especially recommended for most areas.

	'85	'86	'88	'89	'90	'94	'95	'96	'97	'98	'99	'00
WHITES												
French:												
Alsace	24	18	22	28	28	26	25	23	23	25	23	25
Burgundy	24	24	18	26	21	22	27	28	25	24	25	–
Loire Valley	–	–	–	26	25	22	24	26	23	22	24	–
Champagne	28	25	24	26	29	–	24	27	24	24	–	–
Sauternes	22	28	29	25	27	–	22	23	24	24	–	20
California:												
Chardonnay	–	–	–	–	–	21	26	22	25	24	25	–
REDS												
French:												
Bordeaux	26	27	25	28	29	24	26	25	23	24	22	25
Burgundy	23	–	22	26	29	20	26	27	25	23	26	–
Rhône	25	19	26	29	28	23	25	22	24	28	26	–
Beaujolais	–	–	–	–	–	–	22	20	24	22	24	–
California:												
Cab./Merlot	26	26	–	21	28	27	26	24	28	23	26	–
Zinfandel	–	–	–	–	–	26	24	25	23	24	25	–
Italian:												
Tuscany	26	–	24	–	26	23	25	19	28	24	25	–
Piedmont	25	–	25	28	28	–	24	26	28	26	25	–